A Celebration of Poets

Appalachia
Grades 4-12
Fall 2011

A Celebration of Poets
Appalachia
Grades 4-12
Fall 2011

An anthology compiled by Creative Communication, Inc.

Published by:

PO BOX 303 • SMITHFIELD, UTAH 84335
TEL. 435-713-4411 • WWW.POETICPOWER.COM

Authors are responsible for the originality of the writing submitted.

All rights reserved. No part of this book may be reproduced or transmitted in any form or by any means, electronic or mechanical without written permission of the author and publisher.

Copyright © 2012 by Creative Communication, Inc.
Printed in the United States of America

ISBN: 978-1-60050-478-5

FOREWORD

In January of this year, I was watching the Miss America Pageant. I thought of all the accomplishments that culminate in this one ending competition. These outstanding women had decided what they wanted, paid the price and now were reaping the rewards of their hard work. While watching the pageant, the finalists were on stage and a few of their accomplishments were written across the screen. For Miss Arizona, Jennifer Sedler (who ended as 3rd runner-up), one of her accomplishments was having a poem published in 5th grade. In checking our records, it was our company, Creative Communication, that published her poem "Hawaiian Seas" in the Fall of 2002.

Jennifer wrote to us about the experience of being published:

"I had a poem published by Creative Communication in 5th grade, and I will never forget how special and inspired it made me feel. I have since gone on to win numerous essay contests, many which earned me scholarship money for college, and I may have never believed in myself if it wasn't for Creative Communication. And as Miss Arizona, I write pages and pages of creatively-written updates for all of my followers. Now of course I still take time on my own to read, study, and write poetry. When you choose to be an active learner and writer, I think you will find, just as I did, that truly anything is possible."

When a poet enters our writing contest, they are students like everyone else. As they move on in life, talents are developed. A 5th grade student becomes Miss Arizona. Another student, novelist Angela Bishop, also wrote to me the following:

"My name is Angela Bishop, and almost ten years ago you selected one of my poems to be published in the Southern edition of your book. I was 15 and it was the highlight of my young life. Although it has been nearly a decade, I just wanted to finally express the thanks I have felt all these years. I cannot thank you enough for accepting my work and publishing it. I have been writing since I was a child and have continued to write. I am currently working on my second novel. So, thank you, thank you, for the confidence you unknowingly gave me in 1999. I plan to keep writing for as long as I possibly can. Your poetry contest is a wonderful thing, and you open a window for tomorrow's great writers to find their way through and gain the confidence in their work. Keep it going, you are making dreams into realities."

To both Jennifer and Angela and the students in this anthology, I am glad that we are here for you. We helped you in creating an accomplishment that you can be proud of and add to your resume. When students wonder if they should enter a contest, I give a strong affirmative. You may not be accepted to be published, but if you don't enter, there isn't a chance of being published or being a Top Ten winner. Sometimes you have to take a risk and enter a contest. It may change your life. Just ask Jennifer and Angela.

I hope you enjoy the poems that are included in this anthology. We are pleased to help provide the spark that makes lifelong writers. Each of these students took a risk in entering and has the potential to achieve great things in their lives. Good luck.

Tom Worthen, Ph.D.
Editor

WRITING CONTESTS!

Enter our next POETRY contest!
Enter our next ESSAY contest!

Why should I enter?
Win prizes and get published! Each year thousands of dollars in prizes are awarded throughout North America. The top writers in each division receive a monetary award and a free book that includes their published poem or essay. Entries of merit are also selected to be published in our anthology.

Who may enter?
There are four divisions in the poetry contest. The poetry divisions are grades K-3, 4-6, 7-9, and 10-12. There are three divisions in the essay contest. The essay divisions are grades 3-6, 7-9, and 10-12.

What is needed to enter the contest?
To enter the poetry contest send in one original poem, 21 lines or less. To enter the essay contest send in one original non-fiction essay, 250 words or less, on any topic. Please submit each poem and essay with a title, and the following information clearly printed: the writer's name, current grade, home address (optional), school name, school address, teacher's name and teacher's email address (optional). Contact information will only be used to provide information about the contest. For complete contest information go to www.poeticpower.com.

How do I enter?

Enter a poem online at:
www.poeticpower.com
or
Mail your poem to:
  Poetry Contest
  PO Box 303
  Smithfield UT 84335

Enter an essay online at:
www.poeticpower.com
or
Mail your essay to:
  Essay Contest
  PO Box 303
  Smithfield UT 84335

When is the deadline?
Poetry contest deadlines are August 16th, December 6th and April 9th. Essay contest deadlines are July 19th, October 18th and February 19th. Students can enter one poem and one essay for each spring, summer, and fall contest deadline.

Are there benefits for my school?
Yes. We award $12,500 each year in grants to help with Language Arts programs. Schools qualify to apply for a grant by having 15 or more accepted entries.

Are there benefits for my teacher?
Yes. Teachers with five or more students published receive a free anthology that includes their students' writing.

For more information please go to our website at **www.poeticpower.com**, email us at editor@poeticpower.com or call 435-713-4411.

TABLE OF CONTENTS

POETIC ACHIEVEMENT HONOR SCHOOLS	1
LANGUAGE ARTS GRANT RECIPIENTS	5
GRADES 10-11-12 HIGH MERIT POEMS	7
GRADES 7-8-9 HIGH MERIT POEMS	89
GRADES 4-5-6 HIGH MERIT POEMS	189
INDEX	261

STATES INCLUDED IN THIS EDITION:

KENTUCKY
NORTH CAROLINA
TENNESSEE
WEST VIRGINIA

Fall 2011 Poetic Achievement Honor Schools

*Teachers who had fifteen or more poets accepted to be published

The following schools are recognized as receiving a "Poetic Achievement Award." This award is given to schools who have a large number of entries of which over fifty percent are accepted for publication. With hundreds of schools entering our contest, only a small percent of these schools are honored with this award. The purpose of this award is to recognize schools with excellent Language Arts programs. This award qualifies these schools to receive a complimentary copy of this anthology. In addition, these schools are eligible to apply for a Creative Communication Language Arts Grant. Grants of two hundred and fifty dollars each are awarded to further develop writing in our schools.

All Saints' Episcopal School
Morristown, TN
Betty Golden*

Bearden High School
Knoxville, TN
Virginia Thurston*

Berkeley Springs High School
Berkeley Springs, WV
Vanessa Fox
Heather Lorigan*

Bernheim Middle School
Shepherdsville, KY
Jimmy Carnes*

Bradford High School
Bradford, TN
Kim Pierce*

Buckner Elementary School
La Grange, KY
Heather Sparks*

Centennial Elementary School
Dickson, TN
Kim Walton*

Coffee County Central High School
Manchester, TN
Joyce McCullough*

College View Middle School
Owensboro, KY
Tina Hare
Debbie Hendrix*
Wendy Wells*

Dillard Drive Middle School
Raleigh, NC
Connie Duerr*
Amber Leahy

Dyer Elementary & Jr High School
Dyer, TN
Lee Fesmire Hudson*

Elkton School
Elkton, TN
Teri Mize*

Evangelical Christian School Ridgelake Campus
Memphis, TN
Vita Swindell*

Fuquay-Varina Middle School
Fuquay Varina, NC
Shirley Dunn*

George M Verity Middle School
Ashland, KY
Billie Menshouse*

Germantown High School
Germantown, TN
Billy M. Pullen*

Grimsley High School
Greensboro, NC
Jennifer Brady Wilson*
Karyn Collie

Heritage Middle School
Maryville, TN
Marie Richardson*

Hunter GT Magnet Elementary School
Raleigh, NC
Angie Parham*

J Graham Brown School
Louisville, KY
Neysa Jones
Allana Thompkins*

Leesville Road Middle School
Raleigh, NC
Vicki Newland*

Longest Elementary School
Greenville, KY
Tara Whitmer*

Loretto High School
Loretto, TN
Trisha Moore*
Brandon Weaver

Memphis Academy of Science and Engineering
Memphis, TN
Deshonda Johnson*

Middle Creek High School
Apex, NC
Joshua Matteau*
Melissa Smith

Mineral Wells Elementary School
Mineral Wells, WV
Darcella Maul*

Montgomery Central Middle School
Cunningham, TN
DeAnne Murphy*

Moyock Elementary School
Moyock, NC
Virginia Gioia
Denise Jewell
Kathy Maxwell
Mary Pepe

Paint Lick Elementary School
Paint Lick, KY
Pam Canter*

Pigeon Forge Middle School
Pigeon Forge, TN
Laura Turner*

Providence Academy
Johnson City, TN
Janet Branstrator*
Pam Holben

Ramsey Middle School
Louisville, KY
Ashley Howlett
Kerri Medley*
Dianne Nettles*
Valerie Rueger

Poetic Achievement Honor Schools

Riverside High School
Belle, WV
Nella Toppings*

Saint Pauls Middle School
Saint Pauls, NC
Donald Weller*

Sissonville Middle School
Charleston, WV
Diane Ferguson*

St Agnes School
Fort Wright, KY
Nancy Dwyer*

St Nicholas Academy - South
Louisville, KY
David Trueblood*

Starmount High School
Boonville, NC
Kathy Taylor*

Sycamore High School
Pleasant View, TN
Larissa Haynes
Emily VanBrocklin

Tates Creek Elementary School
Lexington, KY
Brenda Jackson*

Temple Hill Elementary School
Glasgow, KY
Kristin Norris*

Wakefield High School
Raleigh, NC
Carlie Bowman*

Walton-Verona Middle School
Walton, KY
Deborah C. McNeil*

Weddington Middle School
Matthews, NC
Susan Williams*

Westchester Country Day School
High Point, NC
Mary Keever*

White Station High School
Memphis, TN
T. Boyd
Sandra Whittington

White Station Middle School
Memphis, TN
Helen C. Erskine*
Ruby Hubbard*
Christy Peterson*

William G Enloe High School
Raleigh, NC
Rita Achenbach*

Woodland Presbyterian School
Memphis, TN
Carol Percival*

Language Arts Grant Recipients 2011-2012

After receiving a "Poetic Achievement Award" schools are encouraged to apply for a Creative Communication Language Arts Grant. The following is a list of schools who received a two hundred and fifty dollar grant for the 2011-2012 school year.

Annapolis Royal Regional Academy, Annapolis Royal, NS
Bear Creek Elementary School, Monument, CO
Bellarmine Preparatory School, Tacoma, WA
Birchwood School, Cleveland, OH
Bluffton Middle School, Bluffton, SC
Brookville Intermediate School, Brookville, OH
Butler High School, Augusta, GA
Carmi-White County High School, Carmi, IL
Classical Studies Academy, Bridgeport, CT
Coffee County Central High School, Manchester, TN
Country Hills Elementary School, Coral Springs, FL
Coyote Valley Elementary School, Middletown, CA
Emmanuel-St Michael Lutheran School, Fort Wayne, IN
Excelsior Academy, Tooele, UT
Great Meadows Middle School, Great Meadows, NJ
Holy Cross High School, Delran, NJ
Kootenay Christian Academy, Cranbrook, BC
LaBrae Middle School, Leavittsburg, OH
Ladoga Elementary School, Ladoga, IN
Mater Dei High School, Evansville, IN
Palmer Catholic Academy, Ponte Vedra Beach, FL
Pine View School, Osprey, FL
Plato High School, Plato, MO
Rivelon Elementary School, Orangeburg, SC
Round Lake High School, Round Lake, MN
Sacred Heart School, Oxford, PA
Shadowlawn Elementary School, Green Cove Springs, FL
Starmount High School, Boonville, NC
Stevensville Middle School, Stevensville, MD
Tadmore Elementary School, Gainesville, GA
Trask River High School, Tillamook, OR
Vacaville Christian Schools, Vacaville, CA
Wattsburg Area Middle School, Erie, PA
William Dunbar Public School, Pickering, ON
Woods Cross High School, Woods Cross, UT

Grades 10-11-12 Top Ten Winners

List of Top Ten Winners for Grades 10-12; listed alphabetically

Maria Capitano, Grade 11
Pittston Area High School, PA

Anna Daavettila, Grade 10
Houghton High School, MI

Anna Groeling, Grade 11
Arapahoe High School, CO

Arniecia Hinds, Grade 10
Germantown High School, TN

Sabrina Maus, Grade 10
Haynes Academy for Advanced Studies, LA

Erin McCune, Grade 10
Bellarmine Preparatory School, WA

Declan Routledge, Grade 12
Webber Academy, AB

Jacob Schriner-Briggs, Grade 12
Liberty High School, OH

Lianna Scott, Grade 11
Xavier College Preparatory School, AZ

Alexander Wimmer, Grade 10
Home School, GA

All Top Ten Poems can be read at www.poeticpower.com

Note: The Top Ten poems were finalized through an online voting system. Creative Communication's judges first picked out the top poems. These poems were then posted online. The final step involved thousands of students and teachers who registered as the online judges and voted for the Top Ten poems. We hope you enjoy these selections.

Blinded

How do you call me ugly?
Do you think it's my fault…
that I'm bare?
I lift my many arms to the sky.
My leaves falling as I cry.
I silently scream, why!?
A stronger voice than mine replies,
Once your leaves fall away,
then they will say…
"How were our eyes blinded?
How could we not see?"
That is why this must be,
so they can realize what was unseen.

Abby Thomas, Grade 12
Apollo High School, KY

Fall

Fall is such
A beautiful season
When leaves
Change colors and start to fall.

When mountains in
The distance look
Like piles of dirt.

When forest
Starts to cover
The ground
And wooly worms wobble around.

Tiphanie Tucker, Grade 10
White Plains Christian School, NC

Boast of Flay

Father Flay, Charles by name
Man of years, much experience
Teaches computers, educating youth
Mother Christine, Chapman by birth
Caring loving, helping others
Career of teaching, the English language
Son Buddy, youth of thought
Boy Scout, working on eagle
Always busy, no free time
Brother Beau, youngest Flay
Caring kind, crazy careful
Kid of fun, joking a lot
Boast of Flay, one of glory

Buddy Flay, Grade 12
Starmount High School, NC

My Location

My location is murder;
My soul has died long ago.
No heart inside my body.
No hope pulsating through my flesh.
Emptiness has devoured me.
Loneliness my only comfort.
Devastation my only new friend.
Hurt and turmoil have turned into my siblings.
Corruption my parent.
I hate this location.
It reeks of rotten flesh.
It feels like demons rubbing off my flesh.
Their touch is blistering.
I lose a little bit more of me every time they look into my eyes,
When they call my name more pieces of me crumble.
Replaced with robotic chunks of their aspirations for me.
I would never wish this on the most horrible sinner.
I don't want their flesh to melt.
Their eyeballs to fall out of their head to ensure to their keeper that they can't see the vision.
The repay I get for trying to free their souls and give them happiness was casting mine away.
Forever in the deep pit of insanity.

Ja'Rae Bolton, Grade 10
Germantown High School, TN

Transformation

Something like being put into a shredder to severely thrown away.
Or a map to a confounding maze.
I have gloomily endured a handful.
Similar as a hurricane to red cross.
Or a open wound to relieving stitches.
I have unexpectedly rejuvenated.
Practically twins to a caliper to a butterfly.
Or a seed to a bold flower.
I have blissfully developed.
Akin to being informed that you'll fail at having babies to giving birth to triplets.
Or enlightened that the world will end in 2010 to living it up in 2011.
I have been entirely astonished.
Parallel to running after cats to trained to know the sit and stay commands.
Or frighteningly drowned in a pool to swimming in a life jacket.
I have finally learned.

Michelle White, Grade 10
Hawthorne High School, NC

The Middle of Nowhere

In the middle of nowhere, sits an arena next to the woods,
light scatters across the sky, rays of sunshine through the clouds,
In the middle of nowhere, is my place of comfort and joy,
my getaway, my tropical beach of endless land and horses,
Has it changed?
Fallen rotted trees, tangled bare wire, no sign of life,
The bad memory haunts the eleven acre farm,
Why do I still think of only bad?
No more visits, no more riding, crickets croak, snorting, a whistle pierces the air,
In the middle of nowhere horses run, we are free

Jade Bruner, Grade 12
North Bullitt High School, KY

Tic-Tac-Toe

Chaos and commotion
Lay dormant in my head.

Until each tic-tac-toe
Box begins to fill with
The bullet-pointed lists
Reminders, and due dates,
All sneering at me,
Challenging me.

Each bullet point
Excites chaos and commotion,

My agenda accumulates
To a conglomeration of constant to-dos.

Time moves constantly, escaping
My grasp; to manage it is an
Almost unachievable assignment.

But the line drawn through
Each defeated task
Reminds me that time is conquerable.

Katherine Hupp, Grade 12
Germantown High School, TN

Grades or Knowledge?

Quizzes, tests, grades, and GPAs
Determine how we see ourselves
In this overly competitive age.
Receiving a "C" is condemned;
And suddenly, being average
Just isn't good enough.
Retaining information?
No one needs to anymore:
Our transcripts sum up intelligence.
What happened to our love for knowledge?
Obligations and humanity?
They're not reflected in standardized tests.
Exposed to new concepts,
While not truly learning anything,
But how to memorize and forget.
If it is this bad for us today,
What will our kids be forced to face?

Radha Patel, Grade 12
William G Enloe High School, NC

Cars

Chevy Camaros
Are so much fun when you drive
When you get to speed
You feel like you are the king
Until you get stopped

Maria Brink, Grade 10
Loretto High School, TN

The Anger That Lies Within

My life has been filled with animosity,
Which led to violence and monstrosities.
There's something that's buried within my soul,
This wicked feeling keeps rising from the depths unknown.
At this point, this is where it begins.
My life and with the anger that lies within.
My life now, I'm in jail, four walls to each cell.
My boundaries are restricted.
This small place makes me feel more and more constricted.
So, day by day, through thick and thin,
I still feel myself about to release, the anger that lies within.
I had plans to meet my mom face to face,
But no, because her body is in a grave, rotting away, almost ready to decay.
The rage that circulates through me
Doesn't help my heart beat fluently.
Please forgive me Lord, for I have sinned.
Give me the strength to find and destroy,
The anger that lies within.

Alec D., Grade 10
Audubon Youth Development Center, KY

Love's Range

Thoughts of her, my mind is always smothered,
Her eyes are as blue as any ocean,
Her voice, I love when it is uttered,
Seeing her smile soothes scathes like lotion,
Skin as smooth as silk, hair long and brown,
Her cute smile rivals her sweet voice,
She admits a sweet aura when around,
After meeting, loving her was no choice,
College will bring a challenging feat, a continual fear that our hearts will estrange,
Separated by thousands of feet,
How far is too far for one heart's range
Through fear and change, one thing is sure, my heart
Will always have a vacancy for her.

Andrew Pardue, Grade 12
Starmount High School, NC

Love Is a Puzzle

Love is a puzzle, never ending always changing
Ideas are the seasons love goes through.
As ideas change, so do we,
Our love was never-ending.
Now we've changed, we're different people, you and I.
Our lives drifted apart,
And took our love for one another with them.
If the puzzle pieces don't connect, it won't work.
Everything has to fit just right, or it falls apart.
Our love has changed; we're drifting apart as we mature.
I'm not the girl you fell in love with, and you're not the man I once loved.
Love is a puzzle, the pieces always fall apart.
Maybe one day the pieces will fit, but 'til then we must depart.

Meghan Ripple, Grade 11
Providence Academy, TN

Sorrow is the Abyss

Sorrow is the abyss
What is and what could be
The space between

With each intervention
For each bridge engineered
The rift only grows wider

Control is artificial
Control cannot change
The abyss remains

Is it possible
For one to care
But not control?

Is it possible
For one to love what is
While knowing what could be?

One path, one path only
Only he can change himself
Only he can cross the abyss

The single path
Neglected time after time
The abyss lives on.

Michael Hopkins, Grade 12
William G Enloe High School, NC

Walls

And I remember,
as your lips moved rhythmically.
Maybe it was a song,
stuck deep inside your head.
Or maybe a quiet chant,
a prayer for me to hear.
If only your words had touched my ears.

But not a sound broke the barrier,
the defensive walls I'd built –
not to keep you out,
but to keep me locked in place.
A place safe from change,
in an ocean of my pain.
Masochistic was my name.

And in this palace of woe, I was all alone.
Without another soul,
I was forced to feed off my own.
I drained myself of love, of hope,
but, in this way, I was broke.
In my tries to safe myself,
for my life I blindly grope.

Katherine McCourt, Grade 10
Middle Creek High School, NC

Imprisoned

I stroll around with a deception of aptness and prosperity,
Though I am imprisoned within my dark past.
I renew my sins again and again until my judgment shall pass,
Then I realize my faults.
It is far too late to repent for my invariable wrongdoing.
I search for a savior as if I never knew of my own.
I consider the possibility that maybe, just maybe my next chance shall come.
Then reality sets, and my fear suddenly appears.
I recognize the individual that my eyes have longed to see.
But not in this manner
Not this soon.
I'm not ready, I'm not prepared.
I haven't done all that is expected.
I have performed what my father has asked of me not.
Just one more chance? ????? Is it really too late?
Surely I deserve your forgiveness.
Nevertheless it's my time.
To those whom I deceived,
My apologies, as I am ashamed of my wrongdoing.
But it is my time.
Amen.

Alexis Taylor, Grade 10
Memphis Academy of Science and Engineering, TN

Progression

Take a look through our heritage
Take a glimpse at our culture
Recognize those who helped us go further
Our people on the move always
Constant continuation
Years ago, even before the Great Migration
W.E.B. Dubois' curiosity started it all
Despite the Restrictive Covenants
Ignoring the segregation in school halls
Marcus Garvey who said let us embrace our skin, our structure, our face
Langston Hughes whose words were so deep and true
People of color read 'em and felt 'em too
Miss Zora, on Miss Zora Neal Hurston
Their Eyes Were Watching God has my emotion and heart bursting
Some may call 'em "Niggers," "Jigaboo" or just black folk…but heroes are
What MOST call 'em
For they were all apart of the Renaissance of Harlem.

BreAnna Thomas, Grade 10
Memphis Academy of Science and Engineering, TN

The Sky

During my gruesome week I walked out for air
At first I thought I was the only one hurt and upset
But when I saw the sky
It was full of depression
Shedding enough tears to cause a flood
Screaming at the ones who did him wrong
Throwing what he could to strike those
So then I realized that I was not the only one that was hurt and upset

Myranda-Lynn Johnson, Grade 11
Richmond Early College High School, NC

My Second Home

Slowly I rise up to the
land of tranquility.
The air smells salty.
The ground like fire.
With its piercing blue color the
Water cools
My burning skin.

The wind calls me
To come closer.
Like a mother's succulent
Voice.
The water pulls me in.
Makes me sway from
Side to side.

This place is extraordinary
Breathtaking.
The place of my wholesome,
nothingness.
The electrified
Radiant,
Beautiful, beach.

Cortni Holloway, Grade 11
Germantown High School, TN

Where Am I From

I am from an antique lamp found in my grandmother's house,
From Kroger branded applesauce and a broken refrigerator
I am from the bustling busy streets of Shanghai, China.
I am from the botanic garden
That holds the rose bush that's beautiful to look at
But dangerous if touched

I am from moon cake festivals and squinty yet thoughtful eyes,
From Yining and Xianghong and Zhang
I am from "Do your best!"
And "Never give up on your dreams!"
From God is great, God is good and let us thank him for our food

I am from an empty unsatisfying hole from lack of faith.
Hearing the word of God every Sunday
But never ever listening
I'm from Waco, Texas but reign from Nanjing, China
Where Peking duck and the lucky eyeball from a fish head are specialties
From my parents immigrating to America with only $200 dollars in their pocket,
To both the wonderful childhood they both gave me and my little brother

I am from the pictures hidden away for no one to see,
A family that's torn and broken,
And needs something to help rebuild their happiness

Helen Zhang, Grade 11
Germantown High School, TN

Bullet

Tonight I can write the saddest lines
Of how a bullet took something
So precious of mine

To walk through those doors
And see the love of my life
In a light blue casket
Dressed up so nice

Tears are welling up inside me
From my heart and my soul
My entire body feels so numb
My surroundings are so cold

The world comes crashing down
My life comes to a stop
My heart breaks into pieces
My stomach ties into knots

I miss him more and more
Each and every day
Tonight I can write the saddest lines
Because my love has gone away

Tiffany Cheshire, Grade 11
Ripley High School, TN

I Am From

I am from old thrift store records,
From Lucky Brand Jeans and cereal for dinner.
I am from the broken kitchen window,
That won't shut and lets the flies in during the summer.
I am from the South Carolina trees
covered in Spanish Moss,
Whose trunks gave me a backrest as I watched the sunset.

I am from hay rides and tall happy people.
I am from Worshim and Gross,
From the sentimental and the move-far-aways.
From the Don't tell anyone! And the Go ask your Mother.
I am from Sunday morning service
Only to forget once the last hymn is sung.

I am from the suburbs of Cordova, carrot cake and fried mushrooms.
From the jacks my father swallowed,
The lake house that I saved, and
The woman who lives in my house, who is not my mother.

I am from the tackle boxes under guest bed,
whose tiny cubbies held family photos and old green stamps.
I am from a stack of postcards,
Whose messages have been long erased.

Kirby Gross, Grade 11
Germantown High School, TN

Cl2

I stare at the bubbling lagoon,
enclosed by levies of fossilized calcium,
and wonder what it has seen.

How many bodies have marinated
in this pool of dead skin and sweat?
This festering, simmering soup
of God-knows-what.

It sees every old man sink
into the brackish water—
mingling his own salty brine
with the leftovers of others'.

It sees each woman settle
into the murky deep,
spreading her toes in the sediment
that lies stagnant at the bottom.

I stare disdainfully at the foamy filth
that settles on the water's surface.
I cast the powdery substance
into the impervious depths,
knowing that no amount of chlorine
can ever erase what this hot tub has seen.

Laura Sharp, Grade 12
Germantown High School, TN

Miles Away

Miles away
Just out of reach
Action becomes thought
Thought becomes speech

Sight becomes memory
Until it's reborn
My understanding is clear
My acceptance is torn

It makes sense in my head
But there it remains
Alongside strange thoughts
That my mind entertains

Emotion and reason
Persist to conflict
But I know that the future
Is mine to predict

Peter Menzies, Grade 12
William G Enloe High School, NC

Midnight Masquerade

When darkness overtakes us
And night has us in her grasp,
We know not what to do,
But slip into our masks.

For night brings with her
The ball of mysteries,
Many who hide their faces
And move as if in dreams.

The masquerade begins as
The clock strikes midnight,
Then all the dancers emerge
And dance in the pale moonlight.

To music played by minstrels
Sad and melancholy,
Swaying to the notes
In masks painted jolly.

Then as the clock strikes one,
The dancers break away,
Then into the shadows
They disperse, and go on their way.

Rebekah Plowman, Grade 10
Union County High School, TN

First Love

I love the way my heart jumped
When my hand first touched yours.
Your eyes, they shine like sunsets
In the fleeting evening sky.

Your smile is infectious.
Full of confidence, but never arrogant.
Instant intimidation,
Yet irrevocable attraction.

The first kiss
Is like nothing else.
My heart erupts with passion
Just thinking of you.

New love is a graceful butterfly
Wrapping its wings around me
Instilling silent security.

Sarah Glick, Grade 12
William G Enloe High School, NC

Broken Glass

Once a whole.
Once something beautiful.
Then someone dropped her
or maybe she fell.

She doesn't remember.
She only sees the present.
A broken mirror,
a shattered mess.

Larger parts can be glued
but it'll never be the same.
The smaller pieces will never be found,
lost somewhere in space.

When you tilt her this way
and the light is just so,
she looks almost new.
She looks almost perfect.

But eventually you see her flaws,
the parts that are beyond repair
You may not mind
but she can't bear for you to know.

Michelle Pleasant, Grade 11
Germantown High School, TN

Facing the Day

My first day of real school.
The alarm clock wakes me up,
But all I want is to hide,
To curl up under the covers,
To never face the day.
I am so scared.

Questions race through my mind.
I'm used to being at home so
Why do I have to go?
What will happen?
Are my teachers nice?
Will I have friends?
Will school change me?

My mind protests the inevitable.
I don't want to go.
Nervous, but somewhat excited,
It's all surreal.
Facing this day, a challenge.

My mom picks me up when the day ends.
She asks about my day.
The truth? It wasn't so bad.

Rebecca Collier, Grade 10
Germantown High School, TN

Which Way?

Two roads diverged in a yellow wood,
one path eroded and worn down,
the other clean and untouched.

I peeked down the path,
although destroyed,
it reminded me
of the comfortable life I lived.
Every mistake I had made.
Every triumph I had won.
My past.

I glimpsed at the alternate path.
Clean and unused,
it resembled the life I could have.
It bled with hope and determination.
My future.
To which path I was going to take
was unknown.
Should I choose what I know
or what I hope will be?

Meredith Dowden, Grade 11
Germantown High School, TN

What Is a Good Poem?

They make us laugh.
They make us cry.
They confound you.
They abound in you.
What is a good poem?

They make you ponder over what was said.
They fill your heart with dread.
They fill you with fear,
or bring about a tear.
What is a good poem?

They fill you with glee
and give cause for a jubilee.
They bring you up when you're down.
They turn your frown upside down.
What is a good poem?

Derek Anderson, Grade 10
Coffee County Central High School, TN

Pendulum

You're my Pendulum…
knocking me down.
Striking, and then…
turning around.
Hoping to hit,
even harder this time.
Hitting with no…
warning or sign.

Brianna Carter, Grade 12
Antioch Christian Academy, NC

I Am From

I am from the dirt,
from those come and gone, the unbreakable cycle of life.
I am from the faded shutters
banging against the side of our ancient home
I am from the aloe vera, the succulent plant
that grows to heal so strong yet dies by the cold.
I am from the bashing of faces into cakes,
and strong temper, from Carbajal and Real.
I am from the insulting words and vulgar phrases,
from do not play with boys and mi'ja study.
I am from late night readings of the Bible.
Self interpretations and preaching what they don't practice,
maintaining a holier than thou attitude.
I am from Cuernavaca and Mexico, chiles rellenos and posole.
From the hat of Tio Nacho Cachetes trampled by his wrath,
the insane lost daughter of Tio Pastor,
and the eye my grandfather lost in a gamble of life.
I am from the top shelf of the closet, the shoebox in a corner,
the mantle over the fireplace. the photos on the wall,
the letters in the drawer, the ancient heirlooms lying dead in dusty attic
I am from the dust of those before me

Paola Herrera, Grade 11
Germantown High School, TN

Where I Am From

I am from refrigerator magnets,
 from Windex and Pine-Sol.
I am from the sandbox in the backyard,
 Still maintaining my footprints from the previous day.
I am from the pine tree swaying in the breeze,
 its strong, knotted limbs hanging protectively over me.
I am from my grandma's cheesecake and falling asleep on the couch,
I am from the how-long's-it-beens and the you've-gotten-so-bigs,
 From Go play! and What do you say?
I am from the kneeling and standing and folding my hands,
 Saying my bedtime prayers, and drinking from the communal cup.
I'm from the city of blues and the place where the pyramid originated,
 Roasted lamb, stuffed grape leaves with hummus.
From the marriage of my grandparents lasting sixty years, to the birth of my sister,
 The innocence of a child.

I am from a family tree, tracing back hundreds of years,
 From black and white photos of smiling people.
I am from gold jewelry, bought long ago in a foreign land.
I am from all of these things — the culmination of past and present,
 Memories and what is to come.

Linda Higazy, Grade 11
Germantown High School, TN

Loss of Words

I am at a loss for words,
My brain does not think.
It just sits there idly staring at me.
I cannot rhyme,
The words seem to run away from me,
They just waste my time.
Can anyone help me.

I am at a loss for words,
So I have lost myself.
I cannot express what I need to let out.
My feelings are caged up sort of like a lion at the zoo.
This is every writer's fear for a loss of words means,
No way let out all of the pain they hold dear.

A loss for words,
Is like a soldier losing his sword.
He will soon lose the battle,
And also the war.
'Cause a writer's greatest weapon is,
A writer's choice of words.

Alex Franklin, Grade 10
Germantown High School, TN

Anger

A red tint starts to take over
A flush of heat rises from my stomach
My bottle slowly starts to fill up
Something inside me has taken over

Aggression is now the answer
Everyone is a walking target
Trouble will always find me
Even though I never start it

Fists are now clenched
Wanting to cause pain
And hoping to receive it
The adrenaline rush is like a drug

Sometimes it's hard not to feed it
I try to fight it off, but deep down I really need it
Blood starts to boil as I start to loosen the cap
I lose sight of what is right

The fireworks are bound to start

Jeremy Willoughby, Grade 12
Middle Creek High School, NC

Dear Old Friend

We've grown apart.
It has been a long journey,
But it's time to move on.
I won't regret your friendship,
Despite the things others say.
Including their comments on your negative influences
Or the way you hinder me.
You've always been a comfort,
You've kept me on the straight and narrow,
And helped through the winters.
No one can argue that you weren't dedicated
Even when others tried to split us apart.

But now we must go different ways.
I'll miss your softness
And the warmth that you provided
However, you've begun to get in my way.
I have goals to meet.
I still thank you for your time,
And all your dedication.
Extra pounds, I'll miss you

Gabrielle Brown, Grade 12
William G Enloe High School, NC

A Different Kind of Renaissance

Your cirrus eyes,
the breadth and Latin slope of your nose
were once as pleasing to me
as the finest works of Monet, the most cubic
Picasso — but your smile was no sultry Mona Lisa,
was bright and easy, came quickly
as a midsummer dawn and lingered
'til nightfall. Gradually, the colors
faded. Your skin of Mediterranean sand
became simply "olive." And though
I cannot revive the graying hues I still feel the most
peculiar rising in my bones when you're with her,
when I perceive her shades brightening in your rich,
steaming cocoa eyes (no —
just brown) in a way I never could —
never dared to dream I would.

Envy
is such a peculiar
shade of
Myrtle.

Marissa Davis, Grade 11
Paducah Tilghman High School, KY

Thoughts of the Night

I stare out into the night,
As the world slows down its pace.
The darkness robs me of my sight,
And yet I see the depths of space.

I see the moon shining its light,
Casting playful silver shadows.
The stars burning ever bright,
Hurling fire like straight-shot arrows.

There is perfection in the stillness,
Unattainable by day,
Only marred by awful swiftness
With which night retreats away.

Thoughts run wild and unafraid,
As they ne'er do below the sun,
I see the fear that does pervade,
And I know I cannot run.

Yet under the moon and stars so bright
I feel revival of strength for life.
I have been given new courage tonight
To dream and make a world without strife.

The sun rises. Let it shine.
Rachel Smoak, Grade 12
William G. Enloe High School, NC

Broken

Today I wake
With my heart broken
Because you take and take!
You have left my heart open.
You are nothing but a fake!
You need to be woken
With a rough shake!
I used to be your special token.
But now I'm just a headache.

But you don't care
How I feel!
No matter how unfair!
I will never be real.
I was just a dare!
You just steal and steal!
Tear and tear!
My heart will never heal!
We were just not the right pair…
Elesia Saunders, Grade 10
Robert C Byrd High School, WV

Here in Harmony

We are all people,
No matter our home,
We breathe, eat and live
While thinking about
Others and their ways
And how we're all one.
We all have something
To bring to the world,
So everyone can
Live, learn, eat and grow
Together at the
Table of the world.
Here, all bring something
To share with people
Of all cultures and
Races to help change
The world for the good
Of all us who live
Here in harmony.
Alex Hughes, Grade 11
Germantown High School, TN

Ave Maria

she taps her fist to his ribcage;
listens.

frustration is plain on her face
when her gaze meets his.

boy; confused, raises a
question:

"what are you doing?"
girl; panicked,
"trying to find the love."

his booming laugh blossoms loud
in her eardrums,
(the) reply:

"no use. was never there, doll,
you know that."

the crazed skittering of her
nails against his flesh,
(her) words:
"what about last night?"
Taylor Stevens, Grade 12
Germantown High School, TN

Insomniac

The toll of those sleepless nights
Begins to find purchase in these days
Just as you feared.

These days have no dates
Surely, you think,
This wasn't meant to be your fate

Frivolous dreams you seek
Of daisies and daffodils
Though, instead you don't sleep
For weeks and weeks

The moment the alarm clock sounds
You feel a weight
Of pounds and pounds

You know It started slow
It didn't start so bad
The days were unhurried
No foul moods, no time to brood,
And no pressing weight

And you hope as you
Try and try to sleep
That this wasn't meant to be your fate
Natalie Shelton, Grade 10
Grimsley High School, NC

Diversity

Diversity has developed over the years
Minorities are no longer unwanted
They are respected as our peers
They are no longer haunted

Times were tough
There was injustice in the world
It was very rough
But it is now a new world

The future looks nice
People are no longer planning to fight
The hate is on ice
The world is looking bright

That's why we need to accept changes
Different views matter
The many ideas range
So they need to scatter

The world needs to accept the many races
People are different and that's okay
We all come from different places
In this new world we can all stay
Ian Schranze, Grade 11
Germantown High School, TN

I Am from Clocks

I am from clocks,
from Rolex and time machines.
I am from under the surface of the ocean.
I am from the potato farm
the Adirondack Blue
whose deep roots I recall
because they trace back to mine.
I am from curry and spices
 from Sayani and Sayani.
I am from the easily-angered
 and the easily-upset.
from Shut up! And Sit Down!.
I am from I prostrate before thee
 with prayer beads in a drawer
 that I choose to ignore.
I am from Chicago and Nani's Well,
 mangoes and spuds.
From the eyes my grandfather lost
 to the use of tobacco,
and the crooked fingers of my cricket playing father.
I am from the memories that will always fade

Aasim Sayani, Grade 11
Germantown High School, TN

Where I'm From

I am from a schoolhouse,
from Gatorade and leaves.
I am from the paint peeling off the walls,
crusty and moldy.
I am from the peach tree
that flourishes in the summer.
I am from soccer and braces,
From Tom and Zoe and Billy James.
I am from common sense and hard work.
From Try Hard!
And Do Your Best!
I am from My Savior Lives
And Almighty is He!
I am from the beach front
And the Scottish Isles,
Coffee and potatoes.
From an arrow in my dad's eye
And the tumor in my granddad's brain.
I am from pictures over the fireplace,
To warm my heart and body.
I am from those feelings that make me who I am.

Tyler Bozeman, Grade 11
Germantown High School, TN

Out of the Storm

Waves toss
And storms rage
Around the bottle, sealed, message within
Sent by Chance or Fate
To a stranger far off, or very near
Or the bottom of the sea.
Its journey endless:
Across the vast expanse of calm waters,
Over the next foamy crest.
No guarantee of anything,
No way to choose its destiny.

So why wait for Chance or Fate
Too long, and it will be too late
Or wrong when it should be right
And all is dark instead of light.

Tossed and battered: still you can win
But only as long as you do not give in
Search until you find what is right
And perhaps, just perhaps, there will be the light.

Elizabeth Porter, Grade 12
William G Enloe High School, NC

Tonight

I'm not throwing you away.
Not tonight, stay in my life.
Don't even pretend like I don't care.
If you're lost in your worries
and things are getting dark,
I promise you're not alone,
I've got tricks up my sleeve,
for the days that you can't see.
Don't be blinded by society,
twisting your image in the mirror.
Your unedited beauty is what they really fear.
I see the pressure killing you,
in your eyes, you'll never be perfect
but in mine you're beautiful and worth it.
So please don't hurt yourself,
stay alive, keep breathing,
don't give up tonight,
cause I'll never give up on you.
You shine like stars in the sky at night,
it's not worth it, trust me
don't you dare take a beautiful life.

Nicole Brunner, Grade 11
Campbell County High School, KY

Autumn

The weather turns cold;
Leaves turn red and gold, then fall;
Autumn has arrived.

Meg Irvin, Grade 12
St Joseph Academy, NC

Leaves

The wind blows gentle…
Leaves fall down like soft whispers,
Whirlwind of beauty.

Ashby Bird, Grade 10
Union County High School, TN

Storm in the Graveyard

The rain splashes
On the unmoving head
Of a demon.
A demon of stone.
The lightning flashes
And lights up the words.
An epitaph.
An epitaph of love.
The wind lashes
And blows the flowers away.
The flowers for a son,
A brother who was well-loved.
The thunder claps
And startles the carriers.
The pallbearers who lay
The boy in the ground.
One last look.
One last kiss.
One last tear.
They will love him always.
Hannah Voyles, Grade 10
Pleasant View Baptist School, KY

Truth

Beauty in silence
stillness of heart
Beating so loudly
as limbs snap apart
Roses have faded
Cold wind doth blow
Forever in solitude
battling foes —
that have raged in wars
Her body enslaved
Though strongly she stands
Age upon age
Her wrists shackled bronze
Her mind chained in gold
Embedded in memory
All truth should be told
Elizabeth Steinauer, Grade 12
William G Enloe High School, NC

John Wayne Gacy

You thought he was kind,
generous Pogo the clown.
You thought wrong!
One after another young men went missing.
Well, they found them under his house.
Twenty seven bodies under his house
and five more in the river.
He was a murderer and a rapist.
But don't worry…
In 1994 the clown was no more.
Jesse Attkisson, Grade 10
Loretto High School, TN

Black

Brown on the outside
But I'm black on the inside
People use my skin color to describe me
Don't look at my skin color and think you know me
People judge me because they think they know my skin color
They don't

I may be black but don't just think I'm bad, uneducated, etc.
Don't describe my skin color
Describe my personality
I'm a good kid, raised by a good family
Yeah, I come for the hood, but that doesn't mean I'm "ghetto"
Yeah, I grew up on food stamps, but that doesn't mean I'll always be broke
I struggle every day, but people keep putting me down because I'm black,
Even other blacks

I didn't make myself a different race
I'm happy with whom I am, a black kid
If you don't like it
Well, that's your loss
I'm Black
Aaron Woods, Grade 10
Memphis Academy of Science and Engineering, TN

Dream

Open eyes
and open mind.
A vibrant realm dances in obscurity.
Each rhythmic beat stimulates a creative trance
As wonders roam uncontrollably.

Haunting reflections of the past taunt muscles itching to rest.
Regret flushes over.

Apprehensive thoughts agonize the present twisting the bolts into stress.
Inhibitions nudge in.

Yearning visions strategically formulate plans to achieve the future.
Ambition oozes through.

A slumbering occurrence filled with jolting rapidity
Hums in the night's air.
Finally, my insomniac dream bursts
Spatters and fizzles into
Peace.
Serenity Martin, Grade 12
Germantown High School, TN

Summer Beaches
This is where the wonders begin,
Sand rubs the toes.
Warmth touches the skin,
The ray quietly goes.
Breezes greet the face,
With a salty sweet.
Then to leave in a warm embrace,
Where the water and land meet.
Waves lift,
Waves fall.

Children happily run,
Hear their laughter.
Having much fun,
And sleep well after.
Mom and Dad wait,
Big balls bounce.
Waves decide the castle's fate,
Children absorb every ounce.
Sun's rays leave the face,
This is where the wonders end.

Mary Keen, Grade 10
Coffee County Central High School, TN

Fall Leave
I see the leaves
Fall to the ground
I see them fall
But they have no sound.

They're all full of color
Throughout the day
They make a crunch when you play.

This time of year is beautiful
It really shows
How God is wonderful.

In my imagination
I can see
God's paint brush
Painting the leaves.

Jessica Tucker, Grade 10
White Plains Christian School, NC

Fighting
Swimming
In a sea of plans
Drowning
In what could—or what should
Slipping
Under the pressure
Fighting
For a better tomorrow

Alina Clarke, Grade 12
William G Enloe High School, NC

Diversity
What makes a forest so pristine?
It's not the trees of the same height and type,
It's the different colors and smells and sizes that make it great,
Since difference, is beauty.
What makes an artwork beautiful?
It's not because it uses only one kind of color and texture,
It's the different shades, colors, and ideas that make it great,
Since difference, is beauty.
What makes a book so interesting?
It's not because it uses the same words, phrases, and ideas that others use,
It's the different story, expressions, and meaning that make it great,
Since difference, is beauty.
What makes our world so great?
Is it because we all look the same, we all dress the same?
Is it because we all think and act the same?
Is it because we all speak the same language or follow the same customs?
No, diversity is what makes us beautiful and great,
Since difference, is beauty.

Savely Zakharenko, Grade 11
Germantown High School, TN

A Letter from Love
It's only when you come to think what love has to bring to you
why does love have to lie when it knows it can stay true to you
Spelling out its words Live Once Value Everything
Well it does bring you friends and can bring you closer to your enemies
So now you think it's defending you —
All along it's been pretending you —
Now you're having flashbacks
that you wish you had never seen
love can by your friend
also your worst enemy
love has to move on —
get another life from here —
pretending you, you, you, and you

Richard Webb, Grade 11
Memphis Academy of Science and Engineering, TN

The Heroic Ones
He makes numerous jump shots, three pointers, and his face is on a cereal box.
He sweats under the fluorescent gymnasium lights with the smell of victory on his fingertips.
She performs in front of millions each night, and writes number one hits.
She shakes in her heels as she sways with guitar in hand, singing her heart out.
They have fans, fortune, and fame.
But they are no heroes.
She misses her children, wishing she could see them day by day.
Her children are playing in a sandbox while she thirsts in the sandy desert.
He doesn't get dinner tonight, or breakfast in the morning.
Yet he doesn't hunger for food, but for the satisfaction of making a difference.
They are brave. They are courageous. They fight for our freedom.
They are the heroic ones.

Sarah Anderson, Grade 10
Coffee County Central High School, TN

Reflection

There is an ecstasy I feel
When pen touches paper.
It begins.
Lights dim,
Adele sings,
Rose-petal candles burn.

It's the epitome of tranquility.
No drug could make me this mellow
Letting out details of a day
Describing life's altering moments.

I've created tears from words,
One hundred smiles.
Hurt me; you're in here.
Loved me; you're in here.

Sheets of white,
Filled with my life — An escape.
The only thing I trust.

Allison Bartram, Grade 11
St Joseph Central Catholic High School, WV

Where Went the Time?

Time flies when you're having fun
It seems our lives have just begun
Starting school, a brand new year
Unaware that the end will soon be here
Preparations made, dances planned
The time is passing with each hand
Football games, basketball nights
Hints of fall and winter's delight
The warmth of spring, the melting of snow
Where oh where does the time go?
The new school year is quick to end
A warm hot summer spent with friends
The cycle never ceases to repeat
As through the years new people we'll meet
On a day in May we'll walk the line
Wondering, where went the time?

Leah A. West, Grade 10
Coffee County Central High School, TN

Morning

The sky is pink
Light and soft
Clear and bright
Soft chirps are heard
Birds have begun to wake
A soft wind blows
And the trees sway
As awaking from a good night's sleep
As the sky brightens, more chirps are heard
For morning has arrived.

Mallory Towell, Grade 12
Middle Creek High School, NC

Finding Myself

If I could disappear, I would fall into an ocean,
And swirls of blues and greens would envelop me and
My hair would spread out like tentacles and I would be the sea.
The darkness would surround me
But I would feel a light in my soul knowing I am free.
The coolness of the water would soak through every pore
And my body would float, having been absolved from its earthly duties.
I would outstretch my arms and feel every particle pass through my open hands.
To be disencumbered by the vast ocean and
Feel the pain being lifted would be enough.
But perhaps my disillusioned mind would discover that the ocean
In which my soul is immersed is a collection of fallen tears,
And I find freedom in my own pain.
This revelation could spark a realization that would grasp me from the depths
And drag me to the surface, where, struggling to find oxygen,
I would breathe
For the first time, knowing
I can save myself.
I can live.
And in disappearing,
I would appear.

Arden Tritt, Grade 12
Bishop McGuinness High School, NC

I Am From

I am from Dr. Seuss books, From Lysol and Sara Lee
I am from my Grandma's kitchen. The sweet aroma that never disappeared.
Always smelling of fresh baked bread and gardenias.
I am from the pink and white azalea bushes the flowers that only come out for a short while
Continuously changing with the seasons.
I am from Christmas cookies and deep set smile lines, From Frank and Jayne
I am from the advice-givers and the life-lovers,
From sit tight! and chin up!
I am from the Thanksgiving blessing, offered up each year
From The First Noel,
Sung at every Christmas Eve Mass since I can remember
I am from the Bible Belt,
From Elvis and BB King
To fried chicken and mashed potatoes.
From the army uniform my grandpa wore way-back-when
To the slight scar on his palm,
Always a reminder of the first date he had with her…
I am from the time-capsule
Holding all my childhood treasures, From a time where dreaming was all that mattered
I am from the stories of my ancestors, Feeling a part of each in me
I am from my past experiences — And the ones yet to come — Wherever they may lead.

Magi Higazy, Grade 11
Germantown High School, TN

The Necklace

I hold in my hand
The diamond encrusted necklace
Given to me by my father
The necklace makes me see things in a better perspective
It gives me strength and keeps me going
It gives me a better and brighter view of the future
With it, I know things will get better
When I fall down, it falls with me and helps me get back up
Whatever life throws at me, with the necklace
I will never give up
Not only do I wear it on my neck
But I wear it in my heart

When I hear the news of my father's death
Boom! The necklace falls to the ground
It breaks open
Leaving pieces all over the tile floor
The necklace is gone with him
That was the only thing I gained from my father
Now I'm not sure about the future
Where's my hope now?

Hedaya Megeed, Grade 10
Middle Creek High School, NC

Snow

The snow fell softly,
littering the ground.
The whole world was silent,
there was not a sound.
The faces looked out,
waiting for a sign.

Waiting unmoving,
no shiver nor shake.
Oblivious to sky,
no thought of ground,
lost in the depths of their thoughts.
Their minds were spinning,
lost to the void,
when all came back,
the sky and the ground,
the trees and the snow,
crouching there and laying low.

The snow kept coming it hadn't stalled,
and the silence continued as all was snow again.

Nicholas Kirkland, Grade 10
Middle Creek High School, NC

Autumn

Leaves crunching on the ground
Colors popping all around
Autumn's light appears.

Mackenzie Graves, Grade 10
Union County High School, TN

Decision

Life is not a train.
Trains make no choices, have no mistakes and no pain.
Life is a unicycle.
It is not easy, nor efficient.
There is no set direction, except for what we tell ourselves.
There is no path to follow, there are others to copy
But that is not life.
Life is adventure, doing the unknown
A road has no mystery; the woods are unbound.
A man makes choices to get where he is going,
But there is no destination; he will die along the way.
But the travels he goes through, and the things that he sees
Are what make the trip worthwhile
The pain that he goes through is what makes him stronger
People say never look back
But it is only then that we see how far we have come
The directions that we have gone.
The choices we make are always with us.
The ones that make us shine
But more importantly, the ones that make us cry
Because life is not a train.

Matthew Ahlers, Grade 12
William G Enloe High School, NC

Diversity Is

A word commonly associated with race
Can't we be diverse in other ways?
There's gender and sexual preference, blonde and brunette
The generation gap that everyone seems to be talking about
Whatever makes you different from the rest of the world
Are we judged and stereotyped by how diverse we are?
The saying is "Don't judge a book by its cover"
Are you the one doing the judging?
Take a second look at yourself, see how diverse you are
There are different faiths and beliefs
Multiple levels in the social community, rich versus poor
How do you treat these people so "different" from you?
Are you kind and understanding
Or mean and closed-minded?
Have you taken the time to get to know those people?
Ha! How are you so sure you have nothing in common with them?
So much to learn
So much to teach future generations
Take pride in your diversity, aim to be diverse
But don't push away others who are "different"
Diversity, be different.

Jevonta Foster, Grade 11
Germantown High School, TN

True Love

You turn it off likes it's a light switch.
But that can't be so.
Once you love, you either always will,
Or never did.

It's such a one-sided verb with you.
You take but never give.
We could profess our love from the mountain tops.
You just wouldn't care.

It doesn't mean a thing to you.
When you've been taught to love all,
Where is the value in the word?
It has lost its potency.

You lost hope in it a long time ago.
You never gave love a chance.
It could be what changes everything for you,
but you see it as a figment of my imagination.

True love has died.
The loss was supposed to make us alive.
It's done nothing but cause death in us all.
Can't we revive true love?

Amber Burris, Grade 11
Campbell County High School, KY

Painted Skies

As each day eventually ebbs away
Leaving fragments of glinted gold
Throughout life's sandy shore – there you'll find
Discarded canvases of painted sky
Enduring everlasting in my mind

Watercolor gradation of cerulean allure
Impasto clouds, expanding formless continuations
Enclosed by outlines of azure
Winged silhouetted figures venture into beyond
Seeking to discover The Deeper Hues
Guides acquainting me with the nature of my muse

I can remember every smudge and smear
Impish man reaching for greater heights
Before the white paint could dry, he daubed his finger
Leaving streaks and contrails behind

Disgracing the divine frescoes that God
So magnanimously exhibits
Yet HE charges nothing for the eye's visits
Painted skies – blue, gold, and clouded purity vie
As night begins to steal the beauty of the display
I anticipate the coming of the next day

Asha Gowan, Grade 12
Northwood High School, NC

The Crying Tree

O beautiful weeping willow,
do they not know of your pain
Once you re-grow your bark,
to be only cut down again.

Always must your beautiful twisted branches,
Be broken and ripped again and again.
That dreadful rain always at your roots,
to simply wash away your sin.

You, so broad, so eager,
so distraught with your strife.
With always that beaming hellish sun,
cast shadows upon your hopeless life.

When you grow old my dear,
wither slowly and die.
So much beauty you bring to the world,
why must you always, only cry.

Must you always feel so down,
and droop so lifeless this time.
Is it because all you ever grew for,
is to truly be alive?

Christopher Young, Grade 12
Belfry High School, KY

The End

It's 4 o'clock in the morning,
and I just can't stop mourning.
I always thought we belong together,
it was supposed to be me and you forever.

Nothing hurts worse than to know,
that this is the end to our show.
I always hoped you'd one day love me back,
to know that you never will, has caused me to crack.

I always thought you were it for me,
twin boys and girls is what I was determined to see.
Wedding bells were soon to ring,
we were supposed to get married at eighteen.

For six years I had a dream,
I woke up to reality with a scream.
We were just kids when we planned this out,
back then there was no doubt.

It's disappointing to know I'm the only one broken,
you could care less from what's been spoken.
All I can do is move away,
and hope that haunted I will not stay.

Cameo Arnold, Grade 12
Ooltewah High School, TN

Shall I Compare Thee to a Tear

Shall I compare thee to a tear
that falls upon a grieving face
that shows emotions so clear
that knows you can't replace

An army of frustration
that shows no defeat
and causes a sad sensation
that cannot be beat

A drop of water so meaningful
but also revealing
yet very painful
but still shows the feeling

After the storm has died down
there is no more need to frown.

Ana Rico, Grade 10
Loretto High School, TN

Inspiration

Inspiration is like rain,
It can wane,
It can storm,
Or it can languish.

Inspiration is like rain,
It can drizzle,
It can flood,
Or it can be a drought.

Inspiration is like rain,
It can be pleasant,
It can be overpowering,
Or it can be annoying.

Jenna Grace Hill, Grade 11
Providence Academy, TN

In Between the Halls

Just in an instant
All productivity stops
Slaving to the bell

Cram all your papers
For it's time for the next class
All things are chaos

Without an order
Students migrate to the door
Class matters no more

For this six minutes
You must dodge all the traffic
An intense graphic

James Goodall, Grade 12
William G Enloe High School, NC

Jewelry Box

A jewelry box so beautiful and rare, outside scratched from life
Injured by individuals, passed down generations,
History hiding in the hinges of the wooden top.
Interior polished to a glossy finish
Mute walls watched unspeakable crimes, witnessed wretched experiences
The shining of the strong, stable wood
Reminds me of the excitement contained in this etched chest of stories.
Tales from each trinket of jewelry, imprinted on my soul now…
Each ring has a previous owner, every necklace linked with luck and love.
Scraps both silver and gold, interlaced with past memories,
Love…both lost and found.
Shimmering silver, drenched with devotion
Glittering gold gleaming with pride.
The cold, dark lid must be closed…
Thinking, sulking is the only thing to do,
Dragging out thoughts that are better left in the cracks of the woodwork.
This precious tiny rectangle is my own world
Where only certain people can hear my tales
Experience life through my eyes in flashback.
Underneath the jewelry so exact, impeccably placed
You will discover me.

Sierra Brown, Grade 12
Simon Kenton High School, KY

Look at Me

Look at me and what do you see?
Can you describe me to a T? Or is there more to be told?

Look at my past and what do you think?
Is it worth the time it took? Or could it just be forgotten
Look at my present and what could you say?
That I'm doing well for myself or do I need to step up the game?
Now take a look at my future and what can you see?
Is it bright and successful, or do I need to do things a different way?

Now tell me can you describe me to a T, or are you just not sure?
Can you tell me how I feel? Or it's not written on my face so do I hide it well?
Can you tell me that I'm original? Or do you need a human dictionary
As anyone can see you not the judge of me
And you know it too. So let me go and we will all be free.

Whitney Sellers, Grade 10
Stanly Early College School, NC

Sleep Forever

There's something about the walls, the way the sun shines through the trees.
The colors, the air were so welcoming and so unknown
my mind wandering through the bricked streets
ideas of the everlasting feel of finding you
ache and confusion numb our reality.
The idea of tomorrow hides me from today
music carrying through the wind
sounds of humming
light of the moon…
follows me home

Becca Sprigg, Grade 11
Sacred Heart Academy, KY

Love

Love is kind
It is the source of all good
It makes people bind

Love is not evil
Love lightens the mood
We all love someone
Or in the end we should

In the circle of life
As long as we have peace together
We will love each other

I am happy to say also
That I love this day
I love my life
And my friends

If no one tells a lie
Love will last forever
To the end of our lives

Brad Northern, Grade 12
McClain Christian Academy, TN

Goodnight Mademoiselle

good night good night mademoiselle
for now I wish to bid farewell
lay your head down to rest
let your hair fall over your chest
sleep so sound
with dreams profound,
until at last you break your fast
it is the next morrow
filled with sorrow,
since thou hast left the place of serenity
which takes thou to a place of divinity
you wait all day
so you may lay
your head to rest
and your hair fall over your chest
I shall bid farewell
good night good night mademoiselle

Edward Wooldridge, Grade 10
North Duplin Jr/Sr High School, NC

Crow's Silhouette

On a withered branch
A crow has settled and paused
Autumn night fallen.

The wind blows briskly
As to match the eerie dusk
The crow goes grimly onward.

Benjamin Knack, Grade 12
Sycamore High School, TN

I Am From

I am from lotion,
 (Sweet smelling take the dry away lotion)
from the brand Jergens and the compound Glycerol.
I am from the green grass in the vast yard.
 (Green, fresh cut, it tasted like green beans)
I am from the pink, sprouting Crepe Myrtle,
 the hedge in the green front yard
 whose sticky thorns I remember as if it was yesterday.
I am from honey bun cake and eyeglasses,
 From the Kendrick and Thomas, from the Anderson and Jefferies.
I am from the truth seekers and the have to hear it themselves,
From the We are Proud of You! and To Do Your Best!
I am from the house that serves the Lord
 with Bible verses and worship, with Ten Commandments that I can recite
I am from southern barbecue and the mighty Mississippi.
 from fried chicken and Thanksgiving Day dressing,
From the big hats of my aunt and to the dramatic flair of her husband,
 and the laugh of my niece.
I am from the attic where all my history lies, From old pictures waiting to be found,
From birth records and Social Security Numbers spilling out from boxes,
I am from these moments documented in time.

Alisa Anderson, Grade 11
Germantown High School, TN

Where I'm From

I am from the residence on Richmond,
    from the peeling paint and chipped wood the neighborhood children all mocked.
I am from the air of the spacious back porch,
    my conspicuous hideaway.
I am from the faux rose bushes that decorated our front yard,
    their fading colors collecting both sunlight and dust,
    lying as dormant as that extensive road.
I am from teaching and song writing
I am from "your side of the family,"
    from Mahalia and Curtis.
I am from the night hawks and the perfectionists
I am from Holy, Holy, Holy
    with the lyrics of my first solo in my hand
    and the butterflies that fill my stomach when I sing.
Propping up our outdated television was an album
    overrunning with pictures,
    my mother's eagerness to capture every moment,
    my own desire to change into clothes I was allowed to play in.
I am from that place,
    undone before I finished,
    a root protruding from the ground.

Victoria Gray, Grade 11
Germantown High School, TN

A Million Sparkles

The morning mist hung around
It was a striking sight
Everything glittered and glistered
The turquoise valley glowed white
It was a million sparkles —
Fallen from a star light

The morning mist hung around
Moisture played on soft ground
Daisies twinkled like jewels
Berries shimmered so bright
It was a million sparkles —
Fallen from a star light

Amanda Sutton, Grade 12
Precept Academy, NC

Shattered

Day by day
I feel it break
Cracked by the pain it absorbs
How much more can it take
Before it shatters

Pieces scattered
Like broken glass
Reflecting the past

Shattered
Scattered
How long can my heart last?

Kiana Ballard, Grade 11
East Ridge High School, TN

Honey Glazed Eyes

Honey glazed eyes,
A soul that never dies
Making others smile
The laughter lasts for miles
With sun-kissed skin,
And a childish grin

Suddenly attacked with hate
Made his heart ache
Still he lived, laughed and loved
Never put anything above
What his heart told him to do
For this he will always be true

Doha Medani, Grade 10
Grimsley High School, NC

A Sometimes Native Daughter

I am dark eyes and child bearin' hips,
blackberry branches and midnight swims.
No stranger to the taste of honeysuckle,
you could call me a flower child.
But often, I'm the girl in the suicide stilettos,
only invincible if I'm packing six inches.

Other times I am barefoot baptisms,
Mississippi tides, and renewed virgin sighs.

But my veins don't always bleed traces of beauty,
I am backwards beliefs and rural minds.
Roots thick with prejudice, that may uplift enlightened tree stems.
I am Pawpaw's racial slurs, and his kind eyes.
Granola crunching and greasy chicken thighs.
Grandma's goodnight kiss,
under the canopy of her confederate quilt.

I am bones carved from the trunk of ancestral strong will.

I am no nukes and Kent State, free love and the ERA, sit-Ins and charred draft cards.
I am the frog farm. Pumpkin pie, and cupped fire flies.
Paul McCartney and acoustic guitars.
At the same time, I am so many stars. Within a vivid blackness that only can be
Kentucky.

Amelia Gramling, Grade 12
Home School, KY

Diversity Is…

Diversity is a Skittles bag,
filled with multicolored candies and tastes.
It is the World, which contains
humans, birds, plants, and many other things.

Diversity is the days of the year,
with each day bringing a variety of occurrences
different from any other day.
It is the diverse nature of humans.
Caucasian, African American, Asian, and many other ethnicities.

Diversity is walking through a mall finding a shoe store, a food store, and a game store.
It is Language.
English, Spanish, Chinese, French, and more.
It is a bag of Chex Mix containing a wide assortment of food.

Diversity is Halloween with goblins and ghouls and witches and zombies.
It is the bag of candy emptied at the end of the day.
It is religion
with Christian and Catholic and many, many more.

Diversity is everything different working in harmony.
It is what makes this world special,
what makes it interesting.
And without it, we'd never be.

Chase Williams, Grade 11
Germantown High School, TN

English Class

Every day,
new challenges appear.
However, I know that I can
face them here.
My English class
is all I need
to make me
see such powerful dreams.
I dream
of writing
and painting.
I dream
of the things
I can achieve.
This is all made possible
by a class
filled with opinions
and dreams.
This one class
opened my eyes
to what I really dream.

Sarah Bandel, Grade 12
Clarksville Academy, TN

What Is Happiness?

What is happiness?
Are we ever truly happy
Or do we feel something
That isn't real
I've heard happiness
Comes from love
Is love real
Or a figment of our imagination
Do we dream of happiness
Or dream of love
But where is reality
The thing that dampens
Our spirits and hurts
Reality is real
Reality is pain
Reality causes our happiness

Alda Royal, Grade 10
Grimsley High School, NC

Lonely Stranger

Lonely stranger, hiding in the darkness
Come forward and show your face
Don't be scared of your bareness
And your intricate race
Be proud and loyal to your family
And humanly to all
Stand out and stand tall

Jeffrey Chandler, Grade 12
William G Enloe High School, NC

Who Am I?

I am from a picture frame,
from Kodak and nice smiles.
I am from the circle of pavement,
I am from the pot of Poinsettias,
the Sunflower whose bright petals remind me of my personality.
I am from family gatherings and well-rounded hips,
from Louella and Emma Grace and Farmer.
I am from the do righters and the do mighters,
from Speak up! and Don't back down!
I am from obey your parents and you will live long on the Earth,
and Bible games, and popsicle stick crosses.
I am from Memphis and Joe Lee's and Webster's tree,
smoked barbecue and Now and Laters.
From the grandfather who was the pastor of two churches,
the uncle who survived during the Vietnam War,
and the aunt who lost her life due to a reckless drunk driver.
In the top of the guest room closet are many large and small boxes,
filled with pictures, birth certificates, and awards,
I sit and look back on all the things that I remember and all the things that I missed.
I am from these many moments,
going in and out of time.

Amber Farmer, Grade 11
Germantown High School, TN

Summertime

When I recall my summer,
A perfect, peaceful time brings my heart aches of longing.
I had no responsibilities, nothing expected of me,
no obligations or nagging worries.
When I remember my summer,
I reminisce of my days in the hazy, sparkling hot weather,
enjoying the seasonal treats and nature's unrivaled beauty.
I spent my nights in oversized flannel T-shirts,
cruising in a car going much too fast.
When I remember my summer,
All I see are endless nights,
stretching out in a seemingly infinite abundance.
Those matchless two summer months,
are undisputed to be the happiest time of my life.
When I remember my summer,
Present dark skies suddenly seem far away,
and again I am visited by the ghost of my past bliss.
The sudden end came much too fast,
the sweetness was snuffed out without warning.
I run to the cherished summertime memories when trouble overwhelms me,
and have to smile in admission of my many blessings.

Abigail Davis, Grade 11
Germantown High School, TN

Never Forever Hers

She dances a dance of her life
She dances it all away.
The crimson seeps, stains the shoes,
And those dry eyes only fool,
Hides the crimson blooming within her,
Blooming as she falls and withers.

The shell of her stops breathing
Finally, after having already lost meaning.
She leaves only those lifeless eyes,
Collapsing without a cry.

And under the white face's spotlight,
In the night of a cold December,
A lady in pink so graceful:
Crimson stains upon her feet,
A sparkle on her finger,
Empty eyes of cold longing,
For his hand, reaching.
The hand that was to be
Never forever hers.

Yon-Soo Lee, Grade 12
William G Enloe High School, NC

Prima Ballerina

I once was loved,
Adored even.
I once was the center of attention,
A thing of beauty.
Always in the spotlight,
Always on the main stage.
I got applause.
I was cheered for.
No longer.
Now I am abandoned.
Cast into the shadows,
My beauty forgotten.
No more love,
No more adoration.
I am nothing.
Alone.

Lauren Horton, Grade 11
Germantown High School, TN

Her Beauty Sings

Once an eagle, lost his wings.
Crushing all his hopes and dreams.
He saw her, her beauty sings.
Thought of her mostly in his dreams.
A fallen angel, what she must be.
She helped him up, helped him see.
She helped him soar, gave him wings.
Away they flew, her beauty sings.

William Mankins, Grade 10
Preston High School, WV

Friday Night

Through the tunnel we march
As the darkness shrouds
Drowning in anticipation, yet for victory, parched
Our heads held high, our expectations in the clouds
We know all too well what lies ahead

We listen to our anthem, followed by a prayer
Then a sound erupts from under the stands and fills the air
From the lungs of these young men, ready for this test
The sound, a battle cry, no less
Reminding us that defeat was not an option, however victory was, instead

When the kickoff is away, the air is electric
Bodies crashing, helmets clashing, the crowd is eccentric
Of blood, sweat, and tears, we have no fear
Let your emotions and passions be fueled by the crowd as it cheers:
"Go Big Red!"

The stadium now dark, the battle has been won
Regrets, doubts, our team has none
For four years, the memories are made
For lifetime, these memories stay
The greatest memories of all being of every other team's dread

Steven P. Everett, Grade 10
Coffee County Central High School, TN

Cancer

There's a cancer growing deep within me…
Tugging at the harpsichords of all the vitality of one's being.
It sucks and steals all of life's joys and wonders.
I need somewhere to hide.
To decay and mold over…
All for nothing, to think.
Was there ever meaning within any of this?
Some are evil…but most are dumb.
And I need somewhere to hide.
This cancer grows deeper…
With more and more vivid signs of decay.
All the sounds turn into the sounds of streets.
Taking its toll step by step…one mile at a time.
The rain is the face of a long lost friend…ever so welcoming.
Just trying to get where you need to be…becoming who I need to be…
This cancer inside me, I welcome it…
It gives me rest through ache along on the extra mile.
The feelings of rejoicing
And the feel of being needed.
All reflect to the uselessness you've overturned…
Just like this cancer.

Nathan Holbrook, Grade 12
Elliott County High School, KY

Sunlight

Sunlight rolls
Off her sweet cheeks
The love rises,
To embrace me.
The sunlight filters
Through the day,
And the cast of Night
Is held at bay.
The sunlight folds
Her sheets of gold,
And allows the light
To shine true, shine bold.
It cannot keep me
Awake much longer.
Soon to the night
Her strength will falter.
Farewell to the day,
Hello to the night.
I'll see you again
At the first morning's light.

Nichole Lay, Grade 11
Havelock High School, NC

"Courage" Is a Thing of Metal

"Courage" is a thing of metal —
That covers the fragile flesh —
And locks away chilling Fear —
All within a second.

"Courage" intoxicates the weak —
Addicts them to its strength —
And the infamous Pride —
Which pleases the Soul.

It emits a feeling of invincibility —
It stupefies the rational mind —
And unless the poison is diluted —
Before reaching the brain —
"Courage" will leave you cold.

Emily Key, Grade 10
Germantown High School, TN

My Brush

This is my paintbrush that sets me free
But what this brush paints nobody can see

This brush by six strings is bound
This brush paints with beautiful sound

It is black and pearl with a covering of gloss
It can show happiness, sorrow, or even loss

This is my guitar I choose to play
I hope it lives on to be played another day

Jared Chandler, Grade 10
Coffee County Central High School, TN

The Second

I wanted to say something really sweet, but…it's just not coming out.
I don't usually have to use my lips to do the talking, since they are usually occupied.
I can see it in your eyes, even though it's dark.
The glimmer I see there absorbs me into a hypnotic stare.
It's the strangest moment, but I see it fit
It's time you saw who I really am and throw a fit
I'm not it. not him. not the one.
I'm the Second.
Clone, clone of a clone moreover.
The DNA scrambled and tests a failure.
Yet I walk with you now, to show I care.
Human emotion, erodication.
Fear, Hate, Love… Vaccinated.
I ask you now… are you the last?
Your a blast from the past, only better.
Better in that I can have you, hold you, keep you.
Not a secret, not confined.
But everlasting and always mine.

Cole McBroom, Grade 11
Phoenix School of Discovery, KY

I Remember…

I remember going to Walmart and getting whatever I want.
I remember when we would go outside and play volleyball and soccer.
I remember sitting and waiting for you to come home, but giving up and going to bed.
I remember all the times you never came home sober or on time.
I remember not ever seeing my dad like other teenage girls.
I remember all the days of my life that meant so much to me that you missed.
I remember all the days you would fight with my mom and then run off.
I remember the day you should have stayed home, but thought fun was more important.
Then…
I remember all the times walking in the nursing home to see you.
I remember seeing you learn to walk again, but not be there yet.
I remember giving up friends' invitations to come see you.
I remember going to church and praying that things would change.

Lauren Tyser, Grade 12
Berkeley Springs High School, WV

Glistening

She strides onto the stage shyly
Bare feet grasp the forgotten glitter and grime from the polished wooden floor:
A faint remembrance of the lively acts before
Dark, delicate curls tangle down her back and frame her gentle, negligible face
All the makeup in the world couldn't make that face anything but ordinary
So she stands at an average height with an ordinary face, and makes her way onto the stage
Toward the grand, obscure instrument introduced by the dim spotlight
She positions the bench awkwardly before the awaiting audience
And sits stiff as a stranger to this brilliant structure
Her childlike fingers run smoothly, swiftly over the keys in flawless rhythm
The piano hums an eerie hymn, perturbing the audience's jovial humor,
Coercing their every will on the tiny girl who sits so naturally before them
This average, common, everyday child surpasses mediocrity in one aspect:
Her music — her rhythm, her harmony, her crescendo, her emotion, her pathos
In this, she glistens

Sydney Davis, Grade 11
Elizabethtown High School, KY

Sonnet #2

Darlin' don't ask if I love you or not.
If I didn't, I'd've left long ago.
If you were gone, I'd feel like I'd been shot.
The boat of our love is still yet afloat.

Now, honey don't you say you ain't perfect.
You always seem to know just what to do.
No, we can't always know the effect,
But I love all you do, just 'cause it's you.

You're everything I ever wanted.
Yeah, I promise you, you're all that I need,
And if you left me, then I'd be haunted
By your sweet and beautiful memory.

I don't do drugs, I don't have bloodshot eyes,
'Cause baby you're all I need to get high.

Dylan Berry, Grade 10
Union County High School, TN

Autumn's Days

As the leaves begin to fall through crisp air
A hay ride passes by down the dirt road
Full of people and wind blowing their hair.
The tractor is slowing with its big load.

The colors, orange and red, peek through the trees.
The children are out going trick-or-treat.
Some are dressed as witches, some go as bees.
The Thanksgiving table is set real neat.

The table is set with corn, beans, and roast.
Children play while the adults sit and talk.
Uncle Hank cooks and Aunt Joanna hosts.
I can't help but to go on a walk.

The beautiful colors should be gazed upon.
Oh, what a day, when Autumn ends up gone.

Leslie Beeler, Grade 10
Union County High School, TN

Heart of Sorrow

I am drowning from lust in his blue eyes,
The sinking will stop through love he emits.
My love is blinded, I cannot see his lies.
His great blue oceans are bottomless pits.
My world is brightened from his smallest sighs;
A love so deep that I am losing wits.
Can he not see the way my sad heart cries?
My head is telling me to call it quits;
What this head says, this love-sick heart denies.
My heart can't stop showing what it submits.
This dear love is no longer in disguise.
He always knew the love my heart transmits.
No more waiting for his love to arise,
I'm ready to face his final goodbyes.

Samantha Couch, Grade 12
Starmount High School, NC

My Mind Is Blank

My mind is blank as I stare at the sheet.
I am no good poet you must understand.
You see, it is quite the struggle to meet.
I realized the time is at hand,
so I met sonnet poems face to face.
I really don't know why you would do this,
It completely leaves my mind in a daze.
I honor Shakespeare for doing this for bliss,
now that I know how hard it really is.
I honestly think this should have been banned.
Yes I know that none are as great as his,
but he was definitely a smart man.
I have defeated the sonnet poem,
growing a much stronger hatred for them.

Kara Wagoner, Grade 12
Starmount High School, NC

Rising of Tidal Mythology

Let the tide wash away the sand
That dirties our feet
And travel to the stallion of the sea
So merry and gay and free
Depicted in a picture that is suspended
On my wall decorated with a mural of its home

Let the child be lost in the sea
Borne of Sea foam
Standing in a clam
Gab to the fish that
Is equipped with a weapon and knows how to fence
And when the conversations become moot
Let the Titans rain down fire and Poseidon upon the shore

Claire Braxton, Grade 12
Isaac Bear Early College High School, NC

Shall I Compare Thee to a Stormy Afternoon?

Shall I compare thee to a stormy afternoon?
You are more swift and fierce.
Thunder rattles the windowpanes of old houses,
Then disappears into the slowly approaching night.
Sometimes the downpour chokes the undergrowth,
And the branches of even grand oaks wilt;
Even the prettiest flowers must decline,
By chance, or by fickle nature's course, lays undiscovered;
But your internal thunderstorm shall not fade,
Or lose possession of your dancing fury,
Darkness shall never claim you,
When you move from East to West,
So long as the wind blows, and life resists,
So long you live, and restlessness gives you life.

Kathryn Dixon, Grade 12
Germantown High School, TN

The Room

The mention by parents is always a constant
They want it done immediately and it must meet their standard
No matter how hard you try they will cast judgment
Children try so hard, but merely end up flustered

They want our rooms clean and spotless
Seldom offering assistance or a hand
The sheer thought of a clean room is bogus
Yet it is expected, and expected at their command/demand

But rooms are not meant to be clean
We slave away and they are cluttered within days
It's not like I can catch a cleaning gene
And even if I did, I'd never even clean my doorway

The bedroom of a child is meant to be welcoming and homey
Never tidy, bare, and lonely

Gizelle Harris, Grade 12
William G Enloe High School, NC

The Gentlemen's Game

I stare deeply into the board,
a wall splotched in black and white.
I see royalty lined up like lambs to the slaughter.
They methodically scatter,
searching for sanctuary,
reaching for vengeance,
constantly fighting a war without reason.
Warriors are felled and positions taken.
The slain are removed from the fray,
a trophy for the victor.
A lord falls.
The long dead and the living return to their lines,
the battle resumes.

Spencer Jones, Grade 10
Germantown High School, TN

Unintentionally Indifferent

The melanocytes in my cheeks are stagnant,
refusing to produce magenta, ruby, rose, or
even the slightest hint of salmon.

Let them turn my face to wine,
so my embarrassment can intoxicate you.

Let the transformed pigment in my
cheeks show for me the pain, the love, the anger that
even I am not willing to give away.

Let me sit here thinking something other than,
"I wish I could blush."

Nadine Worley, Grade 10
Livingston Academy, TN

The History of a Life

I am from jackets,
from Apple and oxygen.
I am from the bedroom.
(Beige, wooden floors,
felt so smooth)
I am from the rose bush
the maple tree
whose long-grown trunk arced
I remember as if it were my own back.

I'm from Saturday tennis and bad eyesight,
from Sriraman and Lalitha.
I'm from the highest caste
and the one to continue the line
I'm from multiple gods to
pray to help
and some holy scriptures I know by heart.

I'm from Colorado Springs and Ramaswamy's Branch,
rice and homemade juice.
From the bridges my grandfather made
to support the people of his country,
the stuff my mom's mom made to keep us happy.

Swamynathan Sriraman, Grade 11
Germantown High School, TN

I Am

I am from rulers, from Converse Low Tops
And baritones
I am from big red pillars out front
Warm, loud, sounds of friends
I am from the magnolia trees in my backyard
The buckeyes, which represent my family's state

I am from Thanksgiving dinner and thick brown hair
From Mary and Jon and the Huber Clan
I am from shouting matches we had
And the tendency to laugh too much
From Santa's existence and the Easter Bunny
From rosaries and the all encompassing smell of incense

I am from Santa Rosa, California and German heritage
Skyline Chili and Buffalo Chicken Dip
From the Fourth of July at my Uncle Dave's house
When AJ almost blew off his leg with
A firecracker
And the smell of hamburgers cooking
On a fiery grill
And the stories of Chris Vetter's
Crazy youth

Michael Loyd, Grade 11
Germantown High School, TN

Gravity

A heart beats for one purpose,
and only one.
Not to keep the person alive;
but to fall in love.
Because without love
a person is dead.
They are lost and alone,
dazed and confused.
When love is found,
they no longer feel
alone or lost.
They may still be dazed;
that's what love does…
It catches you off guard and pushes you over a cliff.
Falling in love;
isn't an option.
You just…
Fall.
Like it or not.
And all you can do is hope and pray
that another heart will be there to catch you.

Lauren Hupp, Grade 11
Holly Springs High School, NC

Beamer's Boast

Her name is Kelsey, kind and kinetic,
An artist, associating body and music. For
On the tips of her toes she twinkles and twirls, with
Pride and passion pointing her to perfection.
To dance she decides, to devote her day,
Only when studies and homework are satisfactory.
Her God she loves with all her heart, and
Sunday means church and meeting with youth.
A kitchen chemist, so you could call her,
With a joy for baking cookies and cake.
Her eyes are her daddy's, a glorious guardian,
Who wisecracks, deer stalks, and delights in mischief.
Her sister Karlie, with a happy face and heart,
Loves, leads, and always listens.
Her mother she misses more each day, yet
Sees a familiar face and smile in the mirror.
For on a Friday a brave fighter flew,
And God greeted an angel at Heaven's great gate.
Her family is small, but dearly devoted
To encouraging, emboldening, and loving each other.

Kelsey Beamer, Grade 12
Starmount High School, NC

Tears

tears
water droplets
from my eye, to my cheek
from deep in my heart, in my soul
sorrow

Kyra Hutchinson, Grade 12
William G Enloe High School, NC

Unedifying Age

I feel time wasting away
Slipping through my fingers,
Days of perfect weather
Fading into an inevitable snowy bliss.
The shiver of knowing childhood is disappearing
Creates an avalanche throughout my very essence
The weight of newfound adult expectations
Flurry down gracefully, increasing inch upon inch on my shoulders.
Father Time and Mother Nature
Smile a satanic smirk —
Building a college fund
Bulky…moderate and meager
Finishing with coal eyes and a carrot nose.
They pelt me with job applications
That burst and disintegrate
At the slightest touch of my warm innocent skin.
Oh, the harsh reality of getting older, growing up
I watch my summer days drift away an hour at a time.
The silver lining?
  There will always be the occasional snow day.

Tori Gabbard, Grade 11
Simon Kenton High School, KY

Where I'm From

I am from hair relaxers,
From Dark and Lovely and sodium hydroxide
I am from the smell of fried home-cooked food
(sweet, tasty, warm like a breath of fresh air.)
I am from family gatherings and pretty,
brown eyes hidden behind eyeglasses,
from Daphnee and Travis and Housley
I am from jokes and jokes
and the laugh-out-live fun,
from "Stop Talking!" and "You go girl!"
I'm from the Almighty God and
the Savior of all beings
and the ten commandments of the Bible.
I'm from Memphis and Housley's House,
spaghetti and rotel.
I am from the frame of pictures
hanging on the wooden wall,
and the laughs and smiles that fill each picture
the memories that we cherish each day,
and the times we will never forget!

Raven Housley, Grade 11
Germantown High School, TN

Triumph

The earth shook and groaned.
When all the dust did settle,
Nothing could be seen.
But finally rising up,
The good overcame evil.

Blake Tyree, Grade 11
Providence Academy, TN

Curtain Close

Eyes that have never held a smile
Only the reflection of another's
Her teeth only shown in embarrassed grins
She's an actress, of the highest regard
Never failing in her act
It's a play that never ends
When will the curtain close?
A puppet master seems to feed her lines
Sayings of "Oh, I'm just fine"
Her nose could be buried in the script
When in reality, she's just trying not to cry
Her friends? They're actors of their own
They tend to forget time and time again
That her story has just begun
But it's heading further from their sun
Everybody seems to be ready for its end,
But she's just an everyday actress
Waiting for her curtain to close
So she might start her actual life
Emily Ramser, Grade 11
Wake Forest-Rolesville High School, NC

Prophecy

Searchers of the chosen way,
Guard the truth you seek.
Hide the light from evil eyes,
Who look only to take.
Beware an evil seeker comes,
A battle near to win.
Discover truth before the day
When finished time shall end.
An era dawns, an epoch fades,
The haunt of time grows dim.
Forgotten sons of ancient rhyme
Shall find their journey's end.
The precious cost of sacrifice,
The chosen son born new.
His gift alone can pay the price
To seal the evil's doom.
Then truth revealed shall guard the hearts
Of those who walk its way.
A greater good than ancient stones
Disclosed by heaven's ray.
Brooke Belcher, Grade 11
Home School, NC

Question

The power to question
A contradicting concept itself
Not because it is such
But how it's distributed is.

As a child:
Don't question your teacher,
Ideals, parents
Or authority itself.

As adults:
Question the law,
Traditions, values
And authority itself.

While young, don't
Yet old, do?
How clear must such be
Before it is challenged?
Robert Sumpter, Grade 12
Woodrow Wilson High School, WV

As the World Slowly Turns

As the world slowly turns
Rivers run black and the forest burns
People cough when they venture outside
No flowers are seen for far and wide

Children feel gnawing pain
Of a hunger the land cannot wane
Under the scorching hot sun they toil
Because of greed that reeks of oil

Fiery shells and bombs explode
People scatter as events erode
Become refugees in foreign lands
At the mercy of others' hands

Those who sit and wait are many
For cleanliness, for peace, for plenty
Without action these are but concerns
As the world slowly turns
Hannah Hogewood, Grade 12
Enloe High School, NC

Alone

Lost in a sea of uncertainty
Unsure of who I've become
I no longer recognize myself
My heart has become numb

I lost myself on a pathway
And there's no way to get back
Too scared to move forward
But too proud to move back

No hand to hold onto
No crutch to help me stand
No hope to lift my spirits
I'm left alone on this deserted land

Uncertain of who I will become
In the process of finding out who I am
But I make it my mission to find out
And break free from this barren land
Jordan Lewis, Grade 12
William G Enloe High School, NC

Endless War

A war is raging, an endless war
Soldiers fight and soldiers fall
Two countries fighting, lives are lost
People crying, loved ones gone
People wondering will it end
People missing, people gone

An endless war is being fought
A mourning heart missing loved ones
Brothers gone to fight this war
Fathers die for your freedom
Husbands leave for a goal
Gone forever, for us gone

Aching hearts, crying children
Mourning mothers, weeping wives
An endless war, many die
An endless war, hopes all gone
Why fight this war and lose your loved?
why fight a war, a losing war?
Mariya Shostak, Grade 11
Clyde A Erwin High School, NC

Unknown

She is unknown
She's a stranger to me
Who is she?
I don't know her
Living life and everything
Appears to be great
Well, everything isn't always what it seems

Sad from abandonment
How could you give up your child?
I have no need for material things
I feel lost
I need to know my background
Where did I come from?
Is she like a twin? Yes, We look alike
Do we act the same? I don't know
I don't know her
She's UNKNOWN

Asia Hendricks, Grade 10
Memphis Academy of Science and Engineering, TN

Precious Time

Crystal clear are his words,
each one slicing deeper than the last.
In no way could they be misinterpreted.
A well-rehearsed script,
that had been engrained in my mind,
shot from his lips.
An excuse.
Something more important than me.
Nothing could leave me more unsurprised.
It shouldn't bother me,
but it does.
My inquiry is just another failed attempt,
to break through the impenetrable wall,
that has grown between us.
Most mornings the glimmer of hope I wake up with diminishes,
to barely a flicker.
Today it was extinguished.
He will never hear his daughter ask for his precious time again.

Heather Yeomans, Grade 12
Germantown High School, TN

Storm

Sitting, thinking of her
I sit here and concur
How one of two are the same
With a joyful heart, I exclaim
Her eyes are like lightning
Looking into them makes my heart brightening
Her voice is like thunder
Hearing it fills me with cheer and wonder
Her face of a cloud
Even at its worst, beautiful, a proclaimed avowed
Her kindness like rain
It pours into me and nourishes my soul, love I only gain
Everything about her is like a storm
An astonishing spectacle in the most heavenly form
Perfection in its purest state, even if she passes through
Seeing her has left a smile on my face, which is like a rainbow

Zachary Steele, Grade 12
Sycamore High School, TN

The Autumn Flame

The firewood was collected
The woods were evergreen
Both waiting to compete with the sun
As night settled, the Earth was cooled
The wood and the trees saw the light
Red, brown, orange, yellow came from the Earth and sky
Slowly the colors spread
And consumed all on their way
As the moon shone
the fire and the bright colors slowed
Burned to the ground
the leaves are nestled in their new home
It had left death and destruction
The Autumn Flame fled
It left only ashes
For the winter storm to eat

Caitlin Bonner, Grade 11
West Wilkes High School, NC

A Place to Lose Yourself In

Libraries
Tons of books adorning the many shelves
People studying — no doubt cramming for some test
The librarian "Shushing" loud teenagers
The sound of several crisp pages being flipped
"New Book Scent"
Coffee drifting from somewhere in the building
Wrigley's spearmint gum
The stale air of the building
Glad to be immersed in the world of the book I'm reading
Content, for now, until I have to leave
A place to lose yourself in

Ivory Brown, Grade 11
Berkeley Springs High School, WV

Into the Blinding Storm

Building rain
Outside in this tempest dream
The sky is a writhing, roiling mass of dusky clouds
And black winged birds
Invoking, conjuring, bringing forth
Buffeting, whipping winds of western displeasure
Amid their dark timeless feathers
Summon the loose, milky exile of the brain
And the pretty excesses of our tapered hands and fingers
We sweep upon the crying child
Out in the blinding storm
Alone.

Hope Siler, Grade 10
Gibson County High School, TN

High Merit Poems – Grades 10, 11, and 12

Inflamed

The fire's mesmerizing flames,
dance in front of me
in an elaborate pattern.
Constantly moving,
never performing with the same partner twice.
The persistent crackle of the wood
is like a glorious symphony to my ears.
Warmth from the fire,
weaves a blanket around me,
that I encase myself in.
When I start to shut
my increasingly heavy eyes,
the wind shifts
and smoke from the fire
embraces me.
Forced to move,
the smoke squeezing at my lungs,
I must warm up
all over again.

Carter Eakin, Grade 10
Germantown High School, TN

I Remember…

I remember December 14th, 2000.
I remember a crying baby in my room.
I remember long stressful days.
I remember mom and dad yelling.
I remember dirty diapers and baby powder.
I remember being an only child.
I remember my parents feeding one child.
I remember silence at the dinner table.

Then…

Many different voices at dinner.
A brother I can take under my wing.
A little brother who looks up to me.
A big brother who tries to be a perfect role model.

Aaron Morrell, Grade 11
Berkeley Springs High School, WV

Summer to Keep

The smell of roses give me goosebumps.
As I gaze at the blistering sun, I smile
God is watching, I say in my head quietly
Honeyed dew droplets made the dark vegetation blossom
I was in heaven for a while, as the birds chirped
singing their soft melody.
I praised their passion for their gift
At night I said my prayers:
Now I lay me, down to sleep, I pray
this gorgeous summer to keep
If I should die before I wake
I pray the Lord with me, also the summer to take.

Phillip Bradley, Grade 10
Central High School, KY

Early Colonial Life

Young children skip down the road towards school,
The fall morning air brisk and cool.
They walk by farmers plowing their fields,
And for a head of cattle, they must yield.
In the far off distance they can see,
The approaching wagon of a new family.
A young couple is being wed in the chapel they pass,
But they can't stay and watch, or they will be late to class.
As they scurry inside and find their seats,
They excitedly exchange tales of the weekend's feats.
Their teacher enters, and they gather their things —
Their hornbooks and primers ready for what the day brings.
Later, to their log house they rush to do their chores,
For there will be no dinner unless they are done before.
Afterwards they hurry out in the yard to play,
As their parents sit on the porch, finishing the day.
That night they lay in their beds and pray,
That the good Lord will keep disease at bay.

Jessica Lockhart, Grade 12
Seymour Community Christian School, TN

Darkness

Here in the Darkness, I lose myself.
All thoughts of the day fly away
My only comfort has left me,
What will I find?

Here in the darkness, ordinary people surround me,
The silence is bliss for all of us.
The outside world is chaos,
And only we have left.

In my shroud of silence,
The world flies by.
No pain can heal me,
No words can soothe the bumps that have grown over my mind.

Here in the Darkness.

Brittany Tabor, Grade 12
Ripley High School, TN

Family Tree

Family
like an ancient tall tree
Our roots run deep…
We branch off but always find our way home
Family
like a strong, solid tree
We stand high, mighty
You cannot break us
Family
like a towering, imposing tree
Each held up by a trunk of family
So strong and so silently solid.

Destiny Crain, Grade 12
Simon Kenton High School, KY

I'm on a Mission

Teaching with my life because I was raised on a message of faith and sound teaching,
filled with the holy spirit of God, spiritual bleaching. Now I desire the Lord's wonderful teaching,
because through his word its his voice that I'm seeking.
I don't like to talk about religion because then you get blinded by the rules and traditions,
I'm on a mission to speak on God's love and his divine intervention.
I'm trying to let you know that a relationship with God is a glorious journey, an expedition.
Once you're livin' for God, you live in Christ, you're fixed for life; no technicians.
You just have to know your position and admit submission,
that Jesus, the Lord is your savior
and that he actually came to this world and died on the cross just to save ya.
He took your sin, covered it with blood, the devil's a loser, now you win.
I'm here to let you know that I'm your friend and not your foe
I'm here to spit the truth, no lies like Pinocchio. That's right, God got the best of me
I'm gonna follow Him because he knows what's best for me.
I'm gonna stay at my post reading scripture and teaching
because trying to change the world is the goal that I'm reaching.
So I'm gonna keep a firm grasp on my character and my teaching
because in the end it's us, the youth, who I'm reaching.
I'm here to let you know I'm your friend and not your foe,
I'm here to spit the truth no lies like Pinocchio.
I'm on a mission, to speak on God's love and His divine intervention.

Sean Long, Grade 10
C E Jordan High School, NC

Monsters

What happened to the time when monsters only existed in our closets and under our beds?
When did they move to our souls?
And become personal demons instead of just fears?
What happened to Mom and Dad being super heroes and being able to scare away the monsters?
Why can they seem to no longer help?
When did monsters take physical form instead of just being things that go bump in the night?
How did greed, lust, jealousy, pride, revenge, gluttony, and sloth become actual monsters inside of each of us?
How did we become the monsters?
When did we become the monsters?
Can we ever change back?
Or are we cursed to live life as a monster?
Why did the monsters move into us?
Because we grew up.
Because we changed.
They changed too.

Morgan Payne, Grade 12
Mercy Academy High School, KY

Time Is of the Essence

Time is of the essence. Putting your pants on one leg at a time. Striving for your kids to have things Mommy and Daddy didn't have. Living a fairy tale. Knowing that life is what you make it. Realizing that life is hard. Noticing that time is of the essence. Living sunrise to sunrise. Being surprised by what life throws at you. Emphasizing that time goes by quickly. Literally speaking time has ran out for me. Wasting time in the welfare line awaiting my government check. Pondering what to do next? Confused of the next event. I cannot predict. The future awaits ahead. The doors opens for me instead, for me to realize that I was stalling to buy time. Time is of the essence. Achieving to better than the next person. Not stopping to think. Look in the mirror. Goal one has been achieved. You're better than your parents…Complete! Not necessarily. The road gets longer as the journey gets harder. Understand that life ain't easy. Believe me…I say this because I care. If I didn't I would let you sit there sucking up air. Life will graze with you if you let it. Time Is of the Essence!

Latonya Marble, Grade 11
West Charlotte High School, NC

This Thing We Call Strength

What is this thing we like to call our strength?
Is it a measure of our resistance?
The number of tears we've not let free fall?
Or is it just something to get us by?

Where is it that this strength of ours comes from?
Perhaps from standing in the face of fear?
Could it come from our exposed weaknesses?
Or is it just simply thrust upon us?

Who decides how strong we are?
Is it those who fight to see tomorrow?
Those whose lives have been cast into shadows?
Or is it something that can't be counted?

When is it that our strength reveals itself?
Is it when our hope has been bled dry?
Once we have been pushed beyond our limits?
Or is it presented without notice?

Why have we been chosen to have this strength?
Have we shown ourselves to be deserving?
Are we meant to even know of our strength?
Or is it best to leave it unquestioned?

This thing that we call strength, could it be love?

Corey Irwin, Grade 12
Eugene Ashley High School, NC

What the Dolls Know

Glass eyes on porcelain faces, emotionless
Her only comfort from his eyes, the eyes completely devoid
Of common human sympathy

With a need to kiss desire on the lips, and obtain its terrible object
Enforcing silence with a switchblade tongue
And a violent heavy hammer hand

Armed with lies that could fill a room, a superficial smile
Barricading herself from unwanted questions

Inanimate ears are the only ones that hear painful confessions
Only they see beyond the shattered smile
No stinging judgment, just observation

Time erodes the soul, leaving helplessness
Guilt and pain immobilize
Leaving her caged in familiar skin

The silent watchers sit in the empty tomb
While whispered prayers and tears are pouring on a dark hole
Only the dolls know of his dark passions
Only they know the why she was torn apart
And most of all, they know Hell is the death of a human heart

Sarah Peragine, Grade 12
Grimsley High School, NC

Let Yourself Live

Let yourself fall.
Fall into the vast imagination of the world.
Sinking into your beautiful awakening.
Continue to breathe the precious oxygen.

Let yourself freeze.
Frozen cold with no strength.
With all of your fears immobilized in time.
Allow the whispering white trees to guide you.

Let yourself spring.
Spring into a new beginning.
Connect the dots to a new year.
Catch the dreams that are long lost in your mind.

Let yourself burn.
Burn into the flames that God gave man.
Speak the rage of your broken trust.
Age into the person you thought you would never be.

Let yourself live.

Eden Siskind, Grade 10
Germantown High School, TN

Anger

Anger may be the root or start of all evil
we feed on demons
but we are supposed to be God's people
as emotions soar and flow through our veins
that certain emotion is hard to control or maintain
as if we seek for evil or run from what we know is RIGHT

As a people we let anger push us to kill and fight
we use anger as an excuse
we know that evil comes from the devil
we call it anger issues
if you could fit in my shoes
you would understand my perspective

Don't continue to go on with your anger problems
let this be a lesson

Elijah Wright, Grade 10
Memphis Academy of Science and Engineering, TN

Love?

As I sit in this dark room
My mind starts to wonder
When I become a bride and you a groom
Will we still feel the thunder?
As we did when we was younger?
Will we still be love struck?
Or will we be outta luck?
In a blink of an eye everything can change
But for me I hope it will all remain the same.

Leslie Holland, Grade 11
Muhlenberg County High School, KY

Decisions

Two golden keys from two separate hearts
turn from the darkness to make a new start;
One wants truth, torn from past betrayal,
the other hopes to keep the tender heart stable.

Two broken souls mend together as one,
healed from the pain from which they had run;
Wounded by the troubles thrown in their way,
beginning to doubt the decision to stay.

The meaning of forever caught in a short fuse
makes you stray from the one that you don't want to lose;
You turn from your life, and love turns to hate,
engulfed by regret when anger chose your fate.

The true love you feel cannot be broken
by the pain that you've felt, and a few harsh words spoken;
The Golden path of love, or the dark choice to hide,
The moment is now — it's time to decide.

Amanda Richardson, Grade 12
West Davidson High School, NC

Flavor of Love

If life is like a pack of gum,
You're the piece I never want to chew.
And just in case you didn't catch that,
I really despise you.

Baby, picking you out of the pack,
Was like trying to find a needle in a haystack.
But after many crazy flavors,
You're the one I chose to savor.

How could something once so yummy,
Turn into something so darn scummy.
Once so fruity, delicious, and sweet,
Now you're just a psycho creep.

BrinLee Glass, Grade 10
Loretto High School, TN

Procrastination

The uncontrollable urge
To not do something
Because it is too hard,
Because you're tired,
Because want to sleep,
Because you want to party,
Because other things are keeping you up late at night,
This is too much,
This is just stupid
Are thoughts that come into your mind,
You think it will be done eventually
But you know you will end up doing this project in homeroom,
Where five minutes isn't enough to get even one question answered

Angelica Figures, Grade 12
Overton High School, TN

Was It a Dream?

A dead memory,
the time that we spent together
is nothing more than the past.

A hopeless wish,
no matter how many times I want to forget,
our time of remembrance will never leave me.

Nothing can turn back the time that we once had
and I will erase from my memories the image I have.

Slowly, the shards of my mind,
scatter the floor,
one by one.

The crack in my heart grows deeper and it feels unreal.
Nothing can mend my broken feelings.
Yet, after all that has happened, I still can't help but think:

Was it a dream?

Xena Hong, Grade 10
Middle Creek High School, NC

Love Lost

Pain fills my mind
Like an enemy's words unkind
Every day without you here
Close to madness my heart will near
With every passing day gone by
Another part of my soul will die
Why would God take you away
Without giving me the time to say
I love you with all my heart and soul
Without you here in my life I'll never be whole
Can't you see my dear you're all I want
Visions of you in my mind will haunt
Until the day I see you again
When we meet in the next life free of sin
I'll hold you dear inside my heart
Until God decides we've been too long apart

Spencer Young, Grade 10
White County High School, TN

Time

There used to be time
Time for you, time for me
Time to swim across the endless sea
Our bodies entangled like endless twine
"What's yours is yours and what's mine is mine"
Became our mantra over time
Like star-crossed lovers our tale came to a violent end
That no soft-spoken words could ever amend
The pain we felt belonged to you and I
As we said our goodbyes under the evening sky.

Gabriela Phillips, Grade 12
William G Enloe High School, NC

Fairy Tale

A place where violence
Does not exist.
The battle ax
Was never real.
Fire never roared
To life.

A place serene,
With chlorine skies—
Where centipedes
Hum in whispers:
Sweet songs from innocent days
Rising like a morning mist.

A place where deadlines
Are fictional horror stories.
Where children believe
In magic and miracles,
That a sprinkle of fairy dust
Can change the whole world.
Katie Armstead, Grade 12
St Joseph Central Catholic High School, WV

I Remember…

I remember an innocence
I remember a happiness
I remember the Dreamer

I know an evil
I know a darkness
I know the Monster

This ain't the Saint
This isn't from one joyous
I'm no superman
I can't fly
I'm no one's little girl

I remember a dream
The Dream is Dead!

I remember the dreamer
She is no princess
She isn't beautiful
She will never fly

I remember a dreamer
I close my eyes and turn around
And it was years and fables ago.

For all the lost souls
Dzidzai Muyengwa, Grade 12
Roanoke Rapids High School, NC

Tricked Heart

Flows like rivers
Blows soft in the winds
Black like darkness
I still give in

A beat so hollow
Silk and soft like velvet skin
I'll fall and follow
Love I still give in

Sounds of pain
Yet a joy-hearted spin
Happiness in rain
Yet I still give in

Rose red my dreams
Sky blue also dim
It is how it seems
We gave in happily

With mute sounds
Blind and vividly see
Heartbeats pound
We gave in finally
Aaron De Lilly, Grade 11
Woodrow Wilson High School, WV

Old Friend

I hear the clock ticking
The heartbeat of an
Old Friend

He whispers in my ear
Tells me to listen
Apprehend

Immersed in His riddle
I lose the point of
Beginning

Only to discover
In His beginning
No end

Softly sung lullabies
Lull my weary mind
To peace

And He carries me thus
Gently into His
Eternity
Ruby Au, Grade 12
William G Enloe High School, NC

To My Precious Older Sisters

To my precious older sisters,
if only you knew
what all was going on down here.
I wish you could help me through.
Mom and dad divorced
a long, long time ago.
I wasn't angry then,
but now it's starting to show.
Today, things are tough.
It's my senior year.
It's supposed to be amazing,
but I'm only filled with fear.
Mom and dad still say
they miss you very much.
It was really hard for them to see you two
within death's evil clutch.
I love you guys so much
even though we've never met.
The fact that you're my sisters
is a fact I won't forget.
Courtney Goodwin, Grade 12
Campbell County High School, KY

Foal

Deep eyes blink behind ebony lashes
Nostrils quiver on a slender face
Tiny ears perk at the rustling grass

Long legs, awkward to stand on
Support his tiny frame
The foal slowly walks forward

Tentatively, he approaches
His dark eyes are curious
His face, quizzical

Fragile wings flap lazily
Red and gold mix together
Sensing no danger
The foal moves closer

A dark nose edges in
Whiskers brush gentle wings
On a breeze, the butterfly floats away

Eyes wide in wonder
The dark foal watches
All must be observed
Caroline Dischell, Grade 11
Grimsley High School, NC

Press Play

I listen closely as the singer begins, and concentrate on every lyric,
Processing the meaning in my mind.
I press replay over and over again, until I memorize every word,
And can sing along in nearly perfect harmony.
I miss something every time, an obtuse "ooh" or "ah,"
A high note I can't quite grasp, a line I can't manage to hold out long enough.
I start over, this time ignoring the vocals,
Instead focusing on the piercing pitch of the lead guitar,
The chords tumbling forward in an exact cacophony,
Flowing effortlessly from a humble rhythm to an elaborate riff.
Again, I memorize the arrangement, and again, I overlook a note here and there,
I then analyze the subdued rumble that is the bass,
A crucial layer underneath the prominent guitar and vocals,
A mere, hard to recognize murmur, the most distressing element to learn by heart.
The pulsing beat of the drums is next, from beginning to end a fundamental factor of the melody,
The easiest to distinguish, simplest to retain,
But still I consistently miss a beat, no matter how hard I try.
I finally listen to the song as a whole,
My concentration flitting from one component to another,
Struggling to keep track of them all at once,
Although I know it's unattainable.

Sarah Bogdal, Grade 10
Germantown High School, TN

Making the Transition

A cold winter wind whips through the trees
A blank fog is all I can see
Snowflakes covering the dead frozen ground
Icicles hanging all around
Breaths are spotted and Father Winter is heard
Where are all the melodious birds?
Dark skies venture ahead
Like woodland creatures, we hibernate and head off to bed
My attention span in school hangs by a thread
Frigid temperatures loom ahead
Therefore toboggans cover various chilly heads
Is there anything not to dread?
Winter comes but once a year so celebrate and spread love and cheer
Once winter comes to an abrupt halt and spring has sprung,
I will be able to catch rain drops on my parched tongue
The radiant sun glistens like the stars and it shines through my shades as I stroll down the boulevard
Lilies sprouting from the ground
The buzzing of bees and chirping of birds are such soothing sounds
Fresh-cut grass, lavender, and fresh air concoct a sweet aroma that awakens people from their winter comas
Probably the most joyous part of spring is when I hear the final school bell ring
Vacation time has arrived and the world starts to come alive

Brooke Hager, Grade 12
Poca High School, WV

Heartless Words

You wonder why I tell you the truth. The facts are I've been hurt and abused by you for too long and too many ways. You have tortured, cussed, and put me down so many times I've wanted to run far away. Your need is my tears. These may be heartless words, but I'm stronger than I would have been without you even though I absolutely detest you. You are not what stops me now. You are little to nothing to me. Through all your heartless words I still thank you for making me stronger.

Jasmine Goodwille-Contreras, Grade 11
Lawrence County High School, TN

Four Seasons

First we will start with season one
That would be spring because it is so much fun
The snow is melting and things start to bloom
The green grass grows and everything's new

Now onto summer it's getting warmer you see
Things are in full force
You get the heat and the breeze
Swimming, and cookouts and late nights out
Camping and fireworks and this season out

Now onto fall the best season of all
Though things are dying they change many colors you see
The leaves fall to the ground
And you get the colder winds and breeze

Now onto winter the coldest one yet
We play in the snow and get soaking wet
Go into the house and drink Cocoa to get warm
The days are shorter Oh, God, I wait until it's warm

Brandon Krupia, Grade 10
Robert C Byrd High School, WV

The White Cliffs of Normandy

Sailing at sea, as comrades they lived
Facing the ups and downs, gazing at the white Norman shore
The sky turned gray, and the sun was beyond their view
They charged from the craft, as the gray shells began to pour

Towered by the white cliffs above, they made straight for the coast
Trudging forward, boots leaving deep imprints in the sand
The assault ebbed and flowed, forward and backward
Slowly, men began to fall
Yet, there were still some who strode forward to overcome the wall

There are crosses that line the white cliffs of Normandy
The sand on the beach is changed by the tides of time
The waves ebb and flow, forward and backward
Waves slowly cover the footsteps of the men who are gone

Karthik Ramasubramanian, Grade 12
William G Enloe High School, NC

Life

Life is a game of tug and pull
You never know if you will get the best of the game
Life is like dice
You will never know what you will roll on
Life is like the game of basketball
You will never know who you're up against, but just fight for the win
Life is like a closed door
You never know what's on the other side
What I'm saying is life is difficult
You can make the best of it
Life is Life

Daniel Boles, Grade 10
Memphis Academy of Science and Engineering, TN

With Just a Look into Your Eyes

Auburn and sage peer over at me
Peeking from underneath curling lashes of onyx
A smile seeps out onto my face
Displaying a small glimpse into how I feel inside
That nauseating
Invigorating
Breathtaking
Feeling in the pit of my stomach
Just seeing your name flash across my phone
Sends me into a frenzy
The sweet nothings that escape from your lips
Leave me speechless
The goofy mistakes you make because you're focused on me
Make me laugh
Everything so intoxicating
Captivating
Heart containing
Better yet just amazing
With just a glance of your eyes into mine

Rachel Rials, Grade 10
Lee County High School, NC

Love

Love is a myth.
Passion, pure lust.
That "love in the air" is now just dreary dust.
I remember the old days and what we used to be,
But all of that now seems like a distant memory.

Love is artificial.
Games of the heart.
We toy with emotions like an intricate art.
I remember those games and the pain I went through,
Yet somehow I can say I'm still not over you.

Love is blind,
Just as Ignorance is bliss.
So why is it love is the one thing we always miss?

Alexandra Mayo, Grade 12
Providence High School, NC

Death

Death is an unavoidable thing in life
Death is something most people fear
But, death can either be your friend or your enemy
When death comes, people then realize the importance of life
People don't realize who loves them while they are living
When they finally wake up, death has come
Sometimes death is always on the mind
But I don't worry about death; I have enough time
I don't worry about death taking this life of mine
Just give your life to God; He'll protect you all the time
Death can either be a good or bad consequence
But going to heaven will be my accomplishment

Lee Hart, Grade 10
Memphis Academy of Science and Engineering, TN

A Letter from Christopher Marlowe

My dearest friend, Shakespeare, would you help me?
A gang of crazy men are on my tail.
I am caught up in a conspiracy!
I need a secret kept, please do not tell.

I'm leaving town, it's not safe anymore,
They think I'm a spy for the government.
If caught, I can't be, I'm good to the core,
In jail the rest of my life will be spent.

I have for you a collection of works
I wrote; it won't be recognized as so.
You take the credit, you get all the perks,
You say you wrote them, only we will know.

Get these works published, written in your name.
If not, anonymous you will remain.

Kasey Gilmore, Grade 12
Trinity High School, KY

Shall I Compare You to the World's Most Beautiful Sight?

Shall I compare you to the world's most beautiful sight,
That everyone and anyone would love to see.
You're like the glorious sun shining so bright,
I got lucky that you're the one that's meant to be.

The way you treat me and I treat you,
Is the way it should be forever.
My favorite part is you're my dream come true,
Our hearts blend perfectly together.

The comfort and warmness the sun can give
Reminds me of the look in your eye.
It's phenomenal how you both are supportive,
Though you're a little more loving than what's in the sky.

Both the sun and your wonderful self will have bad days,
But I know as well as you should, I'll love you always.

Mycalyn Saucier, Grade 10
Loretto High School, TN

All That Matters

They paint the world with their eternal faith
Itchy wool slides covering her bare arm
Reach her fingertips and we find his warm hand
Wading in sync through the fall debris
Crunch, crunch; the sound of the ginger leaves —
The ending noise, not of their authentic hearts,
But the ignorant whispers of the enemies
The burning tang of the lone wood
The distinct brisk wind, encircling their trust around them,
An untouched rose bush in a twisting cyclone
Ignoring the external obstacles —
All they need is trust

Caroline Klausing, Grade 12
Assumption High School, KY

Shall I Compare Thee to a Black Hole?

Shall I compare thee to a black hole?
You're mysterious enough, to be sure,
and I'm certain your heart is black as coal.
(For *that* there is no cure.)

From galaxies away, people stare;
to them you must seem quite benign.
My treatment of you may seem unfair,
but their hearts are not broken like mine.

You drew me in when I came near,
luring me with false affection.
You soon became my deepest fear,
but it was too late to change direction.

You're the one who took the light from my life,
and you are the cause of all of my strife.

Jessica Vaughn, Grade 10
Loretto High School, TN

Happily Ever After

Shall I compare life to my childhood ways,
so when things get tough I can play pretend.
I wouldn't have to focus on the problems of today,
and every moment wouldn't feel like the end.

So I could go back to when Santa did exist.
When Disney World was the best place to be.
The time when my dad was the only boy I kissed.
When the only movies I was allowed to watch were rated G.

When writing my name was the only problem that came
Skinned knees were the only thing to make me cry.
And I knew without a doubt nobody would change.
When I was too young to know how to lie.

Can I go back to the time with no hurt, only laughter,
The time when everybody lived happily ever after?

Ashley Johns, Grade 10
Loretto High School, TN

Remember Me?

Remember that mole on your left cheek I teased you for? I do.
Remember the hours in my car spent talking about life? I do.
And remember when we laughed so hard that we cried?
Or when we promised to tell each other everything?
The time I actually did tell you everything?
When we promised we'd never leave each other?
The time we kissed and time didn't exist in the first place?
How about the time I screamed "I hate you!"
You screwed me up, making me love you.
The time I wished I never saw you again?
The time I got what I wished for?
Remember that mole on your left cheek I teased you for? I love it.

Drew Murley, Grade 12
Germantown High School, TN

Oh How I Love Fall

Oh how I love fall!
All the smells
And all the colors,
Make me feel so swell.

The cool crisp air
With a light breeze blowing
Through my hair,
As I watch my skirt flowing.

The smell of pumpkin pie,
The laughter of the kids
Makes me want to sigh,
As I start to sit.

Watching the children
Playing in the leaves,
Makes you want to say,
"Oh how I love fall."

Hannah Webb, Grade 10
White Plains Christian School, NC

Destroyer

You're sick and twisted
A monster of your own making
I can't breathe in your presence
Sometimes I believe it's better that way

If I can't breathe, maybe I'll black out
Asleep there is no waking,
Gone are the subtle noises to disturb
No resounding screams left in my mind

I made a dreadful mistake,
I don't know why I looked at you that way
I should've saved myself
I might've had the chance

But, it doesn't matter now
I'm far too lost to ever look back
You've attempted self destruction in my eyes
You seem to have destroyed me instead.

Ashly Summers, Grade 10
Dupont Manual High School, KY

Meteors

Vermillion and gamboge rocks
streak across a glittery sky,
numerous ecdemic bullets
from the final frontier.

Above the towering trees
sparks continue to soar,
colors reflecting the shades
of falling leaves

I lounge by the fire as it pops
and quietly ponder;
what's beyond
this bare maple's top.

Is it all chance
or great sign?
mere coincidence
or drastic design?

I know not
what directs
the show
in the
sky.

Zachary Dougherty, Grade 12
St Joseph Central Catholic High School, WV

My One and Only

There since birth
Watching over me
Keeping me safe from harm

My hero as a child
My enemy as I grow older
Yet, you never left me behind

Struggles and fights
Damage our bond
But, never our love

You tear me down
Yet, I do the same
In the end, we only grow closer

My one and only
The man I can count on
My Dad

Courtney Geiger, Grade 12
Lee County High School, NC

Dry Ice

Her veins,
Resembling live wires,
Course like icy rivers
Beneath her dense skin.
Cold fire
Stirs in her
Smoky arctic eyes,
Bestowing light
To peek
At the frosted depths
Of her rigid soul.

Burning like dry ice,
She is a crystal sculpture
That moves
Like frozen dreams.

She never lets
Anyone in.

Not even herself.

She is a stranger
To her own
Frostbitten heart.

Arniecia Hinds, Grade 10
Germantown High School, TN

Zero to Hero

Zero to hero
In 24 months
My time will come
No longer a dunce

To rise above
Beyond all
Past my hardships
I'll stand tall

All my troubles gone
I wait as it nears
Darkness upon us
I release my fears

I can protect myself
I learned from the best
To fight these demons
This is my test

Kathrine Ball, Grade 10
Coffee County Central High School, TN

The Place I Come From

I am from thumbtacks, from Coca-Cola and hot pizza.
I am from the blue and gray walls of my very own room.
(Bright, exciting, it looked like a football stadium)
I am from the fishpond, the sun whose light
glistened into my window.
I am from honey ham and blue eyes, from Charles and Debra.
I am from the logical and the sarcastic.
From "Have fun while you can" and "Work hard when it is time."
I am from the Ten Commandments, the twelve apostles,
and the one almighty Lord.
I'm from Irvine, Scotland,
From sweet tea and turkey dressing.
From the sweet touch of my grandmother
and the strict discipline of my grandfather.
In my den was a fireplace, whose blaze warmed up the winter,
and signified Christmas was near, that was my favorite time of year.
My family was all around, filled with joy and laughter.
That is where I am from, the family that brought me here.

Jacob Irvine, Grade 11
Germantown High School, TN

A Stand

She sits while tears well up inside her eyes
The silence of the room cutting sea deep
In quiet is noise, her mind screams its cries
Now holding back the end, the choice, the leap

In a day she's fake with all who come close
Those who think they are all so high in might
They who themselves need take a larger dose
Medicine given so freely as right

So many that are weak enough to take a sip
But she no longer will be their victim
Better yet will they be left with a tip
And all who did her wrong, unpunished slim.

Laura Baldwin, Grade 10
Union County High School, TN

Presence of God

I see many things that represent God
I see Him in my skin color
This time He made a beautiful one
I see nature as it goes His way

Never did I know He could make a woman so strong
Never did I know He'd send the perfect man this way
I wasn't able to fathom how much water He brought that day
Never did I know He'd watch me as a man I slayed

He sent me a man of age and wisdom
He sent me a man of money, control, and power
Two died of three
Through the Presence of God I shall prosper

Eric Scott, Grade 10
Memphis Academy of Science and Engineering, TN

Boarding

Metal boxes on wheels,
Doors open, we follow in.
The rolling starts.
Trees and grasses pass, tracks go on and on,
A memory catches up to me; we are one in the moment,
Caught in the images of an ancient Polaroid,
Still rolling.
My head is on the back of the seat,
lulled by the slight shiver of a rumbling engine.
Soon I'll arrive, but today, even if just for a moment,
Time flips back and forth, it's surreal.
I wait,
Watch as the pieces, the proof of time's passage whiz by,
An old shop, withered and crumbling,
stands defiantly as the tangled web of earth pulls downward.
Overgrown trees and vines, still grasses go on and on.
My time is not now, but I will join the defiant old shop.
Images flash by; I soak them up and revel in the familiarity.
Stumbling backwards but always moving forward,
Flashing streams of color burst through the tangled woven webs.

Jordan Russo, Grade 12
William G Enloe High School, NC

The Scars of War

Cold hearts breaking.
Hands on guns shaking.
From all of my combat training
I see that there is nothing worth gaining.
Bodies left in the snow
of the people we'll never know.
Were they sucked in to it like us or volunteers?
Were they bitten by the power bug or left in tears?
All I'll ever know is that
nothing is worth a fight. In fact,
I wish this war was never fought.
Smoke is blinding all my thoughts.
And as I lay me down to sleep
I pray the war my soul won't keep.
If I should die before I wake,
Spare the news for family's sake.

Mariana Burns, Grade 12
William G Enloe High School, NC

Riots

Smoke rises from the riots below
Children have been torn from what they used to know
Lies, love and hate are now one selfish game
But we won't be fazed by this threatening craze
There are too many days worth fighting for
And too many lives being broken over silent torture
All of our pride is invested in things that aren't worth dying for
There are wars that could be settled
And paths that could be traced
But it's really hard to reason with a gun pointed in your face.

Sara Boling, Grade 11
Gateway Christian Schools, TN

I Wear the Mask

I wear the mask, the one you see
The one that cares what people think of me
A nervous feel yet a warm smile
Another day, another mile
Fitting in, it's all worthwhile

Every day, we go to school
Trying to figure out what defines "cool"
Always smart, never a fool
I wear the mask

Why does it matter what we do?
Does anyone here have a clue?
I'll just do my thing and act like me
I don't care what people think or see
I will live happy and carefree
I no longer wear the mask

Rebecca Lane, Grade 12
Berkeley Springs High School, WV

Politics in America

Spinning, spinning
The room is spinning
Dervishly whirling
And spinning.

Everyone is falling
Everyone is tripping
The walls are crooked
And spinning.

Up seems down
Right seems left
The people are crooked
And spinning.

Crash.

Pavithra Suresh, Grade 12
William G Enloe High School, NC

Distance

I am held by murky waters,
And all these earthly things,
Desire, pride, to name a few,
and sometimes even shame

I am blinded by the sun
As I yearn for more
You watch me from your golden sands
As you wait on calmer shores

An ocean lies between us
Moving much too fast,
But somehow all too slow

Hannah Wilson, Grade 11
Grimsley High School, NC

Holocaust Survivor

What more needs to be said to show your great strength,
Enduring harsh, ruthless, merciless cruelty, you defeated the battle within.
You were subject to death, but instead you strove to win,
Not letting your present day circumstance determine your end.

Truly you are a HERO to be recognized,
No one can understand the tears that you have cried,
For the loved ones who died,
Who lost the greatest gift…their LIVES.

I can't even begin to imagine the pain,
How did you remain, sane?
Was it simply that fight for survival that helped you sustain,
You lost much, but from this horrific event what did you gain?

HOLOCAUST…and what a cost it was,
From this memory how do you continue to love?
Do you ever get weary, or constantly you strive above?
Always soaring to new heights, like that of a dove.

You conquered many battles, overcame trials and tribulations,
The words you shall speak will change generations.
For you are a voice to this nation,
With no hesitations, please come and enthrall us with your revelation,
As we give YOU a standing ovation.

Trikeria Johnson, Grade 12
North Mecklenburg High School, NC

You Are Success

Discouraging words come along the way as you are finding success,
You notice you may find yourself with your head hanging down,
Your first step is to look high up to the sky and know in your heart "You Are Success,"
You are someone that can make a difference in the world with the talent you have.

Prepare, work hard, and dedicate yourself for a high level of education,
Education is the key to becoming successful in today's world,
Block out negative thoughts or words that come to your mind and say, "I Am Success,"
I know someone is out there willing to encourage me along this long journey.

"You are success" is my favorite quote to get the day started because it motivates me,
It reminds me that I am never done until I reach the top,
The second step is to surround myself around proactive people throughout life,
Slowly, time will come along when I see everyone applauding me towards victory.

Read encouraging books or poems each day to keep you strong-minded,
Something must keep you happy and your belief is that you are the world's greatest,
You should want to overcome anything in life and know there are challenges,
Proceed, don't slumber, and don't look back upon the past and mistakes.

The third step is to look in the mirror and see success reflects upon yourself,
Head held high, plenty of smiles, and laughter upon the day,
You know you made it and a difference in life when it's your last time crossing the stage,
So I look to everyone out there proud as I can be to let you know "You Are Success!"

Brittany Tyrone, Grade 10
Roanoke Valley Early College, NC

The Decision
A bump, a small one
Barely noticeable
A worried and frightened face
What to say, who to tell?
A decision is made.
In a cold white room
Wicked faces surrounding her
Mixed emotions inside of her
Confusion, sadness, fear, pain
Then suddenly,
Life flashes before her eyes.
Days, months, she has wept
Regretting the day
She made a decision
And let go of life…
Jenifer Cardenas, Grade 10
Grimsley High School, NC

Lost
I am lost
Nowhere left to run
Facing of my own demon
As it got darker my fear got worse
As I ran from them
As my sweat ran down my face
I began to see a light
As you came closer to the light
I felt more alive
I looked where the light leads
A peaceful part of the woods
Where I heard a voice
Of a face I missed
You see I wasn't lost at all
It was all in my mind
Bryton Knotts, Grade 11
Preston High School, WV

Free Falling
Never stalling,
Embracing,
No placing,
Just chasing.

Deeper and deeper
The thrill
As I feel the air chill.
I'm alive, because of a cliff dive.

I plunge,
Take a lunge,
Try to grasp,
My happiness, I clasp.
Daisha Gauze, Grade 11
Sheldon Clark High School, KY

Love
Why not just remove the breath that you gave to me,
that I might stop from hurting you again?
Just cut off my crippled wings,
it's not like I know how to fly.

Remove the spear from my heart
because I can't bear it any longer.
But if you do choose to let it be,
at least clean the trail of blood behind me so that no one will see my pain.

I've kept the ashes of what once was happiness and a relationship.
I pray that the dead feelings will rise again.
And I hope with my plastic smile
it may prevent whatever turns the world upside down and will make things right again.

Maybe if I save the glass beads
that fall from my eyes in a
box under my bed and wipe the marks away with makeup
you will love me.

Maybe I desire too much to be loved.

It's a strange feeling, love.
My only reason to live, yet the only reason I'm dying.

I love you. I just wish I knew what that meant.
Mary Martin, Grade 12
Campbell County High School, KY

Just Alone
There is a man who sits by himself in a small cafe.
Passerbys glance toward him
And turn away with looks of pity plastered on their faces.
"Look at that poor man." They whisper,
"All alone, with no friends nor family to keep him company."

What they do not know is that this man is simply alone.
He is not lonely, nor does he need their pity.
He simply likes the peace and quiet of being alone.
He has a family and many friends.
But none can ever compare with the company of himself.

He is old, yes, and he has seen many places,
met many people and done many things.
But through it all, no matter where he was,
He could always withdraw, get away from this world, and just be alone.
Not lonely,
just alone.

Often these words (alone, lonely) are thought of as twins.
But I, and the man sitting in this cafe, say differently.
Sometimes I sit, alone. Just to think.
I am not lonely,
just alone.
Renée Blevins, Grade 10
Germantown High School, TN

Letter to Me
If I could write a letter to me,
I'd send it back in time to myself at 17,
I would say, hang on tight,
This will be a bumpy ride,
Buckle up, and fight it girl. 'Cause,
There are holes in the floor of heaven,
You have many more eyes than two!
And oh, you've got so much going for you going right,
But I know at 17 it's hard to see past Friday night,
It's your life, what are you gonna do?
Make it to the next grade level?
Or your next thirty years?
Just remember,
You're still around to write this letter to me.
When you get where you're going,
Don't think about backing out,
Just remember, you made it through the toughest years.
That's what I'd say
If I could write this letter to me.
Melissa Riggleman, Grade 11
Berkeley Springs High School, WV

The Fire
Love is eternally burning passion,
It ignites deep within and it consumes.
It is bliss and sorrow in any fashion,
It lets you see, it makes you assume
That she loves you, when she knows you are blind.
You yearn for her when she plays games with you.
You chase her and yet she plays with your mind.
Years go by and she at last loves you, too.
Through the trials, you strengthen.
Through it all, you find your completion.
In the end, you find a soul has lengthened.
In all, your soul grows from depletion.
In the beginning, you cry, scream, and pout.
In the end, love only dies when lights go out.
Jeremiah Turner, Grade 10
Union County High School, TN

Winter
Cold like ice
Yet warm like a fire's wood
You bring joy to kids and love to lovers
You're sometimes long and sometimes short
You urge to grab a sheet and build a warm fort
You bring frost to my windowpane
And a sweet treat to my cookie's glaze
From making the perfect drink mixings
To decorating with all our wonderful fixings
You come once a year,
And every year you bring cheer
A gift of warm laughter
To grace the face of those now, and those who come after.
Hilda Diggs, Grade 12
William G Enloe High School, NC

I Lost Myself
I look in your eyes
and I sense the pain
every where you look
your eyes are dim
your smile is gone
all you are is fake
I lost my friend
I lost my love
I lost myself
in you
no matter how much I struggle to get you back
You're one with the distant moon
I smash the mirror
and look at you then
your eyes are wide with fear
tears are falling
the frown is showing
as you finally try to come near.
Haley Duke, Grade 10
Partnership Academy Alternative School, NC

Thanksgiving
Thanksgiving is the time of year,
When the family gathers,
Eats some turkey,
And maybe some deer.

Thanksgiving is the time of year,
When we each take time,
And thank God for delivering us,
From our fears.

Thanksgiving though should be all the time,
Not just when holiday comes;
Thanksgiving should be every day,
Because Jesus paid for you the ultimate crime.
Mason Lyons, Grade 10
White Plains Christian School, NC

Missing You
Oh how much I miss you.
You left my life without saying goodbye
I miss all the times we had.
This is the second year that I couldn't spend the holidays with you.
Every year around Christmas time, I want to see your face.
I want to hold your hand.
I asked God why did he take you from me.
As birthdays passed, for you I'm wishing.
Why did you have to go?
You left me in a cold world
In my dreams, I see your face and I wish you were here.
I know you're in a better place
If it's part of God's plan
Maybe, we will meet again.
Caylan Parks, Grade 10
Memphis Academy of Science and Engineering, TN

We Conquered

It is the beginning of the end
One book is now closing
But one is waiting for you to open
After all of these rigorous tasks

Night after night filled with deadly piles of homework
Morning after morning filled with depressing emotions once we have departed from our deep slumber
Constant "she said this"
Constant "he said that"

Tears filled with frustration due to our procrastination
Anger arises when pop quizzes appear
Maelstroms of students rushing through the halls
Hearts mending and hearts breaking from our belief in almighty true love

For we are now done
It is the end for this chapter, but not for good
This previous lifestyle will guide us to our future
When conflicts occur, we shall overcome

When a ball is thrown at us, we will know to knock it out of the park
This is our time, class of 2012, to light up this room
As this comes to an end
We all can say:

We came, we saw, we conquered

Kat Elliott, Grade 12
Grimsley High School, NC

Where I'm From

I am from the back yard,
   from swing set and bicycle.
I am from the kitchen,
   always warm with the pleasant aroma of dinner cooking on the stove.
I am from the tall grass,
   the magnolia tree, its branches worn smooth from the hundreds of times the
   neighborhood kids climbed to the top.

I am from trips to the beach and bad eyesight,
   from Jill and Tracy.
I am from the perfectionists and fun-lovers,
   from Do what your mother told you! and Go have fun!
I am from Jesus loves me, from Sunday school and church choir;
   my church friends are my second family, they know me better than anyone else.

I am from Germantown and the South,
   from pecan pie and chocolate milk.
From the brown sugar my father's great grandmother fed him out of a box,
   because his mother told her not to feed him white sugar out of a bowl,
   from the cabin where my grandfather was raised.

I am from the photo album in the house library,
   with pictures from times before I was born to a family portrait from just a few months ago.
Those pictures tell my story better than I ever could on my own.

LeeAnn Bailey, Grade 11
Germantown High School, TN

High Merit Poems – Grades 10, 11, and 12

Word Weaver
I am a word weaver,
Spinning rhymes and emotions,
Tying in the right colors,
Knotting in memories and thoughts.

Spinning a tale of misfortune,
Spinner of love and deceit,
Of adventures thrilling,
Where allies and enemies meet.

Sometimes I wish I could paint,
The perfect picture in my mind,
But alas,
Only in my imagination can my dreams come to life.

I weave words to make you see,
What is in my mind and feelings,
To make you believe you're here or there,
To trust and believe in yourself and others.

So fly with me on a whirlwind,
To lands far in existence,
Filled with journeys to travel,
While I spin and weave.

Elizabeth Lee, Grade 11
Sullivan South High School, TN

Serendipity
Have you always been there, sitting across the room?
Oh yes, it's nice to meet you, and who are you?
Your name is Jess,
Oh why didn't I guess!
You say you've always been here with me?
How did I miss you, oh how could it be?

I can't believe it's been three years!
But you and I — is there something going on here?
Why has my stomach sudden started to become queasy
Every time you come near me?
This is an odd feeling, Jess!
It makes me happy, nevertheless.
I love to see you smile, you know.
It touches my heart, and makes me glow.

We've grown old together, dear good Jess!
I believe the end is near, but I am not stressed.
You've been my life, and I have been yours.
You're my best friend, and I keep loving you even more!
Thank you for always being there for me.
I love you, my friend, and I have no regrets.
To me, it seems that best friends are always meant to be.

Samantha Wallace, Grade 11
Surry Central High School, NC

We Wear the Mask
We wear the mask that shows our teeth.
It hides the tears that run down our face.
We like to dress up and wear lots of makeup.
But still all the couples seem to break up.

We go out to eat and don't know what to order.
Because half of us have an eating disorder.
So we stuff our face with worthless waste.
We wear the mask.

We pregnant women cry a tear.
Because our boyfriends aren't around to hear.
Nine months pass and we see our baby's face.
Once again tears run down our face.
Why aren't you here with me?

We wear the mask.

Kimberly Johnson, Grade 12
Berkeley Springs High School, WV

I Found the Sun
I love the sun; the bright, warm elegance fills the sky
I wait for the time to pass by until the next sunrise.
Sunrise, sunset, life isn't over yet.
When I found you, life had begun,
When I found you, I found the sun.
Your arms spread wide to greet me.
The black core of you deceives me.
I look to you for love and care,
But sometimes I wonder if I should dare.
Although you will leave me someday,
You will always be loved anyway.
When I found you, I found the sun.
When I found you, I found my only one.

Jillian Schlader, Grade 12
Sacred Heart Academy, KY

Baseball Dream
Just one more chance is all that we ask for
One more chance to make the game-winning play
Bottom of the ninth and a losing score
Expectations are high to save the day.
The ball is hit and toward you it comes
You know what to do but can you pursue
Tying run on third and away he runs
You make the catch and the throw is on cue.
The play at the plate is called an out
You're in disbelief but you see it's true
Running to the dugout, crowd screams for you.
Everyone tells you how great you've done
You tell them thanks and that you play just for fun.

Dillon Fields, Grade 10
Union County High School, TN

Adventures with You

Run away with me.
We will run farther than the eye can see.
We'll run into the dead of night.
Not even a bat would dare to take flight.
We will run up the mountain, and in to the stars,
Past the moon and land on Mars.
An adventure I never had dreamed,
But an adventure I take because of you and me.

Run away with me.
We will run farther than the eye can see.
We'll sail across the ocean blue.
I'll be happy because it's just me and you.
We'll go from shore to shore.
A daring adventure I've never taken before.
But that will be just fine with me,
Because it's just you, me, and the sea.

You leave in the morning to be back on your own.
And I'll be back to adventures alone.

Emily Bosak, Grade 12
William G Enloe High School, NC

We Are Two Peas in a Pod

We have been with each other for sixteen years.
You are the only one who knows who I am.
You are the one who knows my secrets.
We trick our friends and teachers.
We laugh at each other and remember good times.
We may fight but we forgive in five.
You are my second half.
You are the second piece of my heart.
If a boy doesn't like then they fall off my chart.
You are my sister and dear friend.
God gave you to me so I have a twin.
I love you my sister and always will.
Sorry girl but we are a packaged deal.
We will always be together forever.
We are like two peas in a pod.

Lana Hartin, Grade 10
Coffee County Central High School, TN

Revolution

A revolution of 2013 is what the world needs.
We need a place where peace conquers all
and politicians don't lie.
Let the new generation take a stand,
one the old regime cannot withstand.

Stop the prophecy of 2010.
It says that bankers will cry,
while polar bears die,
and Uncle Sam will weep
next to a dying rose.

Justin Morgan, Grade 11
Campbell County High School, KY

Watch Me

Look into my eyes
Can you see past the light brown?
Deep into the black pupil
right past the pain
past the happiness
past the love
right over the insecurity
through all the anger
directly at the humility
but past that right at a form
a humble but beautiful form
that gives off an eerie emotion
that feels my own emotions
anger, jealously, humility, stupidity
do you know what it is
does it have a name
let me name it F.C.H.W.
not a word but an acronym
Faith, Consistency, and Hard Work
look into my eyes and see my soul
Watch Me

Everett Spears, Grade 10
Memphis Academy of Science and Engineering, TN

He Who Solves Problems

I asked myself a question this morning
Why do I try to fix my friend's problems?
It's because I care more than anything
Not because I just want to solve them

I try to heal pain that I know they feel
But this kind of pain only God can heal
They say they don't believe that He is real
But I know He has offered the best deal

You know He sent His one and only Son
And I know He felt incredible pain
He took all our sins and the war was won
On the day His son Jesus Christ was slain

You wonder why I am saying all this
Because my friends need to know what the truth is.

Saige Gilliam, Grade 12
Starmount High School, NC

Water

Water is what it is
It has no form in which it takes
It prefers no one or anything
It can be harnessed but not controlled
It can create, and it can Destroy
It can begin life to the ones it touches
Or it can invoke fear into the ones it nurtures
But Water is what it is

Julian Smith, Grade 10
Memphis Academy of Science and Engineering, TN

Encore

The curtains rise,
A radiant woman graces the stage.
Her silky black dress and glossy red lips
Capture the eyes of the audience.
They release faint "ooh's" and "ah's."
She opens her mouth,
And a sound of pure beauty
Escapes from the diaphragm of her stomach.
The rhythmic highs and lows flow through the crowd.
As she closes with her final long note,
Tears fill the eyes of everyone.
They applaud her.
Voices fill the room.
"ENCORE!"
"ENCORE!"
"ENCORE!"
Her humble heart is filled with joy.
She takes her final bow and exits the stage.
The curtains fall.
The show is over.

Taylor Riley, Grade 10
Germantown High School, TN

We Wear the Mask

We wear the mask that hides our thoughts
Never taking blame afraid to be caught
Standing up for something right
Always afraid of people's sight
It hides our shaded eyes

Why are we such hypocrites
Believing one way, but yet we do bits
Do you really wonder who you are?
We wear the mask

We wear a certain face
Walk with a certain pace, but yet it depends upon the place
Never knowing what to show
Why don't we just say what we know
We wear the mask

Rebecca Martz, Grade 12
Berkeley Springs High School, WV

Time

Time
Is more precious than the most valuable jewel.
Diamonds are forever,
But time is bound to end.
Gold may always have its glimmer,
But time's life span is much slimmer.
From seconds and minutes
To hours and days,
Make sure that time is spent wisely
In every way.

Zan Newkirk, Grade 12
William G Enloe High School, NC

Panic

Cracking glass,
I rush around,
my heart pumping,
sweat flowing,
blood running,
in a race that cannot be won.

My brain exploding with awful thoughts,
fears directing my body,
making it shake, making it numb.

I force my brain to open my eyes,
ready to see it.
My nerves are torn,
expecting it;
the cruel, the shock, the end.

A bright light,
a biting pain,
killing my vision,
feeling like the final knife,
stabbed into my chest.
Is it over? Am I dead?

"Honey, you really need to get your butt out of that bed now!"

Laura Balke, Grade 10
Germantown High School, TN

Tie-Dye

With a virgin base it begins,
Ripe and ready.

Pulled together close,
The tensions build,
All wrapped around a central issue.
Still the base remains pure.

It is then soaked with the blood of the ocean,
But that is not the end.
It is drenched again
but now with other colors.
Seemingly pointless splatter
Has a specific reason.

Forced to sit for many hours,
The ink dries but does not fade.

And then it is washed again,
But the clear flow used to wash it becomes impure.
The impurities flow away,
But they show that many still stay.

Over time, however, the colors fade,
And the base may become clean again.

Subodh Selukar, Grade 12
William G Enloe High School, NC

Lost Ones

I believe that they all deserve a chance
Whether it's right or wrong they need help in advance
They still need help in order to survive
It's as if everyone has forgotten their cries
Poverty lurks where they stand
They are only asking for a helping hand
We are struggling ourselves
This we can't deny
But for them another day loses another life
Strife is something they've always known
But now what are they to do
Now that their home is gone
Little shelter, less food, starvation at peak
What do you think about when you're ready to eat
Do you ever thank God for what he's blessed you with
For them just breathing is simply a gift
Loved ones still lost in the dust and stones
Every time I think of them I hope that heaven is their home
Lost within a crowd wishing they could be found
They scream and cry for help but no one hears a sound

Kianna Vinson, Grade 11
West Mecklenburg High School, NC

Diversity Means…

Diversity is what America does not see in its eye
Our proud, arrogant, ways cause us not to see
Other countries very clearly
We think we are the big shots
When we should be helping them out
Everyone is equal yet we do not
Treat other countries as such
Now nationalism is appropriate
But it should not overpower
Our responsibility to treat other countries right
Let's all just come together and be one
People from different walks of life
Mingling with each other and sharing cultures
Diversity truly means
Lifting the veil from our eyes
And seeing the world through them

Andrew Bryant, Grade 11
Germantown High School, TN

Maze

I am lost and alone.
No light to lead the way home.
I have no map, no directions to get out.
I hear nothing, not even a whisper.
I see nothing, not even a star in the empty dark sky.
The cold air washes over me.
Then drops of water hit me.
One by one they make me feel more and more hopeless.
I am cold and tired.
I am lost and alone.

Savannah Smith, Grade 10
Overton High School, TN

This Love

This love is pure; this love is kind…
This love keeps filling up my mind.
This love is light; this love is sweet…
This love can knock me off my feet.
This love can calm; this love can heal…
This love is all that I can feel.
This love won't break; this love won't leave…
This love won't ever cease to be.
This love moves mountains; this love slows time…
I'm glad to say this love is mine.
This love might stumble; this love might quake…
But it's not more than we can take.
This love is strong; this love is wild…
This love can always make me smile.
This love stays close; this love stays near…
With this love, there's nothing that I fear.
This love is real; this love is true…
This love is shared by me and you.
When my world comes crashing down,
It's this love that brings my heart around.

Kelsey Armes, Grade 11
Trinity High School, KY

Instruments of the Dark

Ominous, haunting darkness looms about the room.
The subtle evil captivates its onlookers,
Filling their hearts with admiration and doom.
The sudden glint of a light in the dark
Follows the slow, graceful movement of a bell.
Hark!
One must listen with vigilance
For these chimes do not ring.
These bells, somber but radiating of brilliance,
Sound with deep, harmonious tones.
Gleaming gold and shining silver
Captivate those who look.
Those who listen, however,
Are hypnotized
By these ominous low brass voices.

Ling-ling Phongsa, Grade 10
Coffee County Central High School, TN

Imagine

Look down on thy weeping and still thy cold hand,
If not to console then lay thy no brand,
Raise praise to the Lord and the giveth will come,
Spread belief and surely to gather will all His great sons,

Not the gait of the man not his merit nor knowledge,
But the cry of our God to only we pay homage,
To stand by His side in the darkest of night,
And to break through the black to meet the new day,

Imagine a world that was free of decay.

Jessica Graham, Grade 12
Berkeley Springs High School, WV

Society and Its Cruelty

Lighten the shadows in my heart,
take all the reasons from my mind.
Maybe then, a change will start?

We aim for perfection;
why must the world be so cruel?
It seems to have no affection.
Me against myself, it seems to be a duel.

It's a vindictive and misleading world
society tricks us into thinking what beauty is.

Screaming – yeah, I'm screaming.
Maybe then I can scare this monster away.
The tears, again, start streaming;
because once again it has taken over; more than halfway.

Still, I can't find the strength to care.
Now people all start to stare…

She once believed she was too fat,
but we have society to blame for that.
Life was a game, but she seems to have lost.
She was finally a piece of perfection in her eyes,
but what was the cost of all those lies?

Victoria Blaisdell, Grade 10
Lincoln County High School, TN

The Greedy Four

The last school bell rings in the children's ears
A warm breeze blows leaves across the street
Spring has ended; Summer is here
The warm earth beneath his feet

Then Winter, with her icy fury
Jealous of Summer's reign
Is plotting Summer's demise with Fall, her accomplice
Fierce determination to be Summer's bane

And so went Fall, to break Summer from his power
And down Summer came, though he thought he'd never
And Winter sat on her throne
She thought Summer was gone forever

But Spring was discontent and sought to bring Winter down
And she and Summer sat where Winter had been
But Fall and Winter wanted power back
So Winter got the throne again

But the everlasting argument awakened the great twins
Equinox and Solstice, the celestial pair
The arbiters, teachers, of the seasons
And finally, the siblings learned to share

Mae Carter, Grade 11
Germantown High School, TN

24th Century Farming

Drifting upon an endless sea of castaway opportunities
Waves of memories roll past and leave me downcast
Rejected as a mistake by high society
They sent one hundred others and me with all propriety
"Out to the stars, into a farmstead" their holograms would say
Turn us from orphans to workers and send us on our way

Distressed by these thoughts I turn to my side
As I lay down within a massive transport ship where I reside
And glance out of my only solace and comfort
A tiny porthole that the designers managed to insert
Next to my daybed, a tiny peephole
Onto the deep black expanse that lies beyond
That severs the tentative bond
With the only place I could call home

As I look out to space thinking, I see
Stars scattered among the darkness
And that is when I began to realize
Each star gives their surrounding planets a brilliant sunrise
These tiny pinpricks of light serve to remind me
That I was never known to be cowardly

Michael Peralta, Grade 12
William G Enloe High School, NC

One Last Thing

Unwind, relax, and be set free
Powerless among the winds
Flows so smooth like water going down a stream
Happiness of such delight
Love, patience, thinking right
Relieve this pain of the always wanted
Forget those things that never amounted to be what they seemed
Hardness just by letting people see what I once was
A tree in the fall letting go leaves
Leaving behind the others that stayed by me
Forgive those who never were forgiven
Help those who always wanted my help
Hear those who needed me to listen
Understand those who misunderstood me…
One last thing…
Love…
Love all whoever it may be

Chastity Good, Grade 12
Grimsley High School, NC

My Path

as I walk through the woods the leafs crinkle under my feet
the shining moon is the only thing that lights my path
as the moon grows darker I began to see more
I see the baby faun being born and taking its very first steps
the bear and it cubs laying down to rest after a weary day
when I reach the end of my path god is waiting to take my hand

Hailey Morgan, Grade 11
Polk County High School, TN

Standing Out

A brilliantly beautiful wildflower,
in a field of oats and wheat.
A redwood tree, the only survivor,
after a brutal fire and blazing heat.
A single colored girl,
drowning in a sea of white.
A hospital patient with a rare disease,
one in a million, continuing to fight.
A ragged old homeless man,
begging for warmth and money.
A billion buzzing bees,
guarding their precious, golden honey.
A mustard yellow mallard duckling,
whose egg was switched at birth.
Following its new mother goose closely,
oh the many wonders of the Earth.
Diversity means originality,
being yourself, a shining star.
Living in the moment every second of every day,
standing out will take you far.

Kaitlin Murray, Grade 10
Simon Kenton High School, KY

This Little Light of Mine

I long to see the sky blue without a sin,
And to feel the furtive brush of the breeze upon my skin,
But the air is dank and imbued with a chill.
Your words heavy like a boulder, almighty and still.
I'm trapped in a web: your gossamer of lies,
No longer knowing why truth and kindness you despise,
You flourish in hate and lurk in despair,
And you break the souls of those who can care.
These walls, they divide me. They split me in half,
They hide my spirit under constant attack,
It's no laughing matter, no meaning obscure,
I am no longer the girl that sits shy and demure.
I feel the quiet eloquence of the dark,
Shaping my vision, leaving no sight unmarked,
I see the words which you beleaguer the weak,
You prey upon those whom are modest and meek.
But my love is the single candle in the corner,
Which halts your words, lays them still and forlorn,
My passion for life is the gust that blows open the door,
Letting in the light to shine ever more.

Megan Groff, Grade 12
Oak Ridge High School, TN

Wisdom

Wisdom is a gift
Wisdom is a gift from God
Wisdom is priceless
Without it, we cannot live
Treasure it much in your heart

Sarah Methvin, Grade 10
Loretto High School, TN

The Forest

The forest is quiet and dark,
Yet I hear the sound of a lark.

The wind is blowing fiercely,
All I can hear are trees.

Looking for a way out,
I begin to shout.

I see a bright light,
Is it the sun or just a flashlight.

I move towards the light,
With a lot of fright.

I make it out,
Yet I can't help but shout.

The forest has scarred me for life,
I will never enter that forest again in my life.

Rob Franzen, Grade 11
Campbell County High School, KY

The Hero

Through the rocky plain to the water's edge,
Round the castle's gates, loyalty, I pledge.
I charge onward, my feet graze land,
I'll fight off all with sword in hand.
Across the courtyard, no time to be waste.
A slash behind me which quickens my haste.
He dives at my back, but he hits nowhere.
Two hearts fused together race in cold air.
I turn to battle, I intend to kill.
Surely I won't die here, but maybe he will.
The eyes of my prey then lock onto mine.
Heavy breaths are seen and all is not fine.
Our common feeling, which shall matter not,
Will soon be shattered by one careful shot.
An opening comes, a thrust to the gut.
He falls to the ground with his eyes closed shut.
I dart for the door and open it swings.
I hear my Dear's voice who guides as she sings.
Bounding the stairs to the room up above,
Fulfilling my quest to find my lost Love.

Alexandra Coleman, Grade 12
Campbell County High School, KY

She Died Too Young

How sad, sad it is
That she died so very young,
With life left to live;
But I'll always believe,
That she's looking down on me.

Rachel Freeman, Grade 10
Loretto High School, TN

Balance

When I was young,
My imagination was filled with possibilities,
A realm of my own.
Potential waiting to be tapped at the right moment.
But as time came to pass, and I grew older,
It was clear responsibility outweighed all.
It waited, dormant, somewhere within,
Restrained by the brick wall of reality,
One could not exist while the other lived.
And after getting married, this seemed absolute.
Until the wisdom that comes with age, in all its guidance,
Sparked in the vast confines of my mind.
Imagination and Responsibility,
Each does not restrain the other;
Survival weighs upon equality,
Yin and Yang.
My first book was published later that year,
A celebration of remembrance.
As each anniversary passed, with a new book released,
Satisfaction began to suit me,
While peace carried me to my grave.

Adrienne Lim, Grade 11
Merrol Hyde Magnet School, TN

Click, Click Boom…

Nowadays people take life for granted,
You could quickly meet your doom,
Every day should feel as if enchanted,
It can all be taken away with a click, click boom…

Now don't tread on it so lightly,
Because someone may have to end it all,
Nor should you walk around all big and mighty,
You may be faced to watch all your dreams fall…

A lot of people didn't listen,
So heed my warning,
But then they go up missin'
Or you may not even see tomorrow morning…

so stop and think before you say,
or maybe just stop and pray…

Tanner Nelms, Grade 12
H L Trigg Community School, NC

If I Had the Chance

If the chance came by, I would pursue a bird
I would perch on a bough and watch the forest below
I would search for food on the forest's floor
I would build a nest to house my young
I would chirp a good morning lullaby to the rising sun
And I would sorrowfully sing goodbye as night settled in
Then I would soar through the sky, quietly beating my wings
And I would sit on my bough and slowly fall asleep

Joanna Bolyard, Grade 10
Preston High School, WV

Written in the Sand

Closed in on answers, beyond the key
For love is a test, but the answer isn't me

Time is in matters, the farthest to stare
Beyond the horizon, the wind in our hair

Everywhere we go, it is determined to follow
Whether fate has our hand, or our mind is hollow

So here lies our future, an honorable choice
Because we all die a hero, but all have a voice

Our mark in Heaven is written in sand
Our voice is a pendent, luminous in hand

And I feel as though I've lost my mind
When all other humans seem so unkind

But whether our footsteps have yet to follow
Our fate lies lifeless, under the willow

Tommy Lofgren, Grade 11
Wilkes Early College High School, NC

Quack! Moo! Neigh!

Ring! Ring! Ring goes the alarm,
Another day of work for this old farm,
Quack! Moo! Neigh!
Is heard through the barn as the workers feed the animals their hay,
Ah! The smell of fresh grass,
A lot of work to do as the time will pass,
Feed the animals, milk a cow, milk a goat,
Go to the lake with a net and a boat,
Yes, life is moving for the old farmer and his wife,
But they both agree that there is no better life,
The farmer's wife goes about her business of baking a pie,
She looks to the meadow, and with a happy sigh,
Watches her husband as he cultivates the soil,
Then she checks the garden so the plants will not spoil,
Quack! Moo! Neigh! As the farmer finishes his day,
And walks back inside after wiping off hay.

Alvaro Galvan, Grade 12
Memphis Academy of Science and Engineering, TN

Alabama

Alabama home of the Tide
Filled with tradition and Crimson Pride.
Living in a place where the Tide always rolls,
They won't forget the day when the savage winds blow.
Death and destruction to those in its path
The memory of this will forever last.
With spirit in mind and tradition at heart,
Alabama rebuilds part by part.
Life has gone on, we have made gains and strides,
Showing the true spirit of the mighty Crimson Tide.

Kassidy Price, Grade 10
Loretto High School, TN

When It Enters

Slowly, methodically, and inconspicuously,
It crawls in with the utmost burden,
That nuisance which ravages the heart and thoughts,
The beast who tarnishes the luster on life.

He takes what is thought to be true,
And replaces it with dismal hues.
Resisting is nugatory, albeit slightly reflexive.
There is a time when he crosses a line,

Call it a heart string. Happily when he crosses,
he owns these flagitious ways.
The bug knows its consequences will shatter
The capacity to believe in ignorant bliss.

Solemnly, almost with content,
The bug burrows the way out, leaving gaping rives
And holes that will never be filled.
He knows he is only a whispered thought as he exits,

But his pyrrhic victory has been accomplished.
The bug has killed the juvenescent imagination,
But has initiated the impatience of knowledge.

Hunter Morrow-Elder, Grade 10
Coffee County Central High School, TN

Her Hands

They worked the fabric.
Guided the needle with precision,
and fashioned masterpieces for us all.

They chose the canvas.
Waved the brush with tender strokes,
and amazed us with her art.

They broke the earth.
Worked the trowel with determination,
and awarded us nature's beauty.

They held the pen.
Completed the grid with high-speed perfection,
and awed us with her brilliance.

They set the table.
Filled our plates with love,
and sated our hunger.

They hold me.
Wrap me safe in her arms,
and live in my heart.

Laura Dew, Grade 11
Germantown High School, TN

I Am…

I am from tires,
from Goodyear and polyisoprene.
I am from the berry tree beside the garage.

I am from the tobacco leaf,
the plant Nicotiana, strong and dark
I wish I knew it in his jaw.
I am from road trips and big smiles,
from Willie and Yancey and Clark.
I am from the "Tell the truth"
And the "Que Será Será."
I'm from "You are the best" and "Try again."
I am from the Alpha and Omega
the way, the truth, and the life,
Matthew, Mark, Luke, and John.
I'm from Berryhill and The Windy City,
macaroni and sweet potato pie
the banana chips that made
Mom miss the smorgasbord,
I am from captions, precious, most I did not live,
but tell the story of why I am.

Joel Moore, Grade 11
Germantown High School, TN

Soul Mate

Where did you come from?
My Love, my Life, my Dreams.
How did you find me?
Fate, is what it seems.
We've experienced different lives from one another,
Loving, hating, caring for others as we go
Feeling anger, lust, even jealousy
Betraying one's faithful trust.
Here I sit in amazement
Trying to figure out, Why,
Why did you pick me?
Why did I choose you?
Is this relationship just as true?
Or is it a fault?
The next chapter in our lives
The beginning of something new
I know what will happen next
It's not that hard to guess
You'll bestow a question of the ultimate faith
A promise I'm honored to take
Because you are my Life, my Love, my Dreams, my Soul-Mate.

Taylor Cole, Grade 10
Memphis Academy of Science and Engineering, TN

Thinking

I sat alone under a tall, oak tree;
I looked into the sky of endless blue;
Thinking of life and what's ahead of me,
Wondering just what I was meant to do.

Kaycee Roark, Grade 10
Union County High School, TN

Why Can't I

Why can't I realize
that fire once burning has dimmed from your eyes?
And who could be responsible
for leaving your heart with such a drastic hole?
In your center; within your core
can you feel; can you love anymore?
You look in the mirror, but what do you see?
A face filled with sorrow looking back at thee.
Why does your heart ache with such a pounding pain?
Who could have done this; who is to blame?
How could you be the victim; who could have the capacity
to break your heart not in two, but three
million little pieces? Each shard puncturing
every organ so vital; pain rushin'
like a tidal wave. Going insane!
How could this be your fate?
And who are you?
Someone tell me.
I'd look a little deeper,
but I'm afraid I might see
me.
Adelina Salcevski, Grade 10
Robert C Byrd High School, WV

Little Bird

Dream big, little bird.
Dream your wildest dreams.
Dream of dancing about in the heavens
Or of flitting about carelessly in the sky's greatness.
Dream of freedom and independence
Or of flocking with your birdie friends.
Dream yourself full of grace, of agility, of speed.
Dream yourself to be whatever you want to be.
Dream big, little bird.
But for now, rest.
Close your eyes and sleep.
Today you lay snugly in your nest: newly hatched, young.
But soon — ah, soon,
Soon you shall be a great eagle.
So dream big, little bird.
For tomorrow — tomorrow you will learn how to fly.
Alyvia Perkins, Grade 10
Berean Christian School, TN

Waiting for Me to Fall

I feel like at anytime I'm going to fall apart
I feel like I'm withering away
I feel so anxious, so sad, so mad, so lost
I feel like I'm going to be waiting forever
I don't want to move, I don't want to breathe
I feel like a bride left at the alter
I feel like I don't want to leave my bed or go to my next class
I don't feel human, I don't feel happy or complete
You're just waiting for me to just fall apart
Ahdonnica Patterson, Grade 11
Phillip O Berry Academy of Technology, NC

Trapped

Beauty takes on the form of many things;

Sometimes in cliché visions —
Sunsets in paradise,
Roses and pearls,
And cheesy love lines;

Or in simple sights —
Children playing in the snow,
Fathers dancing with their daughters,
And handmade birthday presents.

We observe beauty with our eyes.
We appreciate it with our senses.

But what if beauty is engrained much deeper than appearances?
What if it was birthed in the abyss of the human soul,
Sprouting and reaching for the outskirts of the physical body,
Only to be trapped by humanity's ignorance.

Beauty only wanted to highlight the tangible world.
But its true roots lie within us,
Feasting off our personalities,
Dreams, intentions, and desires.

What if we looked at the world from the inside out;
And saw the true beauty lying within?
MaryKate Thomas, Grade 12
Germantown High School, TN

The Wheel's Turn

In start, the stiff engine crept
along steel lines
hard enough to break
with a cylinder for head that panted smoke
tied with Euclidian segments
to boxed cars dragged for tail.

Then, it shifted towards the mobility
of a shaky Model-T
scurrying in skinny city streets
as a replacement for Nature's diligent chariot
that ate and wasted,
breathed and adapted.

Now, our carriers strive for an organic face
that zooms through skies
with curves, bent and warped
so to zip across mounted carbon islands
hugging, embracing, the guide
yet gliding as a seal in water.

As the machine advances
less mechanical in sight, motion, and response it comes.
Madeleine Hanson-Colvin, Grade 12
William G. Enloe Magnet High School, NC

Trust

Why trust.
Trust. Betrayal. Hurt.
Always the same.
Why trust.
Without trust there's no more betrayal.
Without trust there is no more pain.
Without trust there's no reason to tell all.
Without it no cause for shame.
Beyond trust there is no more friendship.
Without it a man's just a man
Alone with a world full of hardship —
A ship stuck on a child's box of sand.
With trust there's hurt for a burden,
But with trust you never stand alone.
There's always a shelter to run to —
When all's lost it's the one thing you own.
So trust.
Get hurt. Receive help. Help in return.
Always there.
Always the same.

Noah Belanger, Grade 12
Belanger Home School, KY

Little One

I dance down the halls I twirl my little tail,
I chatter my teeth together. They scream as I go by,
But I don't care.
I scurry to the wooden box. I sniff the air nearby,
I eat the food. It was left on the floor,
But I don't care.
I stiffen as I hear a noise, I peer around when the footsteps start,
I see a large girl. She opens the door and shoos me away
But I don't care.
I find a place to sleep, I curl up in the hay,
I wrap my tail around me. The cold air creeps in and nibbles my nose,
But I don't care.
I start my next day, I realize it is just the same,
I wonder why life is that way. My mind begins to think,
But I don't care.
I am running in place, I am running in time,
I am the rat in the race. My life as a barn mouse is over,
I am moving on today, to find a better life
Away from all this pain. Away from all the screamers,
Away from all the beasts. I do hope they will miss me,
But I know they don't care.

Rachel Dufour, Grade 11
Germantown High School, TN

American Trash

I, me, mine
I read Facebook like
The way I should
Read a textbook.
I make sure I have
At least a hundred
Followers on Twitter.
Asking me to go
Outside would cause
Nothing but disappointment.

I never have to learn,
Because I never have
To think for myself.
It's like the existence of
Education is as irrelevant
As a shelf of books.
It's such an ignorant bliss
When the whole world
Wants to be like me.

Katie McCoy, Grade 12
Germantown High School, TN

Chance

The sheer intensity of it pervades my soul and I shudder.
I gaze upon the massive blackness ahead of me and I gently, gradually, touch it.
I bound back, in shock of the horrid memories that flood my thoughts,
    like a surge of cold, gushing water demolishing a dam,
      a dam built of Determination, Dignity, and Denial
        acting as a façade to the outside world of all that is so
          deeply and deliberately
disguised.
I calm myself.
Cautiously, apprehensively, another attempt.
    NO!
I refuse to reenter the dark abyss of Chance and repeat the Mistake I so greatly Regret.
My mind struggles with the opposing screeching of my screaming heart.
The instinctual Logic I so desperately cling to is suddenly crumbling
    and I stumble upon thoughts I dare not think for fear of my own
      Demise.
The endless, ominous, expanse permeates my very being once again, this time with a
    Torturing Tenacity that approaches parts of my core concealed for so long.
Again, I noiselessly ponder.
Finally in a moment of mental blindness I
    Plunge into the penetrating depth and —

Giannina Rokvic, Grade 11
Notre Dame Academy, KY

I Want This Forever

Every time I see you I can't help but smile
I love hugging you as if I haven't seen you in a while
I fem for your kisses your voice and hugs
That's one thing about you that I love
I want to be with you so much
I enjoy each and every one of your touch
When I see you my heart skips a beat
You're like candy oh so sweet
To me you are more than a crush
When you stare at me I can't help but blush
You are A.C. unit when I'm hot
In my heart, yup that is your spot
You understand me from a point nobody do
That is another reason why I love you
You are everything I ask for and more
Your smile I can't help but adore
Can't find the perfect brush to paint how I feel
I hope this dream of us one day comes real
I know we was made for each other
We protect each other like sister and brother

April Hunt, Grade 10
Overton High School, TN

Who I Am

I'm a black handsome young man
who has a college plan
so I can be a better man
That's Who I Am

I am a young tree trying to reach high and see
how my life will be
That's Who I Am

I will reach my goals and seize control
That's Who I Am

I play basketball
I'm a player trying to succeed
in a better life for me
That's Who I Am

Jawon Jenkins, Grade 10
Memphis Academy of Science and Engineering, TN

Hated

Hated because of the men I've dated
No one knows the pain I've taken
There's a thin line between love and hate
Disgraced because of my faith
I thought I could love a man until feelings began
To run all over my mind
I felt as though a piece of me left
That left my insides hollow
The love I had inside of me turned
Into something that I never thought it could be

Blair Newborn, Grade 10
Memphis Academy of Science and Engineering, TN

A Dreamer's Story

I squint into your fluorescent eyes
But your inner light emerges from within,
registering me blind.

I don't know where to go from here.
I lost the sight of your piercing gaze,
I lost the touch of your warm hand within mine,
I lost the sound of your gentle voice,
whispering,

"Always and forever."

Reality bends,
My perception is off.
I am not kissing two perfect lips,
But instead the air of where you once were.

Now I am not blind with my heart,
but with my mind.
Reaching, Grasping, Searching,
for past memories that have been altered with my insanity.

I am now rendered oblivious
to the hastened time lapse of
moving on.

Marisa Scavo, Grade 12
Middle Creek High School, NC

Coke

Acid engulfs my mouth, biting at what is left of my sanity.
This chemistry experiment is dyed brown,
but in reality it's the color of chlorophyll.

I see its image almost everywhere I look,
dressed in the seductive shade of red,
with a body of glass shaped with curves in

just the right places.

I also can't get enough of the taste
as I chug it down my throat.
It makes me happy;
it is my drug of choice.

However, too much of anything is dangerous.
I notice my own figure engorge after
weeks of overindulging on this substance.
I have to stop before it kills me.

Caffeine is also its most treacherous weapon.
It keeps me up at night
in the darkness of my room.
Now I am left awake to
regret my past all over again.

Lois Charm, Grade 12
Germantown High School, TN

Lost
I am lost in who I am.

Spending so much time searching for me,
myself was forgotten in the process.

Is one to be defined by the sins of the past?
If so, I am truly lost.
If not, I must continue.
Searching.
Waiting.
Dreaming.
Hoping.

Hoping that someone will find me.
That I will find me.
I need me.
Where am I?
Where have I gone?

I am lost in who I am.
Ashley Hawkins, Grade 11
Buckhannon-Upshur High School, WV

Dude Really?
It may not be the knife
but it is the feeling.
You blindly stab the people inside the circle
who try to hold you up
but you only cut them down.
Why push and pull to get your way?
Compromise is a way of friendship
like a selfless devotion.
Now you are beginning to walk alone.
The circle closing in as those who give way
to defeat give up on you.
The circle is slipping away one by one.
Open your eyes, it's that simple.
Don't believe you are blind
they are closed
before you're completely alone.
Jesse Souza, Grade 12
Oak Ridge High School, TN

The Nutcracker
The arms and legs flung with passion.
The fingers flowed to the music.
I sat mesmerized by the hands.
Her legs flew with grace around me.
Her body jerked to the movement.
Her face twisted with hurt and pain.
The music suddenly cut off.
The girl stood still looking around.
I relived the moments of this,
and felt her hurt and pain in me.
Spencer Crumley, Grade 11
Oak Ridge High School, TN

Losing My Way
The enormous wooden porch overlooks the vast,
Endless lake of water.
The water looks as inviting as the open arms of a mother.
The wind blows through the water.
White foam cascades from the waves.
The water giggles as it shoots in the air from the speed boat passing by.
The moment I get on the jet-ski,
A weight releases me.
I simply feel free.
The water takes me.
The sky meets the water's surface,
And I race to beat the sun to it.
A life-filled lake seems to never sleep.
I speed, I surrender, and I breathe.
The jet-ski then takes full control of my hands.
The water takes us away.
The wet, wild water washes me,
As I plunge further down.
The water becomes cloudy,
As I lose my way.

Kinsey Gardner, Grade 10
Germantown High School, TN

My Brother's Drum
Raucous racket, a menacing melody. . .
Out of tune and out of order
Loud, annoying, obnoxious –
Drums.
Hearing the cacophony coming from the drums
I write down in my journal all of my thoughts and feelings –
but the noise breaks my concentration.

Fun instrument to play, annoying to hear. . .
A brand new player, but not a new set of drums
Missing parts, missing tunes, missing beats –
Shaky and undefined, it makes me angry
Makes me go out of mind, out of being.

Interrupting my time of rest, my time of peace from the outside world –
Frustrating, the thought of it never ending. . .
Hearing beats to songs I don't know.
I yell Stop!
Yet ignored by my brother's drum.

Alyssa Hoffman, Grade 10
Simon Kenton High School, KY

Far from Exuberant

I sit alone in the dark
Crying, slow, frustrated, scared, reclusive
Far from exuberant
I do nothing right
My actions always end in disaster
Forced to listen to yelling, but no one hears me
How do I change?
Negativity surrounds me
All I wish for is to see a glimpse of hope
I hear the words "I love you." But it's hard to believe them now
When I don't know what's up or what's down
I push myself on day by day
Do what I think is right to help
But it turns out it's just another day to endure
To endure the sadness. The hate
I can't eat can't sleep It's always on my mind
   So here I sit writing this
Alone in the dark
Crying, slow, frustrated, scared, reclusive
Far from exuberant

Ashley Nelson, Grade 10
Stanly Early College School, NC

Mankind

The third planet,
The location where life was set,
A place of war,
And oil spilling onto sand-filled shores,
Carbon dioxide emissions,
And prisoners of conflict being beaten into submission.

Yet, despite all these shortcomings,
The sun remains shining,
And together the human race,
Stands ready to face,
Any and all difficulties,
With utmost bravery.

We are mankind.

Trevor Lythgow, Grade 10
Coffee County Central High School, TN

Eyes of Wisdom

Eyes are like the sun in the sky
When you look up it always shines on you.
Sometimes when you look at things; they seem clear
But, when it gets scary, close your eyes.
Life can get scary but only if you are scared
I wished that you could see my long wavy hair
When you open your eyes, it may be blurry.
When you are mad, your mind is raging with fury.
You don't have to be mad all the time
You can just use your "Eyes of Wisdom."
Wisdom of mine…

Mickie Mapp, Grade 11
Memphis Academy of Science and Engineering, TN

Background Dancer

It is obvious you run the show
I stay seated and back down
Here,
Take the leading role but save me the background
Even though I miss my cues
You do forget your lines
This blame game is sickening
But I continue to read your signs
No need to put my name in lights
No need for the starring role
You do nothing but kill me, but for torture you keep my soul
So if you need me I'll be stage right
Too afraid to build up courage to have stage fright
I start to see
That I'm not that impressive
My golden confession
But I am who I am
Just a trail of stardust leading to a wonderful superstar

Donte Jenrette, Grade 11
West Brunswick High School, NC

I Am Love

I am patient
I am the smooth flowing waters that comfort you
I am the time it takes
I am the laughter
   and the pain.
I am the tears that stain
   and the anger that strains.
I am encouragement you long for
   and the criticism you never wish to receive.
I am the small, still voice that speaks so sweetly to your hurting soul
I am more of a want
   instead of a necessity
I am who?
I am love.

Nadia Givens, Grade 11
Germantown High School, TN

Migraine

Glance up, then down — that's all the time it takes
To start a storm that can't be put to rest.
A spot appears, it has the moon's curved shape,
But like a star, it burns with zeal and zest.
Bright as the sun and sparkly as the sea,
This spot — it grows — and soon devours all.
And in the mirror, just half my face I see,
A rainbow swirls and makes a sturdy wall.
But just as quickly as it did appear,
It leaves my sight and moves into my head.
And there it stays, inducing pain so sheer.
As an escape, I lie down in my bed.
Closing my eyes, it's off to sleep I drift,
And when I wake, I hope this storm does lift.

Elizabeth Molinet, Grade 11
Germantown High School, TN

Mom

Beautiful brown hair, soft blue eyes
a smile that matches mine.
Blessed by an innocent kindness with a gentle soul
Creating for my brothers and me a world open and safe
    You were our rock,
    You were our life,
    You were our guidance
Now we carry the memories of you in
our heart, our soul, our mind
Sharing a love so deep,
knowing love never fails
Advice you gave – I constantly rebelled,
Tried proving you wrong
though you were always right
Humor lightened the darkest days we went through
Swearing everything will be okay
Your small hands picking me up when I was down
Kissing every boo-boo we had
only comfort a mother can bring
Never giving up on us and never letting go
    You told us even if we were grown we'd always be your babies
Promising to always be there and to love us no matter what.

Dakota Stafford, Grade 12
Simon Kenton High School, KY

A Tribute to Autumn

As hues of red, orange and yellow grow,
The cool and crisp air brings to me much cheer.
Vibrant leaves decorate the ground below,
Because of this I know autumn is here.

To bonfires and festivals I go,
With friends and family ever so dear.
Pumpkin pies and cider fill us so,
Because of this I know autumn is here.

Halloween and Thanksgiving come about,
With thankfulness, celebrations and fear.
The holiday spirit does spread throughout,
Because of this I know autumn is here.

So close to my heart does autumn adhere,
If only autumn could stick around all year.

Danielle Mosteller, Grade 12
Starmount High School, NC

Cancer

A word that brings the sound of crickets to the room
A word you say and all you hear are gasps from others
It's like a glue pulling family together
It brings tears to all eyes
It's like a never ending suffering
It shows a true survivor in the end

Brianna Wilbur, Grade 11
Campbell County High School, KY

We Wear the Mask

We wear the mask that feeds the lies.
It shelters the truth, it protects us.
The guilt is false, we've done nothing wrong.
With nothing but kind hearts and love,
We are punished for innocence, accused of empty crimes.

Why should we cease to fight?
They beat us with cruel names and
Unfair games. No we stand together.
We wear the mask.

We smile, we cry, we love, and we fight.
Together we can push through the hate and,
Unfairness. We can withstand the discrimination.
We can eliminate the prejudice.
But only if we stand together. Only if,
We wear the mask.

Taylor Risinger, Grade 10
Berkeley Springs High School, WV

Come to Me Now

God saw that you were tired
Of fighting to survive
I know how much you wanted
To be here with your loved ones by your side
And we wanted nothing more but you
But God didn't want you to suffer anymore
Our hearts filled with painful sores
And I refused to understand why
Precious moments with you did fly
It was painful for us to watch you go
But God needed you now
So he gently grabbed your hand
And quietly whispered
Come to me now.

Erica Shepherd, Grade 11
Meadow Bridge High School, WV

Exploring the Marsh

Swinging rope,
Salty marsh,
And faintly aromatic poppies.
Enveloping me,
Slightly brushing against my tattered layer.

Only thirty seconds,
Until, my feet touched the sole of Adam's ale.
Until, a sharp edge shattered my skull,
And pierced my frontal lobe.

Consequenced for my foolery.
I received the ultimate penalty.
A penalty that was seen been by no one.

Antonia Watts, Grade 10
Germantown High School, TN

Dear Sandy

Not a second, a minute or day goes by
That we are not thinking of you and asking why

You were very sick and went through a lot
With your family and the injury that you got

We who love you were there 'til the end
Hoping that your past heartaches you could mend

At the end certain ones did not show
Hope you were already with God and didn't know

We think of the decision we had to make every day
Hoping it was right, that's what we want to say

You know we are watching out for your loved one
So send us a sign of if there's more you want done

We already see your signs every day that goes by
From red birds, sunflowers, rainbows in the sky

Gone but not forgotten that is what we feel
Keeping your memory alive, you know we will

You are not hurting anymore in body, heart or mind
You was funny, goofy, loving, fearful, one of a kind
Deea Pullum, Grade 10
White County High School, TN

Commander

My heart beats rapidly with fear
But my countenance resists
For I am the commander
And self-doubt shall not exist

My subordinates, my friends
Their bodies are mine to command
They know that every mission could mean their end
Yet, they follow me willfully

Remembering the fallen
Drives our core
Leaving us fighting till our last gasp
Pain is to be ignored

Death follows us like a spoiled hound
Always begging for more and more
We struggle to avoid that hole in the ground
Evade our own mortality gets harder as the years pass

Paragon is who I am
And I will not allow preventable casualties
Even though death shadows me
I will never give up until I fade away
Tiara Hobbs, Grade 10
Coffee County Central High School, TN

You Were Amazing!

You were an amazing friend to me
Now looking back we always had a smile
On both of our faces, I loved to see.
Friendship was everything I thought
Now you don't even realize I'm here
For you, We never got caught.
I miss having my best friend
Beside me in everything I do
Never wanted our friendship to end.
Now that you don't see me anymore
I feel all alone these days,
It's like you just shut the door.
The nights we lay, looking at the twinkling stars.
Laughing until we couldn't laugh no more.
Catching fireflies in the big jars.
When do I get to see you.
Can't stop crying over our friendship
Thinking about you all day boo,
Now all I wanna ask is "Do you miss me too?"
Kelsey Griggs, Grade 10
First Flight High School, NC

I Go to Church

Sunday morning around 11 o'clock,
Is when the gangstas move off the block.
They are going to church, you need to go.
When you do grab your kids, your girl, stay away from that.
Keep your pants up, because saggin' is a bad title,
Walk in with your head up, holding the Bible.
They say if you are scared go to church but that's false,
Jesus wasn't scared when they put Him on the cross.
We all need Jesus for plenty of reasons.
Subtracts the pain, and multiplies the blessing.
He's there when you're happy, He's there when you're stressing,
I love my God, I don't know about you.
If you think you're better off, then I think you're a fool.
Just stay holy to His name, always put God first,
Bible basic instructions, before leaving Earth.
Monquall B., Grade 11
Audubon Youth Development Center, KY

Thank You

Thank you for the love
Thank you for no pain
I love you with a passion
A passion with no rain
A passion that shines like the light from the sun
Even though our love has just begun
You keep my head from aching
My heart from breaking
And because of you I shake no more
Shake from the terror that I had before
My love for you is as strong as could be
Because now I don't feel lonely.
Brenda Sanchez, Grade 10
Loretto High School, TN

Single Song

I don't know where I am,
Or where I'm going.
No future is seen on the black roads ahead.
No candles to light my way, I'm all alone.
So I'll play my single song.
My song written just for me.
My song will take me away, and light my road for me.
Just only one song, I'll play that single song.
The song that's designed only for me.

When things are getting tough, and you feel like giving up,
No one by your side, no one there to care.
Your single song will play,
And you will dance the night away.

Just play your single song, that song that fits you.
The song that makes you dance, and
The song that won't make you feel scared.
It's only one song. One single song, that cares.

Lindsey Kidwell, Grade 11
Campbell County High School, KY

Forever Loved

A person with a promise, a promise now broken.
Always to be here, with me, never gonna leave.
Forever became never.

All the fusses and fights, long stormy nights.
You stayed by my side when I'd just try to hide.
You hold me close and whisper it's all right,
But in the back of my mind hid that awful fright.

Together this long, four years.
It makes it even harder to hold back the tears.
Just sitting thinking of you and what you used to do.

I wish that I could change all of this, the way it turned out.
But you and I both know what it was about.

I loved you then, today and tomorrow too.
With all regrets to say —
There's no more me and you.

Kaitlynn Wolsey, Grade 12
Pulaski County High School, KY

No Regret

Some things aren't meant to be,
Impossibility as wide as the sea.
But never, ever compromise.
You will find the strength to rise.
And build bridges that you'll walk.
Waste not a moment on a clock.
So move along through this world.
Never give up, and never waste a word.

Joshua Morris, Grade 12
Sycamore High School, TN

Looking Back

Take me back to the forgotten days
That are covered in a cloudy haze.
From the edges of my mind
Lays the world I left behind.

How simple everything could be back then
With no worries of who, what, where, and when.
All so clear without hidden intention
Pleasurable days without intervention.

It was a simpler time in my native home
When the only thing needed was to let our senses roam.
At certain times I wish to go back
To escape reality's cruel attack.

Yet I know this world will live on forever
In this, life was very clever.
Given the chance to pass on this essence
I give rise to new adolescence.

Bohdan Volyanyuk, Grade 12
William G Enloe High School, NC

Mysterious Time

Each day passes
No different from the last
It becomes impossible
To discern present from past

The hours and days
Seem to only creep by
While the months and years
Do nothing but fly

Time is distorted
Incongruent and inconsistent
There is no rhyme or reason
What is distant is near and what is near is distant

It is a great enigma
The equation of time
But to not savor every second
Would be the greatest crime

Parth Majmudar, Grade 12
William G Enloe High School, NC

Bliss

He is my happy place
He is where I go to escape
He is the answer to my prayers
He holds me close when I'm scared
Our love is strong and true
Even if it's not always on cue
This is my bliss
As he seals the night with a kiss

Brooklyn Dotson, Grade 12
Sycamore High School, TN

High Merit Poems – Grades 10, 11, and 12

Excerpt from "The Bird Faithful"
I sit as of yet,
On my stone, cold rock,
Trying to create another masterpiece.
Darkness envelopes my mind
As I sit, staring blank at the world,
My soul waiting for inspiration.
But through the toils of the storm
I know my flight will come,
When my wings catch the wind
And ride it home.
But now, for creation to flow,
My little bird needs help from
The Mother Wind.

Sometimes I do not need Her help,
And I soar through the sky
On my own accord.
Sometimes Her help does not lift me
To the clear-rainbow sky,
So I climb and scale a tree a step at a time,
To reach closer to the heights of my mind.
Genevieve Versteeg, Grade 12
William G. Enloe High School, NC

More Than Just a Game
Why do we participate in games?
Maybe it is the drive behind the mind
Or is it to become a known name?
Some just want to be one of a kind.

With games, comes character heart, hustle.
Believing in fact that strength is key.
We find out brain can even beat muscle.
But that would distinguish weak from elite.

Competitiveness and teamwork are learn,
Along with pride and sportsmanship
Such as sharing or waiting for your turn
Sports are providing us lifelong tips

Whether the game be sports or cards,
In the long run games will help you get far.
Eugene Billips, Grade 12
Starmount High School, NC

Love
A hug was just a hug
Until I realized I did not want to relinquish
A kiss was just a kiss
Until it made my breath diminish
A dream was just a dream
Until I saw your significant complexion
Love was just a figment of my imagination
Until I met you
Aurora Stotts, Grade 10
Coffee County Central High School, TN

I'm From
I am from the family photo album, from Kodak and dark rooms.
I am from the bathroom scale, stable at times but also jumpy
and amused by the plain black numbers increasing on the dial.
I am from the coffee plant, the roses filled with sweet aroma
I am from the late night celebrations with friends and family and loudness
from Albin and Rosemary and Quinones.
I am from the chatter boxes and the as-the-saying-goes morals.
From stand straight and that everything has its time, place, and age.
I am from rosaries but also keeping to ourselves and questioning along with another.
I'm from Long Island and Colombia, white rice and beans.
From the days of my father being with careless friends taking advantage of their youth,
and the little girl who made trips to the houses of old family money that are long lost now.
I am from the aged and torn flower print box in the game room closet
showing only growth and times of happiness represented by
large smiles and exotic landscapes. From the milestones in life
and the droplets of tears on dated pictures wishing for the return of the simpler times.
Nicole Quinones, Grade 11
Germantown High School, TN

BEaUty
And as she looks into the mirror she sees imperfection,
I see me
She looks into the peep hole to her soul, and imperfection is what she sees
She tries to accept what is destined to be.
And the smear on the mirror is what reflects me.
The strength it takes to love me is as strong as she.
To love a girl full of flaws is like loving the sea;
Her insecurities are deep.
It's as if her motive for a man's love at times drains weak.
She wants his love, yet she can't even love herself
And she will never love herself,
Until she finds self BEaUty.
Brianna Jones, Grade 12
William G Enloe High School, NC

Like a Child
Never mind the fact that the color scheme has changed over the years,
that pumpkin-patch-colored house still resides in my memory.
Peeled potatoes and lightning bugs refresh my nocturnal routine,
and every morning breathes of hot chocolate,
and *Hogan's Heroes*.

Leaving this place replays my adolescent sorrow.
I only did what mama insisted.
Lingering memories question my abandonment,
and remind me of how I stood in that driveway,
and cried,
like a child.

Tanishia Sims, Grade 12
Germantown High School, TN

Words

I never knew how much
Words could mean
Until I gave into the emotions
That defeated me.
They pushed me around,
And bullied me.
I feared for my life
Before the day
That I realized words
Can empower me.
I sat down at my table,
And I began to write
My words.
With that first assignment done,
I knew my words were
The best part of me.
I had a bully no more,
And through my words
I found
That I can find
Myself.

Emily Pfeifer, Grade 11
Eastern High School, KY

I Wear the Mask

I wear the mask that hides the pains
A victim of your silly games
I trusted you with all my heart
Until you tore my world apart
Now only the memory remains

I want to sit and cry all day
But deep down I know it's not the way
So for your return I shall pray
I wear the mask

I gave you one too many chances
To break my heart into pieces
So a smile I shall wear
To cover my despair
I wear the mask.

Breana McNelly, Grade 12
Berkeley Springs High School, WV

In Dance, I Am Creative

In dance, I am creative
The beat I keep
My body is rolling
I feel like I'm flowing
My head's shaking
I am wide awaken
I am free
This is the true me
Nothing can change this feeling

Kelcee Fulton, Grade 11
Berkeley Springs High School, WV

The Noteworthy Things

Sitting in class we glance over.
It was a turn away from our firefighter themed coloring
and the beginning of something.
I'm the best friend you've been looking for.
From playing in the dirt, climbing to the top of the playground,
and an abnormal love of Legos — I had it all. Being a girl was just a plus.

The other boys looked at you funny,
as if there was always a proverbial piece of food lodged in your teeth.
Apparently, playing house wasn't very manly.
Calling you a girl was an insult worth stoning back then,
and sincerely and serendipitously I jumped to your defense.
Like a Junkyard Dog I snarled — "You mess with him and you mess with me"
with my tiny fists in the air I resolved that
we were each other's responsibility,
and our parents wrote it off as Puppy Love
as we talked on our house phones every day
from kindergarten to the fourth grade.

We took pictures dressed as husband and wife
with wide smiles resembling an open gate.
You couldn't even say my name correctly,
but you knew all of the noteworthy things.

LaAndrea Mitchell, Grade 12
Germantown High School, TN

Pages of Protection

Leather binding protects his core.
Each page is demarcated with gold sparkle and a gloss finish,
shimmering with each turn of the page.
As she reads in the calm of her backyard,
the golden edges gleam in the sunlight.
Her fingertips rest as she gently places her palm over Psalm 46:10.
In the brightest hue of scarlet, in the vein of his blood, words abandon their page.
Boundless, they float up her arm.
Whispering softly in her ear, they say,
"Be still and know that I am God."

She draws in the winds of the earth.
Her eyes see indigo specks emerge as her lids shut.
A miniscule drop of forgiveness falls from her lashes down her soft pink cheeks.
As she exhales, black stains roll off of her chin.
They sink slowly into the ground and diminish.
She is new.

Just as her makeup vanishes, her sins do also.
As she closes the book, the pages ripple as they pass over her thumb.
Gold tint and glossy shimmer soak in her skin.
Like water after a day spent in the summer blaze, she is quenched by His words.
Now, leather binding protects her core, too.

Phoenix Pope, Grade 12
Germantown High School, TN

My Teddy Bear

Shall I compare thee to an old teddy bear
To others you seem worn-out and old
I think they're just jealous that I won't share
Without you I feel cold

The memories I share with you will never end
You're the one that made me smile
The wounds you caused might never mend
You were with me through every mile

Loving and caring you'll always be
No one knows you better than I
This is why you mean so much to me
The love in my heart will never lie

You told me you would always care
That's why you'll always be my teddy bear

Brooke Fowler, Grade 10
Loretto High School, TN

Life

I sat down underneath a tree one night
Then I started thinking about my life
How it was long and weary in my sight
It was cutting me as if it were a dull knife

Then I thought it cannot be all that bad
I knew there would be ups and downs
And there would be times that I would be sad
But I get by with magical sounds

Even though there are times I wish for peace
In my heart I know it can never be
Because of this life will come to cease
Because the world of man cannot believe

But in the end we all stay
To die here another day.

Justin Johnson, Grade 10
Union County High School, TN

Sleep

I am the embrace in the dead of night,
Dancing around you, pulling you in and out.
I am the drug you cannot quit,
The one ache and constant desire of your body.
I am the ivy climbing the old brick wall,
An odd yet essential part of the familiar scenery.
I am the decrescendo of the symphony down to nothing,
Music in the silence and ringing in the air.
I am your greatest foe and best friend, both,
Appearing at the worst of times, evading when I'm wanted most.
I am holding captive all your hopes and dreams,
Forcing you to go out and achieve them.

Kayla Sweet, Grade 12
Oak Ridge High School, TN

Love

What is love?
Love is a word often used
Sometimes love give you the blues
I've heard many times "I Love You"
What does that really mean?

Love can be expressed in many ways
It comes and goes throughout the days
Show love in a good way
Don't let your clouds turn gray

If you express love in a good way
You will get love day by day
Love is the good things that appear
If you have love there's nothing to fear

I love you, and you love me
If you love yourself it will make me happy
  LOVE!

Nya Taylor, Grade 10
Memphis Academy of Science and Engineering, TN

Fighting in Color

Live in color, not black or white —
Recognizing your differences, it doesn't have to be a fight
It's not always who's wrong, who's right?

In the end, will it matter what they say?
Does it make a difference, at the end of the day?
Be your own person, make your own way

Tomorrow no one will care
what you looked like, what you chose to wear —
So make a difference, it's a dare.

Have compassion for your fellow man.
Believe in something; take a stand
in color, so life is not blind…

Destiny LaGarce, Grade 12
Sycamore High School, TN

Love

What is love?
So many people have told me that they love me
But, they never really showed it.
Love is a four-letter word
But has a strong meaning behind it
As they told me that they love me; they
Also told many others that same lie

In life you can only have ONE true love
When I meet my true love
I want to be the one and only
He tells "I love you."

Brandi Algee, Grade 10
Memphis Academy of Science and Engineering, TN

Nonsensical Happenings

Some say they want to stay,
Some are begging to leave.
Either way we are here,
destined for a Robert Frost poem.
Some are planning for a future,
a future they haven't realized they can't plan.
Some get better than they expected,
some get worse.
Either way,
I'll enjoy living unplanned days,
in a book page by page.
And at the end,
I will start over,
live through happy and tragic endings,
so I will be prepared and pleased,
with the nonsensical happenings
bound to come my way.

Jessica Baker, Grade 11
Germantown High School, TN

Home Sweet Home

Happiness consumes the area.
The smell of freshly baked
Cinnamon bread circulates in the air.

Jokes are shared and
Laughs can be heard from miles away.
Stories are told,
Bad and good,
As we sit around the table and discuss our day.

The feeling of comfort, support, and love,
Never leave this place.
My home sweet home.

Asha Tate, Grade 10
Germantown High School, TN

Those Special Moments

Walking through Times Square
Awed by beautiful sights.
Watching zephyrs in fields of tare
That guide elegant kites.
Remembering all the joys
Shared with true friends.
Playing with childhood toys
Whose appeal never ends.
Going on a first date
Engulfed with sweet butterflies.
Gazing with a soul mate
At the stars beyond the skies.
Finding the cordial keys
To paths truly beneficial.
With moments like these
How can life not be so special?

Nanda Siva, Grade 10
Parkersburg High School, WV

Life

This world is a scary place,
Unfamiliar faces and unexpected things.

Reality too real,
Fantasies too fake.

A thirst for admiration,
A lust for desire.

A hunger for satisfaction,
Left unfed.

New weaknesses will arise,
Simplicity itself will slowly die.

The time that flies will never return,
The hearts unbroken will never learn.

Those who easily trust,
Break easy.

Embrace all fears,
And shed not one tear.

Those who truly love,
Will always be near.

Live a lie and not live fully,
Live just and complete Life's mission.

Brooke Hall, Grade 12
Dyer County High School, TN

Butterflies

You touched my hand
Tinglezzz
I pull away
You pull me back
Warmth floods my brain
I push you away
Your grip is too strong
Light headed
I feel
Light headed
The Butterflies
Butterflies
In my tummy
They've come back
I try to say
…No…
But the look
The look in your eyes
Those beautiful, brown, eyes
They give me
Butterflies.

Amina Alghali, Grade 10
Grimsley High School, NC

High Merit Poems – Grades 10, 11, and 12

A Dream

What is a dream?
A series of thoughts or ambitions that might happen
Maybe it's a weird force of nature that is in your head
Once as a child people have dreams of being someone
An astronaut, president, or even a famous singer
But some say that it never comes true
It's just a dream.

I had a dream once when I was a little kid
t was to be a professional tennis player
As a kid I had many things that I wanted to be
A famous track and field runner
A doctor or a brilliant artist
It's just a dream.

It can come true or maybe not
I have the potential to make it
Even if I played for three years
Whenever I play tennis it's like an adrenaline rush.
The force and power put forth into the ball
It's just a dream.

Kyriunna Harris, Grade 11
Germantown High School, TN

Last Night and You

This is but a ceremonious unwind,
characteristic of the leaking of my soul.
I try listening, holding softly,
but there is no such way in regard to any senses of mine.
There is no antiquity to my ease,
only something picked at and dirty.
What else can I be?
When the wires have all been ripped out? I am nothing.
It is a devilish ceremony, of compulsion on my behalf,
in contrast of a love so strong.
But how could I ever know, if the truth lies only in action?
How am I to feel? With all this reverberation in my skull?
How am I supposed to live, with all this death inside of me?

Over extension, in the name of I know not what.
To think and dream of creation.
To long for that experience, to be left out of the wake.
Bizarre and strenuous, outraged at the scathingly self inflicted.
There's nothing else I can really do.
Lastly let me tell you last night was a dream.
Lastly, could you tell me, last night was a dream?

Mandie Adkins, Grade 12
Elliott County High School, KY

Winter Walk

My favorite knit
Brisk breeze against my red face
Footsteps left behind.

James Ferraro, Grade 12
William G Enloe High School, NC

I Am From

I am from the powerful desktop computer,
From Nvidia and the expanding landscape of the internet.
I am from the pale red house in the cove,
Bustling and full of children enjoying life.
Front yard enriched with the smell of freshly cut grass,
And back filled with glistening pool water.
I am from the weeds in the yard,
Taking root and staying in place,
Fighting against all odds.
I am from the give-it-your-alls,
From "Don't interrupt!" and "How was your day at school?"
I am from the empty book open to the world,
Raised as a blank slate,
Able to make my own decisions
And decide for myself what I want to follow.
I am from the scrapbook in the closet,
Full of my family's memories.
I am from a supportive family,
Always there when I need them.
I am from many things,
And without them I would be less!

Michael Weinhold, Grade 11
Germantown High School, TN

Where I'm From

I am from the Golden Rod and Cardinal,
  The Yellowhammer and Camellia,
  Whose luscious scent will internally rest in my sensory.
I am from Christmas Vacation and male pattern baldness,
  From Gentry and Moyna and Lovett.
I am from excess flatulence and constant hilarity.
  From, "One thing I noticed out there"
  And, "I thought you did good."
I am from In the name of the Father,
  And of the Son, and of the Holy Spirit,
  And a role modeled scientist.
I am from the NASA capital in Sweet Home Alabama
  And Lovett's roots and Renn's roost,
  From barbecue and all kinds of cakes.
I am from the fireplace mantle
  And the hallway closet,
  From the countless scrapbooks and frames.
I am from memories beyond context
  From a life like no other
  And thanksgiving for such moments
  Snapped or unsnapped.

Renn Lovett, Grade 11
Germantown High School, TN

Children

We wish to return
Back to those childhood days
Days of carefree joy

Robby Cowan, Grade 11
Germantown High School, TN

Confused

Thoughts lost,
and thoughts tangled,
thoughts confused,
mixed and mangled,

I'm confused,
I don't know,
which way to turn?
which way to go?

So I will try,
to think about,
a way to escape,
a way out,

So now I plan,
to clear my mind,
and when I do,
I seek to find,

A way to keep,
confusion at bay,
so I can keep,
things going my way.

Courtney Bartley, Grade 12
Grimsley High School, NC

Love

Love me, all of me
If you can't, leave me
I come as who I am, there is no changing
Love me, all of me

Forget the past, look forward to the future
Great things are in store for our love
But I want to be loved, without a doubt
Love me, all of me

I love you, all of you
Your eyes, your smile, your laugh
The way you hold me
I love you, all of you

Young, puppy love
I hear it over and over
But what we have is real
We are real

So love me, all of me
I'll be the loving girlfriend, fiancé, and wife
We deserve it, we deserve love
I love you, all of you

Taylor Young, Grade 12
Sycamore High School, TN

I'm from Ordinary

I am from French vanilla coffee, from Frequent Flyers and sunburns.
I am from the ordinary suburban home with the smell of freshly mown grass.
I am from the tulip poplar tree in the backyard,
The overgrown garden no one cared to care about.
I am from A Christmas Story every December,
And laughing at jokes we have heard two million times,
I am from academic, sporty and artsy.
From "good night" and "good morning,"
Paired with a particularly annoying nickname.
I am from Adrianisms like
"These hath God married and no man shall part,
Dust on the Bible and drought in the heart."
I am from a tea-time grandmother with an accent everyone loves,
From hot cross buns and pecan pie.
I am from the army base in Germany, playing the harmonica and guitar simultaneously
And setting a school track record with the relay team.
I am from the sad scrapbooking attempts and the toy bucket full of old pictures.
I am from pasting those pictures on projects
And sending them in for school videos.
I am from looking at those photos in our entryway until I move out and move on.

Alexandria Exley, Grade 11
Germantown High School, TN

My Struggle
Faults

Sometimes I hate to care for others, when none care for me.
I sometimes become a doormat, just so I don't have enemies.
I strive so hard to be the best to be loved and adored.
But yet and still I'm scorned by my peers more and more.
When I get someone I truly love, I hold on with all my heart.
But I smother them and they leave, and I'm at the place from which I start.
I looked at these faults and wept, for I thought I was an imperfection.
So worked to change my mind and body, and this became an obsession.
But I stopped and thought about the purpose of these changes.
And found that I am who I am, in Infamy or Fame.
So now I spent my day to live for Me, Myself, and I.
Because I want to truly live and love before I die.
I still work hard and strive to succeed, but I'm not doing it for anyone else.
I'm doing it for me.

Terrence Hogan, Grade 10
Middle College High at NC A&T, NC

The Shadow

The me I have when I'm with you, and the me I have when there's him, too.
I never realize the transformation until I'm alone again with neither of you.

My friends they see a different side, too and no one knows
Only me and you, the unknown shadow in the dark.

The shadow who hears my quiet celebrations, and the mournful morning tears.
The one who never moves to change or fix or interrupt my thoughts.

The shadow that grows when I grow, as the day progress,
And then in the end with the moon grows depressed.

Elizabeth Stillwell, Grade 11
Providence Academy, TN

I Wear the Mask

I wear the mask that expresses a smile,
But I have not been happy for a while.
My body aches and my heart is broken.
My pride is shot because the monster has spoken,
But yet I stand here like a brick wall.

Why am I to blame?
It makes me feel ashamed
Because I am the one in the right.
I wear the mask.

I feel so lost in this world that's so cold,
But in the end I will be the one standing bold,
And then when I am down I feel defeated.
I feel so empty, and lots of love is needed,
But yet I find myself here, alone.

I wear the mask!

Shane Justice, Grade 12
Scott High School, WV

Common Sense

Whatever happened to Common Sense?
Where did he go?
We have lost all of his knowledge,
his understanding,
and his love.
All of those precious guidelines
that helped us live our lives.
We overlooked him, so he left without a trace.
And now we are without him,
our most needed Common Sense.
What has this world come to?
Common Sense is laughing at our ignorance.
If only I could have run away with him,
how lucky would I be!

Sarah Buck, Grade 10
Coffee County Central High School, TN

High School

Welcome to the world of high school
Where there's jealousy,
Abuse! People don't know what to do.
Fighting and fighting trying to find someone to love
Here, there is less thankfulness and pride to our God above
Some never think about humility
Always indulged in someone's stupidity
On a positive note,
They always want to see the friend in me
I'm keeping my grades up
Being the best student I can really be
Welcome to the world of high school
Yea, that's cool
But are you focused on what you're supposed to do?

Jerriney Clinton, Grade 10
Memphis Academy of Science and Engineering, TN

Valentine's Day in Heaven*

A man that's hurt, he's all alone.
He was in a wheelchair, but now he's gone.
This man is my Pappy, I love him so dear.
He now lives in Heaven, God says, "He's here."

Seven years have gone by since the day so sad,
This day was the day that my Pappy died.
February 13th, 2004, the day before Valentine's Day,
My Pappy reached and entered Heaven's door.

As sad as it was, now I can see,
My Pappy's death set him free.
He no longer suffers all of the pain,
He made it to Heaven and had so much to gain.

How wonderful it would be to spend Valentine's in Heaven,
My Pappy has ever since I was seven.

Courtney Booth, Grade 10
Montgomery County High School, KY
In memory of Harry Carter Means

Courage

Not all of us have courage in life
But the ones that do use it, and well
Through all your battles and all your strifes
So keep your brothers close, and this will not fail
Even now you know you may lose, you must fight
Every single odd can be against you
And you still must fight and not think of flight
But not giving up is what you must do
To face all things, no matter what they are
Big or small, everything can fall
Any man can sound tough from afar
But the biggest voice is the one of us all
Courage can be shown in many ways
So stand up for yourself all of your days

Allen Mendenhall, Grade 12
Starmount High School, NC

The Pain of the Sea of Happiness

The vast sea of happiness
How do I get across?
Maybe a boat?
No then I might be swallowed whole by the waves of joy
A plane maybe?
No the gusts of gladness would surely make me
Crash into the same sea I so badly want out of
That's it a plank!
But the sharks of sharp shrieks
Of pure happiness will devour me alive

This is the pain of a sea of happiness

How do I get out?!

Jeanne Cardinal, Grade 11
Oak Ridge High School, TN

I Am From....

I am from bookshelves, from Rowling and Austen,
I am from family dinners, discussions around the table and the smell of home-baked cookies,
I am from oak trees as old as dirt, and fresh cut daisies,
I am from Christmas eve service and small feet, from Mills and Scott and Morgan,
I am from big imaginations and big hearts,
From book lovers and music gurus,
From speak your mind and always respect your elders,
I am from love Jesus and John 3:16,
I am from Memphis, Tennessee and Marks, Mississippi from small towns and big reunions,
From pumpkin and chocolate pie, and Mexican wedding cakes,
From the six little ladies, who still act like they are seventeen,
From the air force and a mixture of world cultures
From the childhood sweethearts that head the family,
From roses left on front door steps and sneaking out to late night movies,
From scrapbooks made with care, from hallways lined with photos,
And slides from Europe, and everywhere the family has been,
From the timeless pictures, each holding a story,
From the loving family that can spend weeks together,
And still laugh about the smallest things,
And from the future generations, whose stories are yet to be written.

Selby Mills, Grade 11
Germantown High School, TN

I Am From

I am from local library tables, from Sharpies and the frequent, late night essay
I am from the makeshift computer table, small, crammed in the corner of a crowded apartment that smells of peanut butter and Pinesol
I am from Crepe Myrtles, the bridge over the pond
I am from Christmas lasagna and bad eyesight, from crazy grandmothers and foreign uncles, cousins that become your best friend
I am from the directionally disabled, the flirty and the husband-hunting
From the crust that mother said was healthy, the things I had to do because she should have
I am from internet churches, lazy Christians, the Sunday afternoon nap worshipers, from the hypocrites who preach and don't follow.
I am from Lancaster, a place like Grover's Corners in Our Town, from which no one ever leaves and they always come back.
I am from the microwave dinner, the easy bake cupcakes.
I am from the mother that chose love over education, the high school sweethearts and college newlyweds.
I am from the disgruntled father who works all day and hates his job.
I am from the familial prison that is missing too many bars, the push of invisible forces, from wanting them to be proud.
I am from the disappointed afternoon when the car never comes, the shakes of heads and the sighs of exasperation.
I am from the diamond rings and fancy clothes they can't afford, the pictures that sit in boxes undeveloped.
I am from the untuned piano in the downstairs hall, the messy bedroom doing homework all during the night.
I am from local library tables, from Sharpies and the frequent, late night essay.

Hanna Hefley, Grade 11
Germantown High School, TN

Humanity

No street lights,
Pure darkness in the dirty streets.
People fight for their lives.
It's a daily struggle.
On the streets they beg for help.
Kids run through traffic, trying to sell anything and everything.
The birth of the human race; yet the death of humanity.

Mariam Diallo, Grade 12
William G Enloe High School, NC

Time Pays

Rush in, rush out,
Life ticks through the mind.
Brothas, sistas, stay running not gunning.
Never to know the full extent of higher learning.
Tick, tock, reaching out for hands to extend, yearning
But alas, grandfather time solemnly reflects
the tragic existence of man.

Devan H., Grade 11
Audubon Youth Development Center, KY

Where I'm From

I am from bullhorns on Christmas morning, from silly string sprayed around the house,
and competitions on drinking the most raw eggs.
I am from the safe, warm, loving and caring feel of home.
I am from the iris flower, the magnolia trees.
I am from family dinners and chaos, from Stephanie
  and Kevin.
I am from finding trouble and seeing how long it takes to get out.
From "always chew with your mouth closed" and always saying yes ma'am and yes sir.
I am from Christian backgrounds, but now from trying to figure out the world for myself.
I'm from Memphis, Tennessee and a family ancestry of who cares, from sweet tea and mashed potatoes.
From my brothers being cavemen at the dinner table, from falling off chairs singing Aretha Franklin,
  and overcoming the troubles in our family.
I am from picture frames on tables, on walls, and anywhere else pictures can be hung.
From paintings by my mom of the four boys during our only innocent times (if innocent at all).

Payton Roedel, Grade 11
Germantown High School, TN

Why?

Why do you do the things you do,
If you know they will hurt someone?

Why do you use the words you use,
When they are killing someone on the inside?
And you know they are…

Why do you make people cry,
And not say anything to them?

Why don't you say you're sorry,
While you still have the chance?

Because sooner or later,
People will get tired of standing up
For all your wrongs

Even if you try,
No one will accept your "I'm sorry's" anymore.
You took too long
And lost your chance for that.

Why would you put yourself through all of that?
When all you have to do is say,
I'm sorry…
And prove that you really are.
Why?

Samantha Spillman, Grade 12
PennFoster Homeschooling Program, TN

A New Girl in a City

Stepping into a new life,
unknown paths, and an unknown world.
New people, a new path,
A new girl in a city.

How should I tell you my story?
Should I tell you through colors or through pictures?
This is tough; it's a long journey…

Walking endlessly, mindlessly,
unsure where the path will take me,
but it was sure that it was you I see,
my companion, friend, angel…

You accept all my troubles,
whenever we're alone,
we'll take this on together.

Come with me, walk these unfamiliar routes.
Our dreams are pouring drop by drop,
you are surrounding all around me.

Look into the distance,
new girl in a city,
you may not know, but the one is all around you.

Change our destiny, and let the footprints lead our way…

Bhavna Singh, Grade 12
William G Enloe High School, NC

The Light

There's always a calm before the storm.
A quiet before the raging sea.
That's what I expect to see.
But prove me wrong and boost my spirits.
Because I'll never find out if no one shines the light.

Detravia Green, Grade 11
Raleigh Egypt High School, TN

A Journey Worth Taking

Life is short lived and tomorrow isn't promised nor will it ever die
So live it to the fullest with God and live His name on high
If you follow His word you will make it by and by
One day meeting your loved ones high in the sky

Jaleen Hatcher, Grade 10
Mount Airy High School, NC

Safety Is Around the Bend

Lost in the woods
Without a map
A broken compass fills your
Pocket.

Nowhere to turn
For a safe embrace.
Confusion in the tree
Tops.

Music in the distance.
Memories are dancing shadows.

Sitting and waiting
For daylight to come
When the trees will move
And things will fade away.

Safety is around the bend.

Lacey Dylan Julian, Grade 12
Bessemer City Early College High School, NC

My Love for Baseball

Sssss…pow…sssss…pow…sssss…pow…strike three you're out!
The batter accepts defeat in the box.
Angrily he slings equipment and pouts,
While I on the mound am the one who mocks.
The opposing pitcher, throwing aspirins,
Short, sweet, hands to the ball runs through my brain.
Focused, my bat is hungry, I'm zoned in.
Sssss…Boom, home run, the pitcher's eyes show pain.
Diving in the dirt, or rolling in grass,
Infield is reaction, outfield is speed.
Ball first, be smooth, I shall not let one pass.
Play, hard, play tough, three outs is all we need.
Baseball for me will soon end at Starmount
But then I will become a Catamount.

Dillon Bray, Grade 12
Starmount High School, NC

Our Relationship

There is no trust between you and me
I wonder sometimes why do
we even try
Things ain't getting better
You change like the seasons
in weather
winter — your heart turns in stone-cold ice
spring — you bloom into a THING I've never seen
summer — you make me want to melt
fall — we change colors and die inside until it comes back around
I'm feeling like I can't
get through to you
Relationships

LaDestinee Williams, Grade 10
Memphis Academy of Science and Engineering, TN

I Will

Do you know what its like
To watch your hair fall out in clumps every day
Knowing one day it will all go away?

I do, because I have cancer

Do you know what it's like for sleep to leave you tired?
To stay up all night feeling anything but wired?

I do, because I have cancer

Do you know what its like to cry, even when you don't know why?
To be given steroids that make your face dry?

I do, because I have cancer

Do you know what its like, having your privacy stolen away?
People wanting to know how you eat, sleep, and spend each day?

I do, because I have cancer

Will you know what its like to say, I survived it all?
Getting up off the floor without having to fall?
Will you know what its like to defeat the battle?
To have survived it all?

I will, because I have cancer

Naomi McIlvaine, Grade 10
Home School, NC

Salt Water

Though the whirligig is done,
Though long ago has set the sun,
I remember.

I remember days of laughter
And of fun.
I remember hallowed silences beneath the summer sun;
They meant more to me than shallow words could ever hope to.

In my tortured spirit your memory rends and roars,
an avaricious beast, not content to be ignored.
Nor will he be sated
Until every thought, every act, every drop of blood
lies beneath his yoke to writhe in torturous bondage.

Though the days we had were passed so sweet
that it was as if gravity forgot my feet.
Though the memories are sweeter still
The most practiced alchemist would be jealous of the skill
with which time has changed honey to bitter salt water.

It stings, it burns, it nourishes me not,
And yet my fractured self would not let it be forgot.

Sean Norton, Grade 12
William G. Enloe High School, NC

Spark Plug from Darkness

A new breath of fresh air occurred after a time of deep sorrow
From a time where people die from an invisible killer
to a time where a man can be inspired to learn and be creative,
this world has changed the world of the past and the world of today.
In the past, chaos and horror reign down the world,
but humanity turned this godforsaken land into a place of motivation.
This new world creates a world of art, science, politics, and literature.
People saw the creation of the famous artwork, the Mona Lisa,
to listening to great stories like Romeo and Juliet by William Shakespeare.
The motivation of the people aided bright ideas that achieved
great advancement to the modern world.

Finally, a reformation of the world occurred after a time of deep sorrow as
if God has given his people a second chance of life.
This time has been described as the Renaissance of 1400 to the 1600.
The people passed the ultimate test of survival and were rewarded with creativity.
If the people of the Renaissance can pass this test, so can people in the modern time too.
The people can't let these achievements go to waste,
so the people must continue their thirst for knowledge in order to preserve the future generation.

Bryant Yu, Grade 12
William G Enloe High School, NC

My Little Bird

Will my little bird come back one day?
Will you ever fly back my way?
I play the tunes we listened to in the old days, in hope that you would hear and come back to stay,
A couple of times you flew around just to tease me,
Made me feel happy, but why, if just to leave me?
Hoping that we could be one again
But you're far away with a new owner,
I want to find you, but it's getting colder
Time is winding down, you will soon be gone for winter
Surrounded in the warmth of another member,
I will be here in the cold, and you, I will always remember
Your face forever in my soul, beautiful images making me quiver
No matter what happens, I will leave my window open
Hoping that you will remember me, and decide to fly back in
So we can forever be one again.

Erica Ross, Grade 11
Overton High School, TN

I Am From...

I am from Microsoft, from Window's phones and Zunes
I am from old computer in the attic that never gets used, and just gathers dust each and every day.
I am from the beautiful American Ash, the gorgeous Aspen.
I am from the cookouts and black hairs, from Hamid and Faranak and Taghavi.
I am from the wise and do-gooders.
From go clean your room, which I never did and why didn't you make a 100, when I made a 99.
I am from the Islam's, which I know little about, but wish I knew more about
I am from Memphis, Tennessee and Tehran, Iran, juicy kabobs and amazing basmati rice.
From the gold medal that my grandfather won in the Olympics for Iran,
that shiny gold medal that I still cherish each every day, and the hard working father that I have,
who works hard every day for us to be happy.
I am from the magnificent memories that I am reminded of every day when I walk into the family room.

Omid Taghavi, Grade 11
Germantown High School, TN

Expectations

Their opinions of me hurt
I cannot be the infallible person they wish for
They think I joke when I'm serious

They try to mold me
But I favor my freedom
Joyous chain free independence

She sets me up to be strong minded
Yet she binds me to idealism
Why not think outside the box?

He binds me to the American boring dream
Hoping that I'll sit behind a desk
Wishing for that white picket fence

Their hopeless wishes are
Chains on my freedom yearning spirit
I apologize for not fulfilling expectation

Natalie Lawyer, Grade 10
Middle Creek High School, NC

Memories

Young child's memories of oceans quickly fade
Recollect your dreams, puzzles still remain
Uncover secrets hiding in the shade
To find new ones awaiting through the rain
Things happen that you cannot change or do
Never regret decisions of the past
Stop, rethink this moment of deja vu
So you can understand this idea aghast
Always remember to never rethink
Choices you pick throughout your lifespan
Cherish little moments, don't even blink
Or you might miss something in God's great plan.

For life is a two-way path with roadblocks
Where memories are tucked away in a box.

Corryne Huxley, Grade 10
Union County High School, TN

School

I sit in this room
and stare at the clock
hoping this day would
just end. while I wait
these people stand in front
of a room, just talking,
but I do not understand.
while they stand there
I wonder why am I still
here, just wanting to leave
but there is something
keeping me here…

Brandon Morgan, Grade 11
Morristown-Hamblen High School West, TN

Coconut

This girl,
once had a lot of friends and a family,
surrounded by a very peaceful environment.
But one day,
somebody took away her parents.
The brown skin,
brown hair,
white fruit juicy inside her body,
told her to not trust anyone anymore.
She saw stickers on her parents' body.
From then on,
she never lets anyone to touch her one more time.
Her hard shell made her feel safe.
The inside of her was so soft.
No one knew how to break her shell,
and never will.
Time went by fast,
her body started to leak.
She thought about her parents,
how painful they were,
and quietly died.

Xuyi Zhu, Grade 10
Providence High School, NC

Strong

She's crying with her family again in the waiting room
The doctor said "The cancer's spread you've only got a week or two."
Sometimes she wonders if it's all worth the fight
But only God has the power to end a life
So she tries her best to see the good in everyone
She holds on to hugs not knowing which will be her last one
And she tells everyone she's OK
You've got to live life day to day
and she just keeps moving on.
She's making amends for all the wrongs she's done
She's meeting old friends and going out just to have fun
She called up her brother she hadn't seen since '92
Just to whisper to him a simple "I love you"
She wonders what tomorrow holds
If she'll make it long enough to know
but she just keeps pushing through.

Julianne Kramer, Grade 10
Holy Angels Academy, KY

My Dad

This figure that stands before me
is always there for me.
Though it may seem prison bars separate us
later we will show how it truly affects us
how it truly helps us.
We might not see it
that's how the world works around us.
I'm glad to say that
this figure is my dad.

Justin Price, Grade 12
William G Enloe High School, NC

Remembrance*

The current wasn't swift,
Nor the water unfamiliar,
But they found his kayak adrift,
And his life jacket very near.

They searched all day
And into the night.
All the while,
His wife filling with fright.
At the break of dawn
They searched again,
Only to find
Nothing more of him.

All of his appointments
And operations canceled.
The hope that he is still alive
Is like the flame of an endless candle.
With my mother's life,
By him whom it was saved.
I will never forget him,
Not a single day.

Alex Beckman, Grade 10
Loretto High School, TN

*In memory of the physician who practically saved my mom's life. Thanks to him, she is still here today.

Who I Am and Where I'm From

I am from Easy Mac, from Kraft macaroni and cheese beginnings.
I am from the unreachable dust in between the cracks of the walls.
(It covers everything that is forgotten, and clogs my lungs with its troublesome nature.)
I am from azaleas and the tulip tree with its long and gnarly roots that I tend to every summer.
I am from waffles and large chocolate brown eyes with pointy ears
From Judy and Richard.
I'm from smart remarks to commands and the comebacks to the obvious,
From "Shush! You're being too loud!" and "The whole neighborhood can hear you!"
I'm from the Father, Son, and the Holy Spirit who gave his life for our sins out of his love for us all.
I am from Ireland and Romania,
From steak and chicken.
From the many places my mother has lived
To the forgotten hometown of my father, who chooses to remember it only once a year.
I am from the numerous yearbooks on the bookshelves,
A remembrance of my naive, grotesque self, something I long to forget.
I am from those atrocious school pictures — pictures taken on my bad hair days —
With my undeveloped smile — but that is who I was and who I have blossomed from.

Kaitlyn Singleton, Grade 11
Germantown High School, TN

Loyalty and Love

Can you stay by my side regardless of hard times? Keep it real with me and always down to ride. We're side by side every time. No one can divide or come between you and I. During the rain and storm, would you say, "We shall overcome?" Can you take me telling you no, even if I haven't once before? If I loved you with all my heart, would you decide one day to walk away? What if I gave my all to you? Would I ever regret doing so? Can I trust you not to take advantage of my love? Would you decide to cheat, beat or destroy me? What if I had nobody to turn to? Could I run to you?

Dominique Douglass, Grade 10
Memphis Academy of Science and Engineering, TN

A Feeling

Trying to describe
the feeling you give me.
It's like magic.
Like you let me breathe.

Being in your arms
means never let go.
You make me feel alive
and make me go with the flow.

Kissing your lips.
Hope to never part.
Causing a soft glow
and a warmth in my heart.

Holding hands together
as if it were the last day.
Showing our love
in every possible way.

Me with you as one
is more then a dream come true.
Just one thing left to say.
That is, I love you.

Nikkita Wilson, Grade 12
Campbellsville High School, KY

Eraser Dust

Eraser dust, the trace of work
That scratched away has been.
Mistakes and stray lines all are gone,
Ne'er to be seen again.

Eraser dust, a trail that follows
Whate'er I try to do.
I'll work and write and make my strokes
Then obliterate, start anew.

Eraser dust, that nagging reminder
That I have erred in way,
And though I cannot see the gaffe,
Still yet it has been made.

But what would happen if this dust
I should cease to make,
And left my errors in plain sight
To look back on my mistakes?

T'would be no pleasure, that I'm sure,
To view what I did wrong,
But a backward glance every now and then
May improve a future song.

Caroline Hughes, Grade 12
Sun Ridge Academy Home School, NC

The Road Less Taken

Two roads diverged when I caught sight of a young student.
Her notes and lab reports,
strewn about the never-ending hallway of mockery and judgment.
I had to make the choice.
To help the young stranger
and become a pariah of the people most have come to call "my clique,"
or to walk away
and maintain what was thought of as superiority.
To turn around and act as though I had witnessed nothing
would be such an easy feat.
It would cause her to know no differently.
I'd be just another of the mocking upperclassmen.
But to lean down and help her off her knees,
pick up her glasses,
and give her the slightest smile
of warmth and reassurance
might make all the difference.

Hannah Melton, Grade 10
Germantown High School, TN

Adultery

They showered her with guilt, which caused her to feel low
She knew who she was, yet the faces of the judging eyes,
Thought they did, but they just didn't know,
Caught up in all of her lies,
The seed she produced from her lover, truth never came 'til the end,
Now she's destined to suffer, sinfully the outcome of her trend,
Forsaken, betrayal below what she really felt,
Taken Captive by her own heart, torn by the pain that she couldn't accept,
They looked down on her, as pity rains from above,
As she sinks deeper each time,
For she was only in love, Is that much of a crime?
Heart of broken stone pieces, glass tears,
Conniving all these years,
With her conscience burnin' her up inside,
Alone she faces the worst of her fears,
Oh how she wishes this sin she could hide…

Tiara Dickerson, Grade 12
Overton High School, TN

Journey of Truth

Hiding under the covers,
and beneath the cushions on the couch,
In the depth of your mind,
behind the teeth in your mouth.
Buried like treasure in the sand of our souls,
being walked all over, and taking its toll.
Lurking behind the curtains like a killer in a film.
Burning in our throats like pottery in a kiln.
Seeping through the vents of the stories that we tell.
Lingering on our tongues as the anticipation swells.
Retreating from the surface just as you think you've found your proof.
Sending you on your way, still searching for the truth.

Bethany Wiles, Grade 12
Preston High School, WV

Forever Remembered*

The emblem on the vehicle reads "Ford," inside are two sisters,
The best of friends, both young, beautiful and full of life.
It is an ordinary day in Alabama,
Leaves are beginning to fall as autumn arrives, October has just begun.

They begin to make their journey down an old familiar road, not thinking of what is to come,
All of the sudden, they hit a bump in the road, the driver loses all control,
They are both thrown from the vehicle, these are their last moments,
For one, the last moments of life, for the other, the last moments with her best friend,
One of the girls hears sirens; the other hears angels singing,
One is asked her name; the other is welcomed into heaven's gates,
One is rushed to the hospital; the other is ushered along the streets of gold,
It is not just a normal day now, it is a day that will forever be remembered.

Life is short, cherish it, hold the ones you love close,
For you never know when an ordinary day,
Will turn into a day, that you will forever remember

Hannah Cozart, Grade 10
Loretto High School, TN
**In memory of Skylar Ann Mays*

As I Donned My Lace

At first glance, they are faded and torn
But underneath are the memories that speak only to me
It takes me back to younger days when friendships were born,
And unforgettable times were made
Staring longer, I see the love that shaped my life for so long
So many recollections are flooding back into the light of my dusty, old attic
Things I did, like singing that song
That day resurfaces in my memory every time I hear it played
I start to wonder when my childhood disappeared and the real world took its place,
But life carried me in so many different directions after high school
That every reminder of the past was lost as I donned my lace
So many things have changed for the better, but the instant I saw those faded photographs
Juvenescence overwhelmed me, reminding me that life took me everywhere I wanted to go
And when I had a chance I would have stories to tell, pictures to show, and memories to relive
Oh how I would travel through time and see how God blessed me so

Kristen Townsend, Grade 10
Coffee County Central High School, TN

Apple

I am from Apple Inc, from iPods and iPhones.
I am from the Apple campus in California, at 1 Infinity Loop.
I am from the apple tree, the apple trees that grew into money trees.
I am from 1976, founded in a garage by 3, from Steve Wozniak, Steve Jobs, and that guy Ronald Wayne
I am from the Apple I, and later the Apple II, the Macintosh, the MacBook, the iMac
From creative minds, and powerful businessmen.
I am from the brainwashed Apple cult, where people buy nearly anything, disregarding the price.
I'm from Cupertino, founded by two Steves. One round and inventive, the other skinny and with pancreatic cancer,
but with powerful marketing skills
From the time the iPhone 2G was released, to the iPhone 4S, and the death of Steve Jobs the next day.
I am from Apple, the land of crazily overpriced goods, and "magical" items that must be bought at all costs. But they work.
I wonder why this poem is written on Apple, I think I need to find something better to write this on.
But I use Apple products, and they are some very interesting little things.

Janak Malla, Grade 11
Germantown High School, TN

A Candle

The world surrounding me
  is foreign
      hostile
            I move.

  The darkness shrinks away
    skirts just outside my reach
      I breathe
  I relax.

With a surge it is back
   pressuring, pounding
 desiring only my gibbering insanity
it fails.

My light wavers
     grows weak from the onslaught
   and I fear it will soon go out
we endure.

In an instant, it grows.
   my light is a beacon cutting through the fog
     revealing the things the dark has to hide
and I start to learn all.

My work has just begun.

Ben Murphy, Grade 11
Germantown High School, TN

I Am

I am from shoes, from Nike and Reebok.
I am from the old, greasy, and stained tile floor.
I am from the long, dusty, and winding forest trail,
  From our only sweet mother earth.

I am from summer and fun, from Dave and
  Louise and Paul

I am from the vacations to and fro,
and stay-cations where we know the streets.
From the usual work then play and we need to stick together.

I am from a strong faith. The believers and bible readers.
I am from my family up north, our Chicago-style deep dish pizza
  And all-beef hot-dogs.

From the time when my father ran his 26.2, the cheers at the end,
  And his family congratulating him on his first marathon.

I am from the memories that fade disappear,
  The memories that get thrown away,
  I get tossed aside, forgotten.
  I am disrespected and ignored
    I carry on

Matthew Ohlwein, Grade 11
Germantown High School, TN

Tears

I stare blankly at the sky
To see if rain falls tonight.
Yet, I realize
They are MY raindrops dancing down my face
From my freshly flooded brown eyes.
I wonder why these tears I cry,
Despite knowing I will never know why.

If only it would rain.
It would be the perfect disguise.
I'm not asking for a mask
Not even a 'downpour'
Just a drop here, there,
And one more.

I try and try, to stop these tears I shed; yet, I cry and cry.

If only it would rain
Just a drop here, there,
And one more.

Thomas Wilson, Grade 12
William G Enloe High School, NC

I Only Want to Be Me

You see me, you judge me.
You try to push me down, but you can't budge me,
So since you can't destroy me, you just begrudge me,
But I don't really care.

I am myself; just me.
You can't tell me who I should be.
You want me in an inferior prison, yet I remain free,
So you pretend I'm not there.

You ignore me, but that's okay:
I don't want to be like you anyway!
I am individual no matter what you say!
Go ahead and stare;
I'm not self-conscious.

Jennifer Armstrong, Grade 11
Preston High School, WV

Life vs Death

I pray to God quite often for more wisdom and faith
But in reality only God knows who's real or fake
Life is my mother and death is my father
I let my anger pour out of me like a cup full of water
Jealousy is the epitome of stupidity; I will withhold my energy

The demons always circle me waiting for me to slip
Is life really all worth it? Does heaven have a membership?
They say God can swipe you down like a credit card using debit
But really when you die…
Death gets all the credit

Antonious Kennedy, Grade 10
Memphis Academy of Science and Engineering, TN

Waiting

How can I tell you the things so dear to me?
My every thought. My every dream.
I gave you all I could. Loved you with every beat.
All the time we shared, all the laughs and all the tears, scorched.
We spoke of soul mates and dreamt of forever.
Kids in love is what they called us. But love isn't just a word or a thought. There's no limits, no age.
Once you find that one that steals your breath, it clings to you.
We met by chance, but we loved by fate. I had you. We were strong. We were one.
The days passed and the stress of miles won.
We forgot what we had. Forgot what made us. We forgot love.
Always there, just waiting to be called, but we pushed it aside and let us fail.
I found my spark of hope when you left, my love for you surfaced once more.
You claim yours has returned, that it was never lost.
But I fear the words you say are just that, words.
There isn't a way I can explain or begin to make you understand.
No gesture or a simple debate.
I've said it all before. I've said I love you a billion times. What's once more?
I have nothing left to keep me whole. Nothing to fill my time.
I'll be here, waiting for you to come home.
Always hoping. Always loving.
Always waiting.

Allexa Bonner, Grade 12
Oakland High School, TN

Une Lutte avec le Demon

Dark and deserted, like wide open seas you're in loneliness.
Waves crashing hard on rocks and sounds of whispering winds running through a forceful breeze.
With no thoughts or devotion, you're blinded in the fall of the pouring rain.
Lightning strikes and thunder rolls, leaving you with nothing but unbearable pain.
Your ship of life crashes, and you drown in the misery of past mistakes.
Life before you flashes while you unconsciously choose your fate.
Salty water gurgles in your throat making you realize now is too late.
You strive your way to the surface as one last breath you intake.
Your few last tears descend down your face,
In extraordinary speeds, as though it's a race.
With merely one last whispered phrase you internally affirm your life's cessation,
And let your soul take you on its new found destination.
Upon arrival you become distressed,
You feel this is not where your soul should rest.
With Diablo you fight though he has much presumption that your soul he can capture.
Lights flash and you're here now in purgatory,
Leaving Diablo behind with no feeling of rapture.
You feel faintly inside, as now you're not breathing.
The thought of your death was frankly deceiving.
You awake to find yourself lying in bed,
This strange misfortune was all in your head.

Faith Stivenson, Grade 12
Berkeley Springs High School, WV

Two Faces

Two faces lit up by the summer sky.
Two bodies soaking in the mid of May.
One love so strong, the world stops in her time.
To grant the wish for her lovers to stay.

Alison Shoffner, Grade 10
Union County High School, TN

My Beacon

You are the lighthouse, and I am the ship.
When skies darken, and I am tossed about,
Your light steers me away from craggy cliffs.
You reach into the storm and pull me out.

Shelby Beason, Grade 10
Union County High School, TN

Just Beginning

At times,
you feel your life is fading
far in the distance.
Not knowing where to turn
or who to trust,
you feel as though nothing lies ahead
this path God has set you upon.
Trapped in a box,
with little air left to inhale,
you gulp the last bit
and fight to be released
from this grievous predicament.
In the end,
somehow,
someway,
we will all be able
to overcome what we have been left with.
We will all survive what we once thought was life-ending.

Lorina Aboulmouna, Grade 12
Tullahoma High School, TN

I Matter

Sounds like a Apple product right?
But no not quite
It poses a question:

Am I happy?
I try to be
I smile even though it doesn't convenience me
Why do I feel this way?
Maybe because of what others say
I need to learn to be myself,
Through all my good times and bad health
Then I'll smile,
Not for you,
But for me
Not for us, or for we
But for I,
Because
I matter

Tronjay Davis, Grade 10
Roanoke Valley Early College, NC

Trapped

We are trapped.
To our desks
To our nonexistent obligations;
That friend request we have to accept,
That video we need to watch…
As the world turns outside
The page on this computer is still loading,
The two will never be in sync
Because every second spent here
Is an opportunity lost there.

Andrew Grimes, Grade 12
William G Enloe High School, NC

You Left Me

You left me
You left my dad, my mom, and my sisters
Everything I came from was because of you
And you just say we're not yours
I want to know stories
I want to know how it was when you were growing up
But no
You left, you're scared
You're running from what you've made
You've been proven wrong once already
Two times would be too much for you
My dad is a great guy
You are missing out on him
I want to know about my nationality
But I can't
Why?
Because you left me.

Marisa Padinha, Grade 10
Berkeley Springs High School, WV

This Is Me

You look at me
You see who you think I am
I look at me
I see who I know I am
I see who I was then
I see who I am now
I see who I can progress to be
You look at my appearance
At what I wear
At how I speak
You analyze my actions
And attempt to label me according to my exterior content
Disregarding who I am on the inside
Not taking notice of the intelligence I acquire
Which cannot be determined by taking a quick glance at me
Either you search deeper, or you should not search at all
I will forever be more than what YOU think I am

Rya Wooten, Grade 11
Germantown High School, TN

Reflection

A complexion scarred
by relentless tears,
stained by grief
pressed into few years.
A quivering lip
never taught to smile;
drained of all hope,
faith that failed trial.
Blank unsheltered eyes,
no door to her soul —
for what simmers there
is darker than coal.

Mary Alice Dann, Grade 11
Germantown High School, TN

Affliction

The stress is too massive,
the constant studying and worrying.
I just want to get away.
The grade is just a letter,
the time is too early,
and the halls are full of gossip.
We are led to believe it is all or nothing.
We are told that it is now or never.

I just want to get away.
To the place where there is no worry,
a place where the grass is greener.
For right now, we live in reality.
I will do what I can with what I have.
I will be the best friend I can be.
With support from the ones around me,
I will make it.

Benjamin Barlow, Grade 11
Germantown High School, TN

The Star That You Are

Shall I compare thee to a star
Your shine never fades away
It never fails to take me far
It never fails to make my day
You live in your own space
Taking no lip from anyone
You are your own Ace
You outshine every star
Even far away, we can still see you
Shining with that light that I love
Your shine is always true
And I will always see you up above
And it is all of this that makes me say
I'll be here with you every day

Rodney Morton, Grade 10
Loretto High School, TN

Thanksgiving (Fall)

Thanksgiving is a time to give praise
To God on high, Thanksgiving is a time
To be happy, and a time to be
Thankful for the things you have.

Thanksgiving is a great holiday
In the season of fall where you eat
That turkey and stuffing.

Fall is a season when the leaf changes
And turns into bright colors of orange,
Yellow and red. It is a season when
The weather changes to get ready
For the dark and gloomy winter
That is coming ahead.

Kristen Sawyers, Grade 10
White Plains Christian School, NC

Drive

I drive
Driving down the road,
I've got the wind in my hand.
The cool air fills my head,
replacing my absence of thought.
Winding through the woods
in the blackness of night, I allow myself to escape reality.

I listen.
The thoughts of others,
disguised by melodies, fill my mind.
They provide an outlet that not even the closest companion could supply.
But even now it's hard to decipher the real from the fake,
the wise from the jaded.

Their words mean nothing without action, my action.
Therefore, I hold the power,
the power to be wise, or to be jaded.
As I grip the steering wheel, I hold the power of free will.
My steering works; I just hope I can turn right.

Corbin Loveless, Grade 12
Germantown High School, TN

The Sun

Her radiance flows like light being transformed into pure glory.
Her hair is like light itself, laid beautifully under her crown.
Her dress is sewn in gold and fine linen.
As she awakes the dawn with her voice and beauty,
She holds all of the marvelous wonders she holds in her hands.
All she is, is a sign that her beauty is still, peaceable, and gentle to all that listen.
The entire universe gives her reverence for her cloven fire laid within her voice and eyes.
As she speaks, time itself, slows down, just to listen to her voice come aloud.
All of the light around her flows, moves, sways, and even breathes,
Her beauty is so warm, so light, and so omnipotent.
Her eyes hold all that is perfect, finished, complete, and still to come.
She is beautiful.
She is bright with colors becoming colors,
Alive with the life of her breath.
She is the sun.

Micah Miller, Grade 10
Hilltop Christian Academy, KY

Tragedy of the Commons

here's to the tragedy of the commons,
connecting with a click; ricocheting between many books of faces
checking the influx of tweets; hash-tagging away through hypocrisy
if a dollar was paid for every tweet, we'd all grow rich;
cancer could be cured, homes could be built
from speaking to texting, to diluting the definition of the origin of the species
we'd all grow wiser if we read Shakespeare,
rather than the faces of the Kardashians
we parade down the streets of veracity, with handheld power
contiguous with our surroundings: me, myself and I.
here's to the tragedy of the commons.

Amishi Desai, Grade 12
William G Enloe High School, NC

Not My Fault

It was early, so early, I just could not get up; his phone calls went unanswered, so he finally gave up.
It was five in the morning, my sleep medicine still infecting my mind. I woke up at eleven, with only disaster to find.
Why so many calls, so many texts? Did someone need me this much?
It was my whole family, it was not social, they needed me as their crutch.

From the door came a knock, it was a policeman with stoney eyes;
He asked me questions about my father, he ignored my worried cries.
In a frantic panic, I headed out the door. When the smell of the hospital hit me, I nearly hit the floor.
Death and new life overwhelmed me…This death is wrongfully his.

Why couldn't I wake up? Why is this gash not on my head
If I hadn't taken my medicine, I would surely be dead.
What if I had saved him? What if I were there?
Now I hide my emotions, pretending not to care.

You left me all alone, you left me here alive,
But if I had been by your side, I would have been the one to drive.
Did you fall asleep? Have a seizure? Was it all on free will?
I was not there, I could not know…I will never know how you feel.

Maybe this is my fault, maybe this is just a dream…
Please, my Bubba, just come back to me.

Emma Scott, Grade 10
Loretto High School, TN

By Choice I Say No

To the drug dealer on the corner of 1234 Spring Street,
By choice I say NO.
To the gang affiliated crews that influence the young minds,
By choice I say NO.
To the young teen boys who allow sex to influence their minds,
By choice I say NO.
To the ignorance of those that embrace racism and inequality,
By choice I say NO.
To the girl stuck in her room wondering how she should try to amount up to everyone else's expectations,
By choice I say NO.
To the young boy trapped trying to make the decision of being popular or successful,
By choice I say NO.
It is my soul which guides all of my decisions,
But until I close my eyes and leave this place called Earth,
By choice, I will say NO to all those things, people, and places that can negatively impact me,
My answer will always be NO.

Ashleyh Korgar, Grade 12
William G Enloe High School, NC

Where I'm From

I am from cymbals, from Drum Workshop drums and the Memphis Drum Shop.
I am from the average brick abode, average in size and average in look, with the deep blue pool.
I am from the tree, the mesquite of central Texas.
I am from yearly barbecues in Texas with smoked brisket and grilled catfish sandwiches and from humor, from Brian and Irene.
I am from superb intelligence, from subtle sarcasm and sheer craziness.
From "Run, go!" and "Too many people in the kitchen!"
I'm from Memphis and Texas and Peru; kolaches and Slovacek's Sausage.

William Piwonka, Grade 11
Germantown High School, TN

I Wear the Mask

I wear the mask that laughs and smiles
It hides my insecurities all the while
I act like everything is peachy keen
Running from nightmares to reach my dreams
No one will ever know the darkness

I can't explain the need to hide emotion
Bottle it in an abyss of the deepest ocean
Let everyone think Leo P is just fine
They will never know this life of mine

I may smile when happiness is far away
Anger and hatred shown on beautiful days
Always hiding from terrible news
Never knowing if it's a ruse
If you seek my emotions you must ask
I will always wear the mask

Isaac Parrill, Grade 12
Berkeley Springs High School, WV

I Wear the Mask

I wear the mask that hides the pain
Let's take a walk down memory lane
You seemed to be everything
Turns out you were just a fling
Guess you didn't want anything more, but one thing

Why did I waste my time on you?
But you wasted your time too
Just for the fact you didn't get what you wanted
I wear the mask

You're just another ridiculous boy I fell for
You weren't the first or the last, there will be plenty more
I wish I could undo you
But those feelings are still there for you
Instead I'll just have to keep hiding it
I wear the mask

Lydia Butts, Grade 12
Berkeley Springs High School, WV

Recovery

My heart is heavy with all that I feel,
How can anything possibly begin to heal,
How much damage has been caused by this climb,
They say all I need is time,
And it's funny, my heart feels light,
I think I might actually be all right,
My heart was broken,
But now so many new doors are open,
I'm freed of you,
But that doesn't erase all that we've been through,
However my outlook has changed,
And I think that you are quite deranged,
I'm moving on,
And the first place I'll start is the salon.

Hayley Lemmons, Grade 12
William G Enloe High School, NC

Deserted Rain

the pattering of rain beating the stone
the dark gray clouds, covering the blue sky
ice-cold wind blowing by, chilling the bone
the cars occasionally creeping by
the train's whistle, traveling through the air
the no trespassing sign, nailed to the tree
the beaten house, with years of no repair
the stoplight reflects on the dark tarred street
most trees, covered in leaves, some, half-chopped down
cars, ready to leave, on the road, so slick
a taxi, waiting, to take guests to town
me, just standing against the cold, wet brick
the battered car, waiting, as if in vain
families, without cars, walking, in the rain

Laura Kummerle, Grade 12
William G Enloe High School, NC

Life Is Ever Changing

Life is ever changing,
not knowing what will happen,
making choices blindly,
praying for satisfaction,
in the end it's disappointment,
people let me fall,
like tears from my eyes,
I fall to the ground and burst into tears,
feeling my hand hit the rocks,
the true pain subsides,
I try to cloak the deep emotions,
I turn around to see the clock,
hands spinning too fast for me to read,
then I realize it's just a dream.

Brittney Thayer, Angel Allen, and Kristen Faith, Grade 11
Berkeley Springs High School, WV

An Ode to Sunshine

Sunshine, sunshine, oh how I adore thee.
I wish to match my brightness with your light.
Sunshine, sunshine, please do not ignore me.
Your rays tan my skin a gold warm and bright.
The peak of your brightest days brings me joy.
I run with greatest of ease in your heat.
That fresh new chance of yours, I shall employ,
and today is the day that you I shall meet.
In your fading light, though, I turn and go,
fearing the obscurity consuming all known.
No light is the absence of joy, you know;
only in that bright light, I know I'm home.
The night brings on a calm sort of silence;
It brings out my darkness, this ambiance.

Sanjana Prabhu, Grade 12
William G Enloe High School, NC

Hello I'm Nobody

I look "weird."
Short, colorful hair laces my head.
Dark red for every strand of anger instilled inside,
Blue for my sadness and the tears I've cried.

I don't laugh.
Only at those girls,
The ones with their pink puckered lips,
Long flowing hair,
And those walking death traps
They call high heels.
Red patent leather pumps,
I would trade those for piercings.
I use to try to talk to those girls,
But to them I don't exist.

I don't have a name.
Another constant "who is that?"
Is muttered when my name is called on role.
Everyone looks around,
But no one seems to know.

I simply say,
Hello my name is nobody, who are you?

Heather Jackson, Grade 10
Germantown High School, TN

Viral Music

Lazily dreaming about the meanders of life,
I am immediately and rudely interrupted
by the intimidation of sound waves.
That, without asking, persists on singing
from the electronic clock.

Tunes I'd rather not listen to
Before my feet touch the ground,
Before the steaming green chai tea is welcomed,
Becoming the honorable guest of caffeine enlightenment,

Like a fly buzzing around my head
cursing my ears with a never ending pestilence,
The cranial revolution of pop songs will come to a violent end
like headlights to a morning fog
I can't clear the music's catchiness.

This is merely a case of the flu.
I am defeating this deafening tyranny.
But such a lyric is bound to attach
to another host of its choice.
There is to be a vaccine.
There is a saving song
to engulf the previous infection.

Daniel Brewer, Grade 12
Germantown High School, TN

Candy Chronicles Pt. 1

The candy is yummy
the sugar, sweet and sour
as I chew, I fear for my tummy

On to the grape flavor
and just as I suspect
the candy is yummy

I grope the Halloween sack
and grip a handful of hot tamales
as I chew, I fear for my tummy

My mouth is an inferno
I unwrap a york patty
the candy is yummy

Next is a nerd rope
swallowed whole with surprising ease
when I should be chewing, I fear for my tummy

Next the chocolate bunny
the head is my first chomp
the candy is yummy
as I chew, I fear for my tummy

Jacob Lay, Grade 11
Oak Ridge High School, TN

I Slipped Away in Silence

The sun had toiled me terrible anger,
I burned the ice and melted the fire.
Rumbling storms and showers I gifted,
Punishment until my mood had lifted.

When my chaos subsided I spied the way down,
Over the edges of heaven's crown.
By the lament of a wisping willow tree,
Sat a scene alone for me to see.

A waiting child draped by coat in doze,
My anger was not a threat to pose,
Against a stubborn drive of nerves and steel,
Abandonment a wound and pain to heal.

The pebbles overturned by sticking toads,
My rain a bleeding scar drips on the roads.
Soft moss it whispers as the birds do fly,
I smell sweet spring in fledglings passing by.

I took this as a sign to leave for me,
It hinted quietly for sympathy.
I hauled away my gales and shoots of rain,
And left in silence nothing there to gain.

Helen Ni, Grade 10
Grimsley High School, NC

Senior Year

Everyone said it would be the best year,
And for some it may be, but in my mind
It's the hardest; I want to shed a tear.
I need more strength, and through God, it I'll find!

The stress of it almost too much to bear,
Like the weight of a brick crushing my chest.
I am not used to this feeling so rare,
Yet I try to do my absolute best.

I refuse to give up or to give in,
But to say it's easy would be pretend.
I know that I can do it and can win,
And my struggles will pay off in the end.

Despair hurriedly creeps into my head,
But God gives great hope to feelings of dread.

Kayla Castevens, Grade 12
Starmount High School, NC

Story Book

Shall I compare thee to a love story,
 such as one in a book?
At first, you were fine in all your glory.
 I wasn't too difficult to hook.

However, I couldn't help it.
You were so beautiful, so amazing.
I would always smile to myself a bit
when I would look and catch you gazing.

But just like a book, it seems we've come to an end.
Like always, one heart is broken,
 a love lost, and a best friend.
Memories are love's token.

Maybe there's a sequel, we'll find out one day.
For when it's true love, it'll always find a way.

Katelin Smith, Grade 10
Loretto High School, TN

Forest

Walking through the forest, I see great things.
So much wonder and magic in this place.
In this unknown world, nature sings.
Odd, how spirits who roam here leave no trace.

Sunlight breaks through the canopy above.
Warm rays on spider webs glisten brightly
Though this world is peaceful, there is no love.
There is no sound, but squirrels stepping lightly.

Dusk begins to fall and dark kills the light.
I cannot bring myself to leave this land.
But it will become dangerous at night.
Knowing this, I must get home beforehand.

It is too late, I was not quick enough
With only moonlight, the trip will be rough.

Kaitlyn Dyke, Grade 10
Union County High School, TN

Caught in the Moment

I'm caught in it, I'm sick of it
When I say sick, I'm referring to all you hypocrites
I try to walk away, try to gain distance
Trying to get on the other side of that picket fence
More like a barrier, a wall that I gotta climb
Ignoring fate 'cause it ignored me for the longest time
I was a bettin' man at life, I kept on gamblin'
Puttin' more money on the table though I wasn't winnin'
So now I'm a work in progress, with a new way to live
Tryin' to live a life that might be focused on the positive
I've been through Hell and back, it's like a simulator

I just explain things and now I'm a demonstrator
So let me demonstrate, the world is cold
Full of liars, haters, and deceivers, or so I'm told
Or so I see, every single day
I wanna be alone, I just need to get away

Cody Savage, Grade 12
Sycamore High School, TN

My Unknown Creator

Since birth, I was abandoned like Romulus and Remus,
 Stranded from knowledge as if trapped in an abyss.
 Voices of invaders spoke freely in my mind,
 Curiosity took hold as I replied in no time.
Is it true? There was something responsible for life?
This creator, have I met it? Is it possible that I might?
 Someday, some moment, my fate will arrive,
 Will I meet it or will it remain unknown till I die?
For years I've struggled with the creator's chains of neglect,
 Conquering fear, pain, and the confusion it has left.
 So will I look? Search? Dwell on it? Why bother?
 My unknown creator, I will never call "Father."

Marcus T., Grade 11
Audubon Youth Development Center, KY

That Day

I had a dream and it was about you.
I smiled and recalled the memories we had.
Then I noticed a tear fell from my eyes
You know why? Cuz
In my dream you kissed me and said goodbye.
My heart lives for you.
My soul dies for you.
My eyes cry for you.
My empty arms reach out for you.
But the day you finally decide to love me,
Will be the day after the day,
I have given up chasing you.

Keantay H., Grade 11
Audubon Youth Development Center, KY

Our Love Has Faded

Like the summer sun
Everything had to fade
The colors mixed with dark hues
Of what we were made.
Coldness has gripped the land
Just like ice has frozen my heart
Everything is barren
And we must part.
Lips do not linger upon mine
Softness no longer cradles my soul
The days have ended
And I am not completely whole.
What we once held so dear
And cherished
Is now dust in the wind
And has perished.
What had been, is gone
And should be buried to the hilt
Just like a plucked rose
My love has begun to wilt.

Brianna Winebarger, Grade 10
North Wilkes High School, NC

Mockingbird

Upon my sill I did see
A mockingbird most lovely
He stood quietly on my side
And his precious time he did bide
He sang his cheery song and then
The bird went quiet once again
I pleaded, begged for him to sing
But he was not listening
I decided to croon on my own
And hoped it would not be alone
Soon enough the mockingbird
Saw me sing and then he heard
My poor attempt to steal his song
He knew this was quite wrong
So he once again spread his cheer
With the beautiful song that I could hear
It was so that I did get
The song that I could not forget
I'm glad the mockingbird did sing
And that I was listening.

James Banner, Grade 12
William G Enloe High School, NC

Colors of My Room

Dear Colors of my Room,
You radiate peace,
soothe my troubles,
smile understandingly.
The color of a peeled banana.
Some say you're a coward.
I say you're sensible,
escaping from avoidable conflicts
and drama.
Everyone glows
in your presence.
You truly are the perfect
shade of wonderful.
Sincerely,
Me

Clara Murphy, Grade 10
St. Joseph Central Catholic High School, WV

When I Say "I Love You"

When I tell you I Love You,
It is not from habit or routine,
But because with each passing moment,
I Love You more and more.
With each beat of my heart,
It grows stronger and stronger.
I will protect you with every breath I take,
Until I take no more.

I Love You truly, purely, and solely,
With every breath I give,
Forever and forever more.
I Love You.

Tyler Matthews, Grade 11
Loretto High School, TN

Your Wish

You shatter my eyes to tears,
like beads from broken thread.
Silence me to your thoughts,
to your daze, to your hate,
to your dreams.
To all of which I'm blind.
Guide me to your mind,
where I surrender,
to the wounds you tore me into.
And kiss me,
deprive me of apathy.
My lovesick guilt —
your endless serenity.
Wake me.
Your arms are not mine.

Shilan Hameed, Grade 11
Brentwood High School, TN

Seasonal Love

Laughs and fun with you,
Love the way you dance with me,
Beneath summer stars.
I'm staring at you,
Your hair reminds me of spring,
Flowing in the breeze.
Consciously watching the way you sleep,
You're so peaceful,
Silent as the summer night.
But your heart is so cold,
Stomping on everyone's soul,
Freezing out winter.
Because things change,
Nothing is ever the same,
I guess that is why they call it seasonal love.

Amber Harris, Grade 12
Berkeley Springs High School, WV

Grades 7-8-9 Top Ten Winners

List of Top Ten Winners for Grades 7-9; listed alphabetically

Leah Berry-Sandelin, Grade 8
Mahoney Middle School, ME

Naomi Davidson, Grade 8
Decorah Middle School, IA

Olivia Estes, Grade 9
University Hill Secondary School, BC

Faith Harron, Grade 7
Horizon Middle School, ND

Lily Lauben, Grade 9
University Preparatory School, CA

Alex LePeter, Grade 7
Oak Knoll Middle School, VA

Sarah Lynch, Grade 7
Holy Innocents School, NJ

Ally Merrill, Grade 9
Hamilton Freshman High School, OH

Shelby Senger, Grade 8
Emmanuel-St Michael Lutheran School, IN

Anna Sixsmith, Grade 7
St Thomas More School, PA

All Top Ten Poems can be read at www.poeticpower.com

Note: The Top Ten poems were finalized through an online voting system. Creative Communication's judges first picked out the top poems. These poems were then posted online. The final step involved thousands of students and teachers who registered as the online judges and voted for the Top Ten poems. We hope you enjoy these selections.

Dream Big

Dream big, that is what I think,
Do not settle for anything lesser than what you think you can aspire to,
Whether your aspiration is to be an astronaut and examine Jupiter, to find a way to cure cancer,
be a plastic surgeon, or be a campaign journalist,
No one can shatter your dreams, they are yours alone that you hold the key to,
I say if you want to aspire and reach your full potential, DREAM BIG
In the end, what matters is did you fulfill your dream you always wanted to accomplish?

Akua Oppong, Grade 9
White Station High School, TN

Open Your Eyes

I pray to the God above to open my family's eyes
not knowing if we set our foolishness aside and open our eyes to see that we are killing our brothers
blood boiling to keep our selfish souls warm doing nothing and expecting a change
open your eyes and without the aid of tobacco and other toxic drugs, without the help of organ killing beverages
we can relax in peace
for there is someone in a the hospital bed begging for life wishing they had opened their eyes sooner
but yet it is too late

Marcus Wright, Grade 7
Dillard Drive Middle School, NC

Strength of Prey

Feet thumping, heart pumping, sweat pouring, legs soaring, I am running from the wolf pack.
Pack growling, I'm howling, pack attacking, we are tracking, he's escaping from our hungry mouths.
I'm escaping, they're still chasing, I'm running, legs gunning, for safety at the end of the path.
He's escaped, we're baked, stomachs growling, pack howling, all for naught, nada, zilch, zero, nothing.

Ryan Williamson, Grade 7
Holly Shelter Middle School, NC

God Is with Us

Tonight as I sleep I know that God is with me. Tomorrow when and if I awake I know that he has not left me. Even when I'm wrong I know our God sits on his throne. What a wonderful God we serve. Do we even deserve? As I think about my life I wonder why he even sacrificed. I'm sure he did it because he loves us. I'm just so happy he thought of us. I hope one day I can show my gratitude for he is above all and that's just so good.

Jordan Johnson, Grade 8
Dillard Drive Middle School, NC

A Winter Wonderland

A winter wonderland
With piles and piles of snow
Falling from the sky
Landing in my yard
Covering all the grass
With not a blade peeking through
Awaking in the morning
Looking out at the inches of untouched snow
Drinking my hot chocolate
Makes me glad I'm inside
But when I do go out
I bundle up with layers
Upon layers, upon layers
Being sure I keep warm
Outside
In that freezing winter wonderland

Catena Wilson, Grade 8
Shepherdstown Middle School, WV

Hatshepsut

Hatshepsut was a beautiful maiden pharaoh
She wore men's clothing because people's minds were narrow
She wanted to show that women could rule
Soon people thought that the woman pharaoh was really cool
She ruled Egypt so strong and bold
Her 21 year reign was over when she became old
Reigning longer than the other women of her time
She had many accomplishments in her prime
Her reign was peaceful but her stepson was not
He overthrew her and her government with his evil plot
It's unknown how she died but after her demise
Her image was removed or at least there were many tries
The erasure of her name almost caused her to disappear
Upon searching the records things were not clear
A queen was in question but the proof was found
Her story was uncovered from deep in the ground.

Emma Crowell, Grade 7
St Nicholas Academy - South, KY

What Is Blue?

When you hear the chirping of birds, and feel the calm breeze,
the sky is Blue.

Blue is not ONLY a visible color, it can be a feeling.
A feeling of happiness and a feeling of content.

If ever you feel the sun on your face,
hear the crashing of the waves and whistling of the wind,
along with the taste of the sea breeze air,
you'll know that the ocean is Blue.

When you hear someone cry and sob with ALL their might,
THEY are Blue.

Blue can be visible and invisible.

Blue is a color AND a feeling.
If not seen,
if not heard,
if not tasted,
then it is felt.

Kolotita Andrews, Grade 9
Western Harnett High School, NC

Mischievous Breeze

Soft, symphonic breezes blow all around
It gently kisses the grass below
As it passes, it hugs you close and
Gives you a sense of security

It stirs up the leaves, making them act
As children running in circles
When the breeze has been vacant for some time
The leaves, ever so softly float into the
Comforting arms of the welcoming grass

Oh, but too soon the comforting grass shies
A-W-A-Y—
Leaving the leaves to be comforted by
A ruthless sheet of white crystals

Jada Bisset, Grade 9
Robert C Byrd High School, WV

If I Could Run the Country

If I could run the country
There would be no more war
If I saw guns, I'd set them behind the door
McDonald's fries would be made especially for me
If that could happen, I'd jump with glee
Chick-Fil-A nuggets would be the best
I would eliminate all the rest
If I could run the country
This is what it would be like
If you don't like it, TOO BAD! Take a hike!

Maria Correa, Grade 8
Weddington Middle School, NC

Imagination Will Push Through When It Does Not Stray

A young emotion blossoms in the heart of a wave,
A great wall it is behind me,
Curling slight over my head and stretching afar,
Around the curved inlet where I stand at its crest,
Of sand.
Granules compact,
Bound without bonds,
Shield me from the wall before its following gate.
Unlocked,
with fresh footsteps in beige…
Ah!
My shield yields the strong wave of uncertainty,
Traversed once before.
Oh! Sand let me by, let me be,
I will sing whilst I am free.
My dire urge will pervade your trusting lock.
I can go around, even make way top.
Your fear of the uncertain,
Will mingle with light-footed certainty,
As I glide through a bond,
Into my imagination's realm.

Maxx Tannenbaum, Grade 9
Grimsley High School, NC

Me

J oyful all the time
E njoying life
S hapes in clouds are fun to find pictures in
S trong leader
I magination is as endless as the ocean
C atching snowflakes in my mouth on winter days
A lways smiling

B asketball player
R unning with my adorable puppy
E yes are looking toward the future
N othing is more important than family
N inja!
A lways trying my hardest
N othing can stop me as long as I try

Jessica Brennan, Grade 8
Dillard Drive Middle School, NC

What Is Yellow

Yellow is like the sun flowing in the sky.
The yellow desert has hills like the ocean waves.
Yellow is like fire burning though woods.
Yellow is like a sunflower flowing in the wind.
The sandy yellow beach is like a blanket.
Sour yellow lemons hang from the tree.
Her yellow hair is like a bar of gold.
Yellow will fill the house with light.
The yellow sun will light the darkness of the sky
as it comes over the horizon.

Derek Daniel, Grade 8
Montgomery Central Middle School, TN

You're Only with Me

You're only with me deep inside my head
Like a lost picture, held captive in my head
You're only with me when I sleep
You're locked in my dreams
Because I lost the key
So I guess you're stuck here with me
Until I wake
When I hope that you will be here
So I close my eyes again
But you're not there
Well I guess you found the key
You're only with me when I sing or write a song
I think about you,
I know that where you are, you do too
You think of me, your grandchild
If you could see me, you would smile
So I'm only with you deep inside my head,
Or when I sleep and dream,
Or when I write a song,
So I guess you've been with me all along

Vertina Hatten, Grade 7
Ramsey Middle School, KY

To My Grandmother

Now that you're gone, away from here
A second life is drawing near,
There is great pain and much sorrow,
I wish it would be gone by tomorrow
I guess there are something's prayers cannot mend
For now it's like a reoccurring nightmare that will not end
I didn't want you to go
But God said it must be so
Come on let's go I heard him say
As he took my beloved grandma away
Now the pain will never cease
Goodbye grandma please rest in peace
Every night I hope and pray
That I'll be with you somewhere some day.

Robin Du, Grade 7
White Station Middle School, TN

Green

What is green?
Green is a lily pad with a frog on it.
It's the Northern lights like spirits at the North Pole.
A cave from a waterfall with a mirror.
Butterflies by a river with running water.
The grass grows within the bamboo leaves.
Where the crocodiles roam the kelly green grass
With a tree snake slithering up a tree.
An olive green fly that is resting on a tea leaf.
A field of kelly green trees out in a field
With an unseen two-headed lizard lurking in the water.
A fresh color between blue and yellow.

Sierra Green, Grade 7
Montgomery Central Middle School, TN

Eleven

My book's called Elev-en
Not 10, 9, 8 or Sev-en
My main character is
Sam, Sam, Sam he is
He has some trouble reading
So that's why this book is a mystery
Mack, that's his granddad
Poor little Sam
As mad as he is
Doesn't know the little white lie
His granddad told him his whole life
He met a girl
Caroline, she's moving soon
She can read and better do it fast
One word in his dreams
Eleven, eleven
Oh what, what, what could it mean?!
On man! Too bad we're at the end of the story
Oh no don't worry
This is just the beginning
Of a lying roller coaster

Allyson Boos, Grade 7
Fuquay-Varina Middle School, NC

Kindergarten

I wish life were like kindergarten,
Where everyone likes you for who you are,
And not how skinny you are, or the way you dress.
Where you can be yourself,
And the biggest problem you have
Is that you lost your stuffed animal.
Where there's no drama and no depression.
In kindergarten no one was emo or gay.
Everyone was just themselves,
The way we should all be.

But instead,
People are judged, and because of that,
They have scars on their arms,
But also,
Their souls.
If only life were like kindergarten.

Kyra Frank, Grade 8
Grassland Middle School, TN

Let God Take Control of Your Life

Get to know God by reading your Bible
Find the seed God planted in your heart
Let Him be your fertilizer
Let your branches fly out through your Christian spirit
Your leaves falling will resemble you shedding your sin
Bear fruit for God
Become a witness of God
Help others through their Christian Life

Katie Arnold, Grade 9
Riverside High School, WV

The Almighty Gift

Never ending
All powerful embrace.

Saving children
Healing the ones who face —
Death,
Destruction,
And waste.

Holding the world in place.

It is kindness,
Peace,
And hope.

It is always present even though the world —
Ignores,
Disgraces,
Turns away,
And refuses to face it.

It is God's love.
Given to the world as a present from above.

God's love is here for us to cherish,
So why do we turn away from His grace?
Why do we turn away from His grace?

Cassie Donnell, Grade 9
Bearden High School, TN

No One Is Spared

In the dark of night
In the bright day sun
  — Death comes to everyone

It comes upon both young and old
Even to the brave and bold
  — Death comes to everyone

Sometimes we lose the love of our life
This may be our husband or wife
  — Death comes to everyone

It comes upon us like a roaring tornado
Sent to us by the Greek god Thanatos
  — Death comes to everyone

Our loved ones are sure to have heavy hearts
As from this world we have to depart
  — Death comes to everyone

We must live each day like it is our last
For all too soon the future becomes the past
  — Death comes to everyone

Madison Davis, Grade 8
George M Verity Middle School, KY

Harry Potter and the Goblet of Fire*

Quidditch match gone bad,
Because the Death Eaters are mad,
The Triwizard tournament too
And whose name in the Goblet, who?
The 4th and final wizard out of three,
Wait that doesn't sound right to me
Harry Potter is the final one
The Triwizard tournament has begun.
On the first task he will be last
But he will accomplish it pretty fast
The golden egg will lead him to two
Hopefully he will make it through
Swimming to rescue Ron
The time is almost gone
He ends up saving two
So now he knows what to do
The maze is 3rd and last
Voldemort is coming back fast
Cedric Diggory has come to an end
His father's heart will take time to mend
Now, Voldemort is back.

Ariel Simpson, Grade 7
Fuquay-Varina Middle School, NC
*Inspired by "Harry Potter and the Goblet of Fire" by J.K. Rowling

Why the Journal

Why the journal lay open on the floor that day
I can't rightly say
All I know is that you took a peep
Unauthorized, not permitted, you sneak
You thought grubby hands would not leave a mark
You gave me check, you gave me snark
Telling me you saw nothing
Why were you blushing?
Didn't try to make amends
Were we really once friends?

Finally when you saw my eyes
And the venom that lies
You hung your tail and slunk back
Back, back, back
To where the grubs belong

Alexandra Corcoran, Grade 9
Grimsley High School, NC

The Pink Warrior

She is strong, bold, kind
When she heard, she kept a smile on her face to keep me in place
Love wraps her like a hand-sewn quilt made from the sun
Having enough room for her and everyone
Even when the weakest, she was the strongest
Leading on with faith in one hand and hope in the other
She has battle scars of victory across her chest
My mother, my rock, is truly the best

Tori Thomas, Grade 9
Wakefield High School, NC

Dragons

Mythical creatures soaring through the sky
On a clear, cloudless night
Wings stretched taut by the billowing wind
Spiraling, looping, circling through the air
Bursts of flame, yellow, blue, or white
Their fiery breath illuminating the night sky
Their power waxing in the moonlight
As dawn breaks
They retreat back to their caves
Protecting their precious hoards
From dragon slayers
Seeking to gain the wealth of these fiends
Who guard their treasure
With claw and flame
These are not monstrous beasts
But gentle giants
Each night
They fly under the vast moon
Basking in its light
Flying over the land of dreams

Jacquelyn Wong, Grade 7
White Station Middle School, TN

If You Could Fly

What would you do if you could fly?
I couldn't though, no matter how hard I tried.
Humans can't do it, don't you see?
That sorely disappointed me.

What would you do if you could float?
I couldn't though, I will not boast.
Humans can't do it, don't you see?
That also disappointed me.

Humans are limited
That is true.
'Cause what would you do
If you flew?

Sion Henry, Grade 7
White Station Middle School, TN

Hatshepsut

Although she was a woman, she had great power.
Thutmose III, her nephew, was quite sour.
He destroyed all her things when she died.
Who knew a nephew could be so sly?
We all wonder what happened to her now.
My guess is: we'll never find out.
If we do find out, it'll be when we're dead.
At this moment, we won't know what was said.
People try to go back in time,
But they'll never discover
What happened to the woman ruler
That ruled so fine.

Taylor Sansone, Grade 7
St Nicholas Academy - South, KY

Where I Am From

I am from Charleston, West Virginia,
from country living,
and wearing sun dresses
I am from disappearing
and my parents worrying.
from chasing butterflies,
to laying out, tanning.
I am from playing in the mud,
and jumping in creeks.

I am from a little white country church,
from a private school,
where I met my best friend!
from a popular girl, and a country guy,
came a baby, blue-eyed, blonde hair, me.

I am from a shoe box,
filled with memories,
from notes and pictures of long lost faces.
I am from bruises and scrapes,
from when band aids made everything feel better!

Nataly Dawson, Grade 8
Sissonville Middle School, WV

My Grandpa and Grandma

This poem is to my grandpa and grandma
whom I love so much.
Whose caring and loving hearts
have taken care of me for part of my life.
Supporting and helping me
through school and through my life.
Watching me grow up
and helping me through some of the decisions I might face.
I will always know that you love me
even if I do something wrong,
because that's the kind of grandparents you are.
The ones who will always love me, care for me, and help me.
This is for you, Grandpa and Grandma.
Love,
Travis

Travis Mackin, Grade 8
St Agnes School, KY

Dance

Dancers flying through the air
Never seem to have a care
As the wind flies through their tied back hair
You just can't help but stare
Before each performance they say a little prayer
Saying that the dresses won't tear
You can't afford a little scare
In the beautiful pink ballet slippers they wear
Never adding their own flare
Always having to be perfect up there

Savannah Russell, Grade 8
Dillard Drive Middle School, NC

High Merit Poems – Grades 7, 8, and 9

Love Lost

My love for you
Is like God's love on a sunny day.
When I met you
My heart fluttered
Like a butterfly's wings.
When we got together
You told me you loved me.
But then this one day
You're ready to end it.
What happened to those happy days?
And promises you made?
I guess they were lies.
Now I'm sitting here
Wondering what I did wrong.
But truth be told,
It was never me.
Yes I made some mistakes,
But that's just part of life.
I will learn from it
And never make that mistake again.

Santana Deese, Grade 8
Orrum Middle School, NC

Where I'm From

Where I'm from, everything is perfect.
Where I'm from, nobody dies.
Life is a carefree playground,
Full of hidden surprise.

Days were filled with laughter and play.
Never a worry went through our minds.
With my rag doll by my side,
Nothing could hurt us,
No how, no way.

Where I'm from is full of baking.
Cookies, cakes, galore
Mixing, pouring, baking, and shaking,
Oh the memories we made.

Childhood is just the start.
We learn to spread our wings and soar.
It is where our journey begins.
Without it, life would be quite a bore.

Regan Sands, Grade 8
Sissonville Middle School, WV

Pikeview

Pikeview
New, pretty
Learning, growing, communicating
Like the school
Academy

Martha Ball, Grade 7
Pikeview Middle School, WV

Hunt of a Lifetime

Dad opened my bedroom door and said, "It's time to go!"
My feet hit the floor and I was nervous from head to toe.

I knew this could be the day that I killed the monster buck.
Oh, how I wished that I would have hunter's luck!

Dad had cooked us breakfast of sausage, eggs, and grits.
I ate it fast and said, "Let's go, I'm ready to see who will win this battle of wits."

I asked myself, "Me or the deer?"
And I prayed the hunter's prayer, "Dear God, please let it be this year!"

Dad and I climbed into our tree stands right before dawn.
I heard a sound and looked down, but it was just a fawn.

Shortly thereafter, I could not believe what appeared before my very eyes.
There stood a massive ten point buck that was going to be my prize.

On this cold, winter, snowy day with the darkness of night slowly fading away,
I made the shot of a lifetime without delay.

When my dad heard the shot he came right away.
There he found me knelt down beside my prey.

With Dad's hands on my shoulders and a twinkle in his eye,
He said in his elaborate way, "That was the best shot of the day!"

I said, "Yeah, because this doesn't happen every day!"
I looked up and thanked God for being with me on this hunt the whole way!

Blake Connell, Grade 9
Cape Fear Christian Academy, NC

Fever 1793

In Philadelphia, the fever strikes again
Thousands of people are getting sick including Mattie Cook's mom
Everybody flees the city to get away from the fever
Even her mom doesn't want Mattie around
But when Mattie and her grandfather get kicked to the curb
Things start to go downhill
Mattie gets sick, Grandpa is weak
They have no food, water, or shelter
A person finds them both and brings them to Bush Hill
Mattie stays in the hot, bloody, fever infested room
While Grandpa gets stronger
When they go back into the city, Mother can't be found and their coffee shop is a mess
There is barely any food but they make do with what they have
But in the middle of the night, robbers take over
While trying to defend himself, Grandpa dies
And Mattie is left alone
The dead are buried with no casket or ceremony
Mattie goes to live with her cook and takes care of a little girl
Then the first frost comes, the fever is over
Mother comes back, farmers bring food and their coffee house is booming
All is well, but Mattie still has a hole in her heart longing for Grandpa

Lindsey Deaton, Grade 7
Fuquay-Varina Middle School, NC

Swishing Leaves
The sounds of leaves swishing in the wind,
Each one with a different size and bend.
Growing on something alive,
But really about to live and die.

They're all above and behind;
But the wind makes a sound,
And they're softly lifted from the ground.
Then they gently fall back with grace,
For another leaf to one day take their place.
Kayla Pauley, Grade 9
Riverside High School, WV

Winter Night
Winter night,
and the snowy landscape
slowly drifts by
through the interminable
darkness —
and a draft of
whispering wind gently
blows coldness
throughout the
frozen, sleeping world.
Sidney Parish, Grade 7
White Station Middle School, TN

My House
In my house
Under the floor
Within the basement
Despite the noise
Without anyone around
Down the hall
Near the back
On the floor
Inside my wonderful book
Of happiness!
Britney Garland, Grade 8
Heritage Middle School, TN

Lights Out
Lights out,
I know this city is loud,
But it's time for bed,
Pray then rest your head.
Tomorrow's a new day,
Don't just stay awake,
I know you have anticipation,
Blame it on your imagination,
Now Darling,
Sleep sound.
Coral Wright, Grade 7
Bargerton Elementary School, TN

The Silver Morning
The cloudy skies are glistening
They're pure white and silver
When it rains, the clouds shiver
I like the breeze that it plays
When rain comes down and washes away
The low clouds, smooth like stone
Unraveled from deep in the earth are silver diamonds
Broken up and split into a million pieces throughout the sky
The cloudy gray skies, calm as can be
They fly up so high
And spread wide like a tree
They're swirly, curly, speedy and dotted
The dotted ones don't like to be spotted
But they are
The best kind is when it snows
It's like a blanket of molten gray metal
Exposed
Or more like millions upon billions upon trillions of preserved fossils
Cloudy skies are interesting
And that's why!
Ryan Cabell, Grade 7
East Millbrook Magnet Middle School, NC

The Mall
If I had my way each and every day would include a trip to the mall;
I'd meet my friend Sianna there and we'd walk down every hall.

My favorite store is Buckle, their clothes are really cool;
we both really like to wear their clothes to school.

Once we've shopped for clothes, we then shop for shoes;
and if we can't find just the right pair, we often get the blues.

But there's more to do at the mall then just shop;
we also like to go to the movies and eat popcorn until we drop.

Yesterday I watched the latest movie in the Twilight series called *Breaking Dawn;*
it was after midnight when the movie was over and we all had a big yawn.

No matter what I end up doing while I'm at the mall, I seem to have a good time;
there are some days when I go that I don't even spend a dime.

You see I suppose it's all about just spending time with my friends;
and I'm sad when I have to leave and all the fun ends!
Hannah Hickman, Grade 9
Parkersburg High School, WV

Samuel Adams
Starting in 1764 Samuel Adams sent Parliamentary policies out the doors
The sugar tax resistance worked better than what Adams tried before
Adams fought to end taxes for the poor
Fellow colonists along with Adams would not listen to Parliament anymore
But at first Adams and his followers were not sure
After many years of protest against the British, Adams won the great tax war.
Richard Hatcher, Grade 8
St Nicholas Academy, KY

Myrtle Beach, South Carolina

Out of the car
In the hot day
Under the sun
Above the ground
On a chair
Near the ocean
Off the coast
During the summer
After spring
Until we have to leave,
    I feel happiness.

Destiny Cotter, Grade 8
Heritage Middle School, TN

Myrtle Beach

In the ocean.
On the sand.
Under the sun.
Beyond the ocean.
Until sunset.
During summer.
Into the waves.
With the dolphins.
Beside the surfer dudes.
As I sit on the beach,
I see beauty.

Alisha Mikels, Grade 8
Heritage Middle School, TN

The River

Down by the river
Near the fish
Underneath a tree
Around dawn
Until I get tired
In the fall
Past the Apple store
Across the street
For me to sit
Beside the river
Full of happiness

Natasha Tate, Grade 8
Heritage Middle School, TN

Halloween Is Near

October is here
And Halloween is near
Candy in the stores
Decorations on families' doors
Trick-or-treaters all around
Every child candy-bound
The smell of pumpkins in the air
Spooky costumes everywhere
Halloween is almost here

Peyton Allen, Grade 9
Wakefield High School, NC

Green

What is green?
Kelly is a shade of green
Maybe green is the color of green peas being eaten
When I see green I think of limes on a tree in the summer
What is green?

When someone says the word green I think of a vegetable garden
Green is the color of grass in the summer waiting to be cut
Maybe green is a park that people walk in every summer
When I see green I think of the green picket fence at my grandmother's house
What is green?

Is green an olive?
When I see green I think of a leprechaun dancing on a rainbow
Maybe green is a happy color
Green is paper being used on a project
What is green?

Brooklyn Elliott, Grade 7
Montgomery Central Middle School, TN

Beauty

I step into the clearing, and I cannot breathe
Before me is a cascading waterfall
Looking so perfect, I think it cannot be.
Under it a pool gathers
Surrounded by rocks, as if they were huddled for a meeting
Past the rocks is the grass worthy to be walked on by Aphrodite herself
Dotted by flowers, placed there as if by magic
I look past the outcropping on which this piece of heaven is perched and
A crashing meets my eyes, roaring with the power of an engine
The sun's warm rays glint the water
Forming glass rainbows in the water droplets
I sit on a rock and now breathe
Enjoying Mother Nature's beauty
Suddenly, however, the skies darken
Reminding me of the sorrows of the world
Only then do I realize
That perfection is fleeting.

Bob Zhao, Grade 7
White Station Middle School, TN

Sunbeams

How radiant, those sunbeams
Shooting like a laser from above the willow tree.
Pointing directly upon the ground.
As I lay there blissfully pondering in the beautiful field of green,
I wonder what it would be like
To be a sunbeam.
The ray of sunlight coming out,
From over the puffy cumulus clouds.
It's a beautiful world and no one ever seems to stop and smell the roses.
The sky, like a beautiful canvas that was freshly painted.
The sunbeams shooting from it, a message of comfort from heaven.
How radiant, those sunbeams.

Victoria LeBaron, Grade 8
New Garden Friends School, NC

Lindy*
Me the beast: Flowers she loves flowers
Beast, beast is what I am
Two totally different things
How could she ever love me?
I tried everything
Gifts and more gifts
How about a greenhouse since she loves flowers?
Yes! She loves it!
Now she wants to study with me!
I have to know everything about this lesson so I look smart
I must make myself at least look like I'm smart
Ha ha like that's possible hey! Not nice
Lindy: how could my dad do this?
Just leave me here
With a complete stranger
He could be a killer or psycho
He gives me gifts like he can just buy my friendship
Like he really wants to be my friend but I'm not convinced
He's gaining on me he's…he's amazing sweet kind,
I…I…I think I love him.

Alexis McLeod, Grade 7
Fuquay-Varina Middle School, NC
*Inspired by the movie "Beastly"

Maximum Ride
Max, Fang, Iggy, Nudge, Gassy, Angel
We stick together, we stay alive
98% human 2% bird
Kids with wings
We were safe…
Until Erasers came and took Angel to the school
Have to go to California
Save Angel from the whitecoats
Try to go back to Colorado…
But Erasers blew up our house
Go to New York City instead
Erasers…half wolf, half man
Flying high above New York
Get a major headache…fall like a hail stone
Finally getting to NYC
Get FREE makeovers
Find a $2000 bank card with my name on it
Spend like no tomorrow!
Find a prison for mutants like us
Set them free
Just a week in the life of Maximum Ride

Isabella Flynn, Grade 7
Fuquay-Varina Middle School, NC

Menace
I love you but you are annoying; kitten.
Stalking my footsteps, you crawl and creep.
I hate when your claws, by which I am smitten.
Wanting to play, when I'm trying to sleep.

Chasing my cursor across the screen,
The annoyance I feel when you give me that look.
I'd call you "menace," but I hate to be mean.
You steal my pencils, you're such a crook.

Enormous cat ears, too big for your head.
You whine and you beg, you are a brat!
I ask you, "Why do you cause me such dread?"
But you can't respond; you're just a cat.

You're fast like lightning, the ninja among us.
You're awful cute, but you cause such a fuss.

Carley Gerdes, Grade 7
Holly Shelter Middle School, NC

I Am Disease
I am Disease.
The creator of cessation and chaos.
My impetuosity is violent, do not anger me.
I show no mercy,
In my eyes, you are all equal,
Whether you are of the poor or the wealth,
You will be taken in disapprobation.
All you love will shun you,
They will take away your arabesque clothes, your wanton lifestyle
I will take away the piquancy of life,
I will leave you alone.
My dominion can overtake any.
I am always there; you may not see me,
But I am always just behind you waiting.
I am not a phantasm, I am real.
I am Disease.

Emma Edwardson, Grade 8
Dillard Drive Middle School, NC

Sunrise
The depressing night's hold on the world
Fading minute by minute into something else
Into fuchsia, lavender, gold, and blue
Transforms into a day of beauty

Madison Adlich, Grade 8
Freedom Middle School, TN

Beauty
Before the rusty red barn
By the last standing willow tree
Near a dark brown muddy pond
Alongside a pile of colorful leaves stands a lonely flower.
During an autumn day the flower was picked.
Despite it dying someone found beauty in it.

Kimberly Massey, Grade 9
Riverside High School, WV

The Year

As the wind does blow
    Across the trees, I see the
        Buds blooming in May.

I walk across sand
And find myself blistering
In the hot, hot heat.

Falling to the ground,
    I watch a leaf settle down
In a bed of brown.

    It's cold and I wait
For someone to shelter me
And take me from here.

    I hear crackling
Crunch, of today's newfound day
    And know it won't last

So I will leave it at bay,
And hope for the best
    This bitter new day.
JT Brenin, Grade 8
Dillard Drive Middle School, NC

I Am From

I am from an 18 hole course
Early humid mornings
Long walks through every hole
Finding golf balls in the water
The hot sun on my back
Dripping with sweat
I am from staying on the range for hours
Or just spending all day at the pool
I am from the fun night swims
And amazing meals at dining room
I am the kid who goes to the club too much
Where everyone knows me
I am from Pinewood Country Club
Wyatt Wellington, Grade 8
Westchester Country Day School, NC

Rumors

Twisting, turning through the hallways
Grabbing every student in reach
This vine strangles even the strongest
Slithering, sliding into your mind
Whispering softly into your ear
As quietly as it travels is
As strong as it destroys
Creeping behind its victim waiting
To pounce, ending it all
Rumors can kill
Arati Joshi, Grade 9
White Station High School, TN

Wind Hollow

The wind blows musically here,
with whispers of love, peace, and happiness.
It tickles past your ears, like gentle lips,
leaving you unaware of its presence,

The rain is sweet like sugar,
and falls in the steady rhythm, of a love song.
It caresses like soft fingertips,
embracing every inch of your skin.

The birds are angelic, their calls and whistles serenading your ears,
Beckoning you to fly high with them, to be lifted to the clouds, and soar.

The sun shines with warmth, keeping this place alive,
thriving with life, and vitality.
It warms your face, with compassion and care,
like a sweet lover's breath.

Close your eyes here, And you will dream.
Not of nightmares, oh no, But sweet alluring dreams.

Dwell here for as long as you like,
time is ceasing to exist in this place of bliss,
Holding you captive to its enchantment.

So close your eyes, and open your heart,
and Welcome, To Wind Hollow.
Melissa Alexander, Grade 9
D H Conley High School, NC

A Mind Rearranged

One day she was a caring mother, nothing wrong at all.
The next day we knew her mind was headed for a fall.
Her thoughts were jumbled, her words sometimes mumbled.
Remembering became a laborious task, something she tried her very best to mask.
A life so changed, a mind rearranged.

As her reality changed and her thoughts became unclear,
I looked in her eyes and saw the real fear
Of what is yet to happen, what is yet to be.
I truly hope she will soon be set free.
A life so changed, a mind rearranged.

A girl in the corner, a man in the house,
Sometimes she sits as still as a mouse.
Each day her anxiety and anger may appear,
And on her face I often see a tear.
A life so changed, a mind rearranged.

I visit and wonder where she will be, will she be with us, what will she see?
Will her thoughts be fantasy, or will they be real, I'm so afraid of how I might feel.
Her thoughts do wander to bygone days, as she visits the past and all her old ways.
Her journey will be long, her reality eventually gone.
A life so changed, a mind rearranged.
Tristan Hazlett, Grade 8
George M Verity Middle School, KY

Lily

This is a poem to Lily
my baby cousin, born in April.
I love it when you laugh and smile
when I come to see you.
Your giggles are contagious
and always make me grin.
You are growing very fast;
I can't believe you're crawling.
Your beautiful eyes light up the room.
Seeing you makes my day.
I will love you no matter what,
Lily, my cousin, my baby.
Kelsey

Kelsey Sucher, Grade 8
St Agnes School, KY

My Guardian Angel

It was a dreary, rainy afternoon
On my way to the hospital
I knew it would be my last time to see him
My heart was breaking piece by piece
Minute by minute
Tears slowly rolled down my face
We arrived to the hospital
I held the hand of my guardian angel
As we said our last goodbyes
I looked at him and said
I love you, forever
Goodbye for now
I'll see you soon

Shelby Bess, Grade 9
Riverside High School, WV

Friendship

Friendship isn't just about
How many laughs or jokes
You shared.

Friendship is about
Who has been there
When everybody else
Has walked out.

That's what a great friendship
Is all about.
So, remember who your
Real friends are.

Shelby McGill, Grade 7
Elkton School, TN

Rainy Days and Sunny Days

When it rains it's so boring
When it is sunny it's so much fun
But they're both okay at times

Reese Kinney, Grade 7
Meredith-Dunn School, KY

Coire Ayres

This poem is to my friend, Coire Ayres.
Whom I talked to a thousand times.
You always listen, even when you don't care.
You're always there which is a very good thing.
Without you there, my world isn't there.
Without my best friend I can't think straight.
That would never happen though we are too close.
I know you are kind and caring, a nice friend who can't tell a lie.
Even when the situation is bad, and you are mad.
You are always there, I can't say that enough,
I will say it till it takes firm ground.
There are many holidays we celebrate together,
But my favorite is November twenty first. That is the best of all.
We do more than ordinary friends.
We bond over football. I don't know most of the players, but you do not care.
So I will write this for friendship, togetherness, and for you Coire
Happy birthday age 13 to 14.
Robert

Robert Witt, Grade 8
St Agnes School, KY

Sledding on the Riverside

As my dad and I pull up in the gray truck, I know this will be grand
Grasping my sled, I run for the slope and
Speedily jump on my sled to begin my descent
With the sound of cheering friends behind me, I swerve onto a snow covered rock
As I catch some air, my hair is blown off my face
The pain in my gut tells me that my stomach is somewhere on the ground
My joyride fades away and my entire life seems to flash before me
I land with a thump of exploding pain
Soon sense comes back to me, and I leap out of the way of other sledders
My feet start the trek back to the summit
Suddenly, against my will, warm tears begin to fall
Sitting down, I taste the saltiness of my tears
My choices are to stay here or try a rerun, so I decide and follow my same tracks
Once again I'm in the air
My sled starts to leave me, but this time I hold onto it
My landing is perfect
Once on my feet again, I raise my sled into my arms
Grand!

Cade Calcote, Grade 7
White Station Middle School, TN

Promises

Should promises really be called promises?
They should be called maybes
It seems as though promises are the bigger disappointment
Why is this?
Is it because we get our hopes up on something that will never happen?
But why aren't maybes so hurtful
It may be the reason promises hurt so much
So does that mean we should believe maybes more than promises?
But will that bring even more disappointment
Promises

Jamonte Grant, Grade 8
Weldon Middle School, NC

The New Testament

Jesus was born like a regular child
He was so sweet, tender, and mild
He was God's son, but he came through Mary.
Many people to heaven he would carry.
Born in a stable in Bethlehem,
Little did Mary know that he would rise again.
Jesus grew up, healing and saving
Ignoring that little guy that we call Satan.
He was crucified; died to save us from sin.
He was put in a tomb with guards guarding it.
Now we are able to be born again
He beat death, and conquered it.
Now he is an even bigger hit.
He came back to life, three days later,
Later on, he ascended into heaven
Now he can save you, even if you're seven.
He'll come back again, you know.
So stay right here, don't go!
Now if we accept Christ to come
Into our heart, he will forgive us,
And give us a brand new start.

Andrea Holland, Grade 7
Fuquay-Varina Middle School, NC

The Tournament

Today's the day, it's time to play
We got a team to beat
So scream and stomp your feet

Our team captain, Caroline
Goes to the center line
The ref tosses the coin in the air
And she picks tails right there

We are lined up and ready to go
I pass to Kelsie and she runs to and fro
She passes to me with a long strong kick
And I knock it in the goal hard and quick

I did it, it's one to zip
With one minute left I did a great flip
The other team couldn't catch up, for we are so fast
We finally won a game at last

With the soccer game won I was finally at ease
Until my dad said, there's another game Elise

Grace Edwardson, Grade 8
Dillard Drive Middle School, NC

The Silent Force

Courage is a rock
steady, strong, unshakable
always trying hard and never giving up.
It smells like cinnamon,
a small amount going a long way,
filling the room.
It tastes like mint,
strong with an everlasting flavor.
It feels like a weight being lifted off your shoulders
for doing the right thing.
It looks like a tree holding strong during a storm
bending, swaying but never falling over.
It sounds like the beat of a drum
steady, always keeping the same beat.
Courage is
the silent force pushing you forward in life.

Abigail Hixson, Grade 8
Leesville Road Middle School, NC

Miracle

So young when it happened,
She was always told that he wouldn't last.
But now that's the past,
Because here is he fourteen years later,
Still full of love…still full of smiles.
Unable to walk, unable to talk,
But he still smiles.
He's a miracle on his own, proving that there's still hope.
He has an angel's smile and a heart of gold.
He's been here before but never this bad.
Tears roll down her face but she tries to hide them.
She won't leave his side,
For she never knows when it'll be the last time,
To see his smile, to see his eyes open, to see his heart beating.
When he mouths that three-word phrase,
She melts because she never knows,
Never knows when it'll be the last.

Danielle Wilson, Grade 9
Parkersburg High School, WV

Confusion

Confusion is a chameleon in a bag of Skittles
You get lost and aren't sure what to do
You get puzzled and can't think straight
Your mind has a billion thoughts going through its brain
You pick what you think first
This is never the right thing

Katherine Baughan, Grade 9
Parkersburg High School, WV

Fade Away

The elegant flower sway
In the tranquil field it lay
Summer coming to an end
Death around the bend
Until next spring, the elegant flower will fade

Mallory Sutton, Grade 7
Pigeon Forge Middle School, TN

Hawk
The dark hawk
Stands still,
Gets set
From on a
Long branch, jumps
Dives quickly with
Narrow eyes turns,
Lands, blended in
With the darkness
Maybe seeing something
Straight ahead
Her wings, large but narrow
And cold, she
Creeps along the
Ground, then she
Dives for the kill,
But wait,
There is nothing but
A leaf blowing
Lifelessly on the ground
Lindsay Orosz, Grade 7
Ramsey Middle School, KY

A World Beyond Ours
Yes we see the breathing trees
Yes we see the dancing stars
But what we don't see…
Is a world beyond ours
Yes we hear the screaming cheers
Yes we hear the sorrowing sighs
But what we don't hear…
Is the world outside
Yes we feel the beating warmth
Yes we feel the breezing chill
But what we do not feel…
Is something much more real
Yes we smell the taunting desires
Yes we smell the refreshing air
But what we do not smell…
Is a place with no affairs
Yes we taste the vengeance
Yes we taste other's dust
But what we do not taste…
Is a world full of trust
Hannah Lichtefeld, Grade 7
Ramsey Middle School, KY

The Basketball Game
Walk in
Shoes squeak, balls bounce
Only winning matters
Giant crowds get us hyped to play
Game time
Nathan Yeo, Grade 9
Bearden High School, TN

The Joys of Christmas
When Christmas comes it makes me want to sing,
Soar above the world on an eagle's wing.

The coolness in the air
Reminds me I should share.

Christmas makes me laugh and dance until I'm worn.
'Cause it's the same time when God sent His son to be born.

You can ask for presents like a hula hoop.
You can also slurp things like hot cocoa and soup.

Decorations can be simple, like a wreath with a bow.
And any Christmas is so special with a little bit of snow.

Picking out the Christmas tree is an event that makes you jolly.
So is singing carols like "Deck the Halls with Boughs of Holly."

An activity for the kids is making a gingerbread house.
Under the mistletoe if you're a grown-up, you just might find a spouse.

Watching holiday specials makes people elated.
Last Christmas we had fun when we ice-skated.

December 25th is a time for family and friends.
It's my favorite celebration of all, and I'm sad when it ends.
Rebekah Holland, Grade 7
The Center for Homeschool Enrichment and Tutorial, TN

The Darkness Within
Does her spirit still dwell near me?
You could say it's not enough to wonder.
Does she want us back in love?
Yet of a night I think I see,
The darkest presence surrounding me.

Tis her I wish to believe.
but her runic rhyme causes fears to well up inside of me.
Dark and strange feelings surround me, so terrifyingly.
But alas breathe besides me.
As if the presence is to reside within me.

So what I want.
Is not what she needs?
Oh please can't anybody, somebody help me!!!
The answer is clear, for the madness neigh the loneliness surrounds me.
Without her arms closed tight around me.

So it is not enough to wonder I just can't make this spirit leave for it dwells within me.
And the sun shall never shine upon me.
For I fear this presence will never leave.
So I could say we are in love.
But I'm not sure hers came from up above.

W'Raven Lollis, Grade 8
George M Verity Middle School, KY

Hidden Melody

The music swells inside my heart
And floats into my ears
Can you hear it too?
It is a song
Of love and caring
Of life.

The music rolls like the ocean waves
Pounding against the shore
Can you hear it too?
It is a song
Of joy and happiness
Of peace.

The music runs with the river
Going, never stopping
Can you hear it too?
It is a song
Of sureness and kindness
Of mercy.

Cheyenne Morris, Grade 9
Craven Early College High School, NC

The Game of Hockey

From the puck drop
Each team wants to be on top
Once the first check is thrown
The presence of hockey is known

A big save
Makes a team brave
And after each score
The game becomes more

The cheer of the fans
And the coaches' plans
All makes an incredible game
And has the crowd going insane
The whole stadium gets louder
As the fans get prouder

When the game concludes
The winner includes
The team celebrating

Cody Murch, Grade 9
Wakefield High School, NC

Pikeview Middle School

Pikeview Middle School
Large, pretty
Bursting, cheerful, glimmering
Beautiful school
Technology wizard

Grace Kelly, Grade 7
Pikeview Middle School, WV

The Beauty of Change

As I stroll through the wood,
the breeze tickles my cheek
it is not yet winter solstice but the temperature is bitterly at a chill.

Even so seldom does a red or golden leaf, the color of the horizon in the very morn,
scurry, twist, and sway in every which direction across an unpaved path,
they stop and stay with the wind only to blow again.

Calls of nearby creatures signal an undisturbed place of nature,
dying flowers lay upon the ground as if stomped by Jack Frost himself,
the blossoms are such a dreary sight,
lifeless and bitter.

Out of the blue comes a magnificent occurrence,
white flakes fall from the sky,
during the warm days I despise winter,
but when it comes I am struck with the feeling of wonder,
I watch as the flurries kiss the land every so lightly,
and so should you.
Stop to watch the beauty.

Kate Hatter, Grade 7
Ramsey Middle School, KY

When?

There is no "light at the end of a tunnel," only true darkness
The ground frigid, the light not visible, I can't see anything but my own soul deformed
I yell for help, but no help is given
I sense an entity listening yet repudiates my unfathomable cries for aid
The space around me gets tighter and tighter
There's no air left, I can't breathe
I remember what my eyes had last seen
For an evil man had aimed a weapon towards my wife and kids and
He was about to shoot my family, when I jumped in front of them and took the shot
Then, I remembered what I heard when I was young
"If a man hasn't found something that he will die for, he isn't fit to live."
I found something to die for, but when shall I live?
I shake and am rapidly pushed and shoved like a rag until…a cessation
A sudden light gleams through my impotent eyes from golden clouds
"Where am I? What's happening?" I then noticed a golden gate open before me
An outer voice suddenly spoke, "Welcome my son, to a place where the benign souls take over the malevolent evils"
I yell in reply, "When will I live again? Tell me when? When?"
I slowly entered the gate as it closed behind me when the outer voice said,
"Now"

Leodan Rodriguez, Grade 7
White Station Middle School, TN

Soccer!!

S occer is something that means a lot to me, I've been playing it since I was young
O n my tournament for CASL, a soccer league, I scored twice
C an't go a whole day without playing soccer
C an do many tricks, I've learned them all from my father
E nough of football season, back to soccer again
R eality, soccer is my life before football

Saad Karaouch, Grade 8
Dillard Drive Middle School, NC

My Room
Around the corner
Past the door
Into the darkness
With loneliness all around
Under my bed lies a secret
Beyond anyone's mind
Without an eye to see my pain
Within my soul darkness lies
With all my thoughts I stay confused
Despite all the hatred I'm always me

Mayson Testerman, Grade 8
Heritage Middle School, TN

The Woods
among Mother Nature
around the wildlife
over the branches and fallen trees
during the sunset
against the breeze
past all people
near a little stream
beyond the world
without technology
I'm at peace with myself

Noah Silva, Grade 8
Heritage Middle School, TN

The "Y" in Townsend, TN
Down at the Y is my favorite place.
Under the bridge is how I cross.
Up on the rocks I stand.
Off the rock, I jump.
Into the water I plunge.
Toward the bottom I sink.
Above the water I float.
Near the shore I swim.
Before I get out of the water.
Within the water will be my happiness.

Justine Lanning, Grade 8
Heritage Middle School, TN

My Favorite Place!
from the sky
towards the ground
until it makes it
down, down, down
around me it falls
beneath my feet
as the world turns white
outside I go
to go to my favorite place
in the snow.

Haley Burns, Grade 8
Heritage Middle School, TN

My Mind Is Like My Locker
My mind is like my locker.
It's dented and messy.
It has words in it I wish it didn't have.
Yet it is full of knowledge and good times.
It has things in it I will need to proceed on with my life, like college and a family.
It helps me with tough questions and the answers I need to know.
My mind is like my locker,
It was made for only me.

Mallory Tidwell, Grade 8
Bradford High School, TN

Grandparents
Grandparents, grandparents what can I say?
They love to spoil their grandkids in every possible way!
They're so wise and kind in their so humble way,
When you're in trouble at home they know just what to say.
You sometimes complain and beg to them just about every day
For without our grandparents we would not be here today!
Young people should listen and learn from what the elders have to say,
You should be so thankful, if your grandparents are still with you today!

Kimberly Ross, Grade 8
Dillard Drive Middle School, NC

I Remember Sisterly Love
I remember my sister; the famous Brianne Trail,
I remember sobbing girls hiding in their room afraid to fight; protecting each other,
I remember hearing the sweet words "I love you" from Kool-aid stained lips,
I remember tender hugs; and wondering where they went,
I remember the smell of sweet rain-like perfume; and how it's no longer there,
I remember my sister; the good times we had
Those memories now forgotten in a lost sea
But, don't forget I love my sister Bri.

Lindsey Sanford, Grade 8
Meadow Bridge High School, WV

Beat to a Heart Called Music
Beat to a heart called music while joy overflows,
Controlling the will and mind, pulsing like a battle drum
In dusk's cold dark while the warrior takes flight,
For joy is joined by rage, taking hold of our souls like a maiden in Moonlight's glow,
Bringing love, greed, and rage through our bodies
For music controls us in dusk's dim light to dawn's light breaking over mountains,
We move to a beat
Beat to a heart called music

Dalton Jones, Grade 9
Riverside High School, WV

Jeremy
Just you and me, those words never sounded so sweet.
Every time I'm with you, I'm nothing but happy.
Remember our first kiss? The taste of my lip gloss and your big soft lips?
Everyone could see how much you meant to me,
Maybe I'll never admit it but…
You might just be one of the greatest things that's ever happened to me.

Samantha Zamudio, Grade 9
Lee County High School, NC

High Merit Poems – Grades 7, 8, and 9

Falling

Falling,
On and on,
Like a rock casually dropped over a cliff,
Nothing to catch me.
In this haze of sadness,
I strain to reflect,
Why did this happen to me?
Why?
This horror,
So fresh and immediate,
Is pulling me to pieces.
I try to think,
To wonder.
I have never done anything wrong to you,
So why me?
I peer through a fog,
Like there is something beyond me,
I am tormented,
To grasp something,
Be it a thought or a person,
Just to be stable and standing once more.
Natalie Adkins, Grade 7
White Station Middle School, TN

The Terrible Day

Daddy, Daddy
where are you
you promised to take me to the zoo
Daddy, Daddy
you need to come home
Mommy can't do this all alone
Mommy, Mommy
where is Daddy,
he didn't come home
Baby, Baby come
here I got to tell you
where daddy is
we put up pictures
and dug their sticks
bricks, and glass I see
the tie you wore today
Mommy, Mommy I see the tie
Daddy, Daddy
I'm 16 now I hear
you say stop crying I'm
home now.
Janey Branch, Grade 7
Ramsey Middle School, KY

Rain

Clouds grow dark with rain
Animals run happily
Animals love rain
Hunter Nethery, Grade 7
Meredith-Dunn School, KY

Nothing

The blank screen, sitting there,
Mocking me,
I look at the clock,
10:00 PM, I feel my eyes start to close,
I slap myself to keep me awake,
My hands go numb, unable to type,
My brain is unable to think of the words,
I look everywhere, trying to find a muse,
Nothing.
My hands start to type,
Like they have a mind of their own,
Like some paranormal entity,
In my own home,
I have no clue what they are doing,
But they are typing something,
It must have been my imagination,
Because when I look at the screen,
Nothing.
Kamron Horton, Grade 8
George M Verity Middle School, KY

Seasons

Winter drones on
with its cold days, forcing me to pick up
my coat.

Then spring comes rolling through with
its cool rain that tickles my nose.

Summer's heat
stops me dead in my tracks.
The sounds of summer
are irresistible; laughter,
mosquitos moving about,
and an ice cream truck.

But fall is my favorite
because of the beautiful
colors and the crisp
cool air.
Abby Bauer, Grade 9
Wakefield High School, NC

Basketball

Hear the fans screaming
Get hyped
Smell the fresh popcorn
Feel the sweatiness of your hands
Fight for the ball
Go in for lay-ups
Foul until you foul out
Form close friendships
Learn how to be part of a team
To be something bigger than yourself
Kailee Rogers, Grade 8
Elkton School, TN

S'mores of Summer

Sitting by the soft, crackling fire roasting
The soft, sweet, marshmallows
The tasty chocolate
Softening against the slightly
Burnt marshmallow
Compressed between
Two graham crackers
The first bite I take
Tiptoes on my taste buds
This turns to a jog
The jog turns to a sprint and
The sprint to a run
My taste buds can't have enough
As a creamy, white sea flows
Over my tongue
The process repeats itself several times
Until the once bright fire
Turns to ashes
Then I look up to see a starry sky
Victoria Robinson, Grade 7
White Station Middle School, TN

Friends

they come in all shapes and sizes
in all different colors
like presents or packages
with a new surprise in every single one
some will be there
when they are needed
others will not be
and shows their true colors
tall or small
thin or round
friends are friends

under the sky
our keeper guides us
to our true friends
that will hold our hand
they're here to stay
forever and ever
Faith Smith, Grade 9
Wakefield High School, NC

Black and White

Light as day
Dark as night
I see no reason
For us to fight

We walk the same walk
And talk the same talk
All of us are equally bright
Whether we are black or white
Nicholas Nguyen, Grade 7
White Station Middle School, TN

Kori's House

In her room
Picking on each other
Swimming in the pool
Walking around
Hanging with people
Staying up all night
Listening to music
Watching tv
Having fun with her
Being filled with happiness

Leah Davis, Grade 8
Heritage Middle School, TN

My Room

Within my room
In my warm bed
With calming quietness
After a long day
Beneath my covers
Without interruptions
into the night
From night to morning
Up not wanting to leave my room
Among all the peacefulness in my room.

Cheyenne Nichols, Grade 8
Heritage Middle School, TN

The Root of All Evil

Money
The root of all evil
Buys many things
True happiness not being one of them

Money buys friendship
But only for a limited time
When money runs low
So does the "friendship"
You thought you had

Ethan Higginbotham, Grade 9
Riverside High School, WV

Gatlinburg

Above the mountains,
On the way,
Near the woods,
During the summer,
With the crowd,
In the stores,
Around town,
Along with my friends,
About the right time,
Around the mountains in glory.

Donavon Williams, Grade 8
Heritage Middle School, TN

My Empty Desk

When you saw my empty desk in English class,
Did you wonder where I was?
Did you think I was sick or
Think I'd skipped just because?

Did you hope I was late?
So when I got there,
You could laugh at my clothes   make fun of my hair?

Maybe you were glad
We weren't in the same room
Because you   can't   stand   the people
Without your shiny hair and perfume.

Did you wonder if I'd never return?
Because I just wasn't cool?
That I was too   afraid   or   ashamed   to come to my own school?

Or did you know I was tired
Of your jokes and your glares?
That I'd   just   given   up?
That I   just   didn't   care?

When you saw my empty desk in English class
And as you went about your day
Did you know that empty desk in English class   would never go away?

Natasha Derezinski-Choo, Grade 9
Grimsley High School, NC

Deep Inside of Me

There's a place deep inside me,
My mind discovered it and my heart adorned it,
When I found this place it was empty and bland,
But made it my home,
And now it's a garden all my own,

When you visit this exotic place,
You find beauty ready to take your breath away;
There's lush green grass sewn carefully into vast valleys,
And forests mightily guarding the ground below,
But when you lurk deep in this forest,
You will find waterfalls carelessly diving into the purest brooks below,

By the brooks there is a garden of flowers,
Each different by design,
With colors bound to captivate your mind,
And dew beaded carefully on each petal,

So what is this place,
No it's not here on the Earth,
You may think this place sounds like paradise or maybe even odd,
But you did not just read any other poem,
You just went inside my mind,
And visited a land sculpted by thought.

Emily Angle, Grade 7
Ramsey Middle School, KY

Mall

I have to go down to the mall again,
To the glass walls and the shops,
And all I ask is a pair of jeans
And a bright array of tops,
And three headbands and one pretzel
And my body is shaking,
And a discount on spring fashions
And music awaking.
I walk in a single-file line, in step with the person in front of me,
Watching to see what kinds of money I see.
The smells of cinnamon rolls fill the air,
But all my friends don't seem to care.
When I look around I see teenagers galore,
Walking around into every store.
I count how many bags I have: one, two, three and so much more,
But I can't figure out why I only have four.
I leave the mall feeling sorry,
So I get on the phone and talk to my sister Marley.

Kennedy Brown, Grade 7
J Graham Brown School, KY

The Hallway of Fire

The hallway filled with smoke, the stairwells are falling,
Like a rock would fall off a cliff, where will I go?
I see my coworker, with his feet out the window, and about to jump,
I scream "NOOO" but it's too late, where will I go?
I'm running out of air, as if I was under water,
I stuck my head out the window, and the sun was shining,
As if it was smiling at me, where will I go?
People are screaming out windows for help,
as if they were screaming bloody murder, but no one can hear them,
where will I go?
I hear the building screeching, and grinding metal falling above,
where will I go?

Ivy Buck, Grade 7
Ramsey Middle School, KY

Me and My Locker

My locker is messy,
Just like me after P.E.
My locker holds many different things,
Like me when I have a lot on my mind
My locker is red,
This explains me when I get angry
My locker is full,
Just like me, full of different things to do
My locker has hooks,
Which also explains me when I get hooked up on things
My locker is surrounded,
Just like I'm surrounded by all of my friends

Christian Prater, Grade 8
Bradford High School, TN

The Way Friends Are Meant to Be

It's always been a little girl's dream
To be a princess.
But when I'm with my best friend,
She makes me feel like I can be anything I want
We could be laughing together
While we burn food in our royal kitchen
Or, we might be fighting to the death
While we are really mad at each other.
But at the end of the day
There is nothing in our way
That will stop us from loving each other.
My best friend and I
Are like pencil to paper.
We are inseparable
We are together forever
We will never be alone
Even when we are far apart
We will love each other
Even after we go our separate ways
And that's how a Best Friend
Should be. Together Forever.

Jasmine-Rose Derenoncourt, Grade 7
J Graham Brown School, KY

The Edge

A dark swirling abyss
Beckons your mind
To swerve ever closer
Dangerously into a bind
Nearer and nearer,
To that sharp and jagged edge.
You see a vivid image, of the dusty surface
Crumbling beneath your delicate weight
And you feel the wind—you feel the shock,
The end is so close,
You can almost taste its bittersweet horror within.
Your eyes dart from the cliff,
To the ground,
In that wrenching moment,
So many sharp memories stab you in your side,
And threaten to drown you.
The ironic smell of death clenches its jaws,
Awaiting your ever-nearing arrival.
And reality jerks you to attention,
Leaving you staring into the writhing darkness.
The edge…

Emma Bell, Grade 9
Home School, KY

Summer

Summer is a fun season.
Summer — you can go to the beach.
Summer — you don't have to go to school.
Summer — you can lay outside.

Corey Curry, Grade 7
Elkton School, TN

How Can Such Evil Exist

How can such evil exist?
As we remember that September no one could ever forget
We remember the gentle building as it begins to break
With the scars in our minds that make us shake.
As the two buildings sitting so glimmering in the sky
They are being attacked but still they rise.

How can such evil exist?
As another plane comes and briefly hits
The battle is not over because still they stand
Way taller and stronger than 1,000 men
Now we hear another command
But still those two Twin Towers we see still stand

How can such evil exist?
As the towers cry out their pain
We sit and watch and continue to complain
As we watch the towers collapse into one
From one side to another comes to be dust
From one knee to another they cry to us
But still we wonder how can such evil exist?

Kiara Harris, Grade 7
Ramsey Middle School, KY

Summer

Summer is my favorite season,
we are out of school and that's one reason.
Oh, I will miss my teachers, peers and friends
but getting to play all day is very pleasing.
I love to play all day with my little brother,
and sometimes we even include my mother.
We go to the park and swing and slide,
but when it gets dark my mom says, "Inside."
Sometimes my mom takes us to the library,
once I got lost in there and that was scary.
This summer I would like to go fishing,
or learn to skate, or even swim in a lake,
but that is all just wishful thinking.
When the summer ends and school begins,
I am excited once again,
I realize I have missed my teacher, peers and friends.

Michael Harper, Grade 7
Elkton School, TN

Kittens

We like to play and pounce
Even though we only weigh an ounce
We like to run
And have lots of fun
To you our love is the only thing that counts

Liberty Wood, Grade 7
Pigeon Forge Middle School, TN

Courage

It is in the little things as we see it.
The first play in a game.
As great as a volcano.
The first time you make a shot or hit
A home run.
The first time you get punished when you're doing wrong.
When they leave you standing in their meanness
And your steadfastness shines.
Later,
Death,
You did not do it to yourself.
You did it with God.
Your courage was living it up until your last days,
That you would show you're not afraid.
If your buddy would be sad
And you'd say you shouldn't be afraid,
Then his courage was strong and brave.
It was the little things that taught us to not be afraid

Abbie Jennings, Grade 8
West Middle School, TN

Blizzardy Shower

Stinging cold wind and dead lifeless trees
Keep you cold and shaking in your knees.
The blinding, everlasting white
Builds on and on each and every night.
The sky, so dull and gray,
Hardly sees light during the day.
Swirling wonder puts on a show,
As the crystals come by and go.
Again and again the snow blocks you in,
You fear you'll never see the ground again.
Piling up more and more each hour,
This cold and miserable blizzardy shower.

Kayla Beauchamp, Grade 7
Jefferson County Traditional Middle School, KY

Process...

I lie abandoned in the shadows of despair,
Broken and hurt, trapped in the path of death
Awaiting for a presence to help heal these wounds.

I stand alone in the darkness of uncertainty,
Paralyzed and damaged, frozen in the steps of negativity
Hoping and longing to feel security once more.

I sit shattered in the isolation of loss,
Sad and weak, encountering the face of Destruction
Wondering when I'll find freedom from the horrid clutch of life;
When I'll find safety from the pain and suffering of/in this world.

Robin Phillips, Grade 8
Church Hill Middle School, TN

Our World

It's crashing down
Everything lost and found
What's happening to us
Always making a fuss
This world has changed
And we can't find a way
Come on everyone listen up
Free some time
And help others out
This is what our world's about
No more with yourself
Put your toys up on a shelf
Go and make a difference
A change in your community
A change in your nationality
We are all one
Living up under the sun
Helping out a little too
Our world needs you
Claire Portilla, Grade 8
Signal Mountain Middle High School, TN

The Lonely Leaf

Piles of leaves all around me,
Once colorful but now dead.
All fallen from the same large tree,
Many feet above my head.

I look up at that tree now,
Nearly empty, nearly bare.
Except for one lonely leaf,
That's barely hanging there.

This leaf is quite a lovely color,
Yes, it's brilliant gold.
But slowly dying, close to falling,
Yes, it's growing old.

Now it can no longer hold on,
It's reached the end of its time,
I watch it drift slowly, to the ground,
Reaching the end of mine.
Kerri Harris, Grade 9
William Blount High School, TN

Camping

Cool, crisp breeze,
Air flowing through the trees,
Majestic hills rolling,
Parker is now at ease.
In my tent,
Napping like a bear,
Going to my own special event.
Parker Walls, Grade 7
Elkton School, TN

Walk Two Moons

There once was a girl,
Her name was Salamanca,
Sal and her dad moved to Ohio,
While her mother went on a trip.
Sal went to go see her mother,
She went to her Grandparents Hiddle
On the way she told a story,
About her friend Phoebe Winterbottom.
A crazy lunatic coming to her house,
Her mother going missing.
Was this the work of the lunatic?
On the road,
Stopping wherever she stopped.
Her grandmother getting bitten,
Going back to memories,
Phoebe's mother getting seen,
Secrets getting spilled.
Where does it end?
Grandma Hiddle passing.
Sal seeing where her mother is,
Moving back to Bybanks, Kentucky
Gabrielle Flynn, Grade 7
Fuquay-Varina Middle School, NC

Depression

I am depression
An egress from your wanton lives
And a bloodthirsty vampire
Sucking the life out of all revelers

You will no longer be hale and lighthearted
Only cruel and horrid
Never again will you be of piquancy
I laugh at you and your foolish hopes
Of wealth and being loved.

I will forever be the chains that
Bind your hands and feet
The voice in your head that says
You will never make it

As much as you may try to
Get me to leave
I will always be there
As the shadow that lurks behind you
Anywhere there is light
Shannon McLeod, Grade 8
Dillard Drive Middle School, NC

Every Day

Every day has its ups and downs,
With its share of smiles and frowns,
But if you'll talk to God a minute,
Every day will have joy in it!
Bailey Robling, Grade 8
North Raleigh Christian Academy, NC

A New Beginning

I'm so sad and blue
All I do is think of you,
I can't sleep at night
Because my dreams I cannot fight

A broken heart is what I feel
Which leads to flowing tears,
I lie thinking of what we had
And all I have are fears,

I don't want to be alone
It's not where I belong
But that's how I feel
Sad, blue and surreal

So I must listen to my heart
And not what others say,
Go on with my life
And find love another day.
Abigail Hamilton, Grade 8
George M Verity Middle School, KY

My Mind Is a Locker

My mind is a locker
It's stuffed up high
It's cluttered and cramped
But it gets by
It gets me everywhere I need to go
It's a locker that won't die

My mind is a locker
It won't ever go away
Stands there every day
I think it may
Locked in are the memories
Even though I'm away

My mind is a locker
The scrapes show I'm not great
Even if I'm late
Once I leave I wave goodbye
To that locker I left behind
Kurtis Hodgens, Grade 8
Bradford High School, TN

Dillard

D ominant
I ntelligent
L earning
L unch time
A thletic
R eaching out
D ragons
Corey Archer, Grade 8
Dillard Drive Middle School, NC

Ormond Beach, Florida

    In the sun
    Among the waves
    On my surf board
    Beyond the sunset
    Through the sand
    Under an umbrella
    Against the shells
    Beneath the skies
    Near palm trees
    Within myself
        I feel relaxed.

Colbie Norton, Grade 8
Heritage Middle School, TN

Dancing and Smiling

Dancing and smiling all the way to heaven
Enjoyed and adored the life he was given
Worked hard for what he wanted
He was hardly disappointed
Papaw was an excellent man
Who didn't have a life plan
Just enjoying every moment with family
Like a kid who'd just bought candy
God took his soul
and I was left in the cold

Kristen Hudnall, Grade 9
Riverside High School, WV

The Woods

In the woods
with birds singing above my head
near a tall tree
beneath a green canopy
without a worry in the world
by myself
except for my dog
on a vine I swing
off I run
into my special place with happiness

Julia Heath, Grade 8
Heritage Middle School, TN

The River

By the river
In my hammock
Under the stars
During the night
Beside my dogs
Over the rocks
Past the hills
Behind the trees
Without the noise
It is pure bliss and happiness

Grace Koella, Grade 8
Heritage Middle School, TN

Forever

To fake your world of happiness,
And begin crumble apart.
To try and try again,
But not everything ends up the way it starts.
Smile and stare upon them,
But the inside, wish your life would be worthwhile.
And that if you could,
Just evaporate into the air.
The leaves around your cluttered world
Begin to fall to the ground and settle down
Calm and lifeless, they lay down to sleep and die.
To decompose into your lies,
And tell your friends that you're happy now,
When you look them in the eyes.
Thoughts of losing everything
And everyone flicker through your mind every day
It's not your fault.
It's only happens because of what prevents you from having a normal life.
You my friend are immortal.
You'll live forever,
And forever you shall live alone.

Hope Genovese, Grade 8
J Graham Brown School, KY

Legs

A child's first step; their most memorable achievement,
everything they perceived came and went.
How they learned to challenge it all,
and how they learned to catch the ball.
They took a chance and never gave up,
they took a chance at beginner's luck.

You may not remember that first day,
that you stood up on two legs looking around you in that curious way.
You took a step forwards; yet fell down,
and almost cried but it was determination that you found.
You never gave up; you never gave in,
you knew like others that someday you'd win.

Ancient and bent; cracked and rusted,
it's the last step you'll take on the legs you've always trusted.
You know you're right where you want to be,
like that first step; you will always be free.
This day you've won like you always knew,
on the final day your legs carry you.

Mikhaila Hillyer, Grade 9
Franklin County Early College High School, NC

Peace

What is really peace?
Why must we be in constant conflict with our neighbors on this Earth?
Harmony is essential
I am sick of hostility instead of empathy
Make peace and art not war.

Zoe Gresham, Grade 9
White Station High School, TN

High Merit Poems – Grades 7, 8, and 9

A New Member

"Do you want to hold him?"
My mom asked gently.

"Sure!" I took the soft, cuddly, and cute
baby into my hands.
He was as soft as a brand new blanket.

"Tarzan! Let's name him Tarzan!"
I said very excited.

"Umm…I'm not so sure about that name
sweetheart. Got any other ideas?"
My mother replied.

"Jake sounds pretty good." My mother said.

We could do everything together.
To this very day I want him to leave me alone.

But I always say I have "best friends,"
but my true best friend is my brother.

Aly Mohn, Grade 7
Ramsey Middle School, KY

I Am Darkness…

I am darkness
I am always around
I am not only all around you but I am inside of you
I play with your mind,
I dull your senses
You may not know, but there is a little darkness in your heart
I feed off of your pain,
Your sorrow
I am a shape shifter
One moment I'm there the next I am not
I slowly, slowly close in on you
And there is nothing you can do to stop me
I am feared by you
But you are not the only one
It is rare to have one that can ignore my mockery
But I will always be waiting
You may say that the sun will always rise another day
But so will I!

Keith Markovich, Grade 8
Dillard Drive Middle School, NC

Paul Revere

He rode thru the night
Shouting "the regulars are out"
The men grabbed their guns
Paul rode till he got captured but lucky Paul
Got 70 minutemen out

Zach Kirk, Grade 8
St Nicholas Academy - South, KY

Better Days

The sweat dripping down my brown-skinned face
The warm hard dirt under my ashy feet
The sun beaming over my big black head
Me in the cotton field, hoping for better days
I see myself leaving. Escaping to a wonderland
No pain or crying
Just happiness and love
But here comes master, with the whip in his hands
Threatening me with harsh words
It makes me want to lay down and die
But I stand my ground
Saying to him I'm black, and he can't control me
I'm my own master
But then he whips me
Blood streaming down my arms and legs
Cuts on my neck and back
He leaves
So I start picking the cotton and hope for better days

Deandre Cole, Grade 9
Overton High School, TN

The Twisting Path of Fury

Anger is a swinging bat
That thrashes around blindly smashing trees and innocent things,
While its goal is to break open the piñata;
It smells like the dumpster,
The pungent smell warns people not to get close
It tastes like lemon,
After a bite one's face will contort into a temporary grimace,
It feels like that moment when you bite your tongue
And tears start to fill your eyes because of the piercing pain,
It looks like a monstrous fire,
Burning down anything that stands in its way
It sounds like thousands of drummers pounding on their drums,
The twisting path of fury make you lose your way.

Christina Song, Grade 8
Leesville Road Middle School, NC

Spaghetti Love Note

Oh spaghetti
How I love you
Sadly, we only meet when my mom makes you
Oh spaghetti
How delicious you are
How I love your compatibility with so many sauces
Oh spaghetti
How I envy your wonderful meatballs
Why do they get to be with you and not me?
Oh spaghetti
Why do you do this to me?
Why must we be from different worlds?
Oh spaghetti

Zoe Chunn, Grade 8
Dillard Drive Middle School, NC

My Cousin
This is a tribute to my cousin, Melissa,
who tries to be there for me.
With Brad being across the ocean so much
you only have the dogs and daughters in the house.
You're the one I can talk freely to
just like you're my friend.
Your brown hair and green eyes
sometimes make me jealous of you.
We don't get to see each other often,
but when we do, we have to catch up.
When you came to visit this summer,
we talked and gossiped just like friends do.
Even though I'm always shy around you at first,
you seem to lighten my mood.
You are one of my very best friends,
and don't you forget that!
Love,
Katie

Katie Stratman, Grade 8
St Agnes School, KY

Mom and Dad
This is a poem to my mom and dad
who are kind and caring.
You are always there for me
no matter what.
Even when I am mad,
you are always there to make me happy.
You never stay mad at me
even when I am bad.
You help me be my best
at school and at home.
You tell me when I do wrong,
and I don't do it again.
I have become wise because of you.
I will never forget what you have taught me.
You are the best parents,
so always remember
I love you.
Nathan

Nathan Sucher, Grade 8
St Agnes School, KY

If Teenagers Ruled the World
If teenagers ruled the world
we would speak in txt abbreviation.
There would be lots of Lol's and BRB'S.
Video gaming would become a national pastime
Adults would also try to overthrow teens.
There would be a lot of lazy rulers.
The new retirement age would be 18.
I do not think this would be the best idea.
There would not be to many rules either.
We all know teenagers do not like rules.

Chase Costain, Grade 8
Weddington Middle School, NC

My Sister
We sign our cars and letters best friends forever
Even though we fuss and fight
My sister has a million ways to make me laugh
She's always there for me through thick and thin
It's so good to have her around
When she got older everything changed
I loved the moments we shared
She's always there till the end
We have each other's backs through anything
She pulls me aside when something doesn't go right
I can tell her all my secrets
Whenever I'm having a bad day she's there to help
I will always love her no matter what
Sometimes I think of ten ways to make her disappear
But we all couldn't live without her
She's also going to be one in a million
It doesn't matter what I say she'll stick by my side
She's like my best friend anywhere we go
She's the one that motivates me
I cherish all the things we do
My sister is my true friend

Ma'Lesha Lanier, Grade 7
Fuquay-Varina Middle School, NC

Red White and She Misses You
All flags are in the air
Fireworks go everywhere
She does nothing but stare
She can't help but remember her daddy over there
Then she suddenly raises her to her chest and says:
I pledge allegiance to the flag
And to all the men in Iraq
And for the men who help him fight, I pray for you day and night
A tear dwells in her eyes
she does not want to cry
for she always hides;
her feelings locked away
but the fear will be gone
once her daddy has returned home
she will no longer be alone
but forever she'll hold on…

Makayla Ratcliffe, Grade 8
Hampton Elementary School, TN

The Declaration of Independence
We are the colonists we demand freedom!
We demand you set us free!
We are people and all people are created equal!
We are in the pursuit of happiness!
We are the people of America!
We won't relinquish at the sight of the British redcoats!
We will fight to the death!
So give me liberty or give me death!
We are the United States of America!

Keenan Newton, Grade 8
St Nicholas Academy - South, KY

Poems

Poems are used to express feelings
Whether it's sad, mad, happy or excited
People make them far and wide
People make the world go round
Without them, we would always frown
They trigger your emotion and imagination
To think about what you'll say
You'll have to use figure of speech
To make them more exciting
So keep in mind
Poems are beautiful

Tori Miller, Grade 7
Elkton School, TN

In My Bed

In my bed
Under my blanket
Toward the tv
Beside my door
Without my dog barking at night
I would be sad
Down the hall I hear noises
Beneath me is my mattress
On top is my cover
Outside my window the moon is full
To a peaceful sleep I close my eyes

Bristol Smith, Grade 8
Heritage Middle School, TN

Paris, France

Beneath the stars
On the Eiffel Tower
Within the night
With my friends
Near the river
Before midnight
Off we go
Through the town
Into many stores
After we're done
We are filled with happiness

Shaina Newcomb, Grade 8
Heritage Middle School, TN

Adrenaline Rush

The thrill of the ride,
The fun rush you feel,
Your blood is pumping,
And you just can't stop.

You should be sane and
Keep yourself alive,
But hear me out now,
Where's the fun in that?

Jay Dharsandia, Grade 7
White Station Middle School, TN

The Destruction of 9/11

"Hey Some people might be buried here"
So I dug from the crystal shards of glass and bricks to
find survivors, just to find nothing but trouble
Generals, officers and innocent workers hurt and dead

Smelling smoky air while recovering zombie-like people
Counting each survivor as we go
As I wonder how many more will we find 5, 20, 30, 50
Oh, how many will I find dead or alive

As we begin to finish up getting survivors
"Creakkkkkk" "Boom" After we heard the loud noises we had felt a rumble,
A rumble so strong and powerful it could have passed for an earthquake
When I look over sadness and shock came into mind

Now here I am a decade after
Remembering the people jumping out windows like skydivers
I remember people running as fast as a race car would
just to get to cover.
It all happened so fast I will never forget what
happened on that day.

Noel Maliwat, Grade 7
Ramsey Middle School, KY

Are You There?

Can you hear me? Are you there?
You're like everyone who stops and stares as my tears fall at your feet.
Are you there? Can you hear me? When I can't fall asleep.
Help me!
I'm living my days through lasting fears.
I know it's hard to see through my tears.
When I'm walking on my knees are you there?
What about in my time of despair?
Are you there?
You see the blood trickling from my feet.
Why aren't you there to help me in defeat?
I feel dead and I am crying in my bed.
Or are you just one of those people who look with blank stares?

Tierra Scott and Bless White, Grade 7
Guilford Preparatory Academy, NC

Faith

Faith is knowing there will be light at the end of the tunnel,
Even if you can't see it yet
It smells of sweet spring berries after a harsh winter
Faith tastes like melt-in-your-mouth cookies,
After a long day at school
It feels like a fleece blanket with a mother's love wrapped inside
Faith looks like the bright sun beating through the gray-colored clouds
It sound like angels singing after a thunder storm,
Music to my ears
Faith lets me know everything is going to be okay,
Even if I can't tell right now
Faith is a beautiful thing

Abigail Holland, Grade 8
Leesville Road Middle School, NC

Grandpa
This is a poem to my grandpa
whom I will love to the end.
With your big brown eyes
you look up at me
and tell me no one compares to me.
The pain of almost losing you
made me really think.
When you looked at me from your hospital bed,
I knew everything was going to be all right.
You know just how to comfort me,
even without your words.
you escaped death the first time,
and now you're here to stay.
I write this for you, my papaw,
because I don't know what I would do
without you.
Love,
Caroline

Caroline Fedders, Grade 8
St Agnes School, KY

Holocaust
Dark, cold winter skies
Big, fearful eyes.
Not a smile in sight
As we watched in fright.
Suffocated in delusion
Not one thing an illusion.
One by one, they all dropped down
In this sick, deadly town.
They look around with their fixed glower
While in this corner we cower.
They control our every move like a puppeteer
And us? We wish we could be anywhere but here.

Naima Alam, Grade 9
Wakefield High School, NC

Knowingly Unknown
She knows me better than I know myself
Always there to comfort me
Dries the tears I cry at night
She's my best friend and my own worst enemy
Helps me and harms me
I don't like her
She always tells me the truth
Even when I don't want to hear it
She takes the pain away when everyone else causes it
She knows just what to do when everything else fails
Every time I turn around,
I see her in my shadow, she follows me everywhere!
I hate that she's ME!

America Hilton, Grade 8
Roanoke Valley Early College, NC

Ode to the Snow
The snow that falls to the ground
is the perfect shade of white
Covering up the dead grass
it lays smoothly over night

Leaving piles of fluff
for children to play among
The trees become decorated
and children twirl catching the flakes on their tongue

The snow sparkles like crystals
twinkles like a new dime
Street lights glare under
collected snow from a matter of time

Just one color to be seen
from miles and miles away
White, shimmering, glowing and gleaming
to make a perfect display

No one ever wishes it gone
its presence is too delightful
A beautiful image to see
the idea of it melting is frightful

Bailie Mustard, Grade 9
Middle Creek High School, NC

The Will of Warriors
Breathless
The air around me intensifies,
Like horses at their starting gates
Yamizura and I take our stances

The look in his eyes assures me
An epic skirmish is about to ensue.
We test each other,
Feinting and waiting
My mind is Confucius in planning
Awaiting every strike, anticipating every move.

The first strike is made.
The air shatters with the sound of battle cries
Our energies clash, souls collide, and spirits intertwine
As blow after blow is exchanged.
Each movement is an agile maneuver
Each blow, a powerful crushing hurricane

It ends as silence makes a triumphant return
And we sit down and ponder
What always makes our battles so intense
We know the answer: the will.

Davion Prier, Grade 7
White Station Middle School, TN

I Saw a Star

I saw a star, burning bright
In the middle of a sleepless night.
I can hear their voices piercing the quiet.
They keep me awake, too afraid of what sleep might bring.
Then I looked outside my window.
I saw a star, burning bright.
Louder and louder their voices grow.
It will all be over soon, I know.
Then I looked outside my window.
I saw a star, burning bright.
The voices stop. The door slams. The car starts.
It is done, finished.
Then I looked outside my window.
I saw star, burning bright.
I hear footsteps on the stairs, then sobbing wails
Everything has gone wrong; nothing will ever be the same.
Then I looked outside my window.
I saw a star, burning bright.
It gives me hope on this sleepless night.

Anna Laura Lobach, Grade 8
Deerstream Learning Center, NC

When the Warrior Lays His Weapons Down

When silence gives way to the hush of darkness,
Flashlights can bring lights but no sound.
People mouth the words with desperate eyes,
But no words escape out.

A helpless cry goes out into the premature night,
Lovers walk miles on end just to reach the lighthouses they see,
Sending beacons of hope,
But alas, the light is so far away that no one can reach.

Fighters punch through the walls their past has created,
But when it is all over the brick is merely crumbling.
With bloody fists. even the warrior drops his weapons,
Life is so long, their hearts are tumbling.

As the young age,
And their fights must become ones that are seated,
There are some who hold on,
But still, they whisper "I will not be defeated."

Hannah McClellan, Grade 8
Moyock Middle School, NC

Common Sense

It rallied a nation and
set the seed of freedom
in our minds. It said the great
words "Tis Time To Part."
Called for common sense
against the royal brute.
All the words written by a single man
whose name is Thomas Paine.

Nicole Clay, Grade 8
St Nicholas Academy - South, KY

The Day I Died

She was the smartest of the whole bunch
No one could make her cry
Alabama December 17, 2010
The fateful day she died
I found out a few days later
I cried and cried
Never wanting to believe it
My best friend gone, in a flash
I never thought she would die before me
Losing her I thought my life was over
That was the day I died
She's gone
I wanted revenge on the guy who wrecked the car
If it wasn't for him
She would be alive, over time I gave up
My heart will never heal
It was shattered, pieces scattered
I felt as if they will never be found
Underground with her

Savanna Cunningham, Grade 7
J Graham Brown School, KY

My Cousin

This is a poem to my cousin, Tate.
Your little face always brings me joy.
Your big eyes shine when you're happy.
Your little hands grasp together,
when you're happy or scared.
I hate it when you cry,
your little face gets red and your eyes swollen.
Always ready to do anything,
even though you're too little.
I remember when I first saw your little face,
four months ago.
You have grown so much since then
into the most amazing person.
I write this for you, Tateman.
May your tiny little face shine,
even when you are hurting.
I love you so much.
Love,
Aunt Anna

Anna Jennings, Grade 8
St Agnes School, KY

Snowing Despair

Hopeless Snow White
Protected by seven loving dwarfs
Hated by one wicked witch
Poisoned by a delicious apple
In her deep despair
Back to reality with a simply kiss
Peace was upon her
Forever and ever

Savannah Wiley, Grade 9
Riverside High School, WV

The Man in the Tree

Take for example, the man in the tree.
He seems quite powerful.
But really is he?

He cowers in fright at the thought of coming down.
He just sits up there and stares at the people in town.
Everyone looks, and everyone talks.
But no one seems to help him, as they continue on their walks.

So one day I decided to take the chance.
I rolled up my pant legs and started to prance.
I made my way up to the top of the tree,
but there was no one to be found.
Not he, just me.

As I looked below me I saw a face.
It was smiling and laughing as if winning a great race.
He said "I am no longer the man in the tree!"
And he ran down the street in a hurried flee.

I looked around, and headed for ground.
But realized I was stuck on top of this mound.

It started to rain, And I started to cry.
For the man in the tree was no longer he,
The man in the tree for now, was me.

Kat Caldwell, Grade 9
Myers Park High School, NC

My World Is My World

In my world
There is no peace,
No limits or reality,
Only my imagination.

My world is a haven for secrets.
It shares and holds me
In a circle of adventure,
Along with fantasy and unimaginable things.

Strange creatures prowl or hunt in my world.
They can fly or vanish,
Or crawl and kill,
All of this helps them survive.

My world is like a game.
You can smell danger in every step of the way.
Survival is critical and a savior.
Traps catch, magic tricks, and fire burns.

Fire is what feeds my world.
It singes and burns terribly.
Like food or water, it gives energy.
My world is like an inferno; it is no place for safety.

This is my world.

Erin Donlon, Grade 7
White Station Middle School, TN

Choices

Choices;
They allow us to make our decisions.
Choices;
They let us choose our side.

Choices;
They allow us to choose our clothing.
Choices;
They allow us to choose our food.

Choices;
They allow us to make a difference.
Choices;
They allow us to choose our own actions.

Choices;
They let us be ourselves.
Choices;
They let us pick the life we want to live.

Choices;
They break down those big decisions.
Choices;
They split up the options that lead us to where we are today.

Jordan Gould, Grade 7
J Graham Brown School, KY

Dreams

Anything is possible
When it comes to dreams
It is unimaginable
To the things we can dream

Dreams are inspirational
They let us know what
We are capable of
And what we can accomplish

The dreams we see
Can be signs
Signs that could lead us
On a journey in this world

You have to have an open mind
When it comes to dreams
Because your dreams are a part of you
And they know everything about you

So you never know
Dreams might be trying to tell you something
Sometimes they are more than
They seem to mean

Raquel Rooney, Grade 8
Dillard Drive Middle School, NC

Tree

Tree
The tree stands
It sways in the wind
The leaves grow in the spring
Then fall in autumn
Soon the bare winter
Hopefully
In
The
Spring
It
Will
Live
Again

Benjamin Embrey, Grade 9
Riverside High School, WV

Grilling

Charcoal or gas
Type doesn't matter
Grilling any meal
Makes my mouth water

Chicken and ribs
Barbecued and smoked
Cooking them outside
Makes me hungry for more

Burgers or dogs
Sizzling and hot
Grilled food on a plate
Is a feast in my mind

Hunter Corbin, Grade 9
Riverside High School, WV

The Beach

The ocean waves go round and round
I hear people talking in the sand
I step into the sand the sun warms my feet
It feels like I am a fish in the water
When I wake up it is cold at night
I feed the birds all day long
I see my family having a fun time
I hear the wind going up and down
I dream that I am at the beach
I see my granny falling in the water
I taste me eating a hot dog at the beach
I see me falling on a sand castle
This is me I am on the beach
It is hot and cold but I love the beach

Gardazly Crawford, Grade 7
Ramsey Middle School, KY

What You Mean to Me

I could say you're the world
But that wouldn't fit
You're more than that

You're the center place
I come to when I'm lost
When I need someone
to help me along

Whether you're right next to me
or we're miles apart,
we will be friends,
no matter what

Through the rough times
or shining moments
you're right next to me through it all

We have lots of things in common
that's why we fit
no one is like us
when we're together

You're more than my world
only four words can describe it
You're my best friend

Caroline Poteet-Berndt, Grade 7
J Graham Brown School, KY

Best Friends

Friends are my life,
They make me complete.
Friends always have your back,
Even through thick and thin.

Friends talk to you on the phone for hours,
Not minutes.
Friends make you smile,
Not frown.

Friends are like diamonds,
They are the gleaming part of your life.
Friends are priceless,
They could never be replaced.

Friends cry when you cry,
And smile when you smile.
Friends never get in a fight,
And always put you first.

Friends make memories together,
And remember them forever.
But my friends,
Are best friends.

Kylie Hall, Grade 7
Ramsey Middle School, KY

False Crawl

The man on the moon stares back at me
As he lights up the night sky
Waves crash on the sandy shoreline
Stars twinkle in the midnight darkness
The wind begins to pick up
Dune grass sways with the sea breeze
Ocean spray hits my face
The only thing visible for miles
Are the dim yellow lights of the pier
Far, far off into the distance
Something grabs my attention
There is a large, dark object in the surf
Scooting her way up the beach
Much older, much wiser than I
She crawls all the way to the sand dune
But, she pivots
And crawls all the way back to the surf
Disappearing into the ocean
Never to be seen again by my inquiring eyes
Just as quickly as she arrived
She was already gone

Allison Dombrowski, Grade 8
Dillard Drive Middle School, NC

The Bicycle

One fall day I was on my bike.
Summer leaves rustling in the
wind. The sun shining down on
me. I was out on my bike
riding down my big hill. Suddenly
my bike wobbled and I looked
down my bike chain ripped in
half. The first thing I knew
I was heading for a face
plant in the concrete.

BANG! I hit the
ground. I was crying for
minutes, I finally got up
after sulking for twenty minutes
I started getting close to my
house. I trip multiple times
what seemed to be forever
I get home my mom
sees me picks me up
and takes me to the hospital.

Ethan Hennies, Grade 7
Ramsey Middle School, KY

Soccer

Enjoyable, exciting
Kicking, running
A challenge to me
Sport

Destini Harney, Grade 8
Elkton School, TN

When I Dance
When I dance,
It feels as if I'm in a trance,
My feet move fast,
My body feels light,
My hair whips around,
I pray that I don't fall down,
My slams get attention,
My spins get a wow,
My jumps get a gasp,
As my feet leave the ground,
I get a laugh from my moon walk,
A smile from my foot work,
And when all goes well,
A trophy for my hard work.
Sarah Bryant, Grade 7
North Raleigh Christian Academy, NC

At Home, Just Me, Mom, and Heff
I am sitting at home,
Just me, mom, and Heff.
I am getting kind of bored,
Because all the others left!

I am thinking of a game to play,
With just mom, Heff, and me.
I need to think of a game,
That you can play with only three.

Here come the others,
Right through the door!
Now me, mom, and Heff,
Won't be alone anymore!
Rose Kinniburgh, Grade 7
Pioneer Christian School, TN

The Rhyme Zoo
Leaping lions, slithery snakes!
A trip to the zoo is all it takes
To have some fun for old time's sake,
Instead of sitting around.

Mischievous monkeys, bothersome bear!
Enemies of the bear BEWARE!
I think you'd better say a prayer
Before he decides to pound.

Zipping zebras, munching moose!
Hey, look! There goes a little goose.
I think I sound like Dr. Seuss,
For my rhymes I am renowned.
Susan Schickling, Grade 9
Merrol Hyde Magnet School, TN

Family Misfortunes
Goodbye Patsy, see you in heaven.
The admired little girl was gone now.
She'll be missed, but no one throws fits.
Aunt Maybell was leaving.
Jessie took care of Ring.

Hunter boys shot,
Boom. Boom.
Ring was hurt.
Jessie must take care of Ring now.
Ring was very fragile.

Papa was gone now,
His mind took a trip to space.
He left behind his place.
Week after week.

Ring, being fragile and hurt,
Said good-bye.
Coyotes came to get the chickens,
Ring fought back, he saved the day.

And papa came back, just in time.
The family was saved.
Ring was a gift.
Crystal Molina, Grade 7
Fuquay-Varina Middle School, NC

Redemption
He became the curse
To save us from the curse
He saved us. Jesus.
The prices that He paid
To take my sin away
He saved us, Jesus

Jesus was born but He knew
The price He had to pay
To take my sin away
And God so loved the world
That He redeemed us
He paid the price for us

He loves us all for us, everyone
Sinful and righteous
He loves us, Jesus
The grace and mercy that He gives
He was dead and now He lives
He lives with us, Jesus

He came, He lived, He loved
He died, He rose

For US.
Katelyn Parker, Grade 9
Powell First Baptist Academy, TN

The Cure of the Sea
In the deep happy water
In the coolness of the waves
After all my trouble
And all my pain

My sorrow lifts above me
And with it gone
I splash away, happily once more

This sight of happiness
The relief of pain
It never matters here
For I am happy
Once again
And here, I always will be

But now I must go
And I must leave
The happiness behind me
For I must find
Another cure
Like the one I found in the sea
Elena Keller, Grade 8
Dillard Drive Middle School, NC

Sometimes
Sometimes
you need
someone
but you
don't have
anyone
so stay close
to those you know
and love
them and
they will
love you back
and chances are
when you
need a friend
they will be
there because
it's hard
to go away
from
someone you love.
Caroline Newberg, Grade 7
Whitworth-Buchanan Middle School, TN

Boston Massacre
Death, anger, sorrow
Fighting, hesitating, strength
War, colonies, end
Austin Sumser, Grade 8
St Nicholas Academy - South, KY

Tree Shadow
Oh, tree shadow, voluminous and
Grand, your mysterious look intrigues
Me, with excitement
And despair, as your tree limbs

Breeze the midnight air.
The starry night proves
Deep and wide like a black
Crystal, twinkle in my eye.

Through the days dark
And bright, your shadow
Still remains the darkest
Under the moonlight.
Craig Dorsey, Grade 9
Robert C Byrd High School, WV

Fishing With My Dad
Fishing is fun,
fishing is great,
the sound of the water,
the smell of the bait.

Seeing the fish come out of their holes,
we gather the nets, the hooks, the poles.
I tighten my line with the fish in sight,
waiting for something just to bite.

I saw the fish swim away as my head shook,
the fish had taken my precious hook.
Nothing is better than a day with my dad,
than seeing the fish we could've had.
Ezra Calef, Grade 9
Robert C Byrd High School, WV

Sleep
Head on a soft pillow
Feathers, poking my head
Breathing slowly
Eyes almost shut

Comfort of home
In soft flannel sheets
Breathing slower
Eyes almost shut

Dreaming
Counting clouds one last sigh
Eyes closed
Sleeping
Kynadee Hoke, Grade 9
Wakefield High School, NC

The Flame
A flame is quivering upon
The wick, its red heart gleaming bright.
It dances higher, on and on,
Red reaches yellow, turning white.
It dreams of burning ever more
And crumbling the walls away.
The magnificent rushing roar
Of flame that toys with leaves: cats' play.
It pounces wildly, burning trees,
Devours the forest hungrily,
Then reaches grass and sips the breeze
While racing uncontrollably.
A tiny light is glowing bright —
The flame is just a small tea light.
Ellen Worthy, Grade 9
Middle Creek High School, NC

Rushing
The water engulfs me,
A sweet, cool embrace,
As I surge forward,
In my steady pace.

I can't help but feel superior,
And I want the water to dance,
While I push myself faster,
I could swim to France.

I don't feel exhaustion or boredom,
Not one ounce,
So I continue back and forth,
Ready to pounce.
Madeleine Nieto, Grade 8
Weddington Middle School, NC

Happiness
Happiness is a flower
Blooming in the sunny morning
It smells like homemade
Cookies fresh from the oven
It tastes like hot chocolate
On a snowy day
It feels like your crush
Kissing you on the cheek
It looks like a rainbow
After a storm
It sounds like the waves
On a day at the beach
It makes you love
Your life
Tyler Beebe, Grade 8
Leesville Road Middle School, NC

Shining Stones
Sparkling, twinkling, and shining, too
The gems are colored,
From yellow to blue.
The black night of onyx,
Or diamond's blue ocean breeze,
This fills with rainbow's color,
Do to light's wheeze.
Gold's great glory,
And ruby's rose red,
Shouts at you with beauty,
And is stored in your head.
Emerald's eerie evergreen,
Sapphire's soothing soft soul,
Topaz's tousled texture,
Silver's silent sensation.
Rings and watches,
Encrusted.
Pray they haven't rusted,
Sitting in the ray.
Hopefully they will be sold
By the end of the day.
Diamond Benson, Grade 9
White Station High School, TN

The Thing About Moms
Arms to fall into
Wrap around me
Like an envelope of warmth
She's always there
Ears to listen
To laughs
Cheers
Hear my teenage tantrums
And teenage tears
She's always there
Eyes to see my transformation
Girl turns woman
The successes I have
The mistakes I make
She's always there
One-of-a-kind
Always watching over me
Protecting
Irreplaceable
Part of me
I love you, Mom
Erin Woggon, Grade 8
J Graham Brown School, KY

Boston Tea Party
Boston Tea Party
Citizens dressed as Mohawks
Threw chests of iced tea
Amanda Hans, Grade 8
St Nicholas Academy - South, KY

Snow Day

The snow curled my hair as it fell
with not a drop of water, nor rain, nor hail.

It fell down with a blissful tune
and lasted, and lasted until mid-noon.

Then the sun came, to decay the day
and the icicles dripped and melted away.

Away it all went, all of the snow
and the water left a beautiful afterglow.

The grass was sprinkled with a silver dew
while the world around it seemed shiny and new.

The snowman had melted, he was gone and flat
and all that was left was his pipe and his hat.

The trees were swaying back and forth
as the wind came rustling in from the north.

The sun shone down upon the ground
and everything was peaceful, safe and sound.

I would like to go on about my snow day
but the next one just seems so far away.

Even though the snow, was melted by the sun
I know that my snow days have only begun.

Mackenzie Clark, Grade 8
Bargerton Elementary School, TN

Leaf

I am a leaf, on this oak tree.
Way up above,
way above some eyes can see.
Hidden in the branches, surrounded by my friends.
I am dancing in the wind, to the beat of its drum.
I sway to and fro,
without a thought in my head.
I am colorful, bright orange as the sun.
I think my life is great until the warm wind leaves
and the cold one comes.
He knocks me off my branch,
sending me flying through the air.
Floating to the ground, light as a feather.
I lay on the ground in fear
when a man comes
and sucks me up in a machine
and dumps me in the street
to be sent to an unknown place to die.
Lonely is what I feel
as I lay here in the dark,
wondering what has become of me.

Hannah Bailey, Grade 9
Parkersburg High School, WV

From Darkness, Into the Light

Everyone has their own path before them,
And you are the one to either go to the right or wrong one.
There are times when you will feel lost and alone
In the darkness with pain and grief,
You walk on a lonely road clouded with your thoughts
Too deep into them and not realizing what's ahead.
You stop and fall with darkness' temptation
To give up hope and abandon all faith,

But you only have two choices to make.
To stand back up to face your troubles head on
And finally fight and conquer your fears,
Or to just lie there hopelessly
To have the darkness defeat you
And slowly fade into nothing.

So make wise decisions and find inner peace,
But for those who think they wander in darkness
Stop and realize the blindfold you are wearing.
Take it off, open your eyes and you will see
The light that is shining so brightly, guiding your way.

Sharmaine Dela Peña, Grade 7
Ramsey Middle School, KY

Baseball Is My Home

I am from no fear, hard work pays off
Practice makes perfect, heart and passion for the game
I am from no pain no gain, the green grass and the brown dirt
Tons of rigorous training, going to workout instead of the movies
I am from failure more than success
Heroes never die but legends live forever
I am from fast and curve balls, groundball after groundball
The seams and the wood, the leather and the metal cleats
Tobacco, sunflower seeds, bad calls and arguments
I am from clearing the benches, bats being thrown
Coaches being thrown out of the game, fans going crazy
The fans singing "Take Me Out to the Ball Game"
I am from popcorn being sold, jerseys being brought
Teams warming their arms up, the National Anthem being sung
First pitch being thrown, umpire saying "Play ball"
I am from Baseball. I am its child.

Nate Mo Blakeney, Grade 8
Westchester Country Day School, NC

Backwards Clock

You see a smile, I feel a frown.
You think I'm up, I know I'm down
I act so happy, but that's just it.
It's an act, life's a backwards clock tock-tic.
A good mood is what I've seen, so I copy without thought.
I'm stealing others' words, it's an act I can't believe you bought.
The price you paid wasn't worth it, neither was mine.
My moods are acts, this is fact.
Life's a backwards clock, tock-tic, tic-tock.

Kirstin Martin, Grade 9
Wakefield High School, NC

Wanting to Be Found

Wanting to be found
I am nothing more than invisible
A ghost from that past that
Nobody loves
Have wanted to die before
But didn't have the guts to try it
Know that it could be so much worse
If I could change what I have done
in the past
I would
The life of a ghost is
excruciating
Nobody would or will love a ghost
How is life worth living if all you are is
Invisible
The scariest thing is the world
that I am afraid of
is being alone
But I guess that is how it is, how it always will be
Alone and Invisible

Taylor Barbrey, Grade 7
Union Middle School, NC

Athletic

I am athletic
I wonder about my future in baseball
I hear the sound of a baseball bat hitting a ball
I see the ball shooting across centerfield
I want the Red Mizuno glove
I am athletic

I pretend I'm pitching when I'm bored
I feel comfortable when I'm on a baseball field
I touch the ball as I throw it across the field
I worry about messing up, and getting yelled at
I cry never
I am athletic

I understand baseball, and it's difficulties
I say never say never
I dream of being a star in baseball
I try to do better at everything I do
I hope to go to the MLB
I am athletic

Gage Sherlock, Grade 8
Montgomery Central Middle School, TN

8:45

8:45 is the time,
8:45 is when we cried,
8:45 is the start of the crime.
It was a beautiful day,
It actually started in a normal way
Birds were singing,
Happiness was singing,
Just a beautiful day.
But out of nowhere,
BOOM BOOM,
It zoomed past their eyes,
Flight 11 has just crashed into the North Tower,
Everything went sour over these hours.
People were all in shock,
They were all on lock,
There were so many tear puddles everywhere
We will remember the 11th of September,
Because 8:45 was the time,
8:45 was when we cried,
8:45 was the start of the crime

Jason Liberto, Grade 7
Ramsey Middle School, KY

Transition

I watch the leaves fall.
They turn the ground from a boring green,
To a playful collage of colors, and I am pleased.
But then I look over at the trees.
Which now are as bare as a lost soul.
"No more colorful trees."
I sigh to myself.
Then again, there was a thought as I reminisced in my mind.
"SNOW!"
I was suddenly filled with jubilance.
Still, I was debating which season I liked best.
It felt as if I was a member of Congress,
Deciding a new law for our country.
I remembered how the smell of fall trees made me want to sleep.
I also remembered the white wonderland winter brought though.
Which season is better?
After a long argument between the seasons, I decided.
It was neither fall nor winter.
It was the transition between the two,
The images that I remember.

Hannah Orgel, Grade 7
White Station Middle School, TN

Yellowstone

Over large mountains
Through wide valleys
Across vast fields
Beyond deep pastures
In a national park
For us to enjoy

Jacob Lavender, Grade 9
Riverside High School, WV

Fishing

Fishing, giggling
Reeling, baiting, waiting
Daydreaming, pretending
Watching and wondering
My ultimate wish:
To catch a huge fish.

Zachary Daniel, Grade 8
Elkton School, TN

Peace Love and Happiness

Peace, love, and happiness,
Is how I describe my friends.
All are great, and
I can't choose which is best,
And I can't live without them all.

Peace is Olivia.
In all our friendship,
I can't remember one fight,
And she is always nice, fun, and friendly.
Olivia is peace.

Love is Alexis.
She was my very first best friend.
We're almost like sisters,
Because we are bigger than friends.
Alexis is love.

Happiness is Emma.
Silly little Emma.
She is always making jokes,
And finding ways to make people laugh.
Emma is happiness.

I love my peace, love, and happiness.
Claire Gerling, Grade 7
White Station Middle School, TN

Schooled

Schooled,
the story of Lionel,
the story of struggles,
of hope,
of proving himself.

Schooled,
an academic story,
of grades,
of skill,
of overcoming.

Schooled,
a very touching story,
where a boy reaches his dreams,
to master basketball,
and help his family.

Schooled,
a must-read story,
a grabbing story,
a wonderful story,
that will have you changed,
and begging for more.
Gabriel Medlin, Grade 7
Fuquay-Varina Middle School, NC

If I Were Nature

If I were a tree I would love
To be the most prettiest
Tree of them all
If I were the grass I would
Never want to be the
Color of brass
If I were the pond I would
Grow rather fond of the fish
That swims in me
If I were the flowers I
Would never cower away from kids
If I were a leaf I would
Keep myself by the trees
If I were nature I would never
Try to endanger myself or those
Around me
So please be nice to me
Linda (Lynn) Ward, Grade 7
East Millbrook Magnet Middle School, NC

Open Temptation

Forever I lay
Bare but open
Still but silent
Welcome all of the uncharted

Heavenly lights bind me now
Hell's temptations draw me down

One thousand hands hidden
By two million eyes
Dare to watch
As I reach for the sky

Silent mouths
Blow silent breaths
Forever screaming echoes
Of eternal death
Lexus Regan, Grade 9
Fairmont High School, NC

Living

Above all other
Beyond your thought
Against all odds
Within your heart
Into your dreams
Beyond tomorrow
Past yesterday
Above and beyond
Beside your best friend
Behind your fears
Toward the end
Until death do us part
Melissa Harper, Grade 9
Riverside High School, WV

The Dawn of Glory

The sunrise still had yet to come,
The morning gray and new,
Spider webs so skillfully spun,
Were shrouded, wet with dew.

At once, a ray of light sprang up,
Arrayed in brightest gold,
And the joy of which I supped,
Began to overflow.

The webs became fine linen,
The dew, pearls were made,
Spiders were now sitting,
On the cloth that they had weaved.

Gone was the dark and cold,
Of the pastel trees,
Gilded now in living gold
A flowing tapestry.

And in the sparkling sapphire sky,
The sun stands proud and tall,
O'er the earth he swiftly flies,
Beaming on us all.
Josh Barbour, Grade 9
First Baptist Academy, TN

Because of You

you were there for me
I was there for you
you're the reason my dreams
came true

you gave me strength
you showed me truth
it makes me wish I was
you

some things were just
out of reach

it made me wish
I was at the beach
as I looked up I thought
I could touch the sky

it's so hard to say goodbye
but, I'm everything
I am because of you

and all I can say is
thank you
Athena Ratzman, Grade 8
Dillard Drive Middle School, NC

The Story of Little John*
I read this book called Forbidden Forest,
When I was done my eyes were the sorest.
In this book there's a man named Little John,
Who has sandy hair and muscular arms.
He was banned from his town,
When he cracked the neck of a knight with brown hair.
In the forest where Little John wandered,
He stumbled upon a man named Red Roger.
He was a sly man thin but quick,
But up his sleeves he held dirty tricks.
He stole from the honest man,
And took coin from the best of hands.
Little John was right with Red Rogers ship,
Until he decided to go on a trip.
Little John threw Red Roger to the floor,
And let himself out the back door.
While wandering in the forest Little John dueled,
A man charming but cruel filled with laughter.
His name was Robin Hood and he promised,
To make John rich and help feed the poor.
If you want to learn more go read some more.

Zachary Bullock, Grade 7
Fuquay-Varina Middle School, NC
Inspired by "Forbidden Forest: The Legend of Robin Hood"

Caught in a Book
Anticipation and suspense fills me.
The words can't be read fast enough.
My nails, once long, are now short and splintered.
My eyes want to close but they can't,
I spare a glance at the clock,
When did the hours pass?
I am caught, in someone else's magical story,
And I must know more.
I smile
I laugh.
Yet I cry,
And I gasp from shock.
I wish it would never end,
Or,
Will it ever end?
But then,
I close it shut.

Rebekah Alvey, Grade 8
J. Graham Brown School, KY

The Course
The feeling of damp hard irons in your hands
The smell of fresh-cut grass on an early fall morning
Sensations you notice on any day
Old, new, broken clubs
Old, young, male, female
Good, bad, slow, fast
It all takes place on a golf course.

Alex Jackson, Grade 8
Weddington Middle School, NC

Christmas
Christmas is the best time of the year,
Christmas is the time of giving,
Christmas is a day to celebrate

Christmas is where dreams come true,
Christmas is a time with family and friends.
Christmas is what lights up kids' faces from presents.

Christmas is the time when it is cold and snowy,
Christmas brings people together,
Christmas bring joy and cheer to everyone.

Christmas is the time of forgiveness,
Christmas makes everyone love one another,
Christmas is the best time of the year

Without Christmas we wouldn't be ourselves,
That's why Christmas is important.
I love Christmas and you should too!

Christina Hyde, Grade 7
J Graham Brown School, KY

Mom
To the strongest person I know,
To the best person I know,
And to the person I look up to each and every day.
Always there for me no matter what,
Never far behind when I need help
Never far behind when I need her.
Spoiled me far too much,
But I always try to be thankful.
We talk like we're best friends,
I tell her every secret and I know it will never get out.
We also fight like we're best friends,
And it's always hard to stay mad at her for more than a day.
I thank God every day for the wonderful mother He gave me.
Thank You.

Alyx Pierson, Grade 8
West Middle School, TN

My Mind Is My Locker
My mind is like my locker, empty 'till I put things in.
I have things inside that I don't need.
When I open it, it can hurt people.
It's small until I put things in it.
It has stuff it shouldn't, and it gets angry it turns red.
It has things I wish I never had.
Things I didn't want to know.
Worst of all it can be very cold.
It hurts when it gets hit.
It stands up for itself and it's stubborn.
Things can get stolen as fast as you blink.
Bad things go through it, and bad things come out.
My mind Is my locker.

Bryan Dudley, Grade 8
Bradford High School, TN

Around the World
I want to travel around the Earth,
To China, Egypt, and Spain.
I dream of going for first class,
With fluffy seats on the plane.

I see mountains,
I see trees,
I see butterflies,
And bumblebees

I drank some juice along the way,
To the Indian Ocean.
I flew the borders of the coast,
I saw a view I adored the most.

I see the Pyramid of Giza,
And the Great Wall,
I wasn't disappointed about this trip at all!
Monique Vaillancourt, Grade 8
Shepherdstown Middle School, WV

My Brother
This is a poem to my brother, Alex,
whom I have fought with many times.
Your education comes in handy
when I am having trouble.
Although we don't get along
as well as we should,
I still love you very much.
You are smart and athletic,
one of the best in Kentucky.
You are humble
and do not brag about what you have.
You are always forgiving and loving,
even when you are mad.
Although I do not thank you enough,
I surely do appreciate
what a great brother you have been.
Love,
Adam
Adam Flynn, Grade 8
St Agnes School, KY

The Accident
Colors blur, lights are flashing
the world is a rainbow.
Children laughing, parents sighing
if only for a moment.
Metals crashing, tires squealing
the whole world seems to stop.
A women crying on the floor.
Colors blur, lights are flashing
the world is a rainbow;
but only through teary eyes.
Michaela Mitchell, Grade 8
Contentnea-Savannah K-8 School, NC

Lost Person
I am a lost person in the dark.
I wonder if I'm the only one.
I hear moaning behind the walls.
I see a light in the dark.
I want out of this place.
I am a lost person in the dark.

I pretend to talk to imaginary people.
I feel someone grab and pull my hair,
I touched and pulled back my hair.
I worry about the pain in my head.
I am a lost person in the dark.

I understand what the moaning is saying.
I say to them, where am I?
I dream to get out of the dark.
I try to get out by running and running.
I hope to find a way out.
I am a found person in the light
Katlyn Ellis-Gainous, Grade 8
Montgomery Central Middle School, TN

The Game
It was the last minute of the game,
My heart was jumping,
The score was the same,
My adrenaline was pumping.

I passed the ball to Curtis,
He didn't know what to do,
He was oh! so nervous,
So we all told him to shoot.

The ball went up high,
I didn't think it'd go in,
I'm not going to lie,
But that shot made us win.

After the game I came to him,
I told him it was a good shot.
Thanks for making us win,
Thank you, thanks a lot!
Hamza Kouser, Grade 7
All Saints' Episcopal School, TN

Cinderella
Cinderella
Kind, caring, beautiful, smart
Who loves dances
Who fears her sisters
Who needs love
Who gives of herself
Who believes in magic
Cinderella
James Hayes, Grade 8
Elkton School, TN

My Parents
This is a poem to my mom and dad
who have forgiven me a thousand times.
You come to support me
at all of my sporting events.
You comfort me when things go wrong,
and help me through if a day is long.
You push me through
all of those days that I have nothing to do.
I should say, "I love you,"
but sometimes it is hard to do
because I'm mad at you.
You buy me things I want that I don't need,
because you give in when I plead.
I should always be open to your love,
because you are both gifts from above.
I will always love you.
Austin
Austin Flynn, Grade 8
St Agnes School, KY

Our Very Special Mother
There is a place we call our mother
The Earth is what I mean
That we live on and should respect
And work to keep her green
She provides all of our needs
Each and every day
So that we can live, work, and play
In our own special way
Even though our mother
Has stood the test of time
We will lose our dear mother soon
For committing so many crimes
So now I declare that we work together
As a human race
To save our mother's life
And keep her right in place
Darian McGhee, Grade 9
White Station High School, TN

Lost in Hope
Hopeless is the steel jail cell bars holding
you captive with no sympathy,
It smells like sweat and energy giving
up for no apparent reason,
It tastes like sticky caramel that
seems impossible to swallow,
It feels like you're tangled in your
own chaos,
It looks like a barren chamber free
of all essence,
It sounds like crying, crying so hard
you can't stop to take a breath,
The icebound river that won't flow.
Maddy Kunkel, Grade 8
Leesville Road Middle School, NC

Second Continental Congress

In June 1776,
The Second Continental Congress,
Decided to write,
A Declaration of Independence,
To free the colonist's rights,
To set America free from Great Britain,
And their king,
To draft the Olive Branch Petition,
Or to start a war,
To make America an independent nation,
And not under the rules of King George III,

So they drafted a petition,
And sent it to King George III,
Who decided for war,
And sent troops to fight,
America prepared for war,
And Washington was in charge,
To shape troops and get them ready for a long war.
The American Revolution had begun!

Amber Willett, Grade 8
St Nicholas Academy, KY

Winter Camping

While camping in the snow,
The white flakes always bring out the true beauty of nature.
The lush forest creates a great place to camp
And hide from the cold wind.

One of my favorite parts of winter camping is
To have no snakes, no bugs to contend with.
With the pests gone,
I easily venture into the snowy woods.

Deep in the woods I find fallen branches,
Pine trees, and wild animals
And am careful not to wake a dormant bear.
Winter camping keeps me energetic, alert, yet peaceful.

Jeffrey Cargile, Grade 7
White Station Middle School, TN

Bluebells

Over the hills and across the river
through fields and valleys a many.
Past lambs and cows and little brown bunnies,
to the place where blue fields lie.
To the little water creek just between the trees
where the bluebells lay all around.
The sweet smell of flowers and buzz of bees
dragonflies lay on the ground.
A slight sway in the breeze as they dance together,
tilting their necks to the shore.
A bluebell is peaceful, perfect and pure.
My mother will love them I'm sure.

Hannah Downs, Grade 9
Wakefield High School, NC

Master of Disguise

His smile is bright and sincere
But his eyes are full of pain and fear
He laughs so joyful and loud
While his heart is breaking without a sound

His mind lingers to thoughts of her
Everyone thinks he is happy; what a clever actor
Stuck in a world of self-condemnation
His mind and heart are filled with frustration

When he was with her it felt like a sugar high
But without her he feels lonely and shy
He seems fine, but another story underlies
Truth be told, he is a master of disguise

His smile is bright and sincere
But his eyes are full of pain and fear
He laughs so joyful and loud
While his heart is breaking without a sound

Sydney Jones, Grade 9
Wakefield High School, NC

Freezing Fear

Fear is the creature at the very bottom
Of the food chain,
The weak victim.
It smells like sweat and blood,
Tastes of bitter soap at the back of your throat.
It feels like sweaty palms,
And sore feet and muscles,
That have worked so hard to escape danger.
It looks like a demon,
Malice ever-present in the eyes and facial expression.
It sounds like a pitter-patter of four feet,
One predator, one prey.
Fear sends chills down your spine,
And freezes your life for that one moment of terror.

Sloane Coble, Grade 8
Leesville Road Middle School, NC

Triangle's Victim

Broken, battered, burned,
She is one of many.
Her family passes by again and again,
But still they do not see.
A glint of gold catches their eye,
And they lean down to another charred body.
"No, not her," they sigh.
They pass her by once more;
Tears fall readily among these rows
Of black, beaten bodies.
Her locket glints, and they finally see.
Home she goes,
For all eternity.

Abigail Hill, Grade 9
Bearden High School, TN

The Balance

Mist through the trees
Flowing, snaking,
Forming shapes to scare children
Guarding the secret it protects
Deep through the trees
A creature lives
Holding the balance in its hands
Keeping good above evil
Evil below good
And in the other world
The same creature resides
Keeping the balance,
But in a different way
For there to be a good world
An equally evil world must exist
Where good is hiding
And cannot be trusted
But in the other
Faith resides
And trust in all things good

Hannah Hemming, Grade 8
J Graham Brown School, KY

I Am

I am Trace Oglesby.
I wonder about the universe.
I hear the sounds of nature.
I see the stars.
I want world peace.
I am Trace.

I pretend to be anything I want.
I feel happy.
I touch the hearts of others.
I worry about the future, good and bad.
I cry only when I feel a crushing pain.
I am Trace.

I understand complicated physics.
I say funny things like a comedian would.
I dream of being an engineer or physicist.
I try hard at everything I do.
I hope that I can live my life to the fullest.
I am Trace Oglesby.

Trace Oglesby, Grade 8
Roanoke Valley Early College, NC

Pikeview Middle

Pikeview Middle
New, big
Exciting, interesting, amazing
Huge building
Creative masterpiece

Matthew Bragg, Grade 7
Pikeview Middle School, WV

Sweet Rain

I step outside of my warm, well-lit house
And into the cold, dark world
The steady drizzle makes me shiver
And goosebumps appear on my exposed arms
But I tilt my head upward, closing my eyes
And the sweet rain continually splashes onto my face,
Leaving me feeling refreshed and wide-awake
I try to catch a few on my tongue, like snowflakes
But the sweet raindrops seem to be deliberately avoiding the dark, gaping cave
In spite of this I become lucky every once in awhile
And the unfortunate subjects disappear into the tunnel of my neck
Then I look around
And all I can see are a few lampposts and the rain
Body and mind are wiped clean of their worries and sins
And I am left feeling calm, clean, and collected
No, I do not mind this cold, dark world
Because the rain is my friend

Divya Prasad, Grade 7
White Station Middle School, TN

Past America

The America that we know today is not that same as past America they say.
The past America was no choice for a person who wanted a say.
It was for a person who always answered with the word okay.
You were taken from love, the love that you had planned on spending your life with.
There was always wonder about the message you would get the next day.
The message that might explain your broken heart.
The message that would change your life.
Whether good or bad you would always see.
You had no say so only if you were a fighter.
"A fighter you'll be and a fighter you shall do well."
Blood tears always being shed to death.
The tears that you cry for the one you love.
Smiles being seen every day on a face.
Because their loved ones are back with them in their rightful place.
The past America might not be to your liking but it is the past that made the present.
And that's how we live in Today's America.

Williesha Banister, Grade 8
Emma B Trask Middle School, NC

Insanity

I am Insanity.
I ingress your mind, a teasing pestilence I am
I have the power to overtake your mind, and will do so as I please.
A blasphemous mockery of how you used to be, and what you fear most.
No one will ever understand you, or stand by you.
You are alone, cut off from the world.
While you revel in your great feats, remember, I am still there.
A sagacious fear, I am.
I have stolen your mind…a mind that was never yours to begin with.
I am Insanity.
I fill your body with convulsed actions of impetuosity.
The life you once knew is a cessation, finished, ending…over.

Julia Mileski, Grade 8
Dillard Drive Middle School, NC

Where I Was Raised

I am from Sissonville
I am from the mountains
I have been playing football since I was little
I play basketball
I play baseball
Good at sports
Athletic and healthy
Favorite TV show when I was little was SpongeBob
Like to work outdoors
I am a nephew of a store owner
Am a good Christian
Love to go to church
Like to hang out with my friends
Love to go hunting
Like to go fishing
Don't like school
Get good grades
Don't like to get in trouble
Don't miss church, unless I am sick
I am a good kid

Austin Burford, Grade 8
Sissonville Middle School, WV

Where I'm From

I am from a region called the south
Y'all and might could are often said from the mouth
I am from mashed potatoes and good bread
And if you don't go to church, you'll sure be dead
I am from fried chicken, any day
Arby's, Hardee's, and maybe some Chick-Fil-A
I am from a land where we used to have slaves
But the Civil War put that act in the grave
I am from a people often called "rednecks"
And some of our states are in a financial wreck
I am from a place where cowboys are everywhere
And even a dusting of snow makes driving a scare
I am from a land of rodeo and horse races
And, for some reason, people like NASCAR chases
I am from many farmers and crops
Everyone drinks sweet tea, till the last drop
I am from a place of much fun
A place where you are free to run
I am from a region that I love
No other place will ever come above

Tommy Boggis, Grade 8
Westchester Country Day School, NC

Where I'm From

The feeling of scoring my first touchdown
The smell of the fresh cut grass
The grip of a new football
The taste of the sweetest victory
These are the memories that last
Overall, football is my best
Football is my nest
Football is my life
And football is my wife
Football is my soul
Football never grows old
I will always play
My beloved football game
Football has begun at home
While football is for me alone
Football is my home
Football has yet to be cheated
While in football, our team will never be beaten
Football is too fun
And football is where I'm from.

Jared Wilkinson, Grade 8
Sissonville Middle School, WV

Gema

Gema I'm hurting, I'm missing you too much.
You're gone, a friend gone, but never forgotten.
The story so unreal, but every word said true.
Baby girl, you're in a better place now.
I'll never forget you,
I'm just waiting to see you again.

October 7th, 2011, a day that scared us all.
October 7th, 2011, the day you left us behind.
I didn't see you on your last day.
I heard you looked gorgeous in your dress.
I couldn't go to say my last goodbye.
I tried and tried but couldn't.

Now you're in heaven,
shuffling with the angels.
I promise I won't forget you,
that's a promise I'll always keep.
Your smile is now the sun in the sky,
and the tears we all shed the stars at night.

Crystal Guevara, Grade 9
Lee County High School, NC

The Sun Provides

The sun provides
It gives us life
Without it, life would cease to exist
Its rays make plants grow
It gives us energy to go throughout the day
The sun provides

Ramsey Mona, Grade 8
Weddington Middle School, NC

A Night of Fright

I hear you, can't see you
Powerful and very strong
I can't wait until you're gone.
The windows begin to shake.
My home starts to quake.
Help me through this night of fright.

Brandon McCoy, Grade 8
Weddington Middle School, NC

My Mind Is Like My Locker
My mind is like my locker;
It often has many dents and bumps,
But always comes back to be useful.
My mind opens up to anyone
Just like my locker!
It sometimes gets slammed around,
But always comes back to be a glowing beauty.
When school starts it is empty.
When school ends, it often becomes empty
And stays that way 'til school starts again.
The walls hold my boundary
And the door holds all my openings to a new world.
It holds all my knowledge,
And has limits of how much it can hold.
Anyone can come by and bother me,
I just hold my ground.
It is high above everyone else,
We are both helpful and always there.

Olivia Barnett, Grade 8
Bradford High School, TN

Forever Love Her
Through the graveyard, I walk alone,
To see my Nana's plaque of stone.
Hades cares not of your sorrows or pains,
So he took my grandmother far far away.
She died in her sleep, on her bed which she laid
I'll forever love her, now and always.

My family did mourn, for what seemed like forever,
Crying for her in this dreadful endeavor.
Our loss did affect us in so many ways,
I'll forever love her, now and always.

I know that in heaven is where she will be,
Smiling and waiting to get to greet me.
Though I do miss her, a better place I know she is in
Her kind gentle smile I know I will miss.
Our happy times, I do count those days
I'll forever love her, now and always.

Cameron Moore, Grade 8
George M Verity Middle School, KY

Where I'm From
I am from a family that's had our struggles and made our mistakes.
But we always come together on a birthday with cakes.
I am from my grandma who I lost way too soon.
And I learned very early suicide equals gloom.
I am from my brother who I look up to every day.
I will follow in his footsteps each and every step of the way.
I am from my dad who has the most wonderful curls.
And I want him to know I will forever stay his little girl.
I am from my mother who is so sweet.
She always makes me the most wonderful treats.

Morgan Root, Grade 7
Ramsey Middle School, KY

A Nightmare's Lullaby
A nightmare's lullaby,
Screamin' bloody murder,
In the center of my ears.
I cry, I scream, but none can hear me,
Over the crucifixion of a dream gone wrong.
My body shakes, my head trembles.
Music plays in the background, it gets louder and louder.
I stop, I try to scream, I try to awake…
But the nightmare just won't stop.
Death creeps behind my closed eye lids.
Life begins to fade.
I see myself in black and white…
All seems to slow down…
My heart beat is baboom, baboom, baboom, baboom.
And at this point the music is as loud as it'll go.
More real than ever, my body goes numb.
I SCREAM.
The music stops,
A nightmare's lullaby.
Meet me at the equinox,
I need you here tonight.

Sarah Baker, Grade 9
Challenger High School, NC

Clint
This is a poem to my brother, Clint,
whom I fight with all the time,
but I know you will always be there for me.
I will miss you when you go off to college,
but I know in my heart,
that we will always stay in touch.
I can't stand you sometimes,
you get under my skin just to make me mad,
but I know we will never stay in a fight.
I cant stand to see you sick, or in pain.
I am there for you always.
You are my brother,
and I will love you forever,
no matter what!
Kayla

Kayla Noble, Grade 8
St Agnes School, KY

The Shot Heard Round the World
The
shot heard round the
world. It is unknown who fired
it. It is unknown if they were British or
Patriot. It is unknown if they were wealthy or
poor. But we do know it began a war. A war over
Independence. It started a revolution. The
beginning of a war that would bring
the most powerful country
to its knees.

Sarah Eichenberger, Grade 8
St Nicholas Academy - South, KY

High Merit Poems – Grades 7, 8, and 9

Lost in the Music
Snapping my fingers to the rhythm
As I sing along
I don't know what this song is
All I know is, I like it.

I feel free
I am in my own little world
Putting all other unnecessary thoughts to the back of my mind.

My parents are saying something
I don't know what they are saying
Focusing on the music
Voices are getting louder now
I am slowly fading off
Back into reality

The music stops
Mom yells
"TURN THE MUSIC DOWN!!!"
I am speechless
Completely unaware of my surroundings,
All I can do is sing.
Brooklyn Blackburn, Grade 7
South Oldham Middle School, KY

Cabin in the North Woods
Secluded in the North Woods of Minnesota.
Hidden along the Gunflint Trail.
Beyond the Fish Hatchery on South Shore Drive
Birch and aspen trees tower above.
The smell of pine lingers in the air.
Vibrant colored lupines dance in the wind.
Wild roses and daises blanket the ground.
A spectacular view of Devils Track Lake
Northern Pike and Walleye tease the fishermen.
The lonely cry of the loon echoes across the lake.
Breathtaking sunsets paint the sky.
The Aurora borealis reveals its splendor.
Constructed of cedar and covered by a tin roof
Built for rest, relaxation, and fun
Heated by a wood burning stove
A peaceful haven away from it all
The Gongoll family cabin in the North Woods
LaRae Crenshaw, Grade 7
White Station Middle School, TN

Hunting
H aving fun throughout the day
U nder the trees as I sit and look for deer
N ight time is approaching, silence fills the air
T ry to hear the movement through the leaves
I see my target through the maze of trees
N estled in my blind
G athering my nerve, as I pull the trigger
Lane Gorrell, Grade 8
Dillard Drive Middle School, NC

Christmas
Snow drifts in the air,
Carols beautifully sung,
The smell of gingerbread cookies tiptoed up the stairs,
To tease me and
It is plain to see,
Christmas is here.

The children wake up early,
And circle the tall, decorated Christmas tree,
Each open presents with bright expressions,
And play with toys with pleasure.

The women enjoy their time in the kitchen by cooking,
While all the men congregate around the TV,
This day is fun for everyone,
For even the babies who babble with joy.

This day is great,
With happiness and cheers,
Everyone makes the most of it,
But it comes only once a year.
Emily Roy, Grade 7
White Station Middle School, TN

Creative Writers We Are to Be
The painter's brush moves over canvas
the image brought out from an unknown place.

A sculptor's hand in the clay creates
the facial expression in mere minutes.

The designer's choice of color turns
the mundane into something wonderful.

Each brings something that wasn't
into this world that is fresh and new.

Our call is to create as those ones have
a futuristic story written on unused paper.

Our links all different in their colors and
with a pencil never tried in another's grasp.

A story to unfold page after page,
and adventure written from a mystery
by the creative writers we are to be.
Olivia Hodges, Grade 8
Weddington Middle School, NC

Big Buck
There once was a big buck I'd been tracking.
His ways to elude me had began lacking.
With one shot to the crown, he fell to the ground.
Now he's in my freezer in assorted packing.
Jordan Spangler, Grade 9
Riverside High School, WV

The Soldier

One morning he got the call
The news was grave
He told his friends and family
That he may not come back
He was going to war
    The flight was long
And he was nervous
Thinking about what was ahead
He looks out the window
He sees the station
    He walks out the plane
Gets his lecture and his gun
Then he and his group went out
He's been gone for 2 days now
And he's already homesick
    After 5 months of torture
He was finally sent home
When he arrived at the airport
His mom was waiting
And all his friends and family were outside
Then they all went to eat

Connor Cambron, Grade 7
Ramsey Middle School, KY

Try Harder

Smiling towards the outside world,
Finding it easier to hide,
Finding it easier to lie,
Trying to try,
Breathing just to get by,
Wishing one day I'll stop crying,
Dreaming someday I'll fly,
Fly higher than the clouds,
Go farther than the moon,
I'll wish upon a star,
Maybe it'll all come true.
I'll dream away,
Wish more today,
Just breathe the same way,
I try a little harder,
Maybe I'll go farther,
Maybe today will be better,
I'll try harder.
Smiling towards the outside world,
Finding it easier to cry,
Finding it easier to try.

Brittany Ripley, Grade 8
Munford Middle School, TN

Forests

Forests hold many things
Birds nesting and herbs growing
Things are plentiful

Jacob Lewis, Grade 8
Pigeon Forge Middle School, TN

Joy of Life

Joy is like being surrounded by trees,
On a bright sunny day;
It smells like dew on grass
In the early morning,
It taste like fresh bread in a bakery,
Making all who pass by smile,
It feels like the warmth of the sun
On a cold day,
It looks like a water fall,
Calming to all,
It sounds like laughter,
Intoxicating,
Bring all who are around in on the joke,
Brings life to the fullest potential.

Sarah Bryant, Grade 8
Leesville Road Middle School, NC

Christmas

It's all about Christmas,
I like to spend time with my family.
It's all about Christmas,
I like exchanging presents.

It's all about Christmas,
I like going sledding in the winter snow.
It's all about Christmas,
I like going to look at the Christmas lights.

It's all about Christmas,
I like going to church on Christmas
What's Christmas all about?
"CHRIST."

Chris Hefler, Grade 7
Ramsey Middle School, KY

Power in Death

Fleeting through the skies,
Burning in the eyes.
Judge's power, set by threes,
Bow before them, on thy knees.
Who has power, none but they,
They who judge, all the day.
Already judged, the dead given power,
Weapons abroad, guarding Judge Tower.
Extraordinary souls, when in life,
Are given power, of gift or strife.
After the living die, then they are judged,
Good or Evil, both are then nudged.
Gift or punishment, every hour,
Only the judges, are given the power.

Cody Strickland, Grade 9
Riverside High School, WV

That Night

Pitch black, nothing to see
Hooting in a distance
flickering lights click, click
Cold breeze slithers down my neck

I hear footsteps
Clicking stops, power is out
All I see is my breath
leaves rustle around me

I see light in the distance
A man stares me down
years have passed by
All I remember is that night

Bako Darwesh, Grade 7
White Station Middle School, TN

Believers

I'm alone again.
I can feel it too.
You lied to me.
I believed in you.
You convinced me to love you.
I fell for it too…
You told me you loved me.
I believed in you.
Stupid me.
Stupid you.
You lead me to fall.
Fall for you.
You abandoned me.
I would've never abandoned you.

Brooke White, Grade 8
Harding Academy of Memphis, TN

Paradise

There is a place, oh yes
Where everything is green
There is not ever a mess
And the trees are tall and lean
The waves crash upon the shore
It is truly amazing
This place is not a bore
It will make you feel like a king
the sun will always shine
It will never rain
This place is amazing
The sun shines
It is truly dazzling
This place is all mine.

Conor Brennan, Grade 7
White Station Middle School, TN

The New Me
Why am I still in love with you?
you broke my heart
you tore me down
you didn't ask me how I felt
so now I'm looking
so you are standing there before me
not saying anything
the love I have for you is over
the long days
the long nights
the lovely kisses
the warm hugs.

Gone

So now all I have to say is nothing
you were never here
and you never have been
you're not worth anything to me
so now I'm moving on with my life
and so far it's good!!!
Vendela Safford, Grade 8
Kinston Charter Academy, NC

We Were Friends
We were once friends
But that all changed
We used to tell each other secrets
Hang out every weekend
You changed our friendship
You got obsessed with boys
I stayed the same
Still wanting to tell secrets
And hanging out on the weekends
I like boys but not like you
I miss us being friends
But you don't even know I exist
What happened to my best friend
You left me alone
And I want my best friend back
You were always there for me
Where are you now
You understood me
You liked me for me
And not someone else
We were once friends.
Marlee Renn, Grade 7
J Graham Brown School, KY

The Geography of Greece
Greece geography
It was a mountainous land
Three seas surround it
Shaye Allen, Grade 7
St Nicholas Academy - South, KY

I Am a Dancer
I am a dancer.
I point my feet, twirl, and jump.
I pirouette, stretch, and bend.
I feel pain from injuries.
I feel defeat from better dancers,
yet I always keep going.
I smile, I practice, and I perform.
I have grace and exquisiteness.
I do not dance because I am happy,
I am happy because I dance.
When I step on stage I hear the applause.
I present my routine and give my best.
Sometimes I thrive and sometimes I fail.
I am brave and strong.
I don't dance for riches and fame,
I dance to express my emotions.
I am talented, loved, and happy.
I represent determination and beauty.
I am a dancer.
Victoria Hudnall, Grade 9
Riverside High School, WV

I Cried
Brutal cries fill the air
As the war rages on
An enemy charges
At me
A man
Is stopped in mid-run
By a bullet
He falls to the ground
Writhing in an amount of pain
That I will never know
I watched
Watched him die
Later
I cried
Pouring what little soul I had
To the ground
I cried
Till I could cry no more
But the war rages on
Rosa Hannah, Grade 9
Middle Creek High School, NC

Plain White
It's as cold as ice outside
Everything is white
Snowflakes are falling from the sky
The wind chips at your face
Nature is dead
Everything's like a blank canvas
Kids are playing
It's like a winter wonderland
Jessica Hutton, Grade 9
Riverside High School, WV

Depths of Her Death
A death that has yet to come,
A beating heart fades,
Hades shall take her soul soon,
Then a once vibrant life,
Shall exist no more.

What shall become of me,
When her death arrives?

The depths of her death,
Shall be severe,
Many shall grieve,
Over this wondrous treasure,
Oh, what a loss it will be.

What shall become of me,
When her death arrives?

A treasured lady,
The biggest spaces in my heart,
One of the many,
Greatest joys,
Of my life

But what shall become of me,
When her death arrives?
Casey Goldey, Grade 8
George M Verity Middle School, KY

Story of My Life
Life is like a citrus grove.
Leaves and fruit are high above
my head. Look at the
glowing orbs of orange.

Contrasting colors seem to show
those goals reserved for when I grow.
They're too much for me yet, since
nothing rhymes with orange.

My future holds a promise, now
but in what way could I vow
to succeed in time when
nothing rhymes with orange.

Like this verse and how it flows:
close, but imperfection shows.
In part, caused by the fact
that nothing rhymes with orange.

I can presently see the flaws
of my poetic design, because
despite my best wishes,
nothing rhymes with orange!
Kayla Beckham, Grade 9
White Station High School, TN

The Sun
In the sky
Above the clouds
Beyond the moon and below the stars
Between Heaven and Earth
Around lie the planets
Within our galaxy
Around, it creates bright light
Across the universe it shines
In the center of all planets
Unto space it lies
Beyond our distance of travel
For it is a golden ball called the sun.
Jennifer Henson, Grade 9
Riverside High School, WV

Color
Rainbow
Holds these loved things
They brighten our day
They darken our night
Yellow sun
Navy night
Skin, eyes, and hair
All beautiful
But different
Through the eyes of the world
They are colors
They are us
Justice Lawrence, Grade 9
Wakefield High School, NC

Supercars
A supercar, a supercar,
loud, colorful, and fast.
Charges down the street,
like a yellow flash!
Supercar, Supercar.
Light, expensive, and bold.
Full of fine materials,
carbon fiber and gold.
What is the point of these,
fast, loud machines?
To entertain the enthusiasts and kids,
to quench their thirst for speed.
Jordan Massenburg, Grade 9
Wakefield High School, NC

Family
Family at times can be very fun
But sometimes they're like sticky gum
They're stuck in your hair
Then they're always there
And until you cut your hair you can't run
Austin Smith, Grade 7
Pigeon Forge Middle School, TN

Masks
When you are not true to yourself it's lying to yourself
which forms a mask that hides the true you
then which blinds the people around you
and eventually blinds yourself and when you
try to find yourself you have nothing to find
And when try to strip that mask off
you wonder what you will find under that mask

The mask whispers mischievously what is there to live for keep me on
filled with confusion you agree
then soon another mask forms, a mask of regret
it is a burden that eats and you become the
host and it becomes the parasite
then soon enough those masks that you have
created will destroy who you are

This leaves questions like why live and who am I
concealed by the mask that answer will
never be found, it would be like trying to
go to the moon without a spaceship, it's impossible
Stanford Louden, Grade 8
J Graham Brown School, KY

Kites
When children sprint
Their feet thump against the hard black asphalt
Colorful streamers trail behind
The smell of fresh cut grass hovers
As they reach the immense, grassy field,
The sun blows warm air into their faces.
White string in hand, a girl dashes across the peaceful meadow
Followed by a boy and another and yet another
Until kites fill the air, slowly inching their way upward
Painting the sky with vibrant colors
Bright red, pale green, orange, dark blue
Squares, triangles, boxes, planes
Pictures of characters or just simple frames
Spinning and flying and loop-de-looping
Like a roller coaster at an amusement park
Suddenly a string twists and breaks
And the colorful kits slowly drifts down to earth
This wind becomes quiet as if waiting to see what will happen.
As the girl approaches the kite, she quickly ties it back on, and begins to jog, and
The wind breathes a sigh of relief as the kites begin to once again rise to the heavens
Sharon Thomas, Grade 7
White Station Middle School, TN

My Favorite Place to Be
The scent of diesel from the John Deere tickled my nose.
I could feel the warm sun beaming down on my back as I slowly got to work.
The sound of the cows mooing made me internally laugh to myself.
The salty tasting sweat trickled into my mouth as the day went on.
I loved the panoramic view of the most beautiful scenery I had ever seen,
Ohh how I love the country life.
Teagan Dupeire, Grade 9
Powell First Baptist Academy, TN

Time Is Running Out

She knows,
    knows as she's looking into the mirror —
                in the mirror she sees a broken body
                      It sneers: you can hardly call that a body.
                              Her call for help many times gone unanswered.
                            time is running out.
                          gone.
                    Many sneers, no stop
                    Cruel words, no stop.
                              words, thrown like daggers, branding her, her lifestyle, as sins.

    knows that she is slowly killing herself
        she is ticking herself off the list
            tick-tock
            tick
            slowly
                                  stop.
She knows.
            tick.
                            time is running out.

Amy Chen, Grade 9
Bearden High School, TN

Cutting Loose

We are learners, scholars, athletes, and coworkers.
We work together, we examine others, like an animal before it catches prey, and we come lurkers.
We help one out even though it's a hassle,
But we know we might need help and we can count on them when it matters.
We make an effort, trying to succeed.
But we make mistakes and try not to complain about our daily issues, because it could be worse.
We tend to become independent as we grow older and wiser,
And this keeps us wondering what the world holds for us, like a story.
As a population makes room to breathe,
We get a little stronger with a push or a shove.
We rise to our own rhythm and dance to our own beat.
We can't help, but sing our own song.
And to cut loose, and be ourselves.

Katelyn Bond, Grade 9
Parkersburg High School, WV

A Walk

The adventure begins at the corner stop sign, worn with age.
Traversing along a cracked sidewalk, I gaze at the sky.
A clear night, with no stars in sight.
The faint light of the moon is all I have to not be enveloped in pitch black.
The air smells like the crisp scent of nature.
One last song of a mockingbird, then all is silent.
The tall oaks hover above me, swaying in tempo with the howling wind.
The hushed sounds of a cricket add nothing but a quarter note to the melody of the dark.
I reach toward a reddish-colored leaf, to find that it is frozen solid.
A sharp crackle fills my ears as I slowly enclose my numb fingers around the newly crushed leaf.
Sighing, I trudge on, battling the whipping wind.
The journey ends where it started, at the corner stop sign.

Srishti Arora, Grade 7
White Station Middle School, TN

Perfect Isn't Perfect

I have brown hair and brown eyes
I have told numerous lies
My teeth are crooked and off-white
Do you think I'm a beautiful sight?
My clothes are out of date
And I'm too small for goodness sake!
I get confused with that old hard math
But I'm still looking for the right path
Sometimes I cry when I get hurt
Sometimes I feel like dirt!
I think to hard on so much stuff
Some people say I'm a diamond in the rough
But I told them I wasn't worth it
But a wise person said "Perfect isn't Perfect"
Those grateful words change my ways
Even to this tedious day
Sometimes I looked in the mirror worrying
Of what might come knocking
But then I just say
"I'm just the perfect that isn't perfect"

Rebecca Chandler, Grade 7
Harpeth Middle School, TN

Emily

This is a poem to my sister, Emily,
whom I've hurt a million times.
You are always there for me,
in good times and in bad.
I can ask you any question,
because I'm almost always with you.
When I'm not, you're on my mind,
whether I want you there or not.
If we get in a fight,
it never lasts long and soon
we are laughing again.
We have so many funny memories
that it's hard not to smile
when we remember them.
We have a connection that only sisters share,
and it always seems to keep us together.
You're the cheese to my macaroni,
the peanut butter to my jelly,
and I kind of love you.
Lily

Lily Thaman, Grade 8
St Agnes School, KY

Winter

Jack Frost knocking on your window sill,
Calling out to you with a smile filled with glee.
The town that you now live in is winter white,
This is all happening on December nights.

Cold white blankets of snow uneven by your footsteps,
Bundled up into many layers of coats.
Christmas holiday creeping up so brightly
Lighting up the town; filled with bright Christmas linings.
Reds, blues, greens, and yellows
Yummy hot chocolate with mini marshmallows.
Winter is here.

Following up after Christmas,
With everyone creating New Year wishes.
The end of winter is soon approaching
With spring coming near.
The trees that were once bare,
Have blossomed into a new flare with spring finally here.
And all the winter whites will be back around next year.

Tiana Washington, Grade 7
East Millbrook Magnet Middle School, NC

Screams and Cries

There is a boom as loud as a train crash, it gets as hot as the sun,
I hear screams and cries, I don't know why.
I reach in my pocket, I get out my phone,
I tell my mom, I can't come home.
I ask why my building exploded,
She says a plane crashed into the building,
She cried and cried and I asked why,
She says because my baby is gonna die.
I told her "I love you,"
She said "I do too,"
I hung up the phone,
Now I'm alone.
I run over to the flight of steps,
I see the smoke as dark as night,
I run and run with all my might,
Finally I run down the last flight.
I ran through the doors,
I'm finally free,
Oh how close that was,
It could have been me.

Skylar Aubrey, Grade 7
Ramsey Middle School, KY

Black Roses

He gives me red roses
He says that he loves me
Red Roses are beautiful
And so are you, he tells me
But will he still say that
When the Roses go Black

Pauline McCurry, Grade 9
East Rutherford High School, NC

The Race

The race
More like a challenge
Not just a sport to me
More of a lifestyle not a hobby
Harder than any other sport you'll ever do
Pyramid Valley is were it all began for me

Jacob Vance, Grade 9
Riverside High School, WV

High Merit Poems – Grades 7, 8, and 9

Fairy Dust

It's that perfect time of year, I say
When the snow and the icicles gleam all day,
Cats and dogs come inside to be warm,
And friends drink hot cocoa while watching it storm;
Snowflakes and flurries are all some might see,
But children's faces give much glee;
Snowmen and angels fill up the streets,
Marshmallows with hot chocolate are the sweetest of treats;
Ornaments and lights hanging on the tree;
This is a winter wonderland, and we all agree;
Sugar cookies in the shape of beloved Saint Nick;
Children will eat them, until they get sick;
Rudolph and Prancer, two of the best reindeer, are excited
Both are excited, for Christmas is near!
Staring at snowflakes, the ice, and the snow,
This wintery bliss be back by next year,
With the same chill, that I love and know;
The fairies that sprinkle icy shimmering dust,
Shall take a rest from their hard labor,
For it's not that easy to create a winter wonderland.

Riley Williamson, Grade 7
White Station Middle School, TN

Shattered Memories

Ever since that day…
It broke my heart
You were coming to surprise me
Until it surprised you…
That fateful day in the hospital
We lost you for a month until you came to…
But that moment when you opened your eyes
You looked at everybody but me…
They say you lost a part of your memories
And that broke me down…
I was hoping for a whole month that we could be together again
But it's too late now that your memories are shattered…
They told me to leave you and move on.
But how could I when we achieved so much?
Now all is lost and the past is past…
I can't forget you so I'll just keep you buried in my heart
I watch you from afar as you laugh and smile with a new girl…
You forgot me in your mind but I know that someday you will know
That in your heart you will remember our memories
Forever not shattered…

Ashley Vang, Grade 8
Weddington Middle School, NC

Music to My Ears

Choices, selection, play
Beat, tempo, groove
Dancing, singing, laughing
Rock, swing, jazz
Happiness, joy, love
Music to my ears.

Caroline Jones, Grade 7
Wendell Middle School, NC

Wildfire

A spark is born during the dead of the night,
For the mighty god has risen once more.
Atop his head rests a golden crown
Dripping with red and orange jewels.
A smoky essence surrounds him
Like a liquid illusion of fear.
No living thing dares to cross his path,
Or he will send soldiers of flame,
And they will cease to exist.
Crack, hiss flick!
Being rooted to the spot,
Trees becomes an easy target.
Blazing showers of power devour them.
He stretches out his arms
Eager to annihilate more innocent victims.
Yearning to destroy but finding his strength spent,
As he grows weaker.
Then the night turns as silent as a dream.
The God of Destruction slumbers again.

Xiya Wu, Grade 7
White Station Middle School, TN

Scraping the Sky

Large as life itself
Ominously gazing down upon you
Seemingly never ending
The doors slide open and you step in
Up, up, up the floors

Hearing the beep as the doors shimmy open
You feel like you're on top of the world; above everyone
Butterflies in your stomach
Know your safety
You are a god
But don't lean on the glass!
People are ants beneath you; so very tiny

The doors slide open and you step in
Down, down, down the floors
Hearing the same beep as before
Still large as life
Still gazing down upon you

Chris Kelly, Grade 9
Riverside High School, WV

Bird Watchers

As the majestic birds
Fly up near the trees.
The bright feathers
Swoop through the open air.
They roam their kingdom
With mystical beauty.
Through the glistening leaves,
They soar sky high.

Briauna Lovin, Grade 7
White Station Middle School, TN

My Mom and Dad

This is a poem to my mom and dad
whom I love with all my heart.
You do too much for me.
Whenever I am in a tough situation,
you get me great things that I sometimes don't recognize.
Deep down I appreciate all you do for me.
I am grateful for my life every day.
Even when I am mad, you comfort me,
you take care of me.
When I am mad at you, you reason with me.
You are kind all of the time,
with your caring spirits.
Whenever I'm down on myself,
you boost my confidence up.
When I'm sick, you help me,
until I restore health.
Even though I seem ungrateful sometimes,
I will still love you,
Nick

Nick Porras, Grade 8
St Agnes School, KY

The Traveling Bee

I walk along the hills I see
following a yellow and black bumble bee.
It stops at a field of flowers
just when I feel the rain start to shower.

Oh, rain, that is ever so calm
You are very soft when you hit my palm.
The sky is becoming dull and gray
everything is starting to fade away.

The bee is trying to avoid the hurt
by tucking in his wings and squirming in the dirt.
He builds up courage when the sun comes out,
starts to fly high above me in the drought.

Jennifer Tassos, Grade 9
Robert C Byrd High School, WV

The Loaned Glitter

As the birds sing out to the morning sun,
the early joggers set out to run;
The sun comes out to meet the sky,
and raise the clouds from where they lie;
As the clouds go up they leave their glitter,
on the ground in which it litters.

But as the morning sun comes out to meet the sky,
the athletes come back to start their lives;
As the clouds start to long for what they had fired,
the grass holds ever tighter to what they admire;
As the moist white tufts take back what they had loaned,
the green turf misses what they had owned.

Joshua Collins, Grade 9
Home School, TN

Onward

I look Onward
I imagine pain and hardship
I hear the doubt their voices brought me
I feel it eating away at my dreams and intoxicating my body
Through my endless nights of longing
And the tears that were lost

But, cry no more for the day has hardly begun
My watch has just started
So do not fret for me
Looking onward does no good
Now

My world has only just started
Finish one day before you start another
Keep Faith

Do not let life kill the dream
YOU dream

Maggie Ford, Grade 8
Ligon Middle School, NC

Winter

Misty nights, cooler temperatures follow us
Creating little puffs of air when we breathe
The sun gradually disappears from sight
Granting the moon a spotlight

Trees float in milky, glacial substances
Humans throw snowballs and make snowmen
Out of it, creating
Human-like creatures

Fire, flames becomes a pal,
Bestowing glowing warmth upon us
Mugs with chocolate, coffee are sighted
Winter, the coldest yet warmest time

Elizabeth Eban, Grade 9
Wakefield High School, NC

When I Pray

When I pray I bow my head,
and get to the foot of my bed
I think of all the good I've done that day...
I say them quietly one by one.
I ask God for forgiveness
for all the bad I did that day
and hope he will understand and forgive me.
I say I'm thankful every day
and I remind myself
God is with me every step I take.
And although I may not be prefect,
I'm reminding myself in God's eyes I'm PERFECT
in every way...

Anna Curry, Grade 8
Elkton School, TN

The Leader of the Pack

The animal looked up, the first light blinding.
He grinned and stood, his legs were buckling.
When he first met the world, he was soon finding
that nothing's the same after you're a suckling.
He was to be the leader of the pack.

He grew to a strong animal, brave and fast.
And he was the leader of the pack.
They looked to him for guidance,
He gave it in love.
They had no doubts that his guidance was
help from above.

He soon grew old, his health was failing.
His legs would bend and fall from beneath.
His eyes went black and his life was sailing
from the body that was once bequeathed
to the leader of the pack.

Madeline Rogers, Grade 9
Magnolia High School, WV

Hurricane Katrina

Oh, hurricane Katrina
With your strong winds
and furious waters

You took down most of Florida
You killed thousands of people
You left many homeless

Why, why would you do this?
Millions of dollars to clean your
mess, why?

But now you are gone,
but even now we are still sad
Never come back, hurricane Katrina.

Many are crying, many are suffering
All because of your fury
Why hurricane Katrina.

Schools, businesses, libraries.
Gone, We worked hard on those,
And you destroy them, hurricane Katrina.

'Til this day, we are still
restoring our beloved Florida.
Why, hurricane Katrina.

Sean Galindo, Grade 7
Ramsey Middle School, KY

Sunlight

Sunlight.
Raining
from the sky.

Trickling
down pink
flower petals.

Drowning
the lush
green grass.

Splashing
autumn leaves,
red and green.

Rippling
on a small
hut's roof.

Squirting
wings of birds
soaring high.

Washing in
shades of yellow.
Sunlight.

Smiti Kaul, Grade 9
Providence Senior High School, NC

Dreaming

The room was filled with silence,
There was so much violence,
Sirens blaring, people screaming,
I felt I must be dreaming,
Confusion everywhere.

In the darkness I could see,
People falling around me,
First screaming in distress,
Then taking their last breath,
Confusion everywhere.

People crying, people dying,
Helplessness filled the air,
How I longed for a time,
When I did not have a care,
Confusion everywhere.

Then the morning light,
Awoke me from this restless night,
How real this did seem,
But it was only a dream,
Only a dream.

Kylie Keelin, Grade 8
George M Verity Middle School, KY

Sweet Simplicity

Ripples in the darkness —
  Spreading out in rings.
Early morning sunlight —
  To the world it sings.

The faded novel binding —
  A child's oldest friend.
Worn and wrinkled hands —
  Knowledge 'till the end.

A newborn baby's cry —
  Innocent and scared.
The song of every mother —
  Showing how she cared.

Although these things are small,
Nothing can quite compare,
To the world's simplicity,
Which comes from everywhere.

Caitlin Lambert, Grade 8
Home School, NC

Dusk

The dusk is upon us
The sun has shone
With darkness approaching
I head for home.

The quietness surrounds me.
All things are at rest
This peacefulness I find
To suit me the best.

Slowly I saunter
Through the vacant abyss
Realizing that dusk
Brings me nothing but bliss.

The time of day
I appreciate more and more
Anticipating the time of dusk
Like never before.

Shaniya Bellefant, Grade 8
Elkton School, TN

Football

F antastic sport to play.
O ver crowded, fans surrounding.
O ur minds dream of our teams.
T ension begins when you start.
B eat the other team.
A wesome.
L onging they are to score.
L ovely activity to play.

Dylan Wilder, Grade 8
All Saints' Episcopal School, TN

Sharpened

The rush of soft graphite against her skin.
Outlines her face.
Next her eyes,
Filled with the bright blue hue of life,
And dreams, interlaced.

Now imagine this, if you will,
As she fades away.
Her skin grows light,
And turns to white,
Leaving an eraser shaving bouquet.

Leaving pessimism behind,
I turn to try again.
Correct her figure,
Align her nose,
And hope you don't make mistakes.

Justin Williford, Grade 9
Southern Vance High School, NC

Poetry Trouble

Having trouble
Writing poetry
Hard as rubble
Writing trouble
I miss thee, good poetry

Writers block
I'm out of luck
It's been so long
I'll write the wrong
I'll make me, good poetry

The past is gone
I've fixed the wrong
Now poetry
Is what's for me
I love thee, good poetry

Thomas Shelton, Grade 8
Leesville Road Middle School, NC

Music Is

Drifting in the wind
Like a bird floating across the sky.
In every ear
Everywhere.
Beautiful and dangerous like the sea.
Soft and fragile like a newborn baby.
Paints pictures in your mind
Scenes of pain, love, or emptiness.
Fills the world with emotions.
From every dark corner to the sun.
It is life.
Music is there.

Emily White, Grade 9
Riverside High School, WV

Thoughts

Thoughts roll over my head
Like the waves of an ocean
As the pen in my hand
Taps against the wooden table
Making the sound of a drum

I stare at this blank piece of paper
As it mocks me
But yet no inspiration comes to my mind

I sit and think
But still my mind is gone
Like a flower petal in the wind

Writing and writing
Every sentence I think of
But yet everything I write down turns to
Dust

I wait and wait
For that one hope of inspiration to come,
But at last it doesn't

I give the clock a glance
Pack everything up
And decide to head home for the night

Allison Liles, Grade 9
Middle Creek High School, NC

The Leaf Game

Leaves play
In the trees
Gently sway
In the breeze

From a great height
They fall one by one
Flashing in the sunlight
Having lots of fun

Drifting round
And round
And round
Until they reach the ground

Dodging children's hands
As they seek to catch one
On the ground it softly lands
Basking in the sun

Here and there they catch one
A triumph to hold
A leaf is won
Orange, yellow, red and gold

Christina Anderson, Grade 8
Dillard Drive Middle School, NC

Goodbye

When I say goodbye I don't know when that will be,
I always want people to know about me,
Before I say goodbye.

Okay, so picture this, you live this okay life.
But then one minute you drift your eyes away,
And it all ends.

Your throat clumps up giving you that emotion,
That you have to say goodbye,
The shed of a tear hurts you inside,
The smile of a glimpse makes you never forget.

So here I stand, this very long, long road,
I'm walking straight,
With no human touch or,
No human soul around.

Here is my passion to drive me to my life again,
To take me back,
From all the fear around me,
And so I say goodbye.

Luciey Garland, Grade 8
Highlands Middle School, KY

The Epic Journey of Apollo 11

The day is July 16, 1969 at the Kennedy Space Center.
The countdown just begun, 10, 9, 8, 7, 6, 5, 4, 3, 2, 1!
Then the rocket boosters ignite!!!
Wooooosh!
The famous words are spoken.
"Houston we have lift off."

After these words they are on the way.
Since they have successfully left Earth's orbit it won't
be too long until they land on the moon.
As time passes people on Earth are filled with
anticipation and excitement.

It is now July 20, 1969, and the crew of the Apollo 11 are
entering the moon's orbit.
They are now navigating the lunar module, The Eagle, to
the landing site, The Sea of Tranquility.
"Houston, The Eagle has landed!"

Neil Armstrong opens the door to the lunar module, he
steps out and speaks these famous words…
"One small step for man, one giant leap for mankind."

Simon Farmer, Grade 7
Ramsey Middle School, KY

Prison Face

I'm so lonely as I spend these restless nights and days
Stuck with this prison face.
I start to embrace
In these cold cells, I call my temporary place.
Breaking the law will put you in this awful place
Where there's nothing to do but sit and pace.
Wishing you were in a better place
Somewhere like outer space.
Every man has his ending place
Only to start his beginning phase.
I'm a prisoner stuck behind these bars
Not being able to see out far.
Daylight seems out of reach
So I sit and begin to preach.
Everything seems unfair.
When all you can feel is the stare
Of the cold air.

Shaun P., Grade 9
Taft Youth Development Center, TN

I am the Unknown

I am the unknown
A silent pestilence
An untenanted dominion of disapprobation
A realm of phantasm
A land of mockery and fools
A hunting shark beneath the water
A freak accident
An untraceable poison
The monster under the bed
The most dangerous nobody of all
Many different faces
Surprise itself
The unknown has many faces,
It is venomous and lethal
But at the same time it is beneficial and saving,
The unknown is the death
And the life of the background.

Noah Clinton, Grade 8
Dillard Drive Middle School, NC

Hometown Pride

Lined up in twos, about to take the field
They kick the cadence
and enthusiasm erupts throughout the stadium
We proudly march forward to our position
The trumpets sound and the drums begin to thunder
The Indian charges to mid-field
The hometown pride is at its peak.

Shelby Varner, Grade 9
Parkersburg High School, WV

A True Friend

A best friend is not an ordinary friend
They usually stick with you through thick and thin
In times of trouble and need
They won't be the ones to leave
A best friend is someone special
Your friendship is certain to stay
Like true love it will never go away

Marisa Russell, Grade 9
Riverside High School, WV

The Lake

As I walk down to the pier
I see ducks flying overhead,
Their glistening wings blending perfectly with the sky.
I smell the nearby cookouts and wood burning in campfires.
Boats pass by at various speeds,
Some pulling water skiers or wake boarders
Always disturbing the peace.

As I lay there I feel completely at ease
With myself and with the world.
The more and more time I spend out there
The lower the sun goes.
As I watch the sunset
I wonder about the days when I cannot see this glorious sight.
As the stars start to emerge they twinkle with such pride,
And seem to be performing a dance,
One that I am unable to explain.
Soon there are no more ducks,
And no more boats.
I slowly drift off to sleep,
In this amazingly peaceful place.

Cassidy Smithers, Grade 7
White Station Middle School, TN

My Aunt

This poem is for my Aunt.
You are the one who held me as a child,
and are here to love me now.
Your love is out of kindness,
our love brings me joy.
You are the person who goes out of your way
just to be with me.
No matter what I do,
you are there to support me,
my sponsor, my relative, the one whom I love,
my great Aunt Cill.
I am now old enough to return my thanks,
by acknowledging you when I see you,
by giving you a hug
for I know you like my hugs.
And I'm sure you already know this,
for I've told you a million times,
I want you to know I love you,
and you're the greatest Aunt of all.
Love,
Nathan

Nathan Wagner, Grade 8
St Agnes School, KY

Ignorance Isn't Bliss

I hate this world we live in
All this odium and pain over skin
I hate that the oceans are as black as night
And some of the caves are lit up in light
I hate that there's still ignorance
And that children are brought up in cluelessness
I hate that love can't conquer all
And that people won't help you if you fall
I hate that innocence isn't safe
And a day at the office could end with strafe
I hate that millions of people are famished
And all the trees seemed to have vanished
I hate that there's no room to breathe
And that the ice is beginning to seethe
I hate that it's us that does all of this
And that this remarkable world can't be healed with a kiss

Destiny Butts, Grade 9
Owensboro High School, KY

My Unique Soul Is Complete

Quarter note, half note, whole note.
These things come together to tell an anecdote.
An eighth note here, a chromatic run there.
Music is the greatest thing you can share.
It picks me up when I am down, and spreads joy all around.
The sound of music makes me dance and sing.
Has anyone ever heard such a beautiful thing?
This music. It is my second language.
Without it, my soul would be but anguish.
Legato, concerto, duet, Da Capo.
These are only a few of the instructions I must follow.
Allegro, fast. Slow, grave.
Music is the thing this mind craves.
The beat of my heart is that of a metronome —
Tick. Tick. Tick.
Music fuels me to be majestic.

JannaBeth Raynes, Grade 9
Riverside High School, WV

Stormy Days

My life is like a raindrop on a stormy day
when the thunder booms and the lightning cracks.
My life splits into pieces
when I try to put my life back together.
The thunder booms and the lightning cracks again.
My life splits into even more pieces
and when the stormy day is over,
my life goes back to the way it
should be.

Cory Carver, Grade 8
Weddington Middle School, NC

The Night Sky

I look up at the night sky.
I see the twinkling stars.
The glowing moon.
The cool wind whispers as I lie on the ground.
The night sky is so pretty.
I love looking up at the night sky.
Until the wind starts to yell.
The skies turn gray and…
Rain pours from the clouds.

Christiny Seagroves, Grade 8
Elkton School, TN

Love

Love is a feeling so deep you don't know what do to with it,
For a person so special everything else around you is a blur,
Something so special if you let go of it even for a second it is the second of your life you regret the most,
Love is something you cherish no matter where you are or what you're doing,
The one slow dance without the one you love is the worst dance of your life, Love is putting faith into another person,
Love is never mistaken when taken care of, Love is fragile, but with care
Will be the thing most valued in everyone's life, we all need to learn to love, for without love all we have is hate,
Love is the picture we always have, in a pocket, a sleeve, or a shoe,
Sometimes love is a secret, sometimes it is open for all to see,
Love is the reason we have two eyes, two arms, and two legs, but one heart, someone else has the other one,
Love is the person whose eyes and smile put city lights to shame, the person who steals your heart,
The person you can tell "heads you're mine, tails I'm yours,"
When you meet you know they'll be hard to forget no matter what you go through together,
Love is like a stone, when you through it away, it is hard to get back,
With love you must be careful, you can't take back a word once it's said,
You can't go back and recover an occasion once it's passed,
Love is as powerful as anger only it brings words of kindness not hate,
Cherish the time you are in love because once that time's lost you cannot get it back,
Love them forever since when they're dead you want them to always know how much you love them,
Once they're gone you can't get them back to tell them,
Love always because love is great, Love is magic!

Amy Michaud, Grade 7
East Oldham Middle School, KY

Together, We Can

Together, we can make a difference, in a world without trust
A world, that has been chewed up, and spit out, a world that is unjust

Together, we can be a democracy, a nation pure and righteous
We can work against hypocrisy, united, we stand strong against those who spite us

Together, we can stop the rain, and sail through stormy seas
Pull a smile through a child's pain, lessen Hatred's need to feed
On the poor, defenseless minds,
Bringing joy to sight, to glisten all over mankind

Together, we can make the old feel youthful, by reliving their memories,
And with our luck, we can establish their dreams

With our mind's eye, we can see through thicker things than water
Together, we can save someone's daughter,
Help our friends out, in their greatest time of need,
Save the souls of the helpless, now, that's a good deed

Together, we can clean the window of the convicted's past, and brighten that dark, scary path;
Together, we will last

Makenna Ezekiel, Grade 9
Bearden High School, TN

March On!

Heels high, don't drop! Please don't drop! Toes point them, sharp as nails the Drum Majors instruct. Katilyn, heels high in the sky blows a triumphant sound from the bell of her trumpet articulate the notes the band director shouts Katilyn does so obediently. The flutes in their high but beautiful pitch come curving around the brass instruments. CRASH! Goes the cymbals. BOOM BOOM! Goes the drums. PING! Goes the triangle. EXCELLENT! EXCELLENT! Shouts the band director!

Olivia Hammond, Grade 8
Weddington Middle School, NC

The Flame

What takes life but gives warmth
What delivers the stability for human life
But can have a deadly price
It is a serious duty even if it seems nice
It is…
The ever brightening slowly dying crimson blazing flame

It sparks and sizzles for all night and day.
It is everlasting flame
What burns the skin but warms the soul
Its burns the brightest for those hearts black as coal
It warms the home of those in need
With its ever brightening, slowly dying crimson blazing flame

The black fumes that corrupt the air
The flames that burn all we care
The singeing burns that leave scars
The sparks that blow up cars
These may be big prices for the indescribable flame

The flames burn strong
No matter how long it need be
Fore it burns with like emotion because it is the
Ever brightening, slowly dying crimson blaze.

Evan Thompson, Grade 7
J Graham Brown School, KY

Katrina

I love you ocean.
When you're happy
You let us have fun
You provide us with a lot of things.

When you're mad
You can bring damage,
Death,
And destruction.

What made you mad enough to do this?
Make a storm called Katrina,
Form over the Bahamas
And affect thousands of people.

On August 23, 2005 I was only six
When I had heard that hurricane Katrina formed
Over the Bahamas
Then made landfall in southern Florida killing a few people.

In the morning of August 29 it made its second landfall
In southeast Louisiana
And killed over 1,500 people
And flooded New Orleans as the levee system failed.

Danny Simpson, Grade 7
Ramsey Middle School, KY

My Family

I have a family,
so short and tall.
Very large,
and funny all year long.

My brother, Greg, got married to Danielle,
on July 8, 2006.
A youth pastor and a teacher,
a cute couple all around.

My sister, Tiffany, married Thomas Clint,
in the Capital Church on June 23, 2007.
They survived through a deployment,
so they can get through anything.

My mom,
she loves me, cares for me, and supports me.
Helps me through anything,
and I love her most of all!

I have a family,
so short and tall.
Very large,
and funny all year long!

Kaitlin Williford, Grade 8
Dillard Drive Middle School, NC

Basketball Fever

Basketball season is finally here.
As I look into the stands, I can hear the fans cheer.
We have practiced a lot and are ready to play.
I am really starting to feel that this is our day.

The team has heard a lot of negative about our skills,
But we didn't listen, because we know the real deal.
They are just jealous because they aren't as good,
And they should be supportive as any real fan would.

The stuffy locker room is full of anticipation,
As the team is huddled together for the coach to assess our situation.
It's the first game of the season, and things are intense.
The plan is to play tough on offense and defense.

The music starts, and we know it's time to go out,
So we put our hands in, say a prayer, and let out a shout.
We open the door, and we hear the crowd chant.
The team is anxious and excited, so don't tell us that we can't.

The captains meet mid court with the referees,
And in our opponents' faces, it is fear that they see.
The whistle blows, and the game begins.
Our team and our coach are looking to win.

James Wilson, Grade 9
Cape Fear Christian Academy, NC

My Christmas

Christmas is that time of year,
Lots of presents and lots of cheer.
I hope I get a lot of gifts,
It's good school doesn't have year-round shifts!
My parents are so nice to me,
Buying gifts we cannot yet see,
When break comes we are happy and free.

There is only one thing you know,
Our special cat, he had to go.
He loved sleeping under our Christmas tree,
He made this time of year so special for me.
This is his first year without his family,
But we have regained special company,
That is our big black dog, Bailey.

Christmas is always so fun,
It is the happiest season under the sun.
It is great when you receive a ton,
it is the season for everyone!
Christmas is awesome, it makes my day,
It takes all my stress away,
And life is great is all I can say.

Trevor Jones, Grade 9
Parkersburg High School, WV

An Autumn Breeze

Two leaves fall straight down
From the branches of a sacred oak
A cool crisp wind interrupts their peaceful drop

From the oaks and pines of a remote forest
The gust carries the two leaves away
On a journey to another world

To the pricks of grasses
On neighborhood lawns
Where children run and play

Then skinning the rough cement
Of city sidewalks
Almost crinkling one leaf

And onto the shaded streets
Where the other leaf is almost ripped apart
Dodging the tires of a car

The barely intact brown, old leaves are brought down
To the soil of a harvested field
Where their rustling stops with a soft landing

Daniel Jones, Grade 9
Middle Creek High School, NC

9/11

10 years ago,
On this 9/11 day,
Changed many people's lives,
From moms and dads to aunts to uncles,
This was a very tragic day,
10 years ago on this 9/11 day.

10 years ago,
More than 2,000 people died,
When two airplanes flew into the sky,
Hitting the Twin Towers,
While people were inside,
10 years ago on this 9/11 day.

As the morning went on,
Moment of silence given to them all,
Tears fall down the family's faces,
Remembering the 10 years that are now gone.

10 years ago to now,
We can hear the screams,
With fear we see people running with tears,
To find safety somewhere near.

Mikayla Brown, Grade 7
Ramsey Middle School, KY

The Trail of Tears

As we walk the trail we experience the unthinkable,
death awaits us at every corner. Many of the
children have died off. But I focus on myself, as
I see the weeping mothers of the dead children
some of which I knew.

I want to sob and cry, but I know only the strong
will survive. We travel along the trail, as the
winter gets more brutal every day. Food is low
along with our spirits. There's not many of us
left. The thought that drives me to go on is that
I've come this far and I will not fail, I will prevail.

The snow falls slowly accumulating. We stay in
silence for almost the whole trip. Only to
hear the poor people weep and our feet
crunching under the blankets of white snow.
Occasionally we would sing songs but we would
soon stop at the sight of frozen bodies from the
people in front of us. And we are slowly losing
hope even I am.

Soon all hope in me is lost. And I drop dead.

Jose Socarras, Grade 7
Ramsey Middle School, KY

How About You Try to Get to Know Me
Look into my eyes and tell me what you see
Is there anything special you see about me
Can you see troubles and my pain
Or are you just staring into a dark abyss

My eyes are the opening to my heart and soul
Look closely, don't over think it
You can see what makes me whole
You can see what I love and what I hate
You can see what made who I am today

When you look into my eyes
Let it all pour out into your cup
Then drink it down nice and slow
Do feel my pain, my sorrow, my trouble, and my shame
Can you see what trampled my heart
Can you feel how dead I feel inside

Because the deeper you get, the more you know about me
So how about you try
To get to know me

Davida Rawl, Grade 9
Rocky Mount High School, NC

Where I'm From
I am the small and forgotten
The one you may never know
The place where concrete pigs stand
The place where those who are red in the neck usually land
The place where the sun always shines
The place where everyone is softhearted
A place with woodlands
A place where the most outgoing live
A place where everyone is related
Even the most different of people
Where everyone and anyone is y'all
A place for new beginnings
A place with the best barbecue
A place with wildlife that is frankly quite tamed
Oh how I love my little hick town
Of Lexington, North Carolina

Kyle Niner, Grade 8
Westchester Country Day School, NC

Halloween
Halloween is almost here.
It is filled with snacks, treats, screams and cheers.
The best part about Halloween is all the haunted places
And on the way, you see many scary faces
So have fun, get scared and enjoy it while it lasts
It's a really fun holiday
But it leaves way too fast.

Briley Gaudette, Grade 8
Elkton School, TN

To Find an Inspiration
Art, music, movies galore,
They are truly something,
That I can't ignore.
From an exciting journey
And the sadness of loss,
To the wars that make us worry — some won and some lost.
To the majestic sounds that sound somewhere — someplace,
And the test that makes you smile with joy,
To the well planned movie ploy.
To the film that tells us to follow our dreams,
And be who we can be
We can retrieve ourselves from anywhere,
And find our way,
In any direction.
But my way to finding a way
Is to find an inspiration, which can be found in anything
So that I can be an inspiration.
And that is why…
…Art, music, movies more,
Are truly something
I can't ignore.

De'Quan Tunstull, Grade 8
J. Graham Brown School, KY

The Cruise
The first time I got on the boat,
I was in shock.
It was so big I wondered how it could float.
Every night there was a huge dinner.
Even the Captain was there
I think his name was Edgar
I hung out with my cousins most of the time
we really enjoyed the smoothies that the boat had.
We had one called the sweet lime.
The boat also had tons of free food.
There were ice creams, fruits, vegetables, and cakes
that put all of us in a very good mood.
We stopped in the Bahamas and Key West
They were both so beautiful,
This trip was the best!
I can't wait to go back again
My family thinks so too,
But we don't know when.

Brian Lawson, Grade 8
Dillard Drive Middle School, NC

Basketball
The sound of a ball dribbling gets my heart racing.
I hear the crowd get anxious when you pull up for a shot.
The 50/50 chance of it going in is a hard wait.
When the ball swishes through the net,
The crowd jumps with excitement and the win is ours.

Zach Zidaroff, Grade 8
Weddington Middle School, NC

Weaker

When a person
Very close to you
Takes a life changing
Turn for the worst
They aren't the strong
Brick wall that was
Standing behind you
For support
When they become weaker
You are weaker
And it's easy for you
To tumble
And become a pile of debris

Lachelle Weathers, Grade 8
Center for Creative Arts, TN

September

Remember September
The month of the year
When summer is going
And autumn is here.

Remember September
When apples grow fat
And pumpkins grow
Even fatter than that!

September is a time for all.
Beginning of school,
Beginning of fall.

Madison Sweitzer, Grade 9
North Hills Christian School, NC

A Wish That Ended Us All

Once upon a wish
there became a star
and through that star
an eye was born.
An eye that could see the world.
Through the world
came a word
and a people was formed.
A people that became a monster.
A monster that became a reality.
Reality that formed life
and then the life that
killed us all.

Liberty Denu, Grade 9
Heritage High School, TN

Butterfly

Fly through the sky
With colorful delicate wings
Gently land on flowers

Lama Fahr, Grade 8
Weddington Middle School, NC

My Mom

This is a poem to my mom.
You look upon me with your great big brown eyes with very high expectations.
Even when I fail to do well and don't meet those expectations,
you are there with wide arms to give me a reassuring hug.
You bring out the good in people and help use that goodness
inside of them in the world.
You think and care for others before you think of yourself.
You would give the shirt off your back for someone in need.
When I look at your face, I see kindness and happiness
that fills the whole room, and I can't help but feel the same way, too.
You are the most important person in my life.
You are there to cheer me up when I am sad.
You are there to understand me when I am mad.
You are there to support me in making difficult decisions.
You are there to guide me through life.
You are the perfect example of how Jesus wanted us to be.
You are a great teacher and a loving mother.
I know you have heard this a thousand times
and when I failed to say it another thousand times.
I love you, Mom!
Coire

Coire Ayres, Grade 8
St. Agnes School, KY

I Am

I am Micah Arrington
I wonder about poor people and how I can help them.
I hear me telling myself to achieve a greater good.
I see my mom and dad telling me to be the best I can be.
I want for the world to be as good as the biscuits my mom cooks.
I am Micah Arrington.

I pretend that Earth is my friend.
I feel pain in my heart when I see something and can't do anything about it.
I touch the heart of others if I can and if they let me.
I worry about the economy and what's happening to it.
I cry when there is a death of someone who made a difference in my life.
I am Micah Arrington.

Micah Arrington, Grade 8
Roanoke Valley Early College, NC

I Am…

I am the salty Cape Cod, battering against the docks…
I am the bikes children ride to the ice cream shops…
I am the beautifully decorated streets around Christmas time…
I am the cold, wet streets on a rainy day…
I am the warm, comforting sun, that lights up the park, where the children play…
I am the sailboats moving forward by the wind…
I am the breathtaking sunset at the day's end…
I am the sapphire blue sky…
I am the grass people lay in, and watch the clouds roll by…
I am the little shops and stores, that sell candy, and old toys…
I am the little children, all the girls and boys…
I am Southport, NC, my favorite place in the world to be…

Emily Gilliland, Grade 8
Westchester Country Day School, NC

I'm a Survivor

Typing on my computer
Around eight forty five
Hear a loud thump
Thinking Maybe I should dive

Deciding otherwise I run for my life
Then I remember I should probably call my wife
There's a group arguing

But hear a man's plea
Not knowing where it's coming from
Searching frantically
The voice as a lead

Smoke fills the room I break through a fiery wall
There's the guy right down the hall
Then I hear a boom

So confused until the next morning
The twin towers have been hit by a plane
This is a horrible game
Next to me is my best friend

"We're brother until the end"
"Alright" and he was out like a light
"Goodbye Twin Towers, Goodnight"

Makenna Hall, Grade 7
Ramsey Middle School, KY

Christmas Time

Christmas time is a time for fun.
At Christmas time we are always on the run.
Between getting gifts and decorations,
it is always a celebration.

Green and red Christmas lights
are always shining bright.
As we decorate the Christmas tree,
we sing Christmas songs with glee.

We will eat delicious gingerbread
while familiar Christmas stories are being read.
Family always gathers near
this wonderful time of year.

Christmas morning white from snow
and people wait around the mistletoe.
Not a present touched in sight
until we finish singing Silent Night.

Christmas time is like a fashion trend.
it always comes to an end,
but it always comes back when
December rolls around so we can start the fun all over again.

Lindsey Mourneau, Grade 9
Cape Fear Christian Academy, NC

Where Wishes Go

The golden hills
Of the great beyond
This is where wishes go
Once they have been wished upon

The white wolves run parallel
The silver streams
Where minnows leap
And lull the rabbits into deep sleep

Who hath seen this fragrant land
Of white wolves and golden hills?
No one knows, no, no one knows
It wishes to remain unseen by man

So wish to your heart's content
And lay down to sleep
Knowing where your wishes go
To the golden hills and silver streams where the minnows leap

Sara Lillie, Grade 9
Middle Creek High School, NC

Family

Family means everything
Family is who you go to when in need
Family is there for you when you feel like you have nothing.
In a family, there can be many different types of people
Old or young, black or white,
A family is all the people that care about you.
But when someone doesn't have a family,
they rely on themselves.
They don't have the pleasure that we have
to come home every day and see their loved ones.
Or when they are going through tough times,
they can't talk about it to each other.
A family means the world
so be thankful for one another.

Samantha Sheaffer, Grade 8
Weddington Middle School, NC

Being Blue

Being blue
smells horrible and it never leaves you,
being blue
tastes as if you tasted something dark and bitter,
being blue
feels like a terrible stomachache,
being blue
looks like a dark cloud on a sunny day,
being blue
sounds like old, slow jazz,
being blue
can be the most unwanted feeling ever,
being blue

Gabriel Hernandez, Grade 8
Leesville Road Middle School, NC

I Love You

I walk in the halls and I see him,
My heart starts beating a mile a minute
In the lunch line, he came up to me and asked if I liked him.
I say yes and smile as big as ever. He says he likes me too.
I start blushing, my cheeks as red as a beet.

That Friday he asked me out, I said yes. Every time he sees me
He comes up to me and hugs me.
I think of him every second of every day. I hope he does the same.
He text me after school, he does it like it's homework.
Every time I hear my phone go off and I see it's him,
My heart goes off like an alarm. I immediately stop what
I'm doing and I reply.

I could not live without him. His warm soft hugs.
He wraps his arms around me.
I could hug him all day because I don't want to lose a
guy like him. Every time we walk away from each
other or we stop talking we say we love each other.
I could not lose him…because I love him.
Forever in my heart.

Destiny Spahr, Grade 7
Ramsey Middle School, KY

Julia

This poem is to my best friend, Julia,
whom I love like a sister.
With a wider view on life,
you see what others can't
and you can find a solution to any problem.
You open your heart to everyone
and think of the good things before the bad.
You have a big sense of humor.
You could be anyone's superwoman,
by standing up to the bad guys.
You love animals like people.
An inspiration to be happy
in the darkest times.
You are an aunt, a best friend,
a sister,
and a joy to anyone who meets you.
Just hang on tight,
because before you know it,
we'll be at each other's side again at high school.
Love,
Abby

Abby Gruner, Grade 8
St. Agnes School, KY

Antiques

Old, mysterious
Looking, collecting, talking about
A lot to collect daily
History

Tyler Owens, Grade 8
Elkton School, TN

My Grandma

This is a poem to my grandma who is a wonderful person in my life.
Your words and actions have helped sculpt me to be
the person I am today.
The wonderful times that I spend with you
make me count the days
until I can come back for more.
You're always at my concerts
and sporting events
and it warms my heart
to see your smiling face in the audience.
You are the one who says
yes when mom and dad say no.
You spoil me rotten,
but you teach me how to be kind and generous.
I may not say it enough,
but believe me when I say that
I love you so much.
When I walk through your door,
and into a big, warm hug,
it makes me love you even more.
Catherine

Catherine Ehlman, Grade 8
St Agnes School, KY

Pump It Up

As the music fills my veins
I begin to feel like I'm soaring through the gentle wind
The vibe smoothens my heart
And the beat jumps on my skin
I tap my foot against the floor
And bob my head to the melody
I start to prance with my fingers
The song is simply awesome
No violence no crooks
Just new ideas and hooks
Replay buttons appear in my past
But not by hand
But by thought
The pitch
The harmony
The highs and lows
The pauses
The decrescendos
And crescendos
Paralyze me
It enhances my soul

Sherrese Silvels, Grade 8
Center for Creative Arts, TN

Fire Fire

Fire fire burning bright
Fire fire in the night
Fire fire waving free
Fire fire in the breeze

Nathaniel Foye, Grade 7
Meredith-Dunn School, KY

My Own

Above our heads,
Across the atmosphere,
After the sun is long gone,
Behind the clouds,
Below the moon,
Through the sky,
From one end of the earth to the other,
Toward the heavens,
Like a night light,
To guide us on our way,
Along the horizon,
Among many like it, is a star I call my own.

Kaleigh McCarty, Grade 9
Riverside High School, WV

The Ultimate Test

Life… is just a big game
Where every level is not the same.
There are no extra lives or bonus coins,
The faint of heart should not join.
Life, is the perfect illusion,
It is the unbeatable enemy.
We are not really afraid of the rain,
We're only scared of getting wet;
Men are not really afraid of losing,
only of the shame;
No one really fears dying,
We only fear the pain.

Sairam Gudiseva, Grade 9
White Station High School, TN

Dad

Early on a cold fall morning
sitting in the woods
Is where you will find my dad
watching, waiting, listening
The wonderful colors of the leaves
are beautiful during this season
Red, orange, and yellow
they blend together so nice
Far in the distance he hears a squirrel
leaping from tree to tree
As dad sits in the beauty of the morning
he hopes the big buck will appear.

Dana Deardorff, Grade 9
Riverside High School, WV

Winter

Winter
Cold, exciting
Sledding, drinking cocoa
Exasperating to see snow
Lovely

Faith Fedoronko, Grade 7
Pigeon Forge Middle School, TN

The Peacock's Dance

As the overhanging ominous clouds create a downpour of glistening rain,
A blast of color erupts from the ground below,
And the peacock begins his cosmic dance.

Freely, he steps from side to side displaying his fan of blue and green,
With only the heavenly beat from above guiding his steps.
He lifts his face and tastes the sweet raindrops,
While his feather sway in the wind,
And he swirls around and dances to his heart's content.

As the rain gently bears down on the earth
And the lightning streaks light up the dark sky,
The majestic creature sways to the beat,
Boasting his array of colors,
While turning peahens green with jealousy.

Then as the clouds move away,
And a rainbow sprawls across the sky,
The marvel of colors comes to an end,
And the peacock steps away from the limelight
As an actor exiting the stage.

Anup Challa, Grade 7
White Station Middle School, TN

Friends

This is a poem to my friend, Rylee,
who is the best person in my life.
You have helped me through the good and bad.
You are amazing.
You are always at my side.
You have felt my pain, my sadness, my sorrow.
We have been together, laughed together, feared together.
You support my artistic advances and are honest all the way through.
We have been wrong in our thoughts
and in our actions
We have been mad at each other,
we have fought with each other and made up to each other.
So I write this for eyes,
eyes that could only be one person's,
yours.
Love, Caroline.

Caroline Horney, Grade 8
St Agnes School, KY

Moonlight

Bright, beautiful, and glowing moonlight shines through my window.
The light shines on my face.
Feeling like someone is there looking at the same moonlight as I,
sharing this same warmth;
Moonlight compares to a feeling like you are not alone in this world.
It is like what people say, there is always someone out there for you.
So you're always looking up and feeling that there is someone out there worth living for.
Something to gaze at.
Moonlight bright, beautiful, and glowing warmly.

Mirian Njie, Grade 9
Wakefield High School, NC

High Merit Poems – Grades 7, 8, and 9

Where I'm From
I am from football,
from tackling to catching.
I am from the house,
where I spent several years of my life.
I am from the sweet tea,
that my mom makes.
I am from the Sunday dinner,
that my mamaw cooks.
I am from the dirt bikes and four wheelers,
that I ride every day.
I am from hunting,
every season with my dad.
I am from the great family,
that I have always had.
I am from the hard work,
on my papaw's farm.
I am from the deer,
grazing in the field.
I am from the great place,
that I live in today.
Cole Wines, Grade 8
Sissonville Middle School, WV

Hurt
When I first saw you
I thought you were cute
We flirted
We went out
When I saw you flirting
With other girls
It hurt
I told you how I felt
You still did it
You told me
You loved me
I believed it
You told me
You liked my best friend
It hurt
Now that we broke up
I still have feelings for you
And it hurt to see you
Dating my best friend
Dereka Baker, Grade 8
Orrum Middle School, NC

Fall to Winter
Colors always change
Leaves are falling constantly
Goodbye to the fall

Temperature changes
Bring out the winter jackets
Hello December
Hayley Shwer, Grade 9
White Station High School, TN

The Season Brings
My eyes are shown the happiness all around me
I sense the love of this wonderful season
I smell the sugar cookies baking in the oven
The coffee mug full of hot cocoa with warm whipped cream touches my lips
The sounds of the carolers and the rush at the mall fills the air
Kathryn Jennings, Grade 9
Powell First Baptist Academy, TN

Speeding by Sideways
It seems like a bullet flying by sideways in the turn
It stinks like burnt rubber as your tire pops on the final lap
It jerks you into the seat by pure power as you punch it in the straight
It makes your ears quake as the cars fly by like a streak of lightning
It reminds you of sweet chocolate as you taste the leak and identify it as antifreeze
Cody Heck, Grade 9
Powell First Baptist Academy, TN

Hockey
The grip of his hand on the stick,
The feel of his skates on the ice,
The chilly atmosphere in the arena,
Lets him know it's time to play.

Fans cheering on the sidelines,
The refs blowing their whistles,
The puck slicing through the air,
Are all comforting sounds of the game.

His teammates streak across the ice,
Coach waves his arms in the air,
The opposition looms in his vision,
As the puck drops quickly to his feet.

A deke to the left and he is in the clear,
His eyes scan the open ice ahead,
He winds up to take the shot,
Suddenly the puck is in the net.
Darin Gooding, Grade 8
Dillard Drive Middle School, NC

The Dark Age
Earthquakes
And fighting among hilltop forts
A difficult time for
The Greeks
Population shifts
Overseas trade
And poverty took hold
Advanced technology,
Iron weapons,
And a Greek alphabet
The Dark Age went from challenging
To excellent
In nearly 350 years
Madison Woods, Grade 7
St Nicholas Academy - South, KY

I Love Him
I laugh all day,
I cry all night,
I didn't know how much I loved him,
Even though he was my friend.

He makes me smile every day,
He looks at me a different way,
I look at him in a gazing stare,
He didn't know I was there.

I dream about him all night,
I think of him even out of sight,
I gaze at the sky thinking about him,
I think I know what is happening.

I don't know what true love is,
I think I see a best friend,
But the thing I didn't know is that,
I think I love him.
Makayla Boyd, Grade 7
Ramsey Middle School, KY

Beach
I ride for seven hours.
Sleeping whenever
Stopping and eating.

One twenty we finally arrive.
Up to the room
I feel you calling me.
With my swimsuit on I'm coming.

With sand between my toes
The air blowing.
Suddenly see the blue water.
Finally I'm here.
Britton Mann, Grade 7
Dyer Elementary & Jr High School, TN

I Am From

I am from the plains of Greensboro,
The place of hot summer days,
And the cold winter nights,
I am from the rainy days,
And the wind filled nights,
I am the temple,
The community of a religion,
I am from the tops of the mountains,
Down to the salty shores,
I am North Carolina

Will Sagerdahl, Grade 8
Westchester Country Day School, NC

Where I Am From

I am from the rink
The smell of roll-on
The cheers of my teammates
The pressure of the race
The feeling of nerves
The sound of the whistle
The push of my opponent
The moisture of my sweat
The happiness of winning
I am from inline speed skating.

Michaela Craycroft, Grade 8
Westchester Country Day School, NC

Green

What is green?
Green is nature
To see the Northern lights
With the lightest shade of green
You'll see the emerald leaves
Dancing in the breeze
While the lily pads are floating
Their way to freedom
With the coqui croaking with joy
To say the rain forest is a good place to stay.

Katlynn Neblett, Grade 7
Montgomery Central Middle School, TN

I'm Done

At the end of the day
When it's all over with
I'm done
I believed every word you said
But now
I'm done
You lied, you cheated and you deceived me
But now I'm done
It's all over now
Because I'm done

Kashanus Hunter-Fleming, Grade 8
Weldon Middle School, NC

9/11/01

On this day,
The worst of intentions poured over us.
As they crashed into the towers they wrecked the lives of thousands.
When they collapsed, lives were crushed along with everything you believed was real.
Grief so strong it still stains the faces of Americans today.
The horror washed over us like the smoke and ashes as they fell.
What once soared high above the ground,
Was brought to its knees by the hatred of the actions of radical people.
Ten years later, bodies have yet to be found.
People who were there to save others went down in the flames.
Stitches could never heal the wounds we have gained because of this.
On the tenth anniversary
we stumble to our feet as we rebuild the towers.
Our nation
And the lives that were smothered beneath the smoke,
To all of the families and loved ones lost,
We will not forget you.
We will remember not only you, but the innocence of your lives that were taken away.
All because of that day...
9/11/01

Abigail Klopfenstein, Grade 7
W O Inman Middle School, TN

Tasha (Mama)

The pain came the tears flew
Who knew how much I would miss you.
Your were taken by the great but I expected it to come late
He took you up and you smile down you're the one who makes
Me show my so-called beautiful smile.
The people say you were great but not to me you were
The queen of all greats, and people seem to think
I have regrets of God taking you but all I want do is thank you.
On earth you wouldn't withstand the pain and
By the time you were 50 you would be insane.
I think that once you passed I arose into a small young man,
And it seems that in your eyes I see the golden gates
And in my mind I see your smiling face,
And I wonder is life really a race?
But I soon realize that up there is a better place.
I'm living up to what I said I would be a young black male that was going to live good,
And make my dream come true and become an NFL star
And make sure you're the one I seek to reach past the end zone and field goal bars.
If I should die before I wake I pray you and the Lord my soul to take.

Darius Tucker, Grade 8
J Graham Brown School, KY

Happiness Revealed

Happiness is a flower, blooming in the fresh spring sun with vibrant colors and a vivid scent
It smells like a newly bloomed honey suckle in the fresh spring sun
It tastes like caramel flowing out of a chocolate bar
It feels like warmth has taken over your entire body and the world is on your side
It looks like snow, slowly and softly hitting the frozen ground
It sounds like birds chirping at the first sight of spring
Brings light and joy to your life.

Morgan Mann, Grade 8
Leesville Road Middle School, NC

Aqua

The way she moves can leave you astonished.
Twists and turns,
Up and down.
No matter where you are,
You'll probably see her.
Nice on some days,
Maybe not on others.
She's been to lots of places before,
Maybe even outside your window.
She is filled with so much beauty,
You just might get swallowed up.
Sometimes she just wants to talk to a friend,
Because very soon,
She'll have to go again.
But she is a part of you,
That shows she is always with you.
Her name is as fresh as you can get to.
Aqua

Saaman Ghodsi, Grade 9
Parkersburg High School, WV

Love Lasts if You Want It To

You know that I love you, we both know it won't last
We've had too many heartbreaks to let our trust past
We haven't known each other to let it really slide
But every time we kiss I feel like I'm flying high!
You say that you love me but I'm not really sure
You never say it loudly you say it when we're alone
You say that it's romantic and I just go along
'Cause I don't wanna lose you but you just let me fall!
Love lasts if you want it to
Nothing you can say or do
I just wish we had each other to hold on to
Every time I wanna stay you give me wings to fly away
I can't count how many times I wanna say "I LOVE YOU!"

Alia Ray, Grade 8
Swansboro Middle School, NC

Suffering

I am suffering
Powerful beyond belief
You may not understand me for no one does
Your pain increases, as does my power
The more you lose the more I gain
I am a mummer of your darkest days
A pestilence you will never egress
I am your disapprobation
Human nature is never perfect
I am everything you despise
Penance need not be paid
I will consume you in your pain
I am suffering a fear you will always endure

Charlotte Nixon, Grade 8
Dillard Drive Middle School, NC

Morning Sound

It's morning
And the sun has risen once again
The cool air brushes my feathers
And the sun's rays strike the land
From where I sit
I can see for miles
There is no sound
As I sit waiting
For just the right moment
Everything is still
Except for the soft whistling wind
I preen my feathers
Waiting for the right moment to come and
Watch the motionless ground below me
And suddenly I hear it
The first call came from a nearby tree
And an exotic burst of birds appeared out of it
I spread my colorful wings and fly with them
Pouring out my heart in a song
We sing the songs of the morning
To welcome yet another glorious day

Amber Jones, Grade 7
White Station Middle School, TN

My Mommy

This is a poem to my mommy, Eileen.
I know you love me, even when I make mistakes.
You give me the world,
so I can have a good life.
I know sometimes I don't show it,
but I am trying to do better.
You show me you love me
by the things that you do,
even though I can be mean to you.
From now on I will do extra things,
so you know that I love you.
For all the taking me places,
and buying me food,
I appreciate it,
and I thank you.
You are the best mom in the world,
and I love you!
Johnny

Johnny Schaffstein, Grade 8
St Agnes School, KY

In My Paradise

I can feel the misty, fresh ocean breeze against my sunkissed cheeks. I can't seem to find a cloud in the sky. I can hear the relaxing sound of a wave crashing down onto the shore. I can smell the drifting aroma of the delicious food coming from the pier. This is my paradise.

Hannah Moncrief, Grade 9
Powell First Baptist Academy, TN

Winding Road
Me,
Caring
Determined
Tender
Wishes to be a doctor,
Dreams to be a soccer superstar,
Wants to travel the world and go someplace far.
Who wonders what life would be, had I not had a family,
Who fears loss of great things and small,
Who is afraid of things that crawl.
Who like to wander and try new things,
Who believes that God will give me wings.
Who loves music
Who loves exotic food
Who loves to live life
Who loves to be in a good mood
Who plans to be successful
Who plans to do everything before I die
Who plans to have kids, live, and get by

Who doesn't have a predetermined life.
Umida Nasritdinova, Grade 9
Bearden High School, TN

Nature's Going
The light squeezing through the trees
Whistling sound of the breeze
Oh grass how you flow with the wind
And the fish dance down the river bend

It's that time again as you know
The leaves were here now they must go
I look up to see nothing but clouds cushioning
the light
It's a most depressing sight

Grasshoppers chirping my heart beating
Oh how I loathe to see you stop tweeting
Right in front of me, nature you're dying
You'll be back next year I hope you're not lying
Brent Norman, Grade 9
Robert C Byrd High School, WV

Fall
Fall is a pretty time of the year.
Where children laugh and play in the leaves
That fall from the trees
There are so many colors in the leaves
Some are so bright
Just like a colorful kite.
I love to see all the colorful leaves
Up in the beautiful, massive trees
That is the best thing about fall
Yes, true beauty for all.
Briana McConnell, Grade 7
Elkton School, TN

Anyway
People are unreasonable, illogical, and self-centered.
Love them anyway!
If you do well, people will accuse you of selfish ulterior motives.
Do well anyway!
If you are successful, you will win false friends and true enemies.
Succeed anyway!
The good you do today, will be forgotten tomorrow.
Do good anyway!
Honesty and truth make you vulnerable.
Be honest and truthful anyway!
The biggest person with the biggest ideas can be shot down
By the smallest people with the smallest minds;
Think big anyway!
People favor underdogs, but follow only top dogs.
Fight for underdogs anyway!
What you spend years building up may be destroyed overnight.
Build anyway!
People really need help, but will attack you if you help them.
Help them anyway!
Give the world the best you have and it may kick you in the teeth.
Give the world the best you've got anyway!
John Kolb, Grade 8
J Graham Brown School, KY

Finding Confidence
Sometimes I wonder where I'm going;
am I to be ordinary, all alone?
A bottled river, corked, never flowing,
do I fit in or stand outside on my own?
Am I to be a brilliant, gleaming sun
or a simple pebble stuck in the mud?
Will my battles, although bloody, be won
or I defeated, falling with a thud?
Sitting trapped by my fears, yearning for more…

Wait! I can't have that! There's so much life to live!
I will make ripples on quiet shores.
I'll make noise in the world. I've gifts to give!
I'll stand tall, stay loud, and never relent,
I'm larger than life for I'm confident!
Tori Lafon, Grade 9
Bearden High School, TN

Yellow Like
The sun…
is born when the sun comes up
lives high in the sky
looks like summer
feels like the sun on my face
sounds like kids playing outside
smells like fresh squeezed lemons
tastes sour, it makes your mouth pucker
is sad when the moon begins to rise
turns to white and black for the stars in the night sky
Haley Garner, Grade 8
Elkton School, TN

Ella Enchanted

Long ago in a village called Frell,
A girl named Ella was under a magical spell.
She did and said whatever you pleased,
And did it all with great elegance and ease.
"Go here Ella! Do this! Go there!"
Ella got so frustrated she was pulling out her hair.
Her stepsisters were mean as snakes,
And her godmother was a cook named Mandy, who bakes!
But nobody at all could vanquish her spell,
So Ella was ready to leave out of Frell.
But she didn't have a way to leave, not even a car,
That's when Ella met a handsome prince named Char.
She fell in love, but was shipped off to school,
He didn't stop her, and felt like a fool.
But they wrote letters, filled with love,
He told her about the ball coming up.
Ella was happy, but even with the spell
She had no way to return to Frell.
Ella wished with all her might, she flew off to the ball that night.
Ella was happy, married and well,
And that was the end of her horrible spell.

Savannah Stokes, Grade 7
Fuquay-Varina Middle School, NC

The Moon

The majestic moon dances in the sky
While he sings me a lullaby
He is a strong, and beautiful lie
His glistening light never fails to shine

The moon is as big as the entire sea
He's the type of mystery I'd like to be
As he glimmers his power, we all take a knee
His modesty tends to enlighten me

The moon is a face that always holds a smile
We must grin back, all the while
His laughter rings as he's a child
Nothing he does is ever vile

The moon's glory is a joyous song
It's tune engages me to sing along

Kasidi Legg, Grade 9
Riverside High School, WV

The Lost Son

Working on his masterpiece, sitting in the dark.
Dwelling in depression, from his long lost son.
He dwells upon the thought of death.
He daily prays for the will to live.
He watches the horizon, longing for the day.
When his son will ride in, coming home to stay.

Davis Hearn, Grade 9
Powell First Baptist Academy, TN

Glass Bottle

Hold it in
Lock it there
Never let go
Don't empty it, bare

When vex steals your eyes and malicious words leak
Be sure to catch them and trap them inside
If you've done wrong and through your lips accidental lies peek
Fit your good character inside

When the agony-filled screams posses your brain
Stuff your voice inside
As blissful blood pumps through your veins
Let it flow inside

And when the pain starts to overcome you
When the heart of love starts to grow still
Just let it all fill
Your glass bottle

Hold it in
lock it there
never let go
don't empty it, bare

Zoey Morris, Grade 7
J Graham Brown School, KY

Magic Rock

In the grass by the trees
Stuck in the hill hidden from Ares
The gods hid it from him when he went to war
But when he came back they said they had it no more.

Ares searched everywhere, high and low
But when he asked again they said it was stolen by Pluto
Ares went down to get it himself
The other gods re-hid it on a shelf.

It fell from the shelf and crashed through the ground
It fell to Earth on to the beach, just in time to be found.
A poet walking in search of inspiration said, "oh the ocean,
I'll look to the ocean." So he walked down to the beach of the ocean.

But then he noticed something falling in motion
He rushed to the scene to observe the commotion.
When he arrived at the scene he saw nothing at first.
But then the rock shot sparks that suddenly burst.

After he observed it and messed with it too.
He did with it whatever it wanted him to do
I leave this poem for you to end
In hope that you make him do something magnificent.

Andrew Boyles, Grade 9
Robert C Byrd High School, WV

Lacquered Tears

Lacquered tears running down one eye
Daring not to look behind
At the untamed horror exposed
That one may never suffer through
Despite this wish, we all do.

When love and happiness cease to be
And all one final, painful remedy
That sun may never shine once more,
But dark luring over raging seas
Filling lives with prolonging grief.

Lacquered tears running down one eye
As if all love is lost through lie.
That life, though not everlasting, shall take a presence forever
Despite wherever one may endeavor.

Raving eyes will feast upon the envious love that shall never be lost
This conception though is soon to die
Along with the lacquered tears you cry
Then sadness will rein once again
And will always, until the end.

Madeline de Figueiredo, Grade 9
East Chapel Hill High School, NC

The Whale

I am
Majestic
Nice
Calm
Peaceful. As far
As I can see, I'm the
king of the sea. Gaze in
my beauty, do not destroy me. I am
killed for OIL and I do not know
Why, I have DONE nothing to you, so
Why must I die. Watch me SWIM in the ocean
where there is no commotion. Waters so enjoyable
blue, and cold where I am happy
and uncontrolled. I am free
for no one can bother me. As large
as we are, we are a morning
Star

Michael Sawh, Grade 9
Wakefield High School, NC

Mosquito

Dark mosquito, vampire of the insect world.
Your fangs sink in my glistening skin.
You suck my blood, juice that sustains you.
I swat to kill you, but you escape.
Your fangs leave a mark, your imprint swells.
The venom you injected makes me itch.
I live in terror of your return.

Autumn Cravens, Grade 8
Weddington Middle School, NC

Basketball

There is nothing like a game of basketball
Vibrant lights glowing on the court.
The sound of excited fans,
ready to see action.
Once I touch the ball,
it's like the ball is melting in your hands
or playing a massive game of hot potato.
You must keep dribbling the ball on the ground,
passing to teammates, and blowing by the defense for the shot
The game is sometimes physical,
with aches and pains the next day,
but at least I know I played hard.
Every time the buzzer buzzes I check the scoreboard
to see if we are winning or losing.
In four simple quarters of play,
time breezes by.
Staring at the scoreboard,
hoping we have won.
My jaw dropped low,
because the opponent was successful.

James Busby, Grade 7
White Station Middle School, TN

Time

It runs wild and never stops.
The future becomes the present
And the present becomes the past.
Some have come, some have gone.
Your time, it won't be long.
It flies and it will pass right by your eyes.
On the clock it goes round and round,
Making that ticking sound.
To the morning, to the noon, to the night
It follows routine just right.
Sometimes we're in a hurry,
Sometimes we're early.
Every time a heart beats, every time your eyes blink,
Just remember that's a second you can't relive.

Jedidiah Jenkins, Grade 7
Elkton School, TN

Divine Demise

Do you feel that?
Lurking in your heart
Do you feel that?
Ripping you apart?
Eating one alive, it rips the flesh from the bone,
Taking one's shelter, leaving thee all alone.
Cold and dark, this creature can be,
Visible through all but one cannot see.
Poison is nursed by this creature, you feed,
The toxin seeps in, filling one with greed.
What is this creature, not from above?
This creature I say, is something called Love.

Isaiah Greene, Grade 9
Myers Park High School, NC

Things Not Seen

I feel the wind gently caress my face
And think, is there really a wind?
There is no evidence, just invisibility.
But if I observe, I begin to notice.
I see trees sway, leaves rustle,
Butterflies being pushed around by the breeze,
Evidence is all around me.
The Mind ignores the small things,
Important things we must not forget.
If we look hard enough, we begin to notice
Details that prove existence.
The Father who emerged from a car wreck unscathed,
The Mother in labor who was dying,
But someone held her hand and helped her through.
When she asked who it was later,
Her Husband replied, there was no one here.
Even though we can't see something doesn't mean it isn't there.
Evidence is everywhere in Beautiful Nature, in the Mighty Storms,
In the Still Small Voice in your head,
Jesus is there.

Seth Flynn, Grade 9
Mountain Heritage High School, NC

Halloween

Halloween night is lots of fun,
Some people are glad when it's over and done.

I like to do things that are scary.
Like jumping out behind people with masks that are hairy.

I like jack-o-lanterns, witches and bats.
While others like ghosts, goblins and big black cats.

Haunted houses are best of all.
The moon always looks spooky in the fall.

When it's over I am always sad.
So I just eat my candy, and make my orthodontist mad.

Kyle Oliver, Grade 7
Elkton School, TN

Waves

Waves can move up and down,
Just like happy faces and frowns,
There are good times in life and bad ones too,
Though the smiles we share shall not be few,

The rivers and streams have no choice but to move on,
Just like we should not linger on things too long,
Winds are what waters need to overcome,
Ours can be illnesses and deaths just to name some,

These events are somehow defeated,
And our love of life can once again become repleted.

Molly Rogers, Grade 7
White Station Middle School, TN

All About Me

I am nice and wonderful to my family
I wonder if there will be world peace
I hear my dog Lady bark all night
I see ghosts all the time at home
I want a Volkswagen Beatle
I am nice and wonderful to my family

I am pretend that I am a WWE super star
I feel good because I am having a good day
I touch a goat's tongue when I feed it
I worry about my dad dying when he is a bounty hunter
I cried at my pop's funeral
I am nice and wonderful to my family

I understand people that are having trouble talking
I say "Thank you" when people give me stuff
I dream about my family getting lots of money
I try new foods when mom makes me
I hope for a new iPhone to keep in touch with my dad
I am nice and wonderful to my family

Carrie Denton, Grade 8
Montgomery Central Middle School, TN

The Move

Immediately my chest was heavy as an anchor
Upon hearing Martha would move away
Salty tears fell on my cheeks
And memories flowed like a river through my head
My best friend —
No more sitting across the alley
Each high up in our green trees
We talked and talked until dark
I could shout across anytime for her
I had to pinch myself
Praying it was a dream
But then her voice spoke again
"Don't worry, I'll be just around the corner."
And she actually is.

Esther Gordon, Grade 7
White Station Middle School, TN

Cory Thomas Davis

Watching the evening news
Hearing that the Upper Big Branch Mine fell in
As my heart started aching
I knew you were gone forever
I wanted to come save you
Bring your soul back to life
You were such a great guy
Big heart, big smile
Your family sheds so many tears
Just because you're not here
But now your gone forever
Good bye for now, hope too see you soon

Kaylyn Carroll, Grade 9
Riverside High School, WV

New Moon*
Heart pounding,
Eyes watering,
Gasping for breath,
When he left,
He walked away in the light,
Sparkling,
Like it wasn't real,
I can't breathe.
How bad I want him,
I don't know how long it's been,
I've been with my best friend,
He said he wouldn't hurt me,
Then he left me,
And doesn't talk to me,
I see him change from a human,
To a big furry beast,
A werewolf,
Are fairytales real?
Should I believe everything now?
I saved Edward with his sisters' help,
Maybe now, things will be okay.

Racquel Bennett, Grade 7
Fuquay-Varina Middle School, NC
*Inspired by Stephenie Meyer's "Twilight: New Moon"

Green
Green is a magical color
It can symbolize many things
Like a tall, fat bristly tree
Just like a beautiful Christmas tree
With its many colorful lights and ornaments
It stands so straight and still
With its bold, beautiful color
In fields and forests where they stand
Many different sizes and shapes
It sways in the breeze
Also it bends and cracks during storms
But still the bold, beautiful color shines through
Making you feel peace and love
Not just at Christmas
But any time of the year
With the color so bold and bright

Kelsey Winfree, Grade 8
Montgomery Central Middle School, TN

Sunset
Over endless green fields
Beyond the flat horizon
Among the fluffiest clouds
Around the world it illuminates
Unto my face the last rays shine
With the sky full of colors
Before the sun vanishes,
Across the world people softly whisper "Goodnight."

Brooke Rumbaugh, Grade 9
Riverside High School, WV

Sanctuary
Protecting me from the outside world
Warmth and happiness engulf the space around me
A lit candle burns and a bright light shines
A fan chops on medium
And a goldfish swims effortlessly in its clean bowl
The deep plum-colored walls surround me
And my white curtains shimmer in the light
I feel guarded
All that is occurring outside
Crime, panic, stress and sickness
Is unavoidable for many
But not for me, I simply flee to my sanctuary
And all is seemingly well
Until morning
My white palm and neatly trimmed nails grasp the door handle
Pushing down hard
Forcing me into a far from perfect world
Until night when I shall return, safely
Into my sanctuary.

Hannah Cheramie, Grade 9
Providence High School, NC

Fall Weather
The crackling and the crunching of the dry falls leaves,
 the silent whistle of the cold, harsh wind.
All leads up to the wasps stealing honey like thieves,
 and how the creek dangerously flows around the bend.

Oh, sun. Shine your warm, bright light on me.
For I am the noisy cricket, so fragile and small.
I sing with all of the others in harmony,
 under the oak tree where the dead leaves fall.

The roses are dying, and the daisies are dead,
 the bees are running out of honey.
I watch the sky as I lie in my bed,
 and I witness the dull sky change to sunny.

Kaitlyn Paugh, Grade 9
Robert C Byrd High School, WV

The One Place This All Makes Sense…
Music blasting, lights burning, sweat dripping
Hoping your make up and hair is perfect,
The one place this makes sense is the stage.
Dancers preparing, choreographers praying, audience waiting
The one place this all makes sense,
Rising curtains mark the start,
Costumes shimmering, toes pointing, knees stretching
Remembering everything I've been taught in the studio,
Every correction, every step, every movement counts,
Curtains close to the beating drums of the audience's hands,
Minds running a thousand miles per minute,
Hoping I've correctly executed the dance.
The one place that all made sense, the stage.

Caroline Danziger, Grade 7
White Station Middle School, TN

My Tragedy on 9/11
The early morning sun was shining as bright as can be,
This day started out to be fun,
At school with my best friend and me.

As I sat in class,
Listening to my teacher speak,
Waiting on time to pass,
I heard a big boom across the street.
On the faces of people I saw fear,
It seemed like time had stopped,
And something tragic was near.

As the building began to fall,
I ran out calling for you, "Daddy where are you" I call,
But no answer.
As I stood there I was comforted by my friend,
And something told me,
I would never see you again.

Kiana Hearn, Grade 7
Ramsey Middle School, KY

911
The first plane smashed into the North Tower.
Plane number 2 crashed into the South Tower.
The third smacked into the Pentagon
In that terror-filled hour.

The last plane was headed west, then suddenly turned back east
It headed for the White House where the president sleeps.
The courageous people on flight 93 decided to fight back;
They sacrificed their lives to prevent a horrible attack.

Plane number 4 nose-dived into the big field in Pennsylvania
Then there were lots of ambulances from the plane crash.
Also the two Twin Towers were on fire slowly collapsed.
At 9:02 people were jumping out of the window.
When the Twin Towers collapsed the smoke filled the sky as
the people began to cry from the horrible collapse.
People were risking their lives to save their men and
country.

Dallas Hyre, Grade 7
Ramsey Middle School, KY

Chasing Pavements
Chasing pavements on and on looking for an escape,
a safe secret quiet place.
Little kids crying because mom or dad's dying from cancer,
and all the poor baby wants is an answer.
Being prompt and also prepared
the young college student waves goodbye but there's no one there.
Poor old woman sad and alone,
with no hopes or dreams, no success and no home.
Chasing pavements on and on
looking for reassurance and that loving nurturing call.

Aquella Allen, Grade 7
Weldon Middle School, NC

Marching Band
Rat-tat-tat go the drums signaling the rest to begin
Marching down the football field to begin the show
Everyone's in line: Brass, woodwinds, percussion, and flags
All eyes from the crowd focus on the band
Drum major on the stand, counting off to begin
Music now playing in the air
The band marching from one place to another
All in rhythm and tune
The crowd is quiet while they play,
Seeing how good they'll play tonight
The band, at attention, waiting for the conductor
Drum major waving her arms, conducting the next song
The crowd barely moving enjoying the lovely sound
The song is over, the band awaits
The crowd applauds to appreciate their show
Four whistles signal the band to march off
The drums play the cadence,
The band marches to the stands
They all congratulate each other for another well-done show
Then they sit and watch the game continue

Angelica Troiano, Grade 9
Meadow Bridge High School, WV

Boston Massacre
B ritain tried calming the crowd
O ne Bostonian cried out, "Are they to be killed in this manner?"
S entry on duty panicked and called for help
T ragic encounter
O ne British officer shouted, "We did not send for you. We will
N ot have you here."

M any people killed and injured
A ngry townspeople
S everal shots fired
S oldiers knocked down
A fter, colonial leaders used the killings as propaganda
C rispus Attucks, a dockworker, was killed
R elations between Britain and colonists grew tense
E ncounter was called the Boston Massacre

Kaitlynn Hicks, Grade 8
St Nicholas Academy - South, KY

The Break Up
The horrible thought will haunt me forever,
The disturbing scene will be glued in my mind,
That one person will nag me for life.
He has hurt me so many times,
Leaving a permanent scar in my heart.
He has lied,
Cheated,
And destroyed
My heart, soul and mind.
Never to be forgiven
But always loved.

Malea Jolly, Grade 9
Middle Creek High School, NC

Heart of the Sunset

The fiery, red sun
Stands weary and fatigued
But in its eyes, I reveal honor and pride
Its majestic atmosphere lighting the daytime sky
The sun gazes at me
Its power flowing into my flesh
Holding such beauty and grace
It steals my heart and takes away my breath
The grand capability of this sun
Dare not be compared to any such nature in existence
The true beholder and the life of my planet
Cannot be challenged, as it is victorious
I wish for the breathtaking moment to last an eternity
To be my life's image for every, counting second
Alas, the brightest moments come to an end
As the tiresome, flaming sun wishes to set
The gorgeous, blazing sphere lowers in yearning relief
Eventually kissing the distant horizon, entwined in the land
A passionate and desirable scene, pleasing my soul
So long, my dear sun, I do hope you come back again

Tarana Sidhu, Grade 8
Crosby Middle School, KY

Laugh

The main purpose of life,
Is to have fun.
To never let things get to you,
Or make life miserable.
We were not put here to be depressed,
or sad.
We are here to make a difference in the lives,
Of other people around us.
We are here to be happy and peaceful.
When people get to us,
We have learned to shake it off.
Just laugh at it…
Look at life as a gift.
Don't hate anyone or anything,
Appreciate everything and everyone.
Because they all have a reason to be here.
Living is when you're 80 or 90,
And you have laugh lines all over your face.
Laugh with your friends and family,
But most of all…laugh at YOURSELF

Cameron Corey, Grade 7
J Graham Brown School, KY

Mom's Cooking

When I woke up today,
I didn't know what to say,
I couldn't help but look,
When I noticed Mom trying to cook.
It was bad.
It was terrible.
It couldn't be worse.
The eggs were talking, the toast was walking
The pancakes were running, the syrup was cunning
The bacon was singing, the waffles were swinging
The sausage was spitting, the milk was knitting
Look up there, in the sky, there goes the orange juice flying by
I wonder, I worry, I don't know what to do
So, I look at my dad and he says,
"Get in the car, McDonald's isn't too far."

Kathryn O'Leary, Grade 8
Kerr-Vance Academy, NC

The Tunnel of Green

The branches intertwine above
Forming a tunnel through the woods
Stretching seemingly forever onwards
Along the well-worn path
Sunlight, filtering through the canopy of leaves overhead
Dapples the ground with splotches of green light
As the crickets chirp their lullaby
And the birds sing their tune
The trees lean in closer
Beckoning for me to relax in their shade and
Time seems to stand still
As the serenity assuages the everyday worries
That always seem to relentlessly assail me
I let my mind slip away
As I drift ever further down the tunnel of green

Aaron Salomon, Grade 7
White Station Middle School, TN

Music

In a land where voices are heard
Lives the woman to whom all musicians refer.
Her eyes are blue; her hair is gold
Her entire person is a sight to behold.
Her voice is that of the angels,
She is a sanctuary when all else fails.
She is the music which fills our hearts,
And sounds that are pleasures to our ears.
But once we fail at our parts,
Then music will fulfill our fears.

Megan Buchko, Grade 9
Riverside High School, WV

Music to Me

My love for music is so great,
To it, I could never hate
It grows with crescendos while weakens with decrescendos
Ever changing are the rhythms,
With each coming measure
One two, two two, three two, I count,
Waiting for my time to play.
Keep with the tempo, the conductor shouts.
Measures pass like seconds and before you know it,
Your song is over.

Harold Fair, Grade 9
Riverside High School, WV

Vanity

She sees; he doesn't
She finds herself watching him when he's near,
But he never notices. For he's too caught up in himself,
To notice what goes on around him;
One day, his best friend tells him that the vain person next to him is not the guy he grew up with.
With those words, he begins to examine his morals.
The girl has also noticed that, maybe, this guy isn't all he's cracked up to be
Eventually, the guy changes himself, and thinks of others before himself,
And finally notices the pretty girl who has been pining after him for so long;
But he's too late, for she's realized that he is not worth it.
He sees; She doesn't.

Sarah Daugherty, Grade 8
Greeneville Middle School, TN

Lock My Heart

I'm like my locker.
I look the same on the outside but different on the in.
I may look like everyone else but I can hold the things that really matter to you.
I can hold your burden that is making your mind spin or love notes that make your heart skip.
You can tell me the lies that you tell or the secrets that weigh you down.
I won't judge I won't hate I won't make you hide in shame.
I'll lock it down keep it safe.
So remember me I'll sit and wait.
For when the time comes
I'll be here being your listening ear.

Olivia Rowlinson, Grade 8
Bradford High School, TN

The Flame

Fire. It is a path of destruction and unwantingness. You cannot control it, nor overpower it. It holds all of the world's sorrow and pain in its soul. It is a wildfire that spreads throughout your whole body. It closes all of the doors to your future. It owns you, like the Earth owns its thrilling waters and driving winds. Fire is the fear, which cracks your thoughts into each little piece. Fire is the anger that stains your happiness with every moment that passes. Pain is choice, but if you pick the wrong decisions, the fire will find you, and it will destroy you. It is hard to get rid of it, but not impossible.

You can act happy, but the fire will not give up. But with patience and a strong mind, you can block the pain of destruction and you alone can open the doors once more, and find a life of freedom. The world is full of fear and pain, but it can all go away if you put out the flame.

Alex Ziemer, Grade 8
Owensboro Catholic Middle School, KY

Nine Eleven, Two-Thousand and One

Dust fills the air, the musky smell of ashes and dirt so horrifying, on that dark hazy night, I sit there on the curb shocked and terrified. A stream of tears rolling down my face, watching people run, walk, cry. Their coughing worries me, but the sound of my own coughing depresses me. "Help, help please, my child, have you seen her!?" She shows me a picture and I nod sadly. The dust and ash coming in like an eagle dashing for a worm, helpless. The little remains of the Twin Towers, the same Twin Towers that the planes crashed into. The thickness of dust in the air makes it almost impossible for you to see anything, The thickness of dust burns my eyes, the stench of burnt debris burns my nose. The sound of sniffles, the sound of moaning, I breathe in the dirty air, only to end with a cough. I cover my face with my hand that smells like depression and sadness; the smell I never smelled until now, The day where America died. The question everybody is thinking, is this the end or just the beginning? The day of nine eleven two-thousand and one.

Jaelynn Penn, Grade 7
Ramsey Middle School, KY

Disney World

Disney World is a place for me to be me.
I can be a princess, a pirate, or a magician.
I can fly with elephants, soar over golf courses.
I can see alligators and crocodiles,
Lions, zebras, and giraffes.

Disney World is a place where I can be free.
I can run and walk, glide and soar.
I can visit other places,
I never dreamed about.

Disney World is a place to meet
And make new friends.
I can play with Pluto, laugh with Minnie,
Goof off with Goofy, and hug Mickey.
To eat with Belle and Cinderella,
To talk with Mulan and Aurora.

Disney World is a place where,
You never are too old to play.
You are never going to forget,
That time when you were there.

Disney World is a place where all the magic happens.

Brielle Hoagland, Grade 7
J Graham Brown School, KY

Friends Forever

Sarah Lee moved to America when she
Was only sixteen, She had no friends
And little family. When the boat
Docked she was terrified but also
Excited to start a new life with freedom.

She walked off the boat and she took a
Glance at the new land, and smiled then
Took her mother's hand. They walked across
The smooth pavement to stop a taxi and got in the
Vehicle and drove away.

Sarah Lee was excited to start a new school
But was scared to make new friends
The name of her school was North East
High, and her teacher's name was
Ms. Valentine. The next day she went to
School and wore a white and blue uniform.

She walked into school and what
She saw was her best friend from Mexico
Who she forgot had moved there and really
Didn't have to be scared because she had a
Friend all along.

Cheyenne Osuala, Grade 7
Ramsey Middle School, KY

The Red Pyramid

A magical dad who cannot be found,
One boy and one girl are not safe and sound.
Out on their own with magical wands,
For magical help, they become very fond.
Sadie and Carter are just two kids,
On a trip to destroy the Red Pyramid.
This brother and sister are usually apart,
While on this quest they become one in heart.
Their quest is not easy but courage will shine,
These two will not stop till their dad they find.
Around every corner danger will be,
From the evil Lord Set, they will not flee.
Sending in evil forces to stop Sadie and Carter,
Only pushes these two to try even harder.
Set's birthday is upon and his power will grow,
How strong he will get they don't want to know.
Save Dad is a must and destroy evil Set!
All before the day of destruction — You bet!
Evil loses, but they lose Dad too,
Only part of the quest, they wanted to do.
Bravery wins, sadness for loss, and hope anew.

Zach Ihler, Grade 7
Fuquay-Varina Middle School, NC

I'm Happy My Dad Is My Dad

I feel safe when he's around
To open my eyes to new places and experiences
He fills my soul with such happiness
And is the best father I know
Although he may not think I see
Or that I haven't heard
The life lessons he offers along the way
I promise I got every word
He is in my personal hall of fame
Deep with my heart
Always my super hero, daddy
Right from the start
I love my dad, and I wanted him to know
I send him love wherever I go
I don't tell him enough how important he is
In my universe he's my great big shining star
That's why I'm happy my dad is my dad

Katlyn Hurst, Grade 7
White Station Middle School, TN

Spring

I wonder if the sap is stirring yet.
If the bees are buzzing.
I wonder if the flowers are blooming at all.
The little animals are frolicking about.
I wonder if the ground is warming up from the blanket of sunlight
For if it is so, then I will know, it's spring!

Timothy Rains, Grade 7
Whitley County Middle School, KY

Living Room
Inside the recliner
On top of me is my dog
In front of me is the TV
Without these things I would be sad
Above me the fan is on
Near me is my cat, Jinny
Up above me she is there
Despite having school, I'm happy
Until dinner I can stay here
In me is true bliss
Tanner Kirby, Grade 8
Heritage Middle School, TN

Fall
Fall is when the leaves
Fall to the grass
And children play in them
And when school is out for a week
And children go places
And have fun
And laugh
And when fall is over
They are sad
Rhiannon Parkerson, Grade 7
Elkton School, TN

Soccer
Soccer is really fun
the soft green grass is trampled
by players rushing to get the ball
they pass and run to score a point.

The ball whizzes past the goalie
it hits the net, score!
The team cheers as the buzzer rings,
they've won the game.
Sarthak Bansal, Grade 7
White Station Middle School, TN

Waiting
She was waiting by the phone
Because she was all alone
You never call
You're always at the mall
She cried as she tried to keep a steady tone
Mackenzie Driskell, Grade 7
Pigeon Forge Middle School, TN

Sun
Sun
Big Red
Hides behind clouds
Extremely hot and dry
Bright
Scott Stazzone, Grade 7
Pigeon Forge Middle School, TN

The Battle of Bunker Hill
June 16, 1775,
Is a day to remember for all that survived.
About 1,200 militia men,
Were about to fight yet again.
Under the command of Colonel William Prescott,
They set up fortifications at Bunker Hill, which they chose as their spot.

The next day the British redcoats,
Crossed the harbor in their boats.
They assembled at the bottom of Breed's Hill,
Weapons drawn they were about to kill.

Although the Americans lacked ammunitions,
They sure did have a lot of ambitions.
Colonel Prescott reportedly cried,
"Don't fire till you see the white of their eyes!"

The Americans ran out of ammunition so they had to retreat,
But the British learned that they wouldn't be easy to defeat.
The British won the Battle of Bunker Hill
But suffered heavy losses, about 1000 were killed.
Angela Tran, Grade 8
St Nicholas Academy - South, KY

My Locker Is Like My Mind
My locker is like my mind
It's red just like my face when I get embarrassed
It's filled with so many things at one time
I have all these thoughts running through my head with every moment
Especially in front of the class with all eyes during the occasion
It doesn't stand out from the rest of them
I try to fit in with all my friends no one likes to be the outcast
It's neat on the inside, but can get very messy
Like my life everything can be going so well and then it all crashes
It's my everyday place where I go to put stuff up
Just like my mom in ways like when I have a rough day
I always talk to her to get rid of my worries or stress I may have that day
My locker is just like me and my everyday life
Samantha Palmer, Grade 8
Bradford High School, TN

Set Me Free
Silence that kills like a sharp silver sword,
Down on my knees praying a sweet prayer to the precious Lord.
My soul is an agonized angel wanting to fly...
Locked inside like an abase prisoner of a dark cold bitter jail,
Growling loud trying to escape

Then a soft, gracious voice comes about saying I'll open the gate...one day
Feel no guilt, sorry about this disgusting, depression pain.
But one day, I'll heal your distressed soul too.
You will smile when your soul enters heaven's shining, bright, vibrant golden gate
Smile today, look forward to tomorrow,
I'll take away all your sorrow.
Brittany Wood, Grade 9
Riverside High School, WV

1941

It was a nice sunny Sunday afternoon
Until "tat tat tat"
I have never heard so much yelling,
At the docks
Then something hits the airfield
Fuel, bombs, and ammo
All exploding one after another
I swear that the whole world shook
I knew I had to help

Then I remembered
That my father was working
At the airfield
He was a pilot of a P-51 D Mustang
I ran home
As I ran I was thinking if he was off early

I could see our house
She saw me at the end of our hill
Then bombs struck the airfield and our house
I am a 15 year old orphan
3 years later I was recruited to the Marines

John McGarry, Grade 7
Ramsey Middle School, KY

Believing*

Young, innocent Ivy never thought a guy like Tristan,
a swimmer
would ever be interested in her turns out he was!
So much in common so little time,
for they had no clue what was to come.
A terrible accident separated them from one another
losing hope.
Suffering and weeping,
having terrifying dreams
Ivy was losing her faith in her beliefs.
Thinking she was all alone not receiving
the signs that were given to her.
For Tristan was trying to connect with her.
Scaring, frightening, not giving up.
For he was God's helper and was on a mission
to protect her but from whom shall that be?

Graciela Stephany Arreola Lopez, Grade 7
Fuquay-Varina Middle School, NC
*Inspired by the book "Kissed by an Angel"

They Say

They say I can't be a model, I'm not pretty enough
They say I can't be a singer, I don't sound good enough
They say I can't be a dancer, I'm not graceful enough
They say I won't be able to do anything right, I'm way too dumb
They say I won't be loved, I'm not lovable

But now every day I live my dreams

Carenna Collins, Grade 9
Gateway Christian School, TN

The Player's Dream

He played the game most every day outside and near his home
The court was fenced and littered
With cans and styrofoam.

He's played in stadiums as well, arenas great and small.
his jump was high, his rush was fast:
"Defeat the others, win them all!"

The coach would play him all the game
He'd never "sit one out"
He ran as though his heart would burst
But "victory!" was his shout.

He won and won and never lost
Because he could not see
That losing was an option
For one talented as he.

His game is only in his mind
You cannot play with him.
He's in a wheelchair where he's spent
The whole of life confined.

Hank Selby, Grade 8
All Saints' Episcopal School, TN

I Am Change

I may seem like a phantasm
But I come as swift as a hawk
And leave you just as quick
Until the day I come again
To bend your life in my hands
Some revel in my coming
Others find it terrifying
Either way I hold sway over your dominion
And even your most sagacious and dauntless men
Have no hold over me
I can bring the cessation of tyranny
Or ingress it back into your society
I bring a wanton attitude
Or a deadly pestilence
I rule you with impetuosity
For I have no master
I am change

Dylan Telkamp, Grade 8
Dillard Drive Middle School, NC

My Pursuit of Happiness

Happiness is a flower bud just waiting to bloom,
Happiness smells like burnt wood from a warm and cozy fire,
Happiness tastes like fresh brownies that just came out of the oven,
Happiness feels like a soft, long blanket on a cold windy day,
Happiness looks like a kid's smile on their fifth birthday,
Happiness sounds like baby's laughter,
Happiness is a wonderful gift, you should never let go.

Miya Whitaker, Grade 8
Leesville Road Middle School, NC

The River's Charade

I know the River's charade
The semblance of her serenity and the truth underneath
The façade that she portrays, lusterless and lifeless

I have felt her frigid fingers gently grab me
And bring me into her austere, glacial embrace
I know how often she can fling a soul into the swift current with cold indifference

But I know how she is when the sun is prolonged in the sky
When the wind blows balmy and the air is thick
Her waters are tropical and inviting, and she suffers the Eagle to swoop under her surface for fish

I know the River's secrets
The estuary that leads to a bluff of jagged cliffs, her prized possession
The place where her azure water is shallow and she lays exposed

I have heard the River sing
The cry of an overheard osprey
Her fingers stroking the rocky shore
Even the silent flight of the elegant heron,
Whose white impression against the dark blanket of night is breathtaking

I know what she looks like
Hardly elfin, but broad faced and gently hunched over, her eyes creased with crow's feet
Her skin is soft like leather that has been weathered over time
Her lips are plush and slightly open, in pursuit of emotion

Keely Hendricks, Grade 8
Harpeth Hall School, TN

Race to the Finish

There were four runners that ran on the cross country team at Ramsey Middle School.
One girl, named Sammy, was nice to everyone she met. She was full of spirit.
There was a tall girl named Katie. She was full of laughter and jokes.
Jonathan was, some would say, not tall but not short.
There was also a shorter boy named Jacob. He was filled with determination and, well, silliness.

Today they had a major race after school.
All four arrived at a field filled with people in different color jerseys.
They all had on the same thing: a blue tank-top with white stripes on the shoulder.

"All 7th grade boys to the starting line," they heard.
All the boys went running, running, running.

The girls waited as the boys came.
But where were Jacob and Jonathan?
They stood up and walked toward the rope.
"There they are!" Sammy shouted.
They had already passed by and they were in first and second.
In just about seven minutes, they came again, sprinting up the hill.
Jacob first then Jonathan, but then coming from behind, Jonathan blew by Jacob and took first.

At the end they congratulated each other.
They knew that they had a hard practice tomorrow, so they raced back to the bus.
The four when home and were ready to do it again the next day.

Jonathan Green, Grade 7
Ramsey Middle School, KY

From Afar
I see you each day
And your eyes looking at me
Knowing that I can only
Love you from afar

I touched your hand
I smiled at you and you smiled back
How do I tell you
I love you from afar

Today I foolishly waited for you at the door
You passed by holding another girl's hand
I saw love in your eyes that Aphrodite gave you
My heart broke from loving you from afar

I loved you, long ago and
When I see you years later
I'll tell you I loved you from afar

The years have passed, and
I still love you, from afar
Veronica Carroll, Grade 8
George M Verity Middle School, KY

The Beach
The Sun is screaming "Look around the beach"
Today is no ordinary day
Waves flowing up and down
Sand guides me to the shore.
I look up at the sky
All I could see is dreams
Everything I saw is not what it seems
It seems unreal.
As the Sun is screaming at me
I'm thinking
Is this really happening?
I look at the shells by the Sea Shore.
I wonder what is coming next
Do I need to rest?
I keep walking
The same things is happening
Happening over and over again
I stop and look up.
Suddenly
I see shells and in the sky I see dreams
And the sun is screaming "Look around the beach"
Kayla Burage, Grade 7
J Graham Brown School, KY

Life
L iving, breathing, things
I n our planet, but what about others?
F lying, running, jumping, scurrying everywhere
E verything that lives and breathes is the definition of LIFE
Alec Comella, Grade 8
Dillard Drive Middle School, NC

My Great Dane Puppy
My new puppy
My new Great Dane
Grey and black
Paws too huge
Pouncing across the lawn
Up and down
Left and right
To and fro
Clumsily falling
Chasing what comes across his land
Dogs, deer, squirrels, boys
Tumbling leaves
Almost too late he stops
Inside and outside always playful
Unsteadily climbing stairs
Jumping on my bed
Puppy oh puppy
Won't you go to sleep?
Save the pouncing, chasing, climbing for tomorrow
Tomorrow again with
My Great Dane Puppy.
Jack Rogers, Grade 8
Dillard Drive Middle School, NC

Tannenbaum
A frosted fir tree is still cold from the snowy outdoors
While outside it's as bitter as the tree's prickly spines
In our home life is brimming with warmth and radiance
Adorned with crackly, sizzling popcorn
The scent brings back long gone memories
Glossy magenta balls directly from Macy's are among
Minute green needles that poke my scarlet sweater while
Perfuming the air with whispers of winter spearmint
A glass ballerina twirls under a spotlight
Of twinkling Christmas tree lights
Tinsel and berries as red as crimson fire set the stage
Dear Grandmother's feathery, frosted bluebird perched near the top
Where upon a skinny branch
Rests an angel with painted icy indigo eyes
Watching over the world and filling it with comfort
On this night of endless joy
Georgia Coles, Grade 7
White Station Middle School, TN

When I Sing
When I sing, I can almost fly.
When I sing, I sing from my heart
Not from my mouth.
When I sing, it comes from my soul
From inside.
My voice feels flawless, powerful and exciting.
I know I might not be the best singer in the world.
I do know that when I sing
MY voice is beautiful.
Tierra Johnson, Grade 8
Elkton School, TN

Superhero

Someone who'll die for the cause,
and not be fueled by the applause,
but by the rage in his heart,
and the love in his soul,
who plays more than his part,
and takes on an even bigger role.
He'll be my superhero.
He'll die
for my rights,
but by no chance will he kill
for the same will.
He's not like the same old hero.
He's on his own
to fend for himself and his home.
That's my superhero.
You won't believe the heights to which he'll go
to protect me and this place I know.
No, He's not part of the show.
He took on his own role.
He's not like them, he's a real hero.
He's my super hero.

Jeanette Holland, Grade 8
Cheatham Middle School, TN

Foggy Day

White mist swirling,
A foggy city twirling.
Damp moist air forming a cloud,
I make it impossible to find anyone in a crowd!
Looking mysterious and eerie,
I can turn a beautiful day to dreary —
I am fog.
Humidity filling the air,
Frizzing out innocent people's hair.
I crept in during the night,
A swirl of grayish-white;
I add a chill to the air, so you'll bundle up tight!
BUT when the sun comes to play,
Slowly,
I *d r i f t* away.

Taylor Buck, Grade 7
Holy Trinity Catholic Middle School, NC

I Miss You

Why,
Why did you leave me here.
All upset, full of questions that can't be answered.
Me myself is full of regrets and non-explainable feelings.

I just miss your laugh, love and unexplainable kindness,
This you always shared near and far.
You were my rock that I always knew I could talk to.
Without my aunt I'm not complete,
Actually I'm empty.

Sarai Baylor, Grade 7
J Graham Brown School, KY

Light and Dark

Light is a beacon of Hope
Prevailing against all evil
Protecting all that stands with it
So that all is good, and the world is safe
But lurking in the void is the Dark
Trying to set off the balance of the Light
Despite its struggles, and its sacrifices
Light fights back and prevails
Leading the Dark to retreat back to the shadows
Waiting to strike again

Dark is the beacon of despair
Threatening everyone, even its own allies
Doing anything to prevail over Light, despite the cost
It lurks within the shadows waiting for an opportunity
To defeat the Light
Usually to conquer the Earth using figureheads as puppets
By manipulation, Dark gains control
Until it is stopped by the Light
Just remember, Light always decimates Dark

Parris Fortune, Grade 9
Wakefield High School, NC

Moonlight

Steeple, steeple burning so bright
sounding your silent war cry through the night.

Revere and Dawes galloped through the night
shouting "the regulars are coming,"
"the regulars are coming" all through the moonlight.

Adams and Hancock ready in defense
to fight whoever was coming for their independence.

Militias and minutemen fought to the death
with the shot heard around the world with men on horseback.

On July 4, 1776 our independence was sung
with 56 pen strokes declaring that we won.

Caitlin Bell, Grade 8
St Nicholas Academy - South, KY

Grief

I am Grief
A result of wanton
I am a bringer of disapprobation
You will never forget what you have done!
Your past mocks you
I will bring you cessation
I am a pestilence that egresses from the inside
You know that you cannot change your past
Why do you still ponder over it?
How does it feel?
Knowing you have caused so much pain

Andrew Billings, Grade 8
Dillard Drive Middle School, NC

Fool's Gold

In a world full of the same
I stand out;
I know it's good though, because
The same nowadays is bad.

Many reasons separate me
From the path I walk,
To the treasures I seek.

Too many find pleasure
In an empty chest of treasure,
Missing the One that will measure
You and me.

Fool's gold is what they're digging for
In an environment of darkness and black ice,
While through His word
I've already reserved
A spot in Paradise.

Christian Villers, Grade 8
George M Verity Middle School, KY

Remember When

Born in West Virginia
Born and raised in a small little town
My childhood is known history I will never forget
Born as a coal miner's daughter
The touch of my skin was so unreal
My soul was so deep I couldn't explain
Remember the actions I used to make
Thoughts that were too deep, that were so hard to reveal
Remember the moments I used to have
Can't forget the good times I had
The memories are still in my head
The beating of my heart was fierce
I could feel the blood vessels running through my body
Know my actions have changed
Remember the times I played outside
Remember the times with my family
Remember the grins I used to make
Remember the looks I used to have
Remember I have them forever

Emileigh Wells, Grade 8
Sissonville Middle School, WV

If Every Month Was December

Snow angels, making cookies and giving special gifts
That's when all of our spirits lift.
One month of jolly, one month of cheer
Is what gets us through that following year.
Smelling fresh pine trees
Snow to your knees
Sets that Christmas mood.
Twinkling Christmas lights
Fill each dark night's
Cold, arctic air.

Decor to adore
Hot coca to share
Fills the season with its love and care.
Peace, love, smiles, friends,
When December ends it's all pretend.
But if every month was December
There would be no Christmas memories to cherish forever,
Or ever remember.

Haley Gorman, Grade 9
Wakefield High School, NC

You Can Find Me...

My life is fun and exciting
And every day I'm curious about what is going to happen next
It is a small town that almost everybody lives in.

You can probably find me out in the yard
With my grandmother planting flowers

You can find me at church every Sunday
You can find me at the Palladium
Going to see movies with my friends
You can find me at Feeny's
Having a nice cup of frozen yogurt

You can find me at Chick-Fil-la
Or Cook Out getting some food to eat
You can always find me at Harris Teeter
Getting groceries with my mom

You can find me anywhere in High Point!

Carrington Lewis, Grade 8
Westchester Country Day School, NC

My Trust for You

My trust for you is great.
When lies are told, I will not believe.
When you are judged, I will defend.
When you are sad, I will comfort you.
When you are happy, I will smile.
When you are right, I will agree.
When you are wrong, I will correct.
When you are gone, I will mourn.

Hannah Leak-Kent, Grade 7
Dyer Elementary & Jr High School, TN

Brother and Sister

A brother and sister are different
One is 8, one is 13
The brother is athletic
The sister is talented
The brother is a math magician
The sister is a reading wizard
They are both very different
But they are both artistic

Amit Patel, Grade 8
Weddington Middle School, NC

My Brother
This is a poem to my brother, Andy.
Though you are approximately
seventy-five miles away,
I think about you every day.
What you're doing,
how you are, how school is,
how your house is,
and how your friends are.
But the most important thing I want to hear,
is that you're safe and everything's good.
If you think about it, you and I are a lot alike.
I guess the reason why
I miss you so much is because
now there's no one like me at home.
I hope you're doing well
and getting good grades.
Tell your friends I say, "Hi,"
And though I don't want to,
I have to say goodbye.
Love,
Paige

Paige Deglow, Grade 8
St Agnes School, KY

Overwhelming Love
Love is a comfort,
that never goes away.
It smells like freezing snowflakes
slowly falling to the ground.
It tastes like warm hot chocolate,
slowly entering your taste buds.
It feels like the cool fall breeze,
against your warm soft skin.
It looks like a red rose,
just picked from its bush.
It sounds like soft raindrops,
lighting tapping your window pane.
Love lets you know that everything's going to be okay.
Your worries are as if they have
floated off into a far distant land.

Chandler Craig, Grade 8
Leesville Road Middle School, NC

Where I'm From
I am from the southern parts
I am from Sanford stadium
Georgia Bulldogs football is what I love
Many days and nights just cheering and cheering
Playing soccer day after day
Hanging out with my cousin Shane
Eating Chicken Express
Watching a lot of movies
Making many pizzas
This is where I am from

Will Argo, Grade 8
Westchester Country Day School, NC

Music Is Life
Music is like life
You start at the prelude, the beginning of a tale
You begin the crescendo up
There are different moments in life
Piano, mezzo forte, fortissimo
There are also accents
Life goes by like sixty-fourth note
You reach the peak
The liveliest part
You live in the moment, hold the note out
Till soon
You start the decrescendo
Life gets less exciting
You love every moment, anticipating the end
Finally
You breathe your last breath
The final note
Silence
The end of the song
The end of life

Ilea Shahan, Grade 9
Riverside High School, WV

Mini-Me
Delilah is my little niece
My love for her will never cease
She has a smile that brightens my day
It's like the sunshine's bright rays
She is very chubby and fat
As a matter of fact
That baby would roll over if she could
She even makes chunky thighs look good
Little stars peeking through on a cloudy night,
Her teeth are poking through and shining bright
Her hair is long and curly
But when she is hungry she can be surly
My little Delilah is as cute as can be
And, you know, it's plain to see
My little niece is a mini-me!

Brianna Hayes, Grade 9
Parkersburg High School, WV

Pride
Look into my eyes,
Deep down inside
You'll see strength that was created by wounds
So when it's time, my wings soar as swift as an eagle
Trying to prove myself, never trying to deceive you
"Beyond average" my pride says
Stop repeating the American story of a young black man, today
Grab my attention for life
And let my time shine
Rising above all else, challenge me to be great
Know that I can, and remember what I put in your mind

Kezionne Pittman, Grade 8
Roanoke Valley Early College, NC

Just Like You

A mother just like you
it's just like you to make
my world go round
it's just like you to make
all my dreams come true
it's just like you
to find the quality of my heart
it's just like you to hold
my hand and whisper…it'll be okay
it's just like you
to shape me into all I need to be
it's just like you
to take all my pain away…so I can be free
it's just like you
to walk me through darkness
it's just like you
to tuck me in at night
it's just like you to wipe my tears in fright
it's just like you to understand me when I speak
it's just like you to pick me up when I'm weak
it's just like you to be mother of the year

JaQuan Nesmith, Grade 7
Fuquay-Varina Middle School, NC

Flowers

I see a lovely thing, a rose
A thing of such great beauty
You would not give one to your foes
You give from love, not duty

Lilies are lovely, white as snow
Singing in the midday sun
I see them shining, row by row
To drink their beauty, one by one

A yellow tulip stands alone
In a sea of other flowers
Its brightness will not be outshone
In the warm summer showers

The flowers of summer will sweeten the air
And remind us of a time when we had not a care

Holly Fields, Grade 9
Riverside High School, WV

If Teenagers Ruled the World

If teenagers ruled the world what would it be like?
Would it be peaceful?
Would there be any school?
Would the parents tell the teenagers what to do?
NO!
If teenagers ruled the world there would be no school,
it would be crazy, and the parents would be our…
SLAVES!

Mitchell Van Dyne, Grade 8
Weddington Middle School, NC

Sandy and the Mean Kid Rap

There once was a boy whose name is Sandy,
He was good at baseball and he's really dandy,
He once was in a conflict with a mean kid,
He was accused a liar for something he never did,
There he was in a store at the wrong time,
He was looking at magazines worth a couple dimes,
Sandy's house isn't big and he isn't rich,
Some people might say he lives in a ditch,
The mean kid and his friends had a hide out,
It was ugly, beat up with a sign that read KEEP OUT!
Sandy started playing baseball for a team called Raptors,
They were talented and cool just like actors,
He was forced to moved because people thought he was bad,
He was frustrated, crying, and really mad,
Now he's playing for the Mudcats, He took a different approach,
The mean kid was there and Sandy called him a roach,
Sandy had told his friends, "That guy is a thief!",
With butterflies and his stomach Sandy let out a sigh of relief,
He was now feeling good that he had told the truth,
He even told the police that he had proof,
That's the story of Sandy, who's dandy.

MoKyus Bagley, Grade 7
Fuquay-Varina Middle School, NC

My Sisters

This is a poem to my sisters
whom I have hurt a thousand times.
You love and forgive me when I do wrong.
You are there to help me
when I am sick or hurting.
You two are my friends forever.
I can tell you anything.
even though I don't express my feelings as love,
you already know I do, when we roughhouse and have fun.
We kid so much,
you already know to know the opposite of what I say.
So, therefore, you are the worst sister ever.
I couldn't have asked for more of what you already do
for me and our family
to make it lots of fun
Love, Kate

Kate Abeln, Grade 8
St Agnes School, KY

Excitement Unending

Excitement is a firework of enthusiasm;
Exploding in the night with a long trill of adrenaline,
It smells like candy in a candy shop,
It tastes like Pop-Rocks on a hot summer day,
It feels like the coastline unending,
It looks like a small child on Christmas morning,
It sounds like the cheers after the winning game,
It alters your life;
Time and time again.

Becca Mountz, Grade 8
Leesville Road Middle School, NC

Death Is Coming
No time to say a short goodbye,
No tears to quench a saddened eye.
    Death is coming to me.

Can do no more to help my cause,
Play became a sudden pause.
    Death is coming to me.

Darkness surrounding in broad daylight,
Life's battles are no longer mine to fight.
    Death is coming to me.

The earth below as I take flight,
Resist his call with all my might.
    Death is coming to me.

Another life is his to claim,
A Siren's call with no one to blame.
    Death is coming to me.

He came with a warning cry,
Silence now where laughter lie.
    Death has come to me.
    Kelsie Floyd, Grade 8
George M Verity Middle School, KY

What Lies Within
Each journey brings forth
a chance to encounter.
Each encounter brings forth
a farewell.

But when a farewell
brings forth a journey,
the worlds open their hearts

To those chosen by light,
or ensnared by darkness.
To friends, who share
the same bonds
though their paths may differ.

When you doubt the path
trod thus far.
When the hand you held,
is lost from you.
Gaze anew,
at the heart that once was…

For all the answers lie within.
    Dylan Bailey, Grade 9
Riverside High School, WV

The Choice
Crashing waves like the sea
Turmoil rises inside of me
Like a being from my past
Strong feelings boiling fast

A slippery grasp, I try to hold
As darkness closes in so cold
I cannot let it dominate
Or it will be my dooming fate

As I say words I should not have said
What is going through my head?
While I ponder about my choice
Should I have raised my voice?

The choice I made was not the best
Now I'll lay my head to rest
Try to figure another way
Tomorrow is a new day
    Hunter Gullett, Grade 8
George M Verity Middle School, KY

Thomas Jefferson
The writer of the Declaration
Tired of being treated less than
To help free our nation
Was Mr. Thomas Jefferson.

Working for independence
One of 56 men
To help our nation balance
Was Mr. Thomas Jefferson

Having many talents in store
A very creative person
Being an architect and more
Was Mr. Thomas Jefferson.

A new president awaits
In 1801
The third to rule the states
Was Mr. Thomas Jefferson.
    Katie Meyer, Grade 8
St Nicholas Academy - South, KY

The Moon
Before my bed;
the moonlight shines.
Could it be frost covering the ground?
I raise my head;
look at the bright moon;
I sit back and wonder
how big space could be.
    Daniel Cheek, Grade 7
St Joseph Academy, NC

Age
Age is but a number
At least that is what I've heard.
Why is it when you're younger,
It isn't really?

Age is rules and restrictions
You're either too young or too old.
You're too young to understand
But too old to act like that.

Age is not always a true testament
To who you are.
You can be fifty-two
But act like you're twenty-one.
A fifteen-year old could have
Gone through more turmoil
Than a sixty-year old has.

Age is not but a number.
    Amy Bosley, Grade 9
Sycamore High School, TN

Love
Love hurts and heals
Sometimes it can steal
Your heart, your mind
But it may be able to bind

It's easy to love. Love be careful
It can be very fearful
If you confront it, you are brave
But it is very easy to crave

If you find it, be sure to say
"I will love you 'til the end of my days"
Such a beautiful substance
It makes women want to dance

When I see him
Or when I hug him
All I want is to see
The things he sees in me
    Heather Tant, Grade 9
Sycamore High School, TN

Love Is
Love is sweet
Love lasts forever
Love is here
Love is there
Love is a bond
Love keeps us going
Love is peace
Love
    Margaret Hamer, Grade 7
White Station Middle School, TN

Where I'm From

I am from a house across the road from a farm.
I am from a house where the TV was always on either Blue's Clues or Bear in the Big Blue House.
I am from a family that has owned numerous pets, but my favorite was my cat, named Fluffy.
I am from a place where I could smell the neighbor's crops every morning.
I am from a place that also had a multitude of tornadoes, and that's why I am now in West Virginia.
I am from a place where a tornado would completely obliterate one side of the street,
And leave the other untouched by the winds.
I am from a town near the busy capitol city of Indianapolis.
I am from a man from Marion, Indiana, and a woman from Wooster, Ohio.

Ryan Long, Grade 8
Sissonville Middle School, WV

One Man's Trash Is One Man's Treasure

Think about it when you're eating food and when you waste it you could've given it to the needy…
One man's lack of education could be one man's straight A/B honor roll…
Just because you don't want to eat veggies doesn't mean throw it away
Just because you don't like those ugly shoes or that ugly dress doesn't mean throw 'em away
Just because you don't want this phone or that camera doesn't mean throw it away

For all we know there is someone out there who needs these things and will appreciate them because "you don't know what you have until it's gone"

Rionne Hayden, Grade 7
Cleveland Middle School, NC

Regret

Regret is an eerie shadow,
Without choice, it lurks behind the good and the evil.

It smells like blood, copper, tangy, and metallic.
It tastes like tears: the melancholy mixture of salt water and memories.
It feels like something constantly tapping on your shoulder, however you are completely alone.
It looks like a funeral: dressed in black, people stand still as statues.
It sounds like rain viciously pelting on a tin roof: short, sharp bursts of pain sent into an already tortured soul.

Sara McCauley, Grade 8
Leesville Road Middle School, NC

Don't Let Fear Take Over

Fear is like a shadow; creeping upon you, and watching your every move;
It smells like a slowly burning candle, its smoky scent filling the air;
The tense flavor of jalepeños interacts with your taste buds;
It feels like a soft breeze passing by your face, as chills run down your spine;
It looks like an empty forest only to be lit by the moon;
The owl's smooth howl carries in the wind throughout the night;
All of the sudden the fear you have been hiding within, makes its appearance, and controls your every move.

Cole Chance, Grade 8
Leesville Road Middle School, NC

About Life

Life is the sum experiences that we encounter as we go through life. Day to day struggles and triumphs are experiences by all of the world's creatures. As human beings, when we encounter a challenge, we have freedom to choose how to react. Every decision that we make leads us down a different road. We never come to exactly the same crossroad. Every decision that we make has significance. The tiniest choice that we make sounds through the entire universe.

Fatima Ezzahra Faiz, Grade 8
Dillard Drive Middle School, NC

My Mom

This is a poem to my mom, Ann,
whose tender eyes and loving heart
are always focused on others.
You only give and never take
no matter what's at stake.
When I am mad and don't show
you my gratitude,
always know that I am thankful for you.
You give me the courage to do what is right.
And when I fail
you are always there to pick me up
and encourage me to try again.
Although I don't show you
I love you enough,
know that it would be impossible
not to love a person like you.
You are always there for me,
and know that I will always be there for you, too.
Love,
Andy

Andy Flood, Grade 8
St Agnes School, KY

I Am

I am creative and skillful
I wonder what the guitar hears
I hear the music flow around me
I see the crowd go wild
I want to give them a night they will remember
I am creative and skillful

I pretend to be one with the instrument
I feel the vibrations race through me
I touch the strings
I worry about a string snapping
I cry that I will someday not be able to play
I am creative and skillful

I understand complicated rhythms
I say always try something a step above your skill level
I dream of becoming a legend
I try to do better than last time
I hope I inspire others to follow suit
I am creative and skillful

Cameron Ramsey, Grade 9
Bearden High School, TN

Red Rose

I walk outside to the garden
'Tis spring you see
I see a red rose blooming there
Water speckled over her petals
Sitting there in her glorious dress of thorns
With leaves and stem the darkest green
Her crown of red looks like spilled blood
Her brothers and sisters cower under her loveliness
I shall not pick her
I shall leave her to allow her beauty to be seen by others
I do not regret my decision
Later that year I walk outside to the garden
'Tis winter you see
She is gone, they are all gone
But, I know they will be back next spring, next year

Natalia Bartkowiak, Grade 7
East Millbrook Magnet Middle School, NC

My Cruel and Hating World

Hatred is a burning cut,
The flesh opening little by little
It smells like molding bread,
Covering it inch by inch;
It tastes like spinach,
Taking over your mouth with little green goo
It feels like your heart has been ripped open;
For everyone to see the cold and aching part of you
It looks like a black hole;
Ready to take over the world at any minute or any second
It sounds like bloody murder
Making you want to hide under bed and NEVER EVER;
Want to come out again
Controlling over your life
One centimeter at a time

Soett Torres, Grade 8
Leesville Road Middle School, NC

Hot 'n' Cold

Spring is a time of life.
Flowers bloom and dance with the wind
In the unlimited field of green.
Birds sing in merry choirs.
The warms sun's rays are splashed on my face.
No season could be any better.
Yet when flowers close,
Birds glide to the warm south,
And the sun hides behind the blockade of clouds,
Then you'll know that
Winter has arrived.

Meead Rahman, Grade 7
White Station Middle School, TN

The Horror of Hostility

Anger is a horrible creature
Waiting to pounce from the shade and devour lives
It has the stench of burning metal,
Stinging your nose and poisoning your heart
It tastes of iron,
the sharp taste of fresh blood
Hostility takes the appearance of a shark's maw
Ready to tear into anyone who comes near
It sounds like a fork being scraped down a chalkboard,
Sending tremors down the spine of anybody who hears it
Rage will tear apart your life

Grant Barkley, Grade 8
Leesville Road Middle School, NC

Twist of a Tragedy
Flight, crash, boom,
Looks like there's as many dead as at Pearl Harbor,
3000 people dead, another hospital bed,
Twist of a tragedy…

There's another plane,
Whoa, this is insane,
Hospital bed, another dead,
Boom, twist of a tragedy…

3 planes, 2 towers, zip,
A boom as loud as thunder,
Another plane, down in Pennsylvania, both towers collapse,
Pentagon, my old man gone, I'm done…

Both towers collapsed,
Total of 10,000 hospital beds, we need a lot of meds.
They are done, 3,000 gone,
TWIST OF A TRAGEDY…
Zachary Fountain, Grade 7
Ramsey Middle School, KY

Limitless
Fear is a bubble inside you,
Waiting to pop and makes the fearless, fearful
It smells like a cloud of secondhand smoke,
Over time it slowly kills your hope;
It tastes like rotten milk,
That makes you sick;
It feels like dry ice on your skin,
It burns you from the outside in;
It looks like a cloud of darkness,
Where you see no light, no existence;
It sounds like a person screaming in horror,
That doesn't warn you when it comes,
It creeps slowly into life
And then attacks one of it many hosts.
Angelica Escobar, Grade 8
Leesville Road Middle School, NC

The All-Powerful Remote
If there was a remote that controlled life like it does the TV
Would it have easy buttons or a voice command
Will it have a help feature like the computer
Could I hold it in my hand or would it be a big machine
Can I surf all the possibilities and if I don't like it I can go undo it
Can I create other animals to find the perfect pet
Could I make dreams come true
Could I create books that have not been written that are perfect
Could I go back in time and right all wrongs
What if it fell in the wrong hands
Would it be the end to life as we know it
I don't want to know
Mainly because I just want to watch TV
Lloyd Young, Grade 7
J Graham Brown School, KY

Fall
There goes the adventures
The blazing sun
The summer in which we had so much fun
The ending of one thing
The beginning of another

There goes the tune of the ice cream truck
Here comes the noise of the gobbling turkey
Green leaves no longer decorate the trees
But hide underneath the bright colors of fall

You no longer scurry down the street
Fighting off the summer heat
Now you start to feel that windy chill
Following you like your shadow on the street

Rejoice in the days of fall
The feel of her crisp cool mornings
The time is near for fall to end
Even though it feels like it is only about to begin

Fall only visits for a while
She leaves and comes back again
To share her beauty and comfort
As a long time friend
Maya Rashad, Grade 7
White Station Middle School, TN

The South
I really love it down south
I feel the taste of sweet tea to my mouth
Step outside, feel the fresh breeze
Unforgettable sight of the green trees

Most people say sir and please
It's not as cold down south so we don't freeze
All the food here makes you say yum
A lot of birds chirping make me hum

From mountains, cities and beaches
To fresh fruit, oranges and peaches
A dog in an old Chevy truck
Try to find that up north, good luck

I don't hate the north, I just love my home
I can't handle skyscrapers shiny like chrome
Go ahead you can think I have too much pride
But I must represent where I reside

I will always stay loyal
The south to me is royal
For the south I try to comply
From my John Deere, I say goodbye
Kevin Page, Grade 8
Dillard Drive Middle School, NC

Mine

The moonlight
Glinting, shining, casting a shadow onto her gown
The gown that makes her perfect
The gown that makes her mine

The moonlight
Glinting, shining, casting a shadow
On his perfect green eyes
The eyes that make him mine

Her smile
Makes me sing
Makes me want to hold her till it hurts
The smile that makes her mine

His words
Make me speechless; elated with passion
Make me skip a beat
The words that make him mine

I am hers
She is mine

I am his
He is mine

Samantha Darpel, Grade 9
Notre Dame Academy, KY

What My Mother Doesn't Know

Sophia and Dylan are boyfriend and girlfriend,
Just an ordinary couple with no rules that bend,
Grace and Rachel are there for Sophia until the end,
Just a normal teenage girl,
In a little city.

Sophia finally finds her true love,
And it isn't who she thought it would be,
She goes to the dance and finds a masked man,
And they dance,
it's like Cinderella because she doesn't know who he is,

Then her friends go on vacation,
And she takes one too,
But it's in her town,
At the art museum.

She finds her masked man,
And they start to date,
Then she has to tell her friend,
About her new boyfriend,

But she doesn't tell them,
She shows them,
Then it's the end!

Alyssa Long, Grade 7
Fuquay-Varina Middle School, NC

My Mom

This is a poem to my mom, Cary,
whom I love very much.
Your heart is as big as the sky,
You will never stop loving me.
Nice blue eyes that will always watch over me,
hands that are always helping others,
who is always smiling and having a good time.
You have been there for me when I needed your guidance.
You are there for me when I need someone to talk to.
Driving me to sporting events,
cooking me dinner and playing corn hole
are the things I appreciate most.
You are always in the stands,
cheering me to victory.
Your thoughtfulness is beyond imaginable,
buying me things I want but don't really need,
forgiving me always no matter what I do wrong.
I don't always deserve your love,
but I love you anyway.
I will always love you,
Kirk

Kirk Tabeling, Grade 8
St Agnes School, KY

Heaven's Light

Never Deny the power of Heaven's Light
Its mighty creator is very great
It's pure and it's perfect and vanishes plight
You'll see it after the path of narrow and straight

As perfect as His promise, tenderness, and care
The Savior waits for the angels' flight home
Loved ones wait for our return, listen to our prayer
They love it when we decide not to roam

We somehow cry when they reach eternal paradise
But they are happy and will always be pain-free
We only have to make a small sacrifice
When you return there'll be a great jubilee

In heaven's light the righteous will rest
And all in its wake shall be blessed

Samantha Stanley, Grade 9
Riverside High School, WV

My Heart

My heart beats like the South African drums.
My blood runs through my veins,
as though it were the rushing waters of the Niagara Falls.
My heart is as steady as a crane, and soars like an eagle.
My heart is as caring as a mama tiger to her newborn cubs,
and is as wild as a southern cowboy on his stallion.
My heart will open to all in need, as far as the ocean is blue.
What does your heart mean to you?

Norah Mitchell, Grade 8
Dillard Drive Middle School, NC

Their Loss

People are cruel and selfish.

They take you high
Only to drop you down again.

They fill you up
Just to empty you again.

They make you think one thing
Then turn out to be different.

They make you love them
Just to break your heart.

They make you trust them
Only so they can lose that trust
And regain it
And lose it for good.

Then they realize what they lost
And what they're not getting back.

Samantha Crisp, Grade 8
Glen Martin Elementary School, TN

Two Way Street

The words you yell,
The expressions on your face.
The brace for my heart doesn't work,
I feel like I'm in the wrong place.
What do I do know?
Don't you see, this fight is endless?
I hear you, but do you hear me?
The tears of sorrow from the night alone,
Could not compete with my roaring moan.
This two way street isn't working out,
Us making up is beyond doubt.
This endless fight was worth a yawn,
But when I woke up, it was barely dawn.
The restless night was difficult to attend,
Will my broken heart ever mend?
Will we ever talk again?
Maybe.
Will we ever make up?
Maybe.
Will we ever be family…?

Diana Hughes, Grade 7
East Millbrook Magnet Middle School, NC

Building My Door

I went down to the General Store,
To get supplies for my door.
They had no nails.
They had no pails.
And now I don't have a door.

Camille Mauk-Olson, Grade 8
Robertsville Middle School, TN

Inspiration

Going astray from what you knew for so long
Will never compare to the happiness when things stay the same
People say change is good and we think then why does it hurt so bad
Why can't people just understand and maybe lend a helping hand
But really what's the point of asking all these questions
If all these evil things will stay the same
But all the good things change
I wish someone gave me a straight answer of why they keep living
Because I could use inspiration
Kind of like the burning blue flame of hatred of the world
No the people and the same hatred goes for myself also
I could say I wish this and I wish that
But as I and many people say why wish if it won't ever happen
I don't like having this feeling of hate
But to keep my spirits up to say at least I have family
It might be corny but it's something I have and appreciate all of my life

Adil Abdurahman, Grade 9
Arlington High School, TN

The 9/11 Problem

Run, run, run away from New York City on its darkest day,
smoke as dark as night gives citizens a fright,
the Twin Towers fell and people screamed, running for their lives horrified as can be.

People yelling "help, help" while watching the planes crash into the towers in fear,
the crash was like a sonic boom, then the people were at their doom,
the towers smoking and on fire, from all the running, people grew tired.

As the towers collapsed, people began to scream,
"help, help me" heat from the fire was hot as lava,
people ran in terror from smoke and debris and prayed for their lives to continue to be.

Timmy Downey, Grade 7
Ramsey Middle School, KY

A Fellow Patriot's Pain*

Innocent to poisoned faith
So did the veil lift
Heroes of a decade past
Through the rubble sift

Errant pain and toxic hate
Worthy of a rift
Instead unite in freedom's pride
Grateful for the gift

Jayde M. Stone, Grade 8
Camden Middle School, NC

*Dedicated to the memory of all the civilians and emergency workers we lost on 9/11.

Popsicle

Juicy sweet ice cold flavorful bone chilling brain freezing
sore throat cure drops of juice drippin' down the wooden sticky stick
tonsil surgery medicine fruitful cool sugary sour slimy cold on my tongue
delicious cherry cold on my fingers melting smooth thick enjoyable
melt in your mouth goodness

Taylor Lacroix, Grade 8
Weddington Middle School, NC

High Merit Poems – Grades 7, 8, and 9

Friendship of Fall
Leaves falling
Friends laughing
Chills in the wind
Secrets flowing ear to ear

Frogs jumping
Girls talking
Birds singing
Children dancing

Friendship is a ball
Friendship of fall
Tori Brasel, Grade 7
Elkton School, TN

Two White Roses
One white rose,
Beautiful and strong,
Tended to its every need,
Petals open wide and confidently.

Another white rose,
Curtained and ignored,
No one cares that it's there,
Still, it mounts charmingly.

Both stand superiorly,
And both will brown and wither away.
Aleah Wordsworth, Grade 9
Middle Creek High School, NC

Different Colors
You see pumpkins
This time of year
Decoration or not
Fall is still here
The trees are turning
Joyful colors this time of year
Happy or not
Fall is still here
Trick-or-Treat
This time of year
Scary or not
Fall is still here
Adam Cischke, Grade 8
Ramsey Middle School, KY

Soccer
Soccer
Brutal fun
Kicking the ball
Winning is the best
Futbol
Dustyn Walker, Grade 8
Pigeon Forge Middle School, TN

I Am from Sea Gull
I am from a camp set next to a river,
Where morning seagulls sing, sea gull winds calling,
A cabin full of new and old friends,
A couple college-aged men supervising,
A rejuvenating meal in the Mess Hall,
Activities to do for the rest of the day,
The meals only interrupted by thunderstorms,
I am from sandy beaches, rocky sandbanks,
Low grass putting greens, a lake with kayaks,
I am from a Camp Four 'shirt tag' and dodgeball game,
Capture the Flag or even Ping-Pong,
A move night watching *The Goonies*,
A midnight dance party and Bojangles,
I am from a slow Chris Cross dance song,
A fist pumping "Party Rock" by LMFAO,
I am from a deep sea fishing trip outside Morehead City,
A fancy dinner at The Sanitary, staying overnight at the Outpost,
Skidding along the Neuse on a Scout, gliding over waves on a Sunfish,
I am from Camp Four, Bayou, Outback, Sliding Door,
Diverse Space, Sacred Place,
I am from Sea Gull.
Montgomery Belk, Grade 8
Westchester Country Day School, NC

I Am a Hidden Truth
An honesty that would rather be hidden than heard out loud.
I am sometimes seen as a blessing, but also as powerful as pestilence.
For all its goodness it has the disapprobation of millions.
I can make your world a heaven or a hell.
No one has dominion over my power and the force of who I am cannot be stopped.
I am part of destiny. I am the part of destiny that creates destiny.
The sound of each of my words can rip a heart apart or fill a heart with hope.
It is said that I set people free. What is seldom said is that I also keep people hostage.
The most sagacious sometimes take me to the grave, or so they think.
I surface even when my keepers no longer exist because I am not controlled by time or space.
I can be your friend or I can be your enemy
But that depends on your conscience and what lies within your soul.
I make you look behind your back and have you fear going forward.
The only way you control me is by facing me
And accepting the consequences of the power I have over you.
Yusef Sabra, Grade 8
Dillard Drive Middle School, NC

My No Place
Welcome to my No Place, an empty waste of mental space.
Come see the clear fading embrace, and the walking voices that show no face.
Count the stars though your blue haze, while empty thoughts graze.
My No Place refuses to be erased, not wanting to be left unplaced.
Watch the trees grow then fall, like souls trying to swim through it all.
See all the empty grace.
See every long lost face.
Welcome to my No Place, that will forever be home.
Misplaced, ungraced, left without a trace.
Trapped in my No Place.
Margie Dotson, Grade 7
Powell County Middle School, KY

Winter

in the winter
inside my room
under the heat
beneath the light
on my bed
by the door
under the roof
near my dog
toward the tv
as I'm relaxing

Grayson Russell, Grade 8
Heritage Middle School, TN

Best Friend's House

In her yard
Under the sun
On the trampoline
With the music on loud
Around the loop we walk
Down the yard playing golf
Up the road looking for sour grass
On the 4-wheelers
Despite going home
At her house happiness is

Kayla Ratliff, Grade 8
Heritage Middle School, TN

Skate Park

Beside my buddy
To the skate park
Up the hill
With my board
On the box
Over the stairs
Inside the bowl
Up the ramp
Between the other kids
Without a fear in the world

Michael Utley, Grade 8
Heritage Middle School, TN

The Racetrack

In Seymour, Tennessee
Into the gates
Under the sun
Between my friends
Around the track
On the concrete bleachers
Out 'til almost midnight
Off to the pits we go
Across from the racecar
Toward the car we go with happiness.

Savanna Merriman, Grade 8
Heritage Middle School, TN

Hollow Heart

A willow tree sits on top of a hill overlooking a beautiful meadow
My soul lies underneath the tree
Such an unusual choice for me to pick to sit
For this was a depressing tree and I was happy and content or so I thought

I look over the meadow it captures me in its beauty
The scent of flowers burn my nose
The sound of giggles rings in my ear
Little girls run through the meadow picking flowers as they go

Sadly this was a memory I never had
I looked out trying to remember the last time I felt compassion for others' problems
Or even a gave a simple smile
I realized I had never done so
I had never shed a tear for others
Crying only for my behalf
No one had given me love, hate, or simply listened to my problems
I wasn't selfish or mean I tried to feel, but I was hollow as the tree I sat beneath
Feeling nothing, but for myself

Lucy Sermersheim, Grade 7
J Graham Brown School, KY

Why Did You Leave

it's fall the leaves are changing
the air becomes crisp
I sit in my room and watch the days fly by
I wondering why did you leave

you said I was your heart and soul
but then you left me in cold
I stood in the snow and watched as your headlights had to go

I swore I would never miss you again
but each time I close my eyes all I see is you
days and day goes by as I watch the sun rise

seasons may change
but my feelings for you will never change
I can't help but wonder what this winter would be if you weren't with someone like me
winter is sometimes cold and dark much like your soul lately
so I leave you with this goodbye

Tiffany Loomis, Grade 9
Hurricane High School, WV

My Mind Is a Locker

My mind is a locker you could easily get distracted in them.
Things fall out and never get put back in.
Certain things aren't easily found no matter where I put them.
My mind is crazy and frustrating just as my locker.
My locker is dangerous to everyone around me.
Many people look right through my locker and me.
My locker has gone through many changes but is just the same inside.
My locker is full of knowledge old and new, seen and unseen.
My mind is a locker.

McClain Pierce, Grade 8
Bradford High School, TN

Faith

F is for Focus. A central point of attraction, attention or activity. Paying attention to the future, advancing the placement of your past. Successful is what you will be. Not because you're just that abundant with greatness but because you have faith.

A is for Achievement. Something accomplished by superior ability. Working hard and fighting with the strong power of self-encouraged determination. Even though eyes can't see what has been placed in the heart of one, continue to seek the destination of emotional and mental comfort. Someone has to light the path of an ample future in which the blind will see.

I is for Include, meaning to contain, to involve. A blind man can still see a dream. A heartless child can still survive. The power of a thousand individuals is stronger than an individual with a thousand powers.

T is for Trust. Belief in something as true. Even though there will be those who don't believe in you, who cares? You must first believe in yourself. Not every one wants you to succeed. That's why you must trust in yourself. Have faith.

H is for Hope meaning to Long or Dream. Hope for what they never expected. Long for what they said you couldn't and wouldn't have. Dream of an extravagant dream that must and will come true. Together these things create something brilliant. You're not all these things because you're just that abundant with greatness, but because you have FAITH!

Kiera Edmonds, Grade 8
Roanoke Valley Early College, NC

Forever Me

I am as if a worn out string, coming undone at times it seems.
Sometimes a smile is a simple deed, but other times you can't get one out of me.
I was raised on the idea of always being strong, but sometimes my ignorance can make me wrong.
Although many times I might lose my head, I will always turn around, and go full speed ahead.
My faith can be as strong as a sturdy base, but sometimes that's not always the case.

I love the feeling when your toes first kiss the water, it's like a mother first saying hello to her baby daughter.
I sometimes like to sit and watch the stars, and wonder how far away they really are.
My family knows what makes me sick, what makes me happy, what makes me tick.
My determination layered deep inside, can overwhelm me at times.
Confidence is always my key, to reach the lock inside of me.
Sometimes my personality makes me pay a fine, but I am who I am, my flaws are mine.

Mary Catherine Gray, Grade 9
Bearden High School, TN

Life

Life is like a staircase.
You start at the bottom and as you grow you climb those stairs.
The stairs of life.
Sometimes you'll trip, sometimes you'll fall, and sometimes you'll make no mistake at all.
Life can be confusing, it can be grand, all you need is to walk hand in hand.
Have a shoulder to cry on, and someone to hold, eventually you'll find 'that one' with a heart of gold.
Life can be rewarding, don't ever give up, just put on a smile, and buckle up.
Keep climbing those stairs, always be you, no one compares, and always stay true.

Have fun, make memories, go wild, and always keep that perfect sense of style.

You may loose some ground, and have to start to again, but trust me when I say, it's worth it in the end.

Kelsey Ritchie, Grade 8
East Jessamine Middle School, KY

The Face

From the beginning of my life I have been looking for your face, but today I have seen it.
Today I have seen the charm, the beauty, the unfathomable grace of the face that I was looking for.
Today I have found you and those who laughed and scorned me yesterday are sorry they were not looking as I did.
I am bewildered by the magnificence of your beauty and wish to see you with a hundred eyes.
My heart has burned with passion and has searched forever for this wondrous beauty that I now behold.
In all of time and space there is nothing to match the ineffable beauty and grace of your unfathomable face.

Keenan Chapman, Grade 7
Lexington Middle School, NC

I Hate You

I hate you
I hate the fact that I can't breathe whenever I'm around you
I hate that my pulse quickens whenever you're near
I hate the fact that you don't have a clue

I hate you
I hate the fact that you don't see me
I hate that you know how to get under my skin
I hate the fact that everyone says we'll never make it

I hate you
I hate the fact that you make me bite my lip
I hate that I tuck my hair behind my ear because of you
I hate the fact that you only care about her

I hate you
your Abercrombie jeans
your Polo shirt
your charming smile
I hate everything about you
but mostly, that you made me fall for you

Hannah Shannon, Grade 9
Lee County High School, NC

Death

I am Death
You fear every aspect of me for
I am that which cannot be out-Heroded
You may hide your insecurities of me behind jokes or slander but
I am that which shrewd people do not jest of
You may try to run but I will catch you because
I am that of which no vesture, walls, or towers could ever hide you
Some of you welcome me with open arms because
I am the ingress into nothing and forever
You may think you're clever but
I am that which even the most sagacious minds cannot elude
You may think that you can escape me but
I am that which there is no egress
You may not realize but I am there in the shadows, always
I am Death and in the end I am the ultimate victor

Sierra Hickman, Grade 8
Dillard Drive Middle School, NC

Manhattan, New York

In the city, the people walk.
Down the steps is the subway.
Through the city is Central Park.
Inside the Statue of Liberty you can't go.
On the sign it says Ed Sullivan Theater.
Near the theater is Times Square.
Beyond what your eye can see, there are people.
Between the billboards, I stand with a camera.
Despite all the people, it's beautiful.
Up in my memory is a peaceful, fun trip.

Brianna Mandrekas, Grade 8
Heritage Middle School, TN

The Very Tragic Day

We shall never forget this tragic day,
It's sad to even express it this way
It's very, very sad at heart,
That these two buildings came apart.

I will tell you this is very sad,
Now some people are very mad
Now all the soldiers say today,
"This was a very gloomy day."

Good love to all that died,
And we are happy that you tried
These buildings came apart like sand,
And we think about you while we roam the land.

The crash was loud like a sonic BOOM!
Now everybody was at their doom
A lot of people died that day,
So never forget this tragic day.

Breanna Rohmann, Grade 7
Ramsey Middle School, KY

Dandelion

Oh Dandelion, standing alone and tall.
Being there all day listening to the cricket's call.
It's quite lonely being there all day and night,
When surrounding you is green and you're the only shade of white.

Then one day comes a cool autumn breeze
You are off on a journey, the destination cannot be seen.
The journey carries on, not knowing when it's done.
Passing by birds, bees, and watching the bunny run.

When you return a seed is planted and you begin to grow
But when you grow up no one really knows.
So whenever you're gone or think you're alone,
Just remember you will always find your way back home.

Corey Carvelli, Grade 9
Robert C Byrd High School, WV

A Mother's Expressions of Love

Tears of delight fall like rain
as a mother holds her newborn child in her arms.

Pride sparkles in a Mother's eyes like midnight stars
as a mother watches her child grow up.

Compassion glows in a Mother's face
as her child spills their own tears of delight.

You don't have to be elegant, funny, or smart
You just have to be "you"

Now that is a Mother's expression of love.

Blair Harris, Grade 8
Camden Middle School, NC

Parents

This is a poem to my parents
who have helped me a million times.
You have given me advice I have rejected,
But you know I will use it later.
You help me do the best I can
in school, sports and life.
You let me make my own decisions
because you know it will help me grow.
You believe
that I can do what is right.
You hold me responsible
so that I do not make the same mistake twice.
You have taught me
to be respectful.
You have been such good teachers and role models
I have matured greatly.
Finally, Mom and Dad,
always remember
I am grateful for your help
and I love you,
Sam

Sam Romes, Grade 8
St Agnes School, KY

To Remember the Fallen 9-11-2001

To remember the fallen
is not to remember how they fell
but to remember why and for what
To remember the fallen
is not only to remember their actions
but to remember the dream for which they fought
is not to remember how they fought
but to remember who they fought for
To remember the fallen
is to remember their reason
To remember their dreams
and to remember those they fought to save
To remember the fallen
we continue their fight
we carry their dreams
and we finish what they start

Casey Warner, Grade 8
Weddington Middle School, NC

The Unwanted

Death is sad for most to see or be
it can consume the life of you or me
unwanted by most but seen by all
easily done reminds me of fall
in the end don't worry, I'll see you in the place to be

Jeremy Heilig, Grade 8
Pigeon Forge Middle School, TN

The Stars

They shine over us all the time,
But we are only allowed to see them at night.
They choose to hide during the day.
Then at night they choose to shine and light up the sky.
Why, oh why, do they hide?

They come out to play as soon as the sun leaves.
They form shapes that we choose to name,
Yet they aren't always the same shape.
They remain there, shining still, even as we sleep.
Why, oh why, do they hide?

The sun comes up again in the morning,
And chases all of the stars away.
No more fun for them,
For now they must leave or be out shown by the sun.
Why, oh why, do they hide?

The sun insists on being the only star during the day.
But night is their realm, the time in which they shine.
They choose to only shine and play at night.
So I must ask once again,
Why, oh why, do they hide?

Madison Pritchard, Grade 8
Dillard Drive Middle School, NC

Thanksgiving

It's that time of year,
The time all turkeys fear,
Thanksgiving Day is finally here!

Dad frying the turkey,
Mom inside making jerky and pudding,
While the family is in the living room starving!

The family together,
This couldn't get any better,
Then night begins to fall.

Let the feast begin,
The people dig in,
And chow down until everything is long gone!

Sitting down in the den,
Indigestion kicks in,
We are all filled to the brim and sleepy.

Getting ready for next year,
The excitement already alerts me,
Cannot wait to see dad fry that turkey!

Madison Pentony, Grade 9
Cape Fear Christian Academy, NC

Bored
Every day at school,
I'm filled with such dismay;
the monotony of the subject
it's the same thing every day!

First there's my science class,
DNA can sometimes be bleak;
from phenotypes to genotypes,
it's even harder to speak!

Then there's Language Arts,
oh, what a mess!
The number of people talking
shows we're difficult to assess!

Then I head off to math,
I'm now starting to lag;
I walk into my classroom
to see billions of people playing tag.

Then finally to Social Studies,
by now I'm very weak,
but wouldn't you feel the same
If you did this every week?
Bradly Terrell, Grade 7
Holly Shelter Middle School, NC

No Home*
Moonlight guides my steps to where?
I do not rightly know,
Each footprint fades behind the other
No matter where I go,
My heart cries out for comfort
A home where I belong,
But these cold hard streets I
Walk upon seem to hum
My sad life's song,
As I long for a home, a home, a home,
A home where I belong

The visions in my mind's eye
of comrades I witnessed die,
Upon that bloodstained battlefield
brings a soulful, heart-wrenching cry,
Why am I left to walk these streets
So cold and all alone
Haunted by my desire to have
a home to call my own,
I long for a home, a home, a home,
A home to call my own.
Madison Poff, Grade 8
George M Verity Middle School, KY
*In honor of homeless veterans

I Am
I am focused.
I wonder about my future.
I hear music playing.
I see children laughing.
I want the best things out of life.
I am focused.
I pretend I am racing.
I feel the tires sliding.
I touch the steering wheel.
I worry I am going to crash.
I cry that I am losing control.
I am focused.
I understand the importance of education.
I say I am intelligent.
I dream about being famous.
I try to do my best.
I hope to fulfill all of my dreams.
I am focused.
Tare Davis, Grade 8
Roanoke Valley Early College, NC

My Grandpa
This is a poem to my grandpa.
Thank you for doing everything
that you can for me.
Every Sunday I go to your house,
and we watch football, baseball or golf.
You used to take me on vacations
with grandma and mom.
You would help me out with math,
and science homework.
Sometimes you couldn't make it
to my sports games,
because they are too late for you,
but I forgive you.
You and Grandma, when I was younger,
would play with me.
Now that I'm older,
I don't see you as much as I used to,
but I still love you
Lee Ludovicy, Grade 8
St Agnes School, KY

On the Farm
In the sun
During the hottest part of the day
Between the barn and the house
Towards the pasture I go
Around the corner are the cows
Along the fence there are hay bales
With my dog we herd the cows
Across the road we go to plow the corn
In the tractor we sit to get out of the heat
Within me is happiness
Jacob Gross, Grade 8
Heritage Middle School, TN

Haunted Forest
There I stood,
fear in my eyes,
fear in my heart,
scared to walk on

"Booom!!!" As I hear
Lightning strike
Even more startled than ever.

Walking slowly as I go
As I continue to hear
"Booom" people banging
on walls, "Ahhh…"
As I listened.

As I hear a chain saw
get started, "OH MY GOSH
I DO NOT WANT TO DO THIS"
I yelled with anger.

My sister commented,
"Too late now Jalen!"
Jalen Summers, Grade 7
Ramsey Middle School, KY

My Sister
This is a poem to my sister Stephanie.
You sit in your office, working vigorously.
Though if I ever need you,
you're there in a hurry.
You can be stubborn at times,
but you're always looking out for me.
My fondest memories are being with you,
you are my best buddy
You set an example by working tirelessly.
You are and always will be my dearest sister,
Stephanie
Love,
Sam
Sam Hacker, Grade 8
St Agnes School, KY

High Energy
On the sharp piercing court
By the jubilant crowd
With a dreadful smack
On the foul line
To the ringing backboard
Down the slick court
Beside my hateful opponent
Around the helpful screen
Up in the air
Toward the bright orange basket
With a joyful score
Karlee Bolen, Grade 9
Riverside High School, WV

The Dictator

Hatred is a dictator,
slowly rising to power;
it smells like sour milk,
making you gag at every gulp;
it feels like a branding iron,
burning into your skin;
it looks like a sweet flower,
tricking you until it has you
completely in its grasp;
it sounds like the screams of
hundreds being murdered;
it takes control of your life
then completely destroys you.

Jason Brown, Grade 8
Leesville Road Middle School, NC

Bursting with Joy

Joy is a field full of blooming flowers,
that bursts with butterflies fluttering.
It smells like the sweet scent of perfume.
It tastes like a scrumptious chocolate cake,
that was freshly baked four minutes ago.
It feels like a smooth touch of silk,
rubbing against your face.
It looks like a beautiful sunset,
as it sets down into the horizon.
It sounds like little kids laughing,
and playing with friends.
This wonderful stream of happiness,
gives life its meaning.

Tollina Banh, Grade 8
Leesville Road Middle School, NC

Is It Possible?

It is possible to fall in love with
something that won't ever love you
back?
To get a feeling so many others feel
when they're around this thing that
you love so much.
Is it possible to let something
nonliving that I love, that I
give life to take over my heart?
Well is it? No one knows the
answer but I do know that I have fallen
in love with the music that
surrounds me every day!

Leigha Smith, Grade 9
Riverside High School, WV

A Day in the Woods

Walking through the woods
A leaf falls slowly by me
Peace, serenity

Jake Moore, Grade 8
Dillard Drive Middle School, NC

A Fire to Remember!!!

I sit around, from day 'till night,
Just waiting for my fire
I clean and cook, sleep and train, and help out with most everything,
Just waiting for my fire
As I prepare for that big day, a disaster appears from nowhere,
A plane just hit the north tower, that is my fire
No more waiting or training, they need all they can get,
I'm finally suited up for my first big trip, this is my fire
I ran in knee-deep with ash and debris, with tons of toxic air surrounding me,
and so many people running out thanking me,
This is my fire
My radio buzzing with mayday more than ever before,
the smell of death in and out my nose what such horror,
smoky ash and tower parts falling above my head, this is my fire
All I could hear is a huge roar, I look out what's left of windows to the south tower,
falling, collapsing, dying, this is my fire
Getting as many people out as possible, jumping through debris and trash,
I make it out with not a second left, this is my fire
Back at the station, firemen sobbing and hugging more than ever,
I may have left with one brother but now I have hundreds,
That was my fire

Katie Heavrin, Grade 7
Ramsey Middle School, KY

Strength

Sometimes I lie in bed and wonder,
Is this going to be another sleepless night?
I've no more tears to cry, yet plenty of hurting left.
I wonder every once in a while,
Will I make it through the raging storms,
Or will they defeat me?
My friend tells me, "God has your back,"
But God sometimes seems far away.
It's days like this, that I wonder where my strength comes from;
But these days also make me stronger.
Waiting to walk on golden streets is a long, hard journey.
I know one day it will all be worth all of this suffering.
All I have left to say is God grant me the strength for one more day.
Even though I have these days, I know God is where my strength comes from.

Savannah Lackey, Grade 9
Cape Fear Christian Academy, NC

I'm From

I'm from a place with rain in spring, all water in the summer,
All leaves in the fall, and sunshine in them all.
I'm from a place with biscuits and gravy, sweet tea and soda.
A place where friendly people are always walking out in the breeze.
I'm from a place where it's always quiet enough to read a book.
I'm from a place where everyone has an accent.
A place where soccer games are always played.
Saturdays are never wasted.
I'm from a place with Friday night basketball and Monday night football.
I'm from a place where everyone's childhood is the same.
I'm from High Point.

Dylan Sellers, Grade 8
Westchester Country Day School, NC

The Softball Field
On the field
In the dirt
Without my bat I play the 3rd
Despite the heat I play my best
With my bat I hit the ball
Around the bases I run.
As the ball rolls to the fence
Past 3rd I sprint.
After the outfield gets the ball
Towards home plate I run
I'm sure I feel great
Taylor Edwards, Grade 8
Heritage Middle School, TN

Dust
One day we will all be gone
Just dust in the wind.

That day we'll all be old
Just dust in the wind

Today we're here to stay
Not quite yet dust in the wind

Who knows about tomorrow
We might be that dust in the wind
Sophie Assadnia, Grade 8
All Saints' Episcopal School, TN

Memories
Memories remind you of the past.
Some of them don't really last.
They can be hard to let go.
Sometimes they are all you want to know.
The past can be bad.
Or it can be sad.
But most are joyful.
And they make you thankful.
Memories can make you learn.
And they can make you yearn.
For a better future.
Kalissa Bannister, Grade 9
Riverside High School, WV

There is Reason
Life is a beautiful thing.
It has its ups and downs
But wasting it so early is useless
Life is meant to be appreciated.
You should be grateful
That you're alive.
If you ever get down,
Put your hand on your heart.
God kept it beating for a reason.
Mackenzie Stevens, Grade 9
Riverside High School, WV

Night of the Living Dummy*
Her dad got her a dummy
A ventriloquist one
She loved with all her heart
She found a piece of paper
Which she found in his coat
She read it out loud
Which came to be a nightmare
The dummy slaps her
Causing trouble for everyone
He would talk for his own
To get her in trouble
She tries to explain
Her parents won't listen
Ending up grounding her
She and her brother
Come up with plans
To get rid of the evil dummy
They try to throw him away
But he keeps coming back
So they sell him to their cousin
Which was not a wise decision
Adam Hodges, Grade 7
Fuquay-Varina Middle School, NC
*Inspired by "Goosebumps: Night of the Living Dummy" by R.L. Stein

Mind + Locker = Me
My mind is like my locker: strange and bursting with new ideas every day
It can think very complex things, which my mouth can't speak
Bursting with memories, and colorful ideas is what gives me bad migraines
Sharp and steady, with everything in its own personal file
Like my locker, my mind has unwanted items lurking on the brink of it's
own little world
So I must wad these up like trashed paper, and throw them in the basket like Kobe Bryant
And I'm free to think more complex things with a cleaner mind to start anew with
Some days I'm focused, others I'm 3 sheets to the wind, not hearing a thing in the world
But there's nothing that my mind and my locker won't hold in forever
But even though my locker may rust and decay, my mind stays shiny and new.
Able to accomplish anything that comes my way
So though my locker may not be nice or flashy, kind of like me
It, like my mind, holds all things dear to me.
Brooklyn Howell, Grade 8
Bradford High School, TN

Short Life
You won't be there like you used to, who thought they should take you away?
Who?
I admired you and yourself,
But you had to go and ruin your health.
By you making a stupid decision
I lost you for life, causing a terrible feeling that made me feel so alone.
It was like a knife to the heart. My heart; aches as you're away,
It craves till the day that we will not be apart any longer.
I miss you;
I can't wait till the day I can see you; once again.
Cheyanna Bayless, Grade 8
George M Verity Middle School, KY

Sports

I like to play every sport
On a field, diamond or on a court.
I never like to lose
But I will always improve.
When I have fun
I always get the job done.
My number is fourteen
When you see me coming you know I'm mean.
I'm a beast
But anything from the least.
I give 100%
That's the message I sent.
I always support my team
No matter how bad the situation may seem.
Just put me in the game
And I won't be lame.
I have a lot of pride
With my team standing side by side.
I just love to play
For my life it's the only way.
I like to play every sport.

Jacob Miller, Grade 7
Fuquay-Varina Middle School, NC

Wheels on an Airplane

Rubber, black top, skid marks, runway
Going off, on, off and on, hour to hour, every day.
They turn, they torque, they retract
Rotating, jostling, landing safely;
Supporting, upholding, helps with safety.

High above, then down upon
The ground, they go.
Ever hanging in the sky?
No, but pull up like an eagle's talons,
Carrying hoards and loads by the thousands.

Landing gently on the runway,
Harboring travelers:
Gone the fun way.
Rubber, black top, skid marks, runway
The wheels of a shuttler going skyway.

Diana Dubites, Grade 9
Riverside High School, WV

Soul Comfort

We each are alone
Each soul by himself
Each soul must find its comfort
Its comfort could be anything
A person, an object, a talent
Something that they could not live without
Some souls may die in vain for their comfort
This is why love is the most dangerous soul comfort of all

Megan Gwyn, Grade 8
Weddington Middle School, NC

Me, Myself and I

I am not like anyone else
I am just simply myself
Being fake is not for me

No more pretending to be something I am not
Because in the end, you're always caught
No more spreading rumors, even if it is fun
In the end, people figure out how it begun

Posers, liars, and cheaters are things people can be
But that personality is not for me
It is not worth being someone like that
Because I think it is totally whack

Every day I try to be myself
And there is nothing else
That I would rather be
Than simply me
I am just me, myself and I

Taylor Warnock, Grade 8
Dillard Drive Middle School, NC

The End of the World

In the middle of winter I asked my friend
I wanted to know how the world is going to end
My friend smiled and laughed at me,
And said "Go ahead and ask everyone you see."
I asked everyone through and through,
And each one had an answer or two.
"The world is going to be in global warming"
"No, We're going to die by acid storming!"
"The Lord will be coming down soon!"
"It's going to be 2012, you buffoon!"
"We are going to have a Nuclear war!"
"No, we are going to die poor!"
I had started a philosophical debate,
Where everyone thinks they may know their fate.

Davies Lee, Grade 8
Weddington Middle School, NC

My Brother

I follow your footsteps good and bad
I listen to your advice because it's the best I've ever had
I try to avoid your mistakes but end up with my own
I love to see you live your life to the fullest
I love the fun we always have together
I love the silly fights we had growing up
I love everything we do together
But most of all
I love that your are my big brother
I love the man you've grown to be
I love everything you are.
You are my role model, hero, and best friend.
I love you with all my heart.

Nora Coley, Grade 9
Riverside High School, WV

A Poet's Inspiration
I pause
As my slender pen
Touches the fresh sheet
Of paper.
Looking up, I feel
The warm sun
Caressing my face,
Hear the robin's melody
When the wind blows gently
Through the open window.

I sigh and close
My eyes
As I draw in the sweet
Scent of the magnolia tree's blossoms
And the lilacs that brush against the house
And then turn to the
View of the green terrace below,
Letting that become my inspiration.
Wing Deng, Grade 7
White Station Middle School, TN

One in the World
Loving
Humorous
Wishes to influence
Dreams of doing what she loves
Wants to travel the world
Who wonders how everything works
Who fears death
But is afraid of no object
Who likes being with others
Who believes solely in God
Who loves to run
Who loves to cook
Who loves music
Especially to sing
Who plans to save lives
Who plans for success
Who plans to experience
Who needs to understand
Who is just one in the world.
Erin Sweeney, Grade 9
Bearden High School, TN

Seasons Come and Go
Leaves are falling on the ground,
Orange, red, yellow, brown.
Frosty mornings come and go,
Ushering in the winter snow.
Soon spring will be on its way
Causing the children to go out and play.
Summer heat is finally here,
But, autumn's cool weather is coming near.
Brooke Holstine, Grade 9
Riverside High School, WV

The Beach
You can have fun
In the sun,
Or catch a fish that
Weighs a ton!
You can find a dollar
In the sand,
And find big seashells
That's so grand!
I can fly in the air
In a sail,
And put all my sand crabs
In a pail!
Going to the beach is
So great,
Next time we go,
I won't hesitate.
Hunter Burgess, Grade 7
Elkton School, TN

I Miss You!
I miss your smile,
I miss your laugh.
I miss your hugs,
I miss the touch
of your hand to mine.

I miss the way you hold me tight
when I get scared during the night.
I miss the way you say,
"I promise it's alright."

I miss telling you I love you
and listening for your reply,
which always seems to be
"Forever and always, Babe!"
I miss you all around!
Siara Criswell, Grade 8
Dyer Elementary & Jr High School, TN

The Ultimate Race
You dive into the deep,
Your feet begin to move.
You feel the icy chill of cold,
Swirling all around.
You see the person next to you,
About to pull ahead.
You hear the people screaming,
As you go all out.
You taste the chlorine, sour,
As you scream and shout.
You smell it all around you,
When you take a breath.
You move your arms and swim fast
And then you finish strong.
Madissen Campbell, Grade 9
Powell First Baptist Academy, TN

Walking in a Winter Wonderland
I see snow everywhere
The trees are filled with it
As I walk
I see the pretty mistletoe
Covered in layers of snow
It looks like Wonderland
And as I walk by
The trees start to sing
The snow starts to fly
The mistletoe starts to shine as the sun
Arises from the horizon so peacefully
As the sun goes down
I have to leave
But I will never forget
Walking in a Winter Wonderland
Gabrielle Milner, Grade 8
Highland Oaks Middle School, TN

The Book
I can see it.
Just a few feet away.
"Boom, boom" my feet go.
"Thump, thump" my heart doesn't slow.
A foot away, I see it.
"Closer, closer" I'm there.
I reach and feel,
It is in my hands.
I can smell the dust.
"Swish, swish" the pages go.
Fading, fading.
I read and read,
But it cannot be,
Away I go
With the memory.
Madison Reitz, Grade 8
Weddington Middle School, NC

Sunset at the Beach
I gaze through my sunglasses
as the sun crawls down
into the glistening sea.
A sniff of the air
tells me how fresh it is.
At that moment,
the seagulls swoop in the air.
Families snap pictures
and pack to leave.
I take off my shades to see
the sky is red and orange
like a person is when he/she is angry.
Taking a final glimpse at the scene
I pack up my belongings
and head home for today.
Anisha Dash, Grade 7
White Station Middle School, TN

This Vicious Fight
It's the angel and the devil,
Upon my shoulders they will lie;
Kicking and screaming and fighting,
Slowly tricking me, so sly.
"Listen up to me," he said,
"I do the Devil's deed,
Just go for it, you'll be fine"
And through those trying lines I'll read.
And up speaks the angel,
Like a captain out to sea.
"Stay strong sweetheart,
What you do is who you'll be."
Now I don't know who I'll listen to,
I'm not sure what is right.
But either way today will not be
The end of this vicious fight.
Michaela Arndt, Grade 8
Moyock Middle School, NC

My Fantastic Mom
I write this to my mom.
my fantastic mom.
You made me who I am.
Your smiles bring people happiness,
your personality brings people laughter.
You are always there
to get me through the day.
and that is something I cannot repay.
You work all day,
You clean all night,
but you still make time for us.
Mom.
My fantastic mom,
You are the best,
And that's no test.
Alex
Alex Hacker, Grade 8
St Agnes School, KY

Swimming
Swimming through the darkness
Swimming through my doubts
Through my fears
Through my past.

Swimming through my anger
Almost getting drowned in my emotions.
Yet swimming still through the storm
Trying to get myself towards the shore.

Swimming through my life
Swimming through my present
Through the light of the sun
Through the joys and sadness.
Alicia Bauman, Grade 9
Bearden High School, TN

Mind to a Locker
My mind is a locker,
It opens up to everything,
A lot of school subjects,
Sometimes I forget to bring them back.
—Once, they put a lock on me,
I just couldn't think straight,
All of this pressure,
It adds up to be so great.
— Just like a locker,
I turn red, from tests,
I just wonder if I passed,
And about the rest.
—Once my owner opens the door,
They see a big 'ol mess,
But I'm not that bad,
I'm just not the best.
John Chappell, Grade 8
Bradford High School, TN

Books!!!!!
Books are very unique
But, nobody seems to care!!
It seems to me that only I care.
Books are all I think of.
Why does no one care?
Books have lasted for a long time.
Books carry history!
Books are better than movies.
Why do people abuse books?
They put them in electronics!
Books are meant to be pulled off shelves
And opened, on the spot.
How many people prefer books?
Not many that I know!
I know one, other than me,
But that is all I can see!
Jacqueline Rowley, Grade 7
Dyer Jr High School, TN

Friends Are…
Friends are a beginning,
They start as nothing more.
Your friend is like your baby,
Forever you care for.

When a friend turns into a rainbow
Its colors shine so bright
Friends are like a sunny day
That never turns to night.

Friends are a memory
That never fades away
Friends are forever
And forever they will stay.
Staci Stanhope, Grade 8
Bargerton Grammar School, TN

Grandpa
He was my savior,
The only person I trusted,
My whole world,
Even though you're gone,
I know you're still here,
Watching over me.
Protecting me.
Loving me.
I love you Grandpa.
Shawna Skeens, Grade 9
Riverside High School, WV

Your Love
Your love is kind.
Your love is sweet.
Your love is real, and true.
You care about my problems,
And help me through and through.
Your love is caring.
Your love is fine.
All I want is for your love
To be mine.
Madelyn Blevins, Grade 8
South Pittsburg High School, TN

My Mind Is a Locker
My mind is my locker
It is my stalker
It sees all of my things
My pictures, clothes, and everything
It is my life
Sometimes it hurts my finger like a knife
At the end of the day
I put my stuff away
I tell it I'll see it again…someday
Hannah Metcalf, Grade 8
Bradford High School, TN

Death/Why
Death
Soul Crushing
People Gather Around
Sadness, Anger, Blame, Regret
Why
Ethan Williams, Grade 7
Pigeon Forge Middle School, TN

Christmas in the City
Lit buildings, wet snow
Lights on poles everywhere seen
No dark anywhere
William Powers, Grade 7
Meredith-Dunn School, KY

Dream Eater

You close your eyes and sleep so softly,
You're ready to dream oh so sweetly,
But I sneak in,
For I am ready to begin,
To steal your wondrous reveries,
Never asking, no pretty please,
For I am the Dream Eater.

Katherine Segposyan, Grade 7
Blessed Sacrament School, NC

Grades 4-5-6 Top Ten Winners

List of Top Ten Winners for Grades 4-6; listed alphabetically

AbdurRahman Bhatti, Grade 5
Cambridge Friends School, MA

Katie Dominguez, Grade 4
St Joseph School, PA

Avery Fletcher, Grade 5
Balmoral Hall School, MB

Foxx Hart, Grade 4
F L Olmsted School, MA

Maximiliana Heller, Grade 5
Stanley Clark School, IN

Sarah Kim, Grade 5
Avery Coonley School, IL

Grace Lemersal, Grade 6
Meadowbrook Middle School, CA

Julia Peters, Grade 4
Toll Gate Grammar School, NJ

Lucas Tong, Grade 6
Chinese American International School, CA

Mallory S. Wolfe, Grade 5
North Knox West Intermediate/Elementary School, IN

All Top Ten Poems can be read at www.poeticpower.com

Note: The Top Ten poems were finalized through an online voting system. Creative Communication's judges first picked out the top poems. These poems were then posted online. The final step involved thousands of students and teachers who registered as the online judges and voted for the Top Ten poems. We hope you enjoy these selections.

Great Vacation

In the summer of 2011,
We took a great vacation
To the wonderful, wild West.

Our first stop was San Francisco
There we rode the trolley,
And crossed the Golden Gate Bridge,
Then we explored the crooked street of Lombard
And ate at busy China Town.

Yosemite was our next stop.
It had amazing views,
We hiked the dense forest,
To the beautiful waterfalls.

We arrived late to Vegas,
And saw the night lights view
There we stayed at the Luxor,
Which was a pyramid-shaped hotel.

Finally we hiked the Grand Canyon,
And rode ATV's,
Through Utah's red rock formations.

We explored many places,
On this great, great vacation!

Garrett Doss, Grade 6
Dyer Elementary & Jr High School, TN

The Pencil

You rub my nose so hard against this white land
When my nose breaks,
You cut up my face!
And you do it again and again!

When you're mad you stab with me and
You break me in two!
And you do it again and again!

I used to be a tree,
Majestic and tall,
Then you cut me up and I am now many
And you do it again and again!

You drilled a hole in me!
You put some rock in
You made a strange nose
With rolling blades
And you do it again and again!

I'll get my revenge
I'll sharpen your nose
I'll rub your nose down and put rock in you
And I'll do it again and again!

Catherine Phillips, Grade 5
Hunter GT Magnet Elementary School, NC

Soldier

With my hands bleeding
and my eyes strained,
I sit there waiting for my allies to catch up.
Mortars exploding like flashes of light
and dust blowing like a storm
blinds me worse than a blindfold.
There I sit with my best friend
waiting for medical treatment.
I try to soothe him, but his cries are too great.
We sit there waiting and hoping to survive.
By the hand of God we thrive to survive.

Louie Dickinson, Grade 6
Woodland Presbyterian School, TN

Twin Towers

It's been a decade,
since the September attacks
that changed all of our lives.
Now we always look back.
But we still shed tears
for the ones in the towers.
We couldn't stop crying for hours.
Some kids came home to no families that day.
Kids like that, what do you say.
This war will end one day,
I just wish it was today.

Carlos Luna, Grade 6
Saint Pauls Middle School, NC

Rivalry

Rivalry. Not just a word. It is a feeling.
Not a feeling of hatred, but of passion.
The feeling is personal and a deep feeling of winning.
Most of the time it is strong friendship.
Wanting to beat a friend is strong.
Army — Navy
Duke — UNC
Friendship
Fighting
A lifetime of enemies
A lifetime of rivalry

Henry Hooks, Grade 6
Baylor School, TN

Christy My Mom

My mom is really fun and she likes to run.
She runs around the block like a wolf chasing a flock.
Once she gets back her hands are cold as ice.
She runs to bed faster than melting ice.
She turns on the TV to watch the weather.
She falls to sleep faster than a falling feather.
She wakes up feeling even better.
She goes to the kitchen to be a magician.
I love her stew and I love her too.

Jared Shelton, Grade 5
Providence Academy, TN

My First School

One day, I came to a place.
The second I came in, I knew I belonged.
Its walls were decorated with various posters.
Some of basic math, science, or English,
Others of encouraging words or quotes.
The place was littered with children.
Some were big, some were small,
All were young, none were old.
This place made me feel special.
It made me feel strong.
This place had one person that was different.
She was bigger than me.
She taught me, read to me,
And helped me with everything.
She was smart, kind, and thoughtful.
She would never raise her voice.
This place was magical.
It made me smarter by the day.
I only wish
I could come back and play.

Will France, Grade 6
Woodland Presbyterian School, TN

About Me

I am an active and fun-loving girl
I wonder about my career in life
I hear the sound of my parents saying "try harder"
I see a river with no old shoes or trash
I want an iPad so I can chat with my friends
I am an active and fun-loving girl

I pretend to be an only child
I feel pressure on myself when I am at my worst
I touch the raindrops and wonder
I worry if I will be a mom someday
I cry when I feel bad about doing something bad
I am an active and fun-loving girl

I understand the moments of life
I say destiny is not a matter of change, it is a matter of choice
I dream about my family when I grow up
I try to accomplish all my abilities in life
I hope I have a great job
I am an active and fun-loving girl

Jacklyn Wimberly, Grade 6
Montgomery Central Middle School, TN

Fall

Fall is when the leaves start to come off.
And you try to jump off steep hills.
On Thanksgiving you can eat till you get full.
Fall is the season that football will come on.
You scream for your favorite team.
Those are the things that you can do in fall.

Connor Kelley, Grade 4
Moyock Elementary School, NC

Holidays

Once upon a time,
There was a little girl who loved holidays.
Christmas was her favorite holiday
Because she got lots of gifts.
Thanksgiving was her favorite holiday
Because she can eat turkey and corn on the cob.
She likes Groundhog Day
Because they come up from under the ground.

Tamika Brown, Grade 4
Southeast Elementary School, NC

Blue

What is blue?
Blue is like the morning sky.
It is cold like ice.
It is the blood that runs through my princess veins.
Blue is the color of the Atlantic Ocean.
It is the bottom of an underwater canyon.
It is the yummy blue Kool-Aid on a hot summer's day.
Blue is perfect.

Arielle Lill, Grade 6
Montgomery Central Middle School, TN

Beyond Me

When you look at me not much to see
My appearance shouldn't determine me
What's inside many cannot see
To others I'm just some girl
If you look closer, deep beyond
I'm somebody is who determined to be someone
My appearance will not get the best of me
So just look beyond to see a new side of me

Zoe Hearn, Grade 6
White Station Middle School, TN

Restaurant for Mosquitoes

Welcome to the restaurant for mosquitoes!
Here we have the best food for all ages.
We have tons of different locations.
We have all types of flavors.
We have Mexican, Asian, American, Japanese,
and much more. So come on down we got it all.
If you are human, you'll be the main course!

Jason Cowart, Grade 6
Woodland Presbyterian School, TN

In My Tree Stand

I smell the fresh-cut corn in the wind,
I smell the early morning dew,
I taste the sweet goodness of the rain falling off the leaves,
I taste the berries that taste like the sweetest candy,
I touch the bow as slowly as possible,
I could feel the weight on the bowstring
there is a gut-wrenching pain, saying "do not miss."

Lane Wilson, Grade 6
College View Middle School, KY

Fear

It stalks you in your slumber.
Devouring your jubilance.

Hopeless you are,
The ashes of your heart is slayed.
Your love for family and friends are banished.

You cry and whimper, your robust body is nothing,
Nothing but treacherous lies.
You can run, but you can't hide from fear.

Orbs of tears fall from your face.
Drip drop, each drop evaporates into steam.

You turn around, you see fellowship.
Your heart recovered. What saved you?
A friend fought fear. A foe for fear itself.
It's like a cosmic collision.
Friends versus fear.

Tejes Gaertner, Grade 5
Nature's Way Montessori School, TN

Queen of Roller-skating Broke Her Arm

Boom
Blazing fast roller-skates glide across the slick floor
Ba boom

As a thump goes around
Silent everything
"snap"
Ba boom

Rushing in pain
Getting everything done
Boom

Examining her arm in a big huge scary machine
She broke her arm
Ba boom

In a huge house waiting there for three straight hours
A scary day for my mom

Julianna Dill, Grade 4
Buckner Elementary School, KY

An Ode to Mr. Turkey

Mr. Turkey don't be afraid.
We're going to heat you up in our microwave.
We found you at the store with a label.
Now you're at our dinner table.
This year you're on our farm.
You better hide in the barn.
Now we're eating pumpkin pie.
I'm sorry that you had to die.

Maxwell Mendelson, Grade 5
West Liberty Elementary School, WV

The End of the Eraser

I get used to make pencil marks disappear
And sometimes I disappear
I make sure I'm all right
But I speak too soon

My sides are always in bad shape
Even though I am a rectangle that has 4 corners
I currently have none
Due to the kids that have used me

When the time comes
I must go
With a little of me left to use
At school is where I usually die

Now everyone must see my end
I feel like I have no matter
Must go away to eraser heaven
Hope I go in peace

Vaishnavi Mavilla, Grade 5
Hunter GT Magnet Elementary School, NC

Puppies

I am Kynzee
I wonder what I'm going to be when I grow up
I hear dogs barking at me
I see puppies in my dreams
I want a puppy for Christmas
I am Kynzee

I pretend to understand puppies
I feel them clawing at my feet
I touch dogs in my dreams
I worry about my puppies Caramel and Baby
I am Kynzee

I understand how dogs feel
I say Caramel is very cute
I dream about Caramel
I try not to hurt my puppy
I hope dogs can fly someday
I am Kynzee

Kynzee Mosier, Grade 6
Montgomery Central Middle School, TN

Veterans

V eterans Day is all about the people that gave us freedom
E veryone is giving what the soldiers gave, their all
T he soldiers are awesome people that gave us freedom
E ven though some have died, we still love them
R isking their lives for us
A re they still with us? Yes
N ever forget the soldiers
S ad that they die, but don't ever forget them

Lily Christensen, Grade 5
Temple Hill Elementary School, KY

Christmas Holiday
Christmas
Christmas,
Christmas.
Sweet Christmas,
Snowy Christmas,
Happy, joyful, blessed Christmas.
Great, loving, smiling Christmas.

These are just a few.

Jolly Christmas
Nice Christmas,
Playful, happy, family Christmas.
Joyful, presents, musical Christmas.
Cold Christmas,
Good Christmas,
Cool Christmas.

Don't forget about restful Christmas.

Last of all, best of all
I like a family Christmas.
Unique Edwards, Grade 5
Tates Creek Elementary School, KY

My Dog
R unning
O ver
C ouches
K ooko
A mazing
F unny
E ntertaining
L oving
L iving
E xcited
R ockafeller
Allison Ingram, Grade 5
Walton-Verona Middle School, KY

Living Room
I sit and watch the babies play
with their toys,
while my mom
sits next to me,
I hear the loud babies
I sit on the soft brown couch
and the TV is loud as it can be
the lit cupcake candle
is dancing with me,
I smell the chocolate cookies
baking in the oven
and I'm in the loving comfort
of my home
Molly Cline, Grade 6
College View Middle School, KY

Best Friend
I have a best friend,
She's more like my sister.
When she goes out of town,
Boy, do I miss her.
We are best friends forever.
Even when I cry,
She is always by my side.
She makes me laugh,
And it's all better.
She is with me at everything
I do.
I just want to tell her,
I'm lucky to have a friend like you!
Hallie Turner, Grade 5
Paint Lick Elementary School, KY

Blue
Blue is a nice bug car
It is the color of the Memphis Tiger logo
A blue headband
Blue crew cheering
Sounds like the marching band walking
The high tide coming in
Tastes like blue cotton candy from the fair
Blue raspberry sucker
Blue cobalt gum
It feels like my smooth blue glasses
Fluffy round pillow
A raindrop on my head
Blue makes me excited
Tori Perkins, Grade 6
White Station Middle School, TN

Yes and No
Yes and no is all I say
No I will not come an d
play people ask me why
I say nay all the time
it is because "I like to"
Yes I will tie my shoes
Yes I like to refuse a lot
Yes I like to agree a lot
Can you blame me?
I mean yes and no
are the main words
in life, yes, no, yes, no but…
…never maybe!!!
Keeley Littlepage, Grade 5
Longest Elementary School, KY

Poking
My poems, my books
They poke me all day long
In my head is where they belong.
Christian Petty, Grade 5
Walton-Verona Middle School, KY

Idaho Mountains
The mountains
Stand tall,
Taller than anything,
Snow
Resting on the mountains
Trees surrounding
Running all around,
On the ground

While great big mountains
Reach up
White clouds
Blue sky
So beautiful
Idaho mountains
Audrey Gast, Grade 4
Buckner Elementary School, KY

Water Is
Water is H_2O
Water is clear
Water is purified
Water is colored
Water is flavored
Water is flowing
Water is rushing
Water is salted
Water is natural
Water is old
Water is cold
Water is hot
Water is bottled
Water is crashing
And that's what water is
Reed Stobaugh, Grade 5
Longest Elementary School, KY

Emerald Lizard
Lizard you are green as an emerald
Your toes a dim color of orange.
And your brown chocolate tail
Is swaying in the wind

Grabbing a bug with its long tongue
Gobbles it up and swallows it.
Racing up to her home like a cheetah
Feeding her babies

Happy and full
Running around to get exercise
Racing back up to their tree
Lizards thinking
This is a great home.
Scott Janssen, Grade 4
Buckner Elementary School, KY

Whistling Air

When you're lifted above
The ground, zooming and flying
Gravity-defying, safe and sound
You feel a sense of weightlessness
Flying above the whistling air
Windows left ajar
Having the wind in your hair
Knowing the distance you passed so far
Seeing the clouds swirling above so high
The sun beaming at you with a sense of fiery pride
Finding something that was always thy
Eagles soaring at your side
When you fly above the whistling air

Arhum Qureshi, Grade 6
White Station Middle School, TN

All About Love

I love you, I love you
I love you as much as the president loves cheese.
I love you, I love you
I love you as much as a frog loves my dog.
I love you, I love you
I love you as much as ants love food.
I love you, I love you
I love you as much as kids love animals.
I love you, I love you
I love you as much as monkeys love bananas.
I love you, I love you
I love you as much as you love me.

Danyka Van, Grade 5
Longest Elementary School, KY

Rain

I drum hard, pitter-pattering on the roof while they listen to me
I'm from the skies, no, from the clouds, I touch everything
Falling everywhere, falling forever
Causing a deluge
Coming like a lion, leaving like a lamb
I'm a plethora of raindrops
Too fast, too slow
Rapidly starting, miraculously stopping
Clearing the skies
Bringing rainbows and puddles
I leave my path all the time
Just to find a new one waiting for me though

Katie Noe, Grade 6
Davidson Day School, NC

My Yard

I hear
   The roaring of the cars in the street
   The chirping of birds in the sky
   The pitter-patter of rain on the ground
   The rustling of rabbits trying not to make a sound

Jack Pollard, Grade 6
White Station Middle School, TN

Sensitive and Curious Boy

I am a sensitive and curious boy
I wonder if there's a God watching over me
I hear voices inside me saying "I'm stupid"
I see homeless people suffering on the street
I want peace in the world
I am a sensitive and curious boy

I pretend that death doesn't scare me
I feel sad because innocent people lose their lives
I touch the hands of pain and anger
I worry if a World War III will start
I cry that my father won't come back for me
I am a sensitive and curious boy

I understand people die of diseases
I say life is not easy
I dream to be successful in life
I try to give 100% in everything I do
I hope there is a cure for cancer
I am a sensitive and curious boy

Hekima Kamau, Grade 6
Montgomery Central Middle School, TN

Baseball

Baseball is my favorite sport
But to be a pitcher you cannot be short

The Cardinals are my favorite team
To play for them is my dream

Baseball is so much fun
You have to hit, field, and run

I like to play second base
To beat the runner is a race

When the runner is very fast
The time to get him is not vast

If you hit a home run you get a higher score
And the crowd gives you a wild uproar

If you score enough you just might win
And then you get to play again!

Logan Arnwine, Grade 4
Evangelical Christian School Ridgelake Campus, TN

Art

Art is not just about the brushes and pastels.
Art is about the way you see the picture.
The way you see art should be unique and magical.
You should never look at your art and think it is unbearable.
If you are artistic your life will be like a fairy tale or a dream.
Be artistic and dream forever and art will always stay around.

Avery Clapper, Grade 4
Moyock Elementary School, NC

Bicycle Wheels: The Real Deal
Bonjour, we are the wheels of a bicycle.
You might be saying:
"Why in the world are these French bike wheels talking to me?"
We'll tell you why!
The amount of work we wheels do is stupendously underestimated!
The cycler, handlebars and seat always receive the credit.
Not any more!

First of all, every other second during a cycling session,
Our faces have to SLAM against the painful concrete or bumpy road.
We're the ones who have to turn in full circles for constant hours!
We suffer from low self-esteem and severe vertigo!

Look at those arrogant handlebars and that overly confident seat.
They don't move at all! Whereas, we're always the ones working!
That human thinks he is so…glamorous!
Those pearly, white teeth and fake smile!
If it were not for us, the bicycle would not even exist!
It's all about us — US! US! US!
Now shush you wretched spectators!
Time for our training session for the Tour de France!
Iman Dancy, Grade 5
Hunter GT Magnet Elementary School, NC

Run, Kid, Run
"Runners set," the whistle blows
We're off, a stampede of kids
Hungry for the sweet taste of victory
Nothing can quench the excitement
As I round the corner, I can hear the roaring of the crowd
The first half-mile
As I stride down the hill, I can feel the raw adrenaline,
Coursing through my veins
At the top of the hill, I sigh, so relieved
One mile down, one still taunting me
In front of the playground, across the road
Aches and pains wrack my exhausted body
Persistent, I shake it off
In and out of Death Valley
Up a slight incline
"You just got to keep running," my dad says
A quarter-mile left
I cross the bridge, my legs in overdrive
30 yards…now 20, 10, 5, finished
I can barely feel my legs but I am still standing
I don't feel like running ever again…until the next race…
Alexander Goodwin, Grade 6
Woodland Presbyterian School, TN

Teammates
Teammates are like your brothers or sisters.
You sometimes fight and get along.
But in the end you must stick together to make a win.
Grace Williams, Grade 5
Walton-Verona Middle School, KY

Grandmamma
How old are you?
What grade are you in?
You've grown five inches since I last saw you.

How old are you?
What grade are you in?
You've grown five inches since I last saw you.

How old are you?
What grade are you in?
You've grown five inches since I last saw you.

I'm waiting for one question.
Who are you?
I'm waiting for the day when Alzheimer's has taken her away.
Evan Bright, Grade 6
Woodland Presbyterian School, TN

I Am Martin Luther King Jr.
I am Martin Luther King Jr.
I am trustworthy and respectful
I wonder if they will like my plan
I hear cheers and booing
I see thousands of heads
I am Martin Luther King Jr.
I pretend that I have confidence in the world.
I feel really really nervous.
I touch the podium where I will give my speech
I worry that my plan won't work
I am Dr. Martin Luther King Jr.
I don't understand why blacks and whites can't get along
I say to them "I have a DREAM!"
I try to convince them they can get along and they will
I am Dr. Martin Luther King Jr.
Robbie Tanner, Grade 4
Mineral Wells Elementary School, WV

Rosy Weather
It's winter, I am bare and cold,
No sunshine, I am dying out
But now it's spring, I'm slowly blooming,
My buds are filled, let's keep it up.

And now it's summer, I'm beautiful,
All red and rosy,
I've bloomed, I've bloomed!
I'm scented with aromas of smooth, red roses.

It's getting cold, fall is upon me,
My leaves are turning brown and gray.

Looks like another year
Of cold, wet, but wonderful weather is about to begin.
Kamellia Karimpour, Grade 5
Hunter GT Magnet Elementary School, NC

Dogs

Dogs are great
They're a person's best friend
They're a companion for life
A real true friend
They'll love you forever
They've love you to death
Even if you have bad breath
So in conclusion, dogs are great
Go out and buy two, four, six or eight

Emilee Nelson, Grade 6
All Saints' Episcopal School, TN

If I Ruled the World

If I ruled the world
It wouldn't be so crazy
And people wouldn't be lazy.
People would be unique and say
We don't tolerate that craziness.
All would follow good rules
And we would have excellent school.
And that sure would happen
If I ruled the unruly world.

Nazire Jackson, Grade 4
E O Young Elementary School, NC

School

School is a place where you go to learn,
A place where teachers go to teach.
There is a principal in every school,
He runs the school.
You go kindergarten through 12th grade,
You could also choose to go to preschool.
When you get out of high school,
Then off you go to college,
To find a good and better paying job!

Haylee Denny, Grade 5
Paint Lick Elementary School, KY

The Snowman

Outside my house
the snowman
black and orange pieces on a white face
his eyes starring into the abyss of snow
like a ghost staying here forever
it shall stay forever until it has to go

Christopher Robertson, Grade 6
College View Middle School, KY

Butterfly

I surf the grass
that covers the ground
as timid as a mouse.
I am as colorful as the rainbow.
My home lies in the fields.

Savana Johnson, Grade 4
Caywood Elementary School, TN

I Am Wilber Wright

I am Wilber Wright. I have a bike shop with my brother Orville Wright.
I wonder if airplanes will advance in the future.
I hear the motor. I smell the fumes.
I see the wide open sands. My brother gives me the OK ready to go sign.
I am Wilber Wright. I am excited to try the airplane we built.
I pretend that I am not a little scared.
I feel enthusiastic about trying my new invention the airplane.
I grip the wrench. It is cold and hard. I must check everything on here.
I worry that it may fail, but I will try again.
I shout: "It's a miracle! It works! It works!"
I am Wilber Wright. My brother is Orville Wright.
I understand that it is not the safest thing.
I say my brother and I will try again and again to make it work better.
I dream that someday we will fly every day.
I try to make many improvements to make our trips longer and safer.
I hope the idea of airplanes will go on forever.
I am Wilber Wright.

William Lemon, Grade 4
Mineral Wells Elementary School, WV

I Am Pocahontas

I am Pocahontas. I am respectful of all people.
I am very smart.
I will marry John Rolfe.
I hear the Indians calling for me.
I see birds in the sky and Indian children playing.
I am Pocahontas.
I pretend that I will become a friend to the Pilgrims.
I feel very happy because I have a family.
I touch the smooth silky deerskin of my dress.
I worry about being baptized.
I cried when my mom died and I had to leave my father.
I must help John Rolfe explain to the King the importance of tobacco as a cash crop.
I say I believe in all our dreams.
I have a son. He never returns to America.
I am Pocahontas.

Shelby Rader, Grade 4
Mineral Wells Elementary School, WV

Christmas and Winter

O, how Christmas and winter bring joy to all.
Winter and Christmas are a great time of year.
You see snow falling down out of the glistening window.
Kids are rejoicing over the presents under the tree.
Beautiful Christmas decorations have frost over them.
The sound of Christmas bells ringing make my ears happy.
The great green Christmas tree with decorations is sparkling.
The pleasant smell of the fresh Christmas air is blowing.
Families gather around the fireplace while trying to keep warm.
Families have blankets piled upon them, also cup after cup of hot cocoa.
That's why Christmas and winter are a great time of year.
Families all over the world are rejoicing each year.
For the magnificent and joyful family time.
Everyone has a dazzling cup of cheer!

Aryelle Carter, Grade 5
Providence Academy, TN

High Merit Poems – Grades 4, 5, and 6

The Doghouse Blues

Mistress screamed in frustration
"Now you've pushed me to the brink!"
I had followed the mailman
And toppled the garbage can
So she put me in the clink

Oh the doghouse, the lockup
That place of dread and woe
Yes the doghouse, the big house
Where all the villains go

But freedom was calling
I couldn't abstain
I was caught in the act
Of chasing the cat
And thrown in the slammer again

Oh the doghouse, the pokey
That place of dread and woe
Yes the doghouse, the cooler
Where all the villains go

Then master came home
Gave me a bone
And I came out of my doghouse
James Donlon, Grade 6
White Station Middle School, TN

The Sassy Girl

There is someone I know
And she's really sassy
She always wears a big yellow bow
She's always so classy

Her hair is in a bun every day
When she uses glue she never gets sticky
She will never go outside and play
She thinks that mud is icky

Dresses are her thing
They are always so pink
And she's all about the bling
At least that's what I think

OH NO!!!
The teachers put us in the same classes
What if I can't see over her bow!
What if she makes fun of my glasses!

Actually she is really nice
And is very kind
She doesn't treat me like mice
She has a very thoughtful mind
Rachel Strawn, Grade 5
Hunter GT Magnet Elementary School, NC

Christmas

Christmas is here
It's going to be a great time of year!
I love to see all the children
Laugh and play in the snow every day.
I like to see all the kids
Open their presents
To see what they got.
I like to see the snow fall
Like little polka dots.
I like to see the lights on Christmas night.
They look like a rainbow
Through the night.
I like to see the Christmas trees.
It reminds me of my mother
That is so bright!
Kaitlyn Locklear, Grade 6
Saint Pauls Middle School, NC

Someone Special

S is for somebody amazing
E is for excellent
M is for mom
O is for optimist
N is for never say never
E is for excited

J is for joy
E is for exit
F is for forever
F is for forgiving
R is for real
I is for incredible
E is for excitement
S is for silly
McKinlee Jeffries, Grade 4
F H Jenkins Elementary School, TN

Helpless

As I lie in the cold, cramped
bed, saddened by what lies
ahead, I think of what I could
be doing if I were not here

I do not think of the days
when I will not be quarantined
in a lonely world of pain and
sorrow

I believed that those days
were too far ahead of me,
though, in reality, those days
are quite soon to come
Daniel Ward, Grade 6
Woodland Presbyterian School, TN

The Terrific Species

Two little feet
Holding on tight
Waiting to lift off
And glide thru the wind
Flying soaring!

A gorgeous creature
With beady black eyes
A smooth elegant tail
Perched on a branch with no leaves

Blue and black feathers
Waving in the wind
Perfectly measure one pencil long

The wonderful species
Of blue birds
Will leave you speechless
Mollie Grace Fox, Grade 4
Buckner Elementary School, KY

I Am

I am smart and strong.
I wonder if my life will ever change.
I hear my mom and dad fussing.
I see my grandpa in the clouds.
I want a better life.
I am smart and strong.
I pretend that I am funny.
I feel the ground with my feet.
I touch the sky with my hands.
I worry if my mom will be okay.
I cry when I think of my friend.
I am smart and strong.
I understand why I get in trouble.
I say things I don't mean.
I dream about my dad.
I try my hardest at school.
I hope I will succeed.
I am smart and strong.
Joshua Cole Rhea, Grade 4
Centennial Elementary School, TN

Green

Green is the color you see
outside every day. It is the
color of the grass. Green is the
color of leaves on summer plants.

I can smell the green air when
the wind blows. Green is the color
of green beans, lettuce, and
peas. Green is the color of my
brother's favorite color.
Sara Gruber, Grade 6
Bernheim Middle School, KY

Cheer
Cheer is fun
We do cartwheels and we do a ton
We cheer on the team and they win almost every game
We won! We won! We exclaim
They love it when we cheer
We are so loud that they can always hear
When the game is almost done and there is a minute to go
We throw our poms in the air and say, "Way to go!"

Hannah Benson, Grade 4
Evangelical Christian School Ridgelake Campus, TN

Thankful
T hanksgiving Day is about…
H aving fun with family and…
A lways having great food.
N ever forgetting the people who serve our country and…
K eeping them in our prayers.
F reedom is what we celebrate in the…
U nited States of America.
L iving life in this country is great.

Jacob Poole, Grade 4
Centennial Elementary School, TN

Mars
What's on Mars?
Are there cars?
Are there people?
Or big steeples?
Are there homes?
Or crazy gnomes?
What's on Mars?
Are there cars?

Holly Huffman, Grade 5
Evangelical Christian School Ridgelake Campus, TN

Just to Say Goodbye
This is for those who have lost their lives.
Who gave everything they had to protect our land,
Who gave everything they had to lend a hand,
Who gave everything they had to save us,
Who gave everything they had for it to bust.
This is for those who have lost their lives,
Who gave everything they had to say goodbye.

Hannah Hollingsworth, Grade 6
Saint Pauls Middle School, NC

Green Is Everywhere!
Green is everywhere I go.
Green is grass, trees and flowers.
Green is the taste of green grapes bursting in your mouth.
Green feels like a worm cozy hug.
Green is the sound of the wind in the trees.
Green is fresh cut kiwi.
Green is a color I will never forget.

Taelor Mattison, Grade 4
F H Jenkins Elementary School, TN

The Awesome World of Disney
All the fun rides,
People having lots of fun,
The beautiful music on the speakers,
Young children laughing and having fun,
The buttery popcorn popped pleasing all people.

Epcot's smells of many cultures,
The juiciness of the restaurant's steak,
The sweetness of my dessert after a fun day,
The metal rails of the queue as I'm waiting for the ride to begin,
The suspense of waiting piled high as Mount Everest.

The rubbery lap bar as we start the ride,
The seats are as soft as clouds for resting my feet,
The wind now runs through my hair as we begin.

This is my favorite place,
I am happy and content.

Eli Cooper, Grade 6
College View Middle School, KY

I Am
I am polite and funny
I wonder if I will be rich when I grow up.
I hear my dad's voice
I see stars
I want a yellow n' black Lamborghini
I am polite and funny
I pretend I am in the NFL
I feel like lying on a cloud
I touch flowing water
I worry if I am going to be successful in life
I cry when I think about grandparents not here
I am polite and funny
I understand what all of the holidays mean
I say I believe in Jesus/God
I dream of being an anesthesiologist
I try to get a's on my test
I hope I get to be an anesthesiologist
I am polite and funny!

Brendan Waltenburg, Grade 6
Bernheim Middle School, KY

Myrtle the Turtle
I was fishing in my boat one sunny day,
when I had a huge tug on my line.
So I gave a quick jerk to snag my catch
and started to reel right away.
I pulled and pulled, but it pulled back,
so hard I thought my rod would crack.
It finally tired out so I could pull it in,
I was surprised to see that my rival had no fins!
I'd never have guessed I was fighting a snapping turtle!
I think I'll keep this turtle and call her Myrtle.

Alex Hall, Grade 4
Love Memorial Elementary School, NC

High Merit Poems – Grades 4, 5, and 6

I Am Adam Sandler
I am Adam Sandler.
I am hilariously funny and very smart.
I wonder if I will get married someday.
I am now walking onto the stage.
I see a bunch of heads.
I am Adam Sandler.
I pretend that I am onstage giving out free tickets.
I feel good, but nervous and amazed.
I touch the grip of the microphone.
I worry that I will let my fans down.
I shout out loud on the microphone.
I am Adam Sandler. I am very funny.
I understand the neat feeling of being onstage.
I say I believe singing can also make me famous.
I dream of seeing my name in lights.
I try to give everyone my autograph.
I hope that everyone listens to my music.
I am Adam Sandler.

Levi Joy, Grade 4
Mineral Wells Elementary School, WV

Basketball
Basketball is my favorite sport.
I like the way you dribble up and down the court.
Stop and pulled up a three.
So you know it's all about me.
Dunk all over you, flip when I get done.
If I feel like it, I might even run.
Let's go. You know all about me.
When I'm on the court, some people call me Kobe.
AIG all day. You already know it's me.
I'm out so you know it's all about me.
When you play against me you better bring your game
Because I play like LeBron James.
In years about four more, I will have my first MVP ring.
I'm like John Cena, you can't see me.
My dad thought I was right
So if you want to see me, you better have good sight.
Good night. Deuces!

Damaris Sheffield, Grade 5
Southeast Elementary School, NC

Friend Me!
Spring, summer, fall, and winter
I find all my friends by pressing Enter

Boyfriend updates and vacation pics
I get all I need in just a few clicks

Twenty-four hours a day without leaving the house
I get all of my info with the touch of the mouse

Laptop, desktop, or on my phone
With social networking, I'm never alone

Madison Colley, Grade 5
Evangelical Christian School Ridgelake Campus, TN

Do You Cuddle with a Cuttlefish?
Do you cuddle with a cuttlefish or visit with a bear for awhile?
Have you ever wanted to become dear with a deer
Or give a beaming smile to a friendly crocodile?

Have you ever been daffy with a dolphin
And laughed great laughs of joy?
Or played with a platypus and had crawfish shells for toys?

Have you ever sashayed with a shark
Or jumped with a kangaroo?
After your race with a cheetah, did you need new running shoes?

It's true not all animals are friendly.
Indeed, some stink and bite and claw.
But even with faults they're each special,
And I truly love them all!

Zoe Doubrley, Grade 5
Nature's Way Montessori School, TN

The Life of Mr. Tooth
Hey don't even think about not brushing me
Your mom is just going to send you right back to the bathroom

I am so excited for our dentist appointment next week
When those dentists clean me it feels as smooth as butter

I am not very sure if you are aware,
That some of my neighbors are turning as yellow as the sun

Sometimes I bleed because you scrub me too hard,
Sometimes I turn colors because you don't brush me at all

Let's face it
I am one of the most important organs in your body
And you will NEVER be able to change it.

Micayla Bell, Grade 5
Hunter GT Magnet Elementary School, NC

An Alligator Meal
Alligators awaited me
Yelling and screaming "feed me"
SNAP!
An alligator bites the small piece of meat
Blue rope dangling off the edge of the railing
Alligators standing there awaiting for more

Gazing down
Wrestling for one tiny piece of meat
Chomp, chomp
An alligator gulps down the fresh food
Laying there with their bellies full
Under the warm,
Hot heating, yellow sun
An alligator meal

Kennedy Park, Grade 4
Buckner Elementary School, KY

God

God is good,
God is great,
God is everything,
he is up above,
Looking down below,
Watching and protecting us,
From all things bad.
God is strong,
God is mighty.
I hope to go to heaven,
For only he chooses,
But for now I am surrounded
By people who love me.

Alea Padgett, Grade 5
Paint Lick Elementary School, KY

Deer Hunting

D aring
E asy
E ntertaining
R ifle

H unters orange
U p in a stand
N umber of points
T ines
I nteresting
N ature
G runting bucks

Layne Simpson, Grade 5
Walton-Verona Middle School, KY

There Once Was a Man

There was a man.
who had a van.

he loved that
van very much.

one day he
married that van.

and they lived
happily every
after.

Dalton Stanley, Grade 5
Longest Elementary School, KY

Cat

I have a very big cat
He's fluffy, nice, and fat
He sits on the couch
Like a very big grouch
And wears a big yellow hat

Amber Westcott, Grade 4
Centennial Elementary School, TN

My Grandfather

I've known my grandfather all my life.
We would go and fish in Florida.
We saw alligators, crocs, frogs, and even lizards.
But all of that will not make up for what happened a few years ago.
His jolly face is stuck in my mind.
His laugh is so cheerful.
His picture on the wall looks at me and I remember what happened a few years ago.
My grandfather got cancer.
He lay on the bed in pain.
That night he died a few years ago.
The sorrow filled my mind.
Tears flowed from my eyes when my grandfather died a few years ago.

Drew Broome, Grade 5
Providence Academy, TN

St. Louis, Missouri

St. Louis Arch, huge and gigantic, even from far away, beckons like a lighthouse
Bush Stadium made to seat more than 200,000 wild fans
Busy streets loud and crazy with honking cars and people yelling at the top of their lungs
Crowds cheering for those crazy Cardinals to win their baseball game
Hot dogs sizzling at the food stand rolling around like rolling down a steep hill,
Sweat on everybody's face and bodies are wet, like a slippery water slide,
Nachos with spicy cheese and corn chips make a fire on my tongue
Ice cold Coca-Cola quenches my thirst like a thunderstorm in a desert,
My baseball glove made from black, smooth leather
A grand-slam home run ball hit by Albert Puhols rams its way into my glove,
Happy and excited

Will Boultinghouse, Grade 6
College View Middle School, KY

Rojo Aka Red

Rojo is in hot sauce, rojo is a shirt, and rojo is a shoe
Rojo is a leaf, it is hair, red is for love, anger and it is for friendship,
And for lost ones

Red is for noises and nails, it's for pens, pencils, it's for rings, it's for a lot of
Stuff like drinks and lip stick!

Brittany Bowman, Grade 6
Bernheim Middle School, KY

The Seasons

The seasons change from winter, spring summer and fall
Winter — as winter starts flakes fall from above
Spring — as spring starts the rain hits the roofs
Summer — as summer starts the sun will blaze in the sky
Fall — as fall starts the leaves start to change
The seasons will always change from winter, spring, summer, and fall

Kasiya Little, Grade 5
Hall Fletcher Elementary School, NC

Butterfly

A butterfly spreads its wings to fly,
I suddenly blinked and it was out of sight.
There it is flying peacefully in the sky.

Sydney Raper, Grade 5
Walton-Verona Middle School, KY

The Valley

The sun comes and goes
The sweet water gives us food
We can now have peace

Abagail Warman, Grade 5
Walton-Verona Middle School, KY

High Merit Poems – Grades 4, 5, and 6

Christmas

Christmas
Christmas
Christmas
Snowy Christmas
Beautiful Christmas
Fun, joyful, extreme, Christmas
Great, exciting, bright Christmas

These are just a few.

White Christmas
Cold Christmas
Very well-earned Christmas
Most happy, joyful Christmas

Present Christmas
Loving Christmas
Warm Christmas
Don't forget mild Christmas

Last of all, best of all
I like giving Christmas
Lashonda Hensley, Grade 5
Tates Creek Elementary School, KY

Bubble Gum and Hot Wings

Bubble gum is tasty.
Hot wings are feisty.
Bubble gum is finger stickin'.
Pop! Pop! Pop!
Hot wings are finger lickin'.
Schlup! Schlup! Schlup!
In time bubble gum will lose its sweet.
And, hot wings will lose their heat.
They were very tasty before.
I think I will have some more.
Harold Willis, Grade 4
Love Memorial Elementary School, NC

Outdoor Scene

The sky is light blue
The grass is dark green.
Add the sun
For an amazing scene.

The wind blows the spiky grass
Side to side.
Animals peek
And try to hide.

In the busy trees
A bluebird has a nest.
Now our world
Is the very best.
Bryton Yarborough, Grade 4
E O Young Elementary School, NC

The Jersey

The Jersey
that special thing
I wear it up and
down the hallway
and on that
special place, the field

It gives me that
special feeling when
I go up to bat
like hitting a home-run
for your team
and everybody watching

That special thing
the jersey
Aubrie Croom, Grade 6
Dyer Elementary & Jr High School, TN

Music into My Soul

Music, music to my ear.
Just come closer and lean near.

The melody flows into your soul.
Just like a breeze on your afternoon stroll.

Take a look around and you will see.
All the rhythm that came to be.

Let the music take you.
Anywhere it wants to.

Feel the beat and just let go.
Let it all back into your soul.
Emily Cooper, Grade 5
Mount Juliet Elementary School, TN

Laughter

It is an untied balloon.
You laugh you blow up,
If you stop laughing you deflate.

You are filled with joy,
like a balloon is with air.

If someone doesn't laugh you pop.

Laughter is filling up the air,
so is the balloon.

If you let go you fly away,
but you always come back.
Savana Canary, Grade 6
College View Middle School, KY

Fallen

From under the dust ruffle
A blue eye peeks.
Glassy round like a marble
How did bunny get there?
Who did this?
Scratch, scratch
Another eye peeks
What is pushing it?
Now I see a gray tail wagging
Like an anxious caterpillar.
Could it be?
It is! Bordeaux!
Bark, bark!
Now I see a jealous dog.
Val Smith, Grade 6
Woodland Presbyterian School, TN

Basketball

Basketball and baseball are the best.
Soccer and football you never rest.
Basketball I like the most.
I know I'm good but I don't like to boast.
I love to play ball,
But when I watch it bounce off the wall.
I like to watch the NBA.
If I could I would play all day.
I don't play when it's wet,
But when I play I always hit the net.
When it comes to basketball,
I got game.
When it comes to rhymes,
I sure ain't lame.
Mess with the best,
Lose like the rest.
Cody Durden, Grade 6
Saint Pauls Middle School, NC

My Dog

My dog is very smart,
He is also very sweet
When I snap my fingers
He falls down at my feet

My dog is like a friend
My dog loves playing ball,
He helps me when I'm sad
And licks me when I fall

My dog and I are buddies
We are a family
I love him with all my heart
He can count on me!
Dylan Hester, Grade 5
Love Memorial Elementary School, NC

Veterans
The soldiers gave their lives,
Fighting for our lives.
They gave everything they had,
For the freedom that we all have.
And they fought for everyone
To be so kind.
And they fought for our lives,
To protect us all.
But it is sad for the lives that were lost
In every war that came to be.
Austin McLellan, Grade 6
Saint Pauls Middle School, NC

Seasons
Spring
Summer
Fall
Winter

I like winter best of all,
Because of the snow and hot cocoa,
But don't forget the reason,
For the season.
Jesus.
Daylan Logan, Grade 5
Paint Lick Elementary School, KY

Halloween
Halloween is a time to dress up,
Sometimes people get so scared they jump.
You see different costumes every year,
Some act like they have great fear.
You can dress up scary or funny,
You can even dress up as a bunny.
I love this holiday,
It's fun in every way!
It's going to be here very fast,
Next thing you know it's already passed!
Josie Lehman, Grade 5
Paint Lick Elementary School, KY

Christmas Eve Night
Every Christmas Eve night,
I go downstairs when no one's in sight,
I creep around the tree and smile with glee,
when I see presents all around me,
I pick up a box without a sound
and then I hope no one's around,
I went back upstairs,
about to pull out my hair,
waiting for Christmas morning to be…
here.
Adrienne Lambert, Grade 5
Penny Road Elementary School, NC

Zooming
Cold blizzard wind
Smacking my face
Like needles shooting
From the shimmering blue sky
Zooming, jerking on the ride
Like giant trees trying to get you

Screaming it is fun any way
Screeching to a stop
Feeling sad
So we get back in line.
Eden Shean, Grade 4
Buckner Elementary School, KY

Summer Days and Night
Summer days and nights are a delight,
You can swim in the day.
Camp out at night.
Have a fire for heat.
And the s'mores you will eat!

Friends can come over.
You can have a sleep over.
Stay up until midnight.
Oh, what a delight!
I love summer days and nights!
Elizabeth Wix, Grade 5
Paint Lick Elementary School, KY

Turkey
You're so yummy
Turkey
You fill my belly
Turkey
I'm so sorry
Turkey
I know you hate it
Turkey
Time to fill me up
Turkey
You were so yummy
Savanah Wisswell, Grade 4
Moyock Elementary School, NC

Soccer
Soccer is fun
Soccer is great
But now it's all done
And that is something I hate.

Soccer is back
Soccer is here
I'm back on track
And have no fear.
Gage Wilson, Grade 4
Centennial Elementary School, TN

How to Write a Poem
So kids this how
you write a poem.
Remember that there are
no rules.

To start off you are
going to write a narrative
poem. Trust me it is
pretty easy.

All it has to do is
tell a story and
to know who your
speaker is.

Then you need to
figure out what form
yours is, free verse, couplet,
haiku, and acrostic of course.

Then off you
go to start
your story of
what happened.
Alissa Meyerhoffer, Grade 5
Hunter GT Magnet Elementary School, NC

What Is Green?
Green is summer leaves,
Green is an apple,
Green is the color of a frog,
Green is a scary grasshopper,

Green is a bracelet,
Green is a pair of socks,
Green is your favorite shirt,
Or your mother's garden,

Green can be a tractor,
Or smell of a big open field,
Green is a big oak tree,
Or a front lawn full of growing grass,

Green can be scissors,
Green can be your backpack,
Green can be the color of your pencil,
Or the color of your lunch box,

Green can be nail polish,
Green can be your sneakers,
Green is the color of the feather in my hair!
Green is anything you want it to be!
Jayme Maras, Grade 6
Bernheim Middle School, KY

Santa's Here

Santa is coming!
Santa is coming!
That's what the kids say.
They put on their PJs,
They get ready for bed.
They leave Santa cookies and milk,
They hear Santa's sleigh,
They see him out the window in the moonlight.
They hear the fire stop,
They hear footsteps.
They know Santa is near!

Mariano Cordova, Grade 5
Paint Lick Elementary School, KY

Savannah

My baby sister Savannah
loves to play.
She loves it when my mom takes her to the park.
It's all fun, till she falls.
She starts to cry.
She runs to our mom
and says "I falled mommy."
My mom says "it will be okay"
and she walks away,
and she continues to play.
And when it's time to go she starts to cry.

Alesha Horne, Grade 6
Saint Pauls Middle School, NC

Tennessee

A small park to play on,
A fancy restaurant to eat at,
Birds beautifully chirping at me,
Squirrels chomping on walnuts as I pass by,
The freshly fried apples are as green as my lizard,
The freshly cut grass blowing through the wind,
The absence of the bark on the sycamore tree,
The rich taste of the tree's leaves,
Brown, yellow, red soaking in the sun,
Crunchy leaves upon my feet,
Spotted squished mud after it rains.

Keagan Simmons, Grade 6
College View Middle School, KY

Bullying

Bullying is uncomfortable.
It is not very healing.
It can also mean teasing.
Bullying can cause a killing.
When someone bullies you,
They are giving you a message
That they don't have what you have and are jealous.
Bullies are not only hurting your feelings.
When they bully, they hurt theirs too.

Nakei'Briana Simmons, Grade 5
Southeast Elementary School, NC

A Day for Play

Excited people smiling from ear to ear.
Immediately, rides are zooming forward.
Small children are screaming in joy.
The distinct click of seatbelts is everywhere.

Crowded, chlorine filled pools,
Fresh, delectable treats surrounding me.
Quickly melting Dippin' Dots on my tongue,
A cold Dr. Pepper is my lifesaver.

I'm shakily grabbing the hard, metal restraints,
And curiously taking fuzzy softballs like an amateur.

I feel like a five-year-old,
Who gets to play the day away
Without a care in the world.

Brienna Alsip, Grade 6
College View Middle School, KY

Granny's House

I would always watch Granny make
gigantic gooey chocolate chip cookies!
I would always get excited
when I saw Granny getting out the old toy box.
I would love for Granny,
to read me old-time stories like "The Three Little Pigs."
Granny singing pretty lullabies
when it was time to take a nap.
The burning of vanilla candle fumes
would always make the room smell good.
Granny's homemade lemonade was always the BEST!
The smooth carpet when I would crawl
would give my hands a massage.
It's my peaceful place, and every time I pass by the house
I just think of the good memories of me and Granny!
I MISS YOU GRANNY!

Natalie Nicely, Grade 6
College View Middle School, KY

Pierre

My pet Pierre is a dwarf mouse.
He is cute, tiny, quick, and very nice.
He runs on his wheel all through the night,
Which makes it very hard for me to sleep tight.
He loves to slide down his green slide.
When people come up to his cage he runs and starts to hide.
He has escaped many times.
Now we cannot hold him in our hands or let him out of his cage.
He is like a nonstop moving machine.
He is not very clean.
He is adorable when he nibbles on his food,
And you can tell that he is in a good mood.
I love Pierre so much,
That I never want him to die.

Elizabeth Brewer, Grade 5
Providence Academy, TN

The High Flying Bird
soaring through the sky
wondering what it could be
brown, white head
a bald eagle
flying 65 mph
catching fish
scraping its talons across the water
8 feet wing span
for flying
high and low
across the water
Christopher Woosley, Grade 4
Buckner Elementary School, KY

Boots
Boots my family dog
Egg shell white paws
Never letting go of your precious heart.

As you protect the good
And cramp the evil.
My love gets deeper into your life
Smashing lies of mean desperations

My midnight dog
Boots
Lucas McCarson, Grade 4
Buckner Elementary School, KY

Rudy
My dog, Rudy, is a golden retriever
with red fur softer than a cloud.
He loves playing fetch.
He also loves long and short walks.
He will play all day.
Rudy loves playing in the snow.
He is pampered.
All of my family loves Rudy.
Even friends love him.
Rudy is nice and calm around people.
He is the best dog ever.
John Chiozza, Grade 6
Woodland Presbyterian School, TN

Riding My Pony
Riding my pony makes me feel free.
After I ride Billy, we rest under a tree.
Riding my pony makes me feel brave.
Riding days on end is what I crave.

My pony lives on a farm.
His barn keeps him from harm.
He is so tall.
He fills up his stall.
Caitlin King, Grade 6
All Saints' Episcopal School, TN

I Love the Look of the Ocean
I love the look of the ocean
And its consuming waves.
When I go out into the ocean,
The waves burst on the shore.
Then I go out farther.
I see something I haven't seen,
A school of fish swimming swiftly.
When I step on the sand,
I feel something sharp.
It makes me want to see.
Then I reach and hold it up,
A seashell that I love.
I see something pink, a jellyfish.
Ow, it stings! The pain burns,
But I still love the look of the ocean.
Luke Thurman, Grade 5
Providence Academy, TN

Thoughts of You
Thoughts of you rush through my head
sometimes, all the time, every time
I think of you,
so kind and true.
You were a friend,
a giving man,
you were always willing to lend a hand.
Thoughts of you rush through my head,
trying hard just to understand
why it ended the way it did.
Thoughts of you rush though my head,
I wish I could tell you how I feel.
I wish you knew just how much I care.
Thoughts of you rush through my head,
all the time.
Lily Miller, Grade 5
Mount Juliet Elementary School, TN

Basketball
Hey shoot me
You have to score to win
Can't you see
The buzzer's going to ring before you score

Shoot! There's only 2 seconds
Aha! You shot
Oh this is scary
Oh dear!
You scored as the buzzer went off

You just won the game
You just won the tournament
And I'm the winning ball
Sweet!
Cameron O'Brien, Grade 5
Hunter GT Magnet Elementary School, NC

The Leaf
I am a leaf
Here to tell my story
To you

One day the wind blew me
Far, far away
As far as any eye could see

I landed on a branch
But not just any branch
A bird's branch

He pecked and pecked
Through day and night
Until he thought I was done

The wind blew me again
Back to where I was

And here I am
Telling my story
To you
Ethan Sichel, Grade 5
Hunter GT Magnet Elementary School, NC

Background
Flowers all dry,
Nothing living in sight,
Nothing at all in this desert site,

Frozen in ice,
Isn't it nice?
Snow everywhere in the glaciers,

Green happy grass,
With golden and brass,
What a beautiful meadow.
Esme Weeks, Grade 4
Nature's Way Montessori School, TN

Best Mom in the World!
My mama is a very nice
Person to everyone and
She is graceful, friendly
And caring to others
And my mom is a good
Nurturing person even
For animals but mostly
My sisters and me
My mom is a very generous
And kind person
If your Mom is mean and you go
To my mom for a day
You might never want to leave
Natwiya Robinson, Grade 6
Saint Pauls Middle School, NC

Smoky Mountains
Bears lying
peacefully
in the cage,
A creek
with water
rushing
loudly against
the rocks.

Heat burning
painfully on
my skin.
Steak burning on
the grill to
taste awesome.

Scared when I go
to see the bears at
the zoo.
Annah Lundy, Grade 6
College View Middle School, KY

Changes
The blooming flowers are showing,
The springtime showers are flowing,
The mornings are crisp and cool,
It's almost time to uncover your pool.

On scorching hot and humid days,
My tongue calls for ice cold lemonade.
The evil mosquitos buzz and bite,
The refreshing pool feels good at night.

Autumn days have given birth,
As beautiful colors fall to earth.
Cool night breezes have begun to blow,
Bonfires are built to toast marshmallows.

Snow has fallen all around,
Children have snowball fights all over town.
Drinking hot cocoa is oh so sweet,
While the roaring fire warms my feet.
Kaleb Sims, Grade 6
Dyer Elementary & Jr High School, TN

Baseball
B all
A sport
S liding into second
E veryone in motion
B ats hit balls all around
A merica's pastime
L ots of fun for all
L et's play ball
Christian Stover, Grade 5
Mount Juliet Elementary School, TN

Falcon
Soaring through the air like
an airplane
Swooping down to get some
Food from the ice cold water

He catches a fresh fish and
Takes it back to his nest to
Feed his young baby falcons
His bright orange claws
Gripping the twigs of the nest
so he does not fall out
of the tree

Sitting on a cold tree
covered in cold cloud
soft cotton called snow
Jake Justice, Grade 4
Buckner Elementary School, KY

Wonderland
Deer roaming the woods
Cotton balls of snow
Everywhere

Bark falling off trees
Frozen branches of trees everywhere
Packs of deer spying
On you

Deer leaping like gazelles
Blending with the snow
Snow blinding white

Deer roaming the woods
Wonderland
Wonderland
Evan Myers, Grade 4
Buckner Elementary School, KY

Christmas
Ho Ho Ho, it is near
oh, Oh, Oh Christmas is here
and presents seem just to appear
right under here

Christmas is rolling by
so fast it makes me want to cry
it is more than meets the eye
when Christmas is rolling by

Now I hate that it is gone
because I had grown so fond
with family meetings with people like John
but until next year, Christmas is gone
Dawson Wood, Grade 6
Bargerton Elementary School, TN

My Darling, Dora
She is a comfort,
She is joy in sorrow,
Happiness in despair,
And my sunshine,
On *every* cloudy day.

She radiated warmth and love.
She was my angel,
My darling,

Her hair was wild;
So was she.
She was encouragement for me.
Each morning I opened my eyes
To see hers filled with smiles.

She and I are adventurers.
Until the darkest is known
All hatred is gone,
And the pain has melted away,
She and I will continue,
Adventurers.
Kendall Sewell, Grade 6
Woodland Presbyterian School, TN

My Best Friend
Cole is my very best friend.
I thought the fun would never
End.
Then one day
He moved away
Then it seemed the sky was
Gray.
I really wanted him to stay.
I wish that he wasn't so far
Away.
Logan Hayes, Grade 5
Providence Academy, TN

9/11
The war is fought,
For freedom we thought.
Peace was sough.
Blood was shed.
Now most are dead.
9/11 was the cause.
The world stopped for a short pause.
We could've gotten over it,
But we didn't.
Osama was careful
Not to get caught,
Yet he still fought.
Now it's his fault
That he's gone.
Jonathon Felton, Grade 6
Saint Pauls Middle School, NC

I See Sunset Beach

Beach houses old and worn rise in the distance as I drive closer and closer
Sand swiftly swaying in the wind piles up and topples over each other like waves
Waves crash onto the shore like thunder
Seagulls become psychopaths as they screech and dive for food
Hamburgers back flip on the grill as their aroma tumbles over my nose
Sun lotion *squirt-squirts* out of the bottle, causing a blast of coconut smell to drift all over the room
Saltwater sprays from the ocean, causing me to gag from its salty taste
Sandwiches crunch in my mouth deliciously with each little bite
Warm, clean towels dry me off as we head home
The beach has always made me feel happy and excited

Maris Dees, Grade 6
College View Middle School, KY

I Am Alone

I woke up and I wasn't in my home. Then I remembered. I had no home. I was Japanese. My home had been torn apart by waves as strong as steel. I am sad as a human watching the last plant die out.

So much destruction, all from water. I feel lost as a puppy fifty miles from home. I know people will help me, but I still feel as alone as the last human on Earth.

Just as I feel as if it can't get worse, my parents, the last link to my home, are swallowed up by the storm. There is nothing left. I am as alone as a single blade of grass in the field of the world.

I am a Japanese girl with her home torn apart, and I am alone.

Natalie Young, Grade 5
Nature's Way Montessori School, TN

Thanksgiving

We came to a new world didn't know what to do, the Indians remembered the world didn't revolve around you.
Out from the shadows into the meadows came the Indians.
One whole year of good crops, the pilgrims didn't want to treat the Indians like mops.
They all had a feast, they had some roast beast.
We remember this day like it was a life changing play.
It is Thanksgiving when everyone is living the life of a king.
You don't have to have smarts, it just has to run in your heart.

Brent Catlett, Grade 4
Frankfort Intermediate School, WV

Leafy Sea Dragon

The blue majestic water overlapping green majestic animals, which would be holding only the greatest creation: the leafy sea dragon.
It has a skinny, long, unusual body floating through the seas, hiding in it's camouflage through which nobody can see.
The greatest creation: the leafy sea dragon.
It is slowly, gliding, blending so that only friends can see. Webbed, water-winged secure in it's spot. Delicately the green, yellow, purple, red, and blue sea dragon. The greatest creation: the leafy sea dragon.

Drake Smith, Grade 5
Nature's Way Montessori School, TN

American Soldiers

The American soldiers may risk their lives for their family,
friends and others back home.
You may pray for their safety,
hope to God that nothing happens to your loved ones.
So pray and pray 'til an American Soldier comes home.

Hanna Greever, Grade 6
Temple Hill Elementary School, KY

My Parents

I love my parents because they are tough on my education
And they give me what I want
And they are caring toward me.
Even when I am bad, I am on punishment sometimes
But I know that they love me.

Elijah Latham, Grade 4
Southeast Elementary School, NC

High Merit Poems – Grades 4, 5, and 6

The Perfect Moment
Time stands still.
Let's keep this moment.
Bottle it up in a jar
Like the replica of a ship
Sailing the empty sea.
I don't want to miss it.
This is the perfect moment.
Why can't it stay like this forever?
Annastasia Hutcheson, Grade 6
White Station Middle School, TN

Fall Days
Fall days are chilly and breezy.
Red, orange, and yellow all over.
The leaves fall.
Dress warmly to go play!
The sun goes down, down very early.
Rake the leaves and jump in the pile.
Hear the crunch, crunch of the leaves.
This is also time for Halloween.
Chloe Brooks, Grade 4
Love Memorial Elementary School, NC

My Mom
My mom is a loving person!
She looks almost like me.
She has brown hair and green eyes!
My mom is caring, loving, and generous.
She makes me happy.
My mom is always caring about people.
My mom loves me and I love her too!
She will live forever in my heart.
Amy Nicole Clark, Grade 6
Saint Pauls Middle School, NC

Summer
In the summer,
It is bright,
In the summer,
I flew a kite.
It was my very,
First time.
I always like,
The summer night.
Dalton Nicely, Grade 5
Paint Lick Elementary School, KY

Deserted
On a beach in Florida
A palm tree
All alone
Red over orange
Swaying in the wind
Calmly and peacefully
Dylan Hamilton, Grade 6
College View Middle School, KY

Fall and Autumn
The leaves turn colors of
brown, yellow, and many different shades of orange.
They fall as if they were in slow motion
It continuously rains during some days of the week.
Every time the sun is out it still is as if you were walking on clouds.
The grass is dry and cold.
Autumn air is moist as if the air was filled from a freshwater river.
People dress with coats, light jackets, wind breakers, and stockings.
People have extra accessories that they wear such as
hats, gloves, boots, scarves, and hoodies.
Fall sports such as football, baseball, basketball, and soccer are played
by children in the autumn season.
Fall or autumn is the best time of the year!
Brandon Haney, Grade 6
Woodland Presbyterian School, TN

He Is the One
He is like a gift from heaven
He was the 1st one I ever had
He goes into hibernation every winter
The rounded off ears on his head are like the rough terrain — rolling about in the Georgia wilderness
Every baby should have one of these loyal companions
…the fur is a weathered, honey brown
The nose is like a scratched up stone sitting by the pond in the rural parts of Mississippi
Some are named Teddy, mine is named Fuzzy
Some are played with to no end; some just lie in a bed all day
You can look bad, smell horrendous, feel anemic…, but he won't say a word
My bear came out of hibernation for me,
And I bet it did for you too!
Ryan Voehringer, Grade 6
Woodland Presbyterian School, TN

St. Louis Missouri
Busch Stadium too small to hold the 50,000 people trying to find their seats
The Arch, an awesome piece of American architecture, arches my back as I look up
Sirens so loud you can hear them on the other side of the city EEOOWW
People whispering to each other trying to keep their conversation a secret
Boats of the Mississippi River pollute her while she flows south to the gulf
Smoke sets up in the air from the grill, cooking the hot dogs
Burnt but delicious hot dogs wrapped in aluminum foil like mummies
Nachos with spicy jalepeños and warm cheese sits in my stomach and satisfies my hunger
Left field bleachers are a wet fish straight from the water because it rained
The car seat as comfortable as a mattress of feathers
Happy and relaxed
Gatlin Humphrey, Grade 6
College View Middle School, KY

Peace
Peace, a thing this world lacks,
A thing this world needs, a thing that would make us better people.
A thing that would end wars and end bad things that some people do.
Peace, a thing this world needs.
Briana Lindon, Grade 5
Walton-Verona Middle School, KY

The World

The world is like a bumpy road,
With places of harm and fear,
With places of joy and happiness,
But sometimes, there is nothing.

The world is like a fire,
Sometimes the fire weakens,
Sometimes the fire strengthens,
But sometimes the fire needs help to stay alight.

The world is like the weather,
Pretty, clear, and beautiful at one moment,
But ugly, scary, and mean the next,
But sometimes it's a little of both.

You see, the world is many things,
It only matters in one's opinion,
But one thing is fact,
The world is always changing.

Christopher Krohn, Grade 6
McGee's Crossroads Middle School, NC

I Am

I am — loving and caring
I wonder — is Dane going to be made fun of?
I hear — me and Dane playing saxophone and recorder
I see — Dane's little cute face
I want — Dane to graduate high school
I am — loving and caring

I pretend — Dane is always next to me in school
I feel — proud of being a good big sister
I touch — his soft hands
I worry _ Dane is never going to stop stuttering
I cry — when I fight with him
I am — loving and caring

I understand — life is rough when you see brothers grow up so fast
I say — life is a climb, is a beautiful view
I dream — to have nieces and nephews
I hope — I make a difference in my brother's life
I am — loving and caring

Kaleigh Foster, Grade 6
Bernheim Middle School, KY

Snow

Soft, gentle, cold, fluffy
As white as the stripes on zebras
Pillow of protection when my brothers tackle me
Mixed with milk, sugar, and chocolate, it is delicious
Makes for an extraordinary ride on a sled
Slipping and sliding makes for great fun
Falling to the ground and making snow angels
But the best thing about snow is, SNOW DAY!!!

George Gallop, Grade 6
Woodland Presbyterian School, TN

I Am Taylor Swift

I am Taylor Swift. I am very talented.
I wonder when I will get married?
I hear my fans screaming, shouting, and singing with me.
I see some of my friends and fans dancing.
I am Taylor Swift. I am a country star.
I dream I am on American Idol.
I feel terrified when I prepare for my next concert.
I touch my guitar and I feel its grand texture.
I worry because I am not a very good dancer.
I shout to my fans: "I love you, thanks!"
I am Taylor Swift and I love to sing.
I understand that my life is hard and difficult.
I say powerful words in my songs.
I dream that I will soon have a husband to share my dreams.
I try very hard to get fans to sing with me.
I hope that many many years from now people will still hear me.
I am Taylor Swift. I love to sing. I love the USA.

Tori Douglas, Grade 4
Mineral Wells Elementary School, WV

I Am

I am kind and brave.
I wonder why some people are very careless to the planet.
I hear the werewolves howling.
I see Africa.
I want world peace.
I am kind and brave.
I pretend to dance like a professional.
I feel trees and flowers.
I worry if the world will end any time soon.
I cry when animals and people die.
I am kind and brave.
I understand that my father will never see me again.
I say that there are a lot of forests near my home.
I dream to be a famous dancer.
I try to listen hard in school.
I hope I live forever.
I am kind and brave.

Skye Story, Grade 4
Centennial Elementary School, TN

Evansville Rocks

Malls are full and ready to explode
Beep boop beep boop echoes from arcades
Cars are honking and speeding like cheetahs
People are yelling and playing in parks
Restaurants are steaming and full of great smells
Barbecues are booming with music and people
Exhaust fumes are as hot as the sun
Steak is juicy with barbecue
Pizza is popping and plowed to the crust
Arcade games are full of coins and happy
Mall doors are huge and open wide
Happiness and excitement with every stride

Evan Marksberry, Grade 6
College View Middle School, KY

Darkness
Darkness
Not external but internal
Darkness
Black is what I see
Dark clouds is what is inside me
Darkness
Scary and terrifying is what I feel
I don't know if I will ever heal
Darkness
The ground is solid cannot bare
To step or I'll tear to pieces
Darkness
Falls wherever I look
I should have taken the correct path
Darkness
Why does everything happen to me
Kassidy Street, Grade 6
White Station Middle School, TN

Love
It started out with a friend
Then ended with a kiss
He held me by the hand
I could hear him whispering in my ear
I loved the soft sound of his voice
Until he left me standing alone
We used to walk together
In the light of the sun
We loved each other very much
On one Valentine's Day
The best one I ever had
He passed me a note
That I will never forget
From that day on
Until I die
My love for him will always be in my heart
Elizabeth Whelan, Grade 5
Walton-Verona Middle School, KY

America's Beauty
I love America…
It is such a great land,
And to think God created it,
By just waving his hand!

I think so hard about
Our great nation…
It is a great place to
Spend a vacation.

It has been adored…
For so many generations.
And I just sit and
Ponder about our great nation!
Austin Crowe, Grade 6
St Joseph Academy, NC

Green
Green is the grass
The fresh cut smell
Beautiful, fresh, moist
And a lot of it.

Green is the trees
And some people's favorite color
I don't know why
But some are shy.

Green is frogs
Jumping all around
Going from lily pad to lily pad
All around the pond.

Green is an alligator
Stalking its prey
From under the water
He's impossible to see.

Green are plants
Giving us oxygen
They're all around
Inside and outside.
Mason Likens, Grade 6
Bernheim Middle School, KY

Yellow
Yellow is the bees
Buzzing through the sky,
Or the stars twinkling from above,
So high!

Yellow is the sweet, yet sour lemonade
Tingling on my tongue.
The salty popcorn,
Making me say "Yum!"

Yellow is the fire,
Burning all smoky.
The big bright sunflowers
With a beautiful aroma.

Yellow is a child's laughter,
Smiles here and there.
Or wind blowing through your hair,
Leaving painted leaves everywhere.

Yellow is that big smile,
All warm bright and shiny.
Yellow can fill a rainy day,
If you just let the light lead your way!
Cali Buday, Grade 6
Bernheim Middle School, KY

Letter to a Cheerleader
I am a pom-pom
Sparkling red and white
I go to practice in your trunk
And then I say goodnight.

Under your bed I go
With those dust mites and shoes
A chewed up apple and a flag that says
"I never lose!"

And did I mention the cat?
She's always checking me out,
Always pulling one of my streamers
So I can yelp "Ouch!"

I go up and down, right and left
Every twist and twirl,
When I finally get to the ground
I feel like I'm going to hurl!
All I'm saying is I'd like for us to connect
Get in touch more often and oh yeah…
HAVE SOME RESPECT!!!
Alyssa Rorie, Grade 5
Hunter GT Magnet Elementary School, NC

Freedom
Freedom is not free,
And it will never, ever be.
For all the soldiers that fought,
They all got something
Money never bought.
For all the families that cried,
Over the ones that died.
All the ones left dead,
And all the blood they ever shed.
This is the price they paid
For our freedom.
Paige McKenzie, Grade 6
Saint Pauls Middle School, NC

Flying Water
Soaring up above flying like
Beautiful water still and flowing
Like a bird in air

Soaring through graceful also free
Like water calm, full of life
Like a bird in air

Soaring calm and graceful
Like water moving
With a bird
Gentle also free
Like a bird in the air
Megan Baker, Grade 4
Buckner Elementary School, KY

Our Everlasting Memories
There she stopped and collapsed
when I ran to her to help she was lifeless
I said my goodbyes and cried
then buried her under her favorite tree to rest

I still didn't want her to leave me
alone for she was my happiness,
strength, and best friend

I still wasn't going to forget any
memories of our times together
because there would be too many I'd have to
erase from my mind

I'll need to carry on without you
until my time comes
and when it does if you'll meet
at Heaven's Golden Gates
we'll walk through together and all
the memories, love, friendship and
fun will last for all eternity
Caitlyn Mayberry, Grade 6
Dyer Elementary & Jr High School, TN

Friends
The best thing in the world is to have a friend
They will stay with you 'till the end

But to keep your friend you need to be nice
That is some good friendship advice

Friends are like your back up, when you're feeling down
You know they'll always be around to keep you off the ground

They are like your second self,
They know everything about you
No matter what mood you're in,
They know just what to do.

Keep them 'till the end of this life
They will keep you out of pain and strife

They are like your sign that says STOP!
They help your brain in that spot
(Stop you from doing dumb things,
Somebody might call the cops! If you do it.)
Frannie Hincks, Grade 5
Walton-Verona Middle School, KY

Ode to Toby
Toby my dog gives me kisses when he misses me.
He barks when he hears cars go up the road.
He chases the cat, but he can't run that fast because he is too fat.
My dog snores, but when I say his name he ignores me.
Colton McAdams, Grade 5
West Liberty Elementary School, WV

Blue
Blue is the sky's color the ocean's best friend.
Blue is what you see at the lake.
Blue is the sound of
screaming Kentucky
fans cheering on
their favorite player.
Blue is the world
around you.
In the tub you are consumed
by the happiness.
Blue is fish caught by
your grandfather.
Blue is the taste of a
warhead candy.
Blue is the smell of the beach.
Blue is the smell
of Heaven after your first whiff.
Terrence Beavers, Grade 6
Bernheim Middle School, KY

Mammoth Cave
Rocks everywhere get to tell me their stories.
Darkness then light.
Writing from slaves on the ceiling and to the side.
Water droplets ahead are pouring out their tears.
Bats flying around like clouds in the sky.
The cool breeze and fresh air dance through my hair.
There's coal from the area to the side of me crying out
Mine me, take me, help me.
A scent that has no name.
Air while it is slow dancing everywhere.
The fresh coldness everywhere is winter floating in the air.
There are slippery rocks that surround my hips
And stay there for seven years.
Excited I am for the journey ahead of me in the cave
Then out again.
Excitement is in the air.
Wondering minds are everywhere.
Chelsea Bailey, Grade 6
College View Middle School, KY

War
War, it is usually never a good thing
It has been around forever.
There have always been days of triumph and victory,
There have been days of horrible losses.
But the world can't seem to
Get away from it.
Many people have been killed,
And many people have been saved in war.
Wars have been started for many different reasons.
We have gained new allies, and made new enemies.
But we are and hopefully always will be,
The strongest — the U.S. military.
Braden Hvasta, Grade 6
Woodland Presbyterian School, TN

High Merit Poems – Grades 4, 5, and 6

The Power of Love
Love is one of the most powerful things of all
Love is the thing I share with the world
Love is the thing that keeps me warm during a blizzard
Love keeps me feeling up when my spirit is down
Love is the flow of all positive things
The thing that opens all hearts
The thing that clears out the negative energy around us
Love drives me to get up and get through the day
Love brings people together
Love stops war and brings peace
Love turns the sad into happy
Love is the thing that fills the world with peace
Love is the most precious thing to me

Jerry Tyler, Grade 6
Weldon Middle School, NC

My Best Friend Ever
My best friend she will be.
She will be the most wonderful girl you'll ever see.
Her name is Tyleka Bizzell and we'll watch
The birds as they fly by.
And we'll watch our kites
Fly in the sky.
When it is school time, we will
Sit beside each other on the bus.
And we like the same holidays.
We also like the seasons of the year.
Her family is nice and intelligent.
Tyleka's pet Katie is the most amazing pet you'll ever see.
Tyleka, you are an amazing friend.

Blessen Simmons, Grade 4
Southeast Elementary School, NC

My Horse, Angel
Angel always runs so fast,
She startles me when she goes past,

My chocolate colored Rocky Mountain mare,

will carry you here, there, everywhere.
She runs like the wind,

Her ears perked up, her head with a slight bend
My love for her will never end!

Jessica Harris, Grade 5
Paint Lick Elementary School, KY

March
M arch is my favorite month
A wesome spring is near
R ight you are! Flowers will bloom
C hristmas has passed, no more snow
H appy I am in March

Taylor Aaron, Grade 4
Evangelical Christian School Ridgelake Campus, TN

What Is Green
Green is the color of the grass
Green is the seaweed on the ocean floor
Green is the color I think of when I'm happy
Green is the lizard climbing a tree

Green smells like freshly cut grass
Green tastes like fresh herbs in your dinner
Green sounds like the seaweed swaying in the sea
Green looks like the palm trees in California

Green feels like the grass on me after rolling down a hill
Green makes me want to go outside and play
Green is my favorite color

Emily Barrach, Grade 6
White Station Middle School, TN

Best Aunt in the World
Ode to my Aunt Daniela.
You are a caring, loving person.
I know why Uncle Scott married you.
You are a funny person, any time I'm around you.
My stomach hurts, I laugh so much.
You care for everyone all the time.
When I'm around you I feel love and support.
Here is a secret —
You are my favorite aunt.
You always make everybody happy.
But, the most important things I love about you
Is that you are you.
You will always be the best aunt in the world.

Ashley Jones, Grade 6
Saint Pauls Middle School, NC

Spring
It's spring time isn't it great
There's no anger nor hate
It's a good time to play outside
Or you could surf in the tide
In this time children scream with glee
While they play with their family.
Spring is even good when you're blind
Because you can go outside and smell the pine.
When the days get longer you can tell summer is drawing nigh
So I guess you'll have to tell spring goodbye.

Steven Snyder, Grade 6
White Station Middle School, TN

Christmas Dinner
Grandmother's house
Warm and inviting
Bricks, stones, warm open fire
Fresh rolls as soft as clouds
All the girls cooking delicious, Christmas dinner

Seth Fenwick, Grade 6
College View Middle School, KY

The Prime Thing
It was the prime thing that
occurred in my life.
I was just two years old
when it occurred.
I didn't have a care in
the world and I always
wondered what it would
be like if they
were still together.
But I'm lucky it happened,
because everything is for a
purpose.
I'm just lucky I have a mom and dad
by my side when I require
them the most.
And I have superb stepparents
that take care of
me too.
Laymon Amagliani, Grade 6
Woodland Presbyterian School, TN

My Dog
I have a Dalmatian,
Who fights for our nation.
He is a fire fighter,
who uses a lighter.
he prances and dances,
he sings his songs
of barks and warnings,
of fires he longs.
He saves cats, he saves dogs,
even a couple of frogs.
But when he comes home
I give him his shiny white bone.
He heads to his bed,
he does some twirls
as his head whirls,
of thoughts his mind thinks
"Why did I decide to do this
Oh well I gotta do it again TOMORROW!"
Kaitlyn Rose, Grade 5
Longest Elementary School, KY

Fairies and Goblins
Fairies are creatures which live in the sky
They are also creatures who can fly
You probably think these creatures…
Are safe and sound
But they are not when goblins are around
They work for Jack Frost, a very mean guy
He hurts the fairies by taking their treasure
But with the help of two girls named…
Rachel and Kirsti, they defeat Jack Frost
And those mean, terrible goblins
Jordan Kriss, Grade 5
Moyock Elementary School, NC

Cross Country
Cross Country was the sport I chose,
I wasn't sure how I'd do.
I wasn't the fastest of them all,
but I always finished the race too.

Two miles seemed
like such a long way,
but now practicing,
I can run it today.

Shelby Farms
was the place to be,
to make new friends
that would run against me.

I am really glad
I decided to run.
It was hard work,
but very fun.
Anna Fracchia, Grade 6
Woodland Presbyterian School, TN

Ode to Family
Family here, family there
Family everywhere for me
They make me see what life really means

They know all the right
Things to say from when I
Am up at night
To when I get in a fight

I love my family
Because they actually
Understand the real me
And they really love me

My family is always there
They really care
I never want to
Leave because I love too much
Shelby Ensor, Grade 6
Bernheim Middle School, KY

Christmas
C rawling through the snow
H ollering through the woods
R udolph flies by
I ce is everywhere
S anta rides high in the sky
T oys fill the house
M aking everything a mess
A sking for a lot
S now melts as Christmas is over!
Bethany Stone, Grade 6
Bargerton Elementary School, TN

Black Lion
Black lion — oh — black lion
with all your might
protect me
Black lion — oh — black lion
with all your pride
teach me

Black eagle — oh — black eagle
with all your strength
protect me
Black eagle — oh — black eagle
with all your speed
teach me

Black lion — oh — black eagle
with both your brains
teach me

Oh lion oh eagle
thank you for all
my friends
But farewell, my friends for now
Joey Canal, Grade 6
McGee's Crossroads Middle School, NC

The Outside World
The rolling, green hills
The snow capped mountains
The pale, blue sky
The wandering creatures
The continuous prairie
Massive waterfalls or slender streams
Wolves howl into the night
Wind rustles the leaves on the trees
Streams' rushing water
Seeps through gaps in the rocks
The sounds of birds pierce the tranquility
Trees of oak, pine, birch,
Maple, ash, and willow
Fill the air with their scent
They are trampled on by
Small woodland creatures
The jagged peaks spiked through clouds
The flat cliffs and mesas
Bask you in magnificence
Shed their glory upon you
Its constant beauty has no end
Tyler Rakers, Grade 6
Woodland Presbyterian School, TN

Being Fair
Wind blows in my hair
Pretty sight and pretty people everywhere
Caring for others, being fair
J'Shaun Redmon, Grade 4
Centennial Elementary School, TN

The Stage

Bright lights burning warm reds, oranges, and yellows
and cool blues, greens, and purples.
Many costumes hanging backstage…
Soft, itchy, sparkly.

Music just blaring during warm-ups and rehearsals.
The audience going wild after the show!

Hairspray and excitement fill the air!
Red lipstick that's on my teeth…eww!
The blond metal from bobby pins that I can't hold with my hands.

The dried out makeup it's like an old woman's skin in the winter.
My stiff hair that's glued down with hairspray.

I feel unstoppable…even if I mess up.
I feel happy, amazing, at peace.

Lillie Mathis, Grade 6
College View Middle School, KY

Ode to Tilly

Tilly you're my dog,
I love to see you run so fast,
you stay on task.

You're so funny,
I can't help but laugh.
I wouldn't sell you for all the money in the world.

When there are crowds,
you can't help but howl!
Your silk fur is so soft and clean.

Be careful when you run in the yard,
because you just might fall.

When you get your bones,
you forget who owns you and loves you.

Casey Wood, Grade 5
West Liberty Elementary School, WV

My Favorite Movie

Twilight is my favorite movie to watch at night
They always show vampires that fight
Jacob Black is my favorite character to see
I like him because he's a werewolf, but he doesn't scare me
Bella and Edward got married in one of the shows
They are in love and everybody knows
Bella didn't care about fitting in
She only had about four friends
I wish we could watch this movie at school
But we can't, because it's really against the rules
This is why my favorite movie is Twilight
And I like to watch it at night

Chantel Kidd, Grade 4
Weldon Elementary School, NC

The Story That Was Left Behind

My cousin and I playing in the yard.
He and I racing from his house to my grandparent's house,
A thumping sound when we run.

Smell the newly fresh grass that has been cut,
The wild flowers are big, round, yellow suns when they grow there.

The warm s'mores that we had some nights,
Taste like a dream come true.
I taste the sunflowers that always grow there.

I touch the rough leaves from the bushes
That dance in the wind.

The rough, bumpy, dark oak trees there,
Feel like a rhino's skin.

I feel sad and feel the flames that burn inside me
When he went away.

Hayley Jones, Grade 6
College View Middle School, KY

Love Ballad

My sister met the man of her dreams.
They're so in love it makes me want to scream.
He was in the army far away.
So they talked and Skyped every day.

From the time she got home till time for bed.
All she thought about was Chris in her head.
Even if you needed it you could never get the phone.
Cause when they were not talking all they did was groan.

She is just as crazy about him yes it's true.
I think they have both gone coo coo.
They are in love it's easy to see.
What a happy marriage it will be.

I think in this family we will let him stay.
Because it's for sure he will never go away.
My sister is happy and so am I.
Because Chris really is a good guy.

Addi Carman, Grade 6
Bernheim Middle School, KY

My Best Friend

My best friend is Ajaney.
First we do our homework, then we can play.
And after that we play with our tambourines.
Finally we can jump on my trampoline.
But wait, there's more.
We can decorate my front door.
Now it's time to go to bed,
But I want to play instead.

Karia Lewis, Grade 4
Southeast Elementary School, NC

Christmas

Christmas, Christmas,
Trees are lit!
Christmas, Christmas,
Grandma knits!
Christmas, Christmas,
Singers are humming!
Christmas, Christmas,
Santa is coming!
Christmas, Christmas,
Rudolph is near!
Christmas, Christmas,
Presents are here!

Madison Hedrick, Grade 5
Moyock Elementary School, NC

Lola

Playful and fun
Smooth and silky
Fur as dark as the night sky

Snuggle in my bed
All night long
Purring like a drum

Small but growing fast
Loving and loyal
Meow

Libby Thetford, Grade 6
Dyer Elementary & Jr High School, TN

The Lake

Over the river and through the woods
Behind Grandmother's house,
Lies a large,
Luscious,
Lake
The lake is as green as an emerald
What else would I want to do
Than sit at this sparkling green lake
With an occasional blue
I would sit on the dock forever
If only life lasted an eternity

Logan Maddox, Grade 6
College View Middle School, KY

Dads

Dads are cool,
They cannot be replaced.
They are your guide books for life.
They'll teach you stuff,
While you're a kid,
Dads have a job,
It's to take care of you.
No matter what, dads will always love you.

Dallas Nicely, Grade 5
Paint Lick Elementary School, KY

I Am Johnny Appleseed

I am Johnny Appleseed. I am going on a long journey.
I wonder if my journey will be good or not.
I hear the birds singing and the wind whistling.
I see birds in the trees and apples on the trees.
I am Johnny Appleseed. I decide to travel westward and plant the seeds.
I pretend that the seeds will be plentiful for the people to eat.
I do feel sad sometimes out here all alone.
I touch the ground it is cold and wet. Winter is coming.
I worry that I may get hurt out here all alone.
I cry because tonight I am very lonely.
I am Johnny Appleseed and my journey is lonely.
I understand that I am helping people by going on this journey.
I am planting seeds that will grow into fine trees for them.
I say to myself that I will succeed on my journey.
I have met a few people and told my story. I hope they remember me.
I try to plant lots and lots of seeds for people that will need them.
I hope people like my apples. You can make almost anything with them.
I am Johnny Appleseed. I have finished my journey. "Now grow my seeds."

Andy Morehead, Grade 4
Mineral Wells Elementary School, WV

I Am From

I am from glittery bows lighting and glowing in my hair.
From playing in the yard while my dad barbecued.
I am from the pink walls of my bedroom.
And a little black day bed.
I am from the strawberries growing in my yard.
They were my dad's but to me they were mine.
I am from an old teddy bear that I sleep with for two days then a special pillow
From Danielle Fuller and Robert Fuller.
I am from brown hair and brown eyes.
And from spinning and prancing around.
From waiting for dance class to come around.
I am from giving my life to Christ a special day at church.
I am from my grandmother and uncle.
From macaroni and cheese and steak on a good day.
From the sad day when I was sobbing when my uncle moved.
And from wishing he would come back and all I had to remember him by was a little doll.
I am from those moments when I was born,
    brought into this world with bows glittering and lighting in my hair.

Madison Fuller, Grade 5
Tates Creek Elementary School, KY

Myrtle Beach, SC

The beautiful waves wildly crashing wherever they want,
The yellow beach umbrellas say hi to the sun as people open them up,
Many small children play in the shiny sand,
Seagulls honk as little kids chase them,
I smell the ocean waves' salty water,
I smell the suntan lotion as people put it on,
I taste the ocean waves' water as cold as ice cubes,
I touch the warm, soft sand, a blanket of warmth over the ground,
I touch the cool relaxing waves as I clean sea shells,
I feel relaxed and calm like I don't have any troubles in the world.

Wayne Daley, Grade 6
College View Middle School, KY

High Merit Poems – Grades 4, 5, and 6

The Forest Untouched
Cool breeze rushing by
Gleaming green glow
Of the forest
A meadow untouched
By humans

Tons of trees
Everywhere you look
Trees, trees, trees
The grass no more
Now bushes, trees, and twigs

Bushes, trees, and twigs
All a perfect green
Air so moist
And non polluted
Animals nearly never thirsty

This meadow surely is
Untouched by the human species
Tyler Hadaway, Grade 4
Buckner Elementary School, KY

Fire
Fire can be blue, white, or red
It can reach to the top of your head
Fierce, firm, and flickering
Burning so bright
At day or night

Wildfires are caused by a
Streak in the sky
The effect is a
Barrage of flames
For wildfires
You have lightning to blame

But you should be grateful too
You wouldn't have toasted marshmallows
If it weren't for a campfire
Next time you have a fire
Don't be so pessimistic
Or would you rather be in the Arctic
Arvind Niattianandam, Grade 6
White Station Middle School, TN

Roses
Roses are a symbol of love
Its beauty and elegance
Where there is beauty there can be pain
Thorns are hidden under its beauty
Which can cause hatred
The rose is a symbol of many things
But you are the one who chooses
Evan Sheppard, Grade 6
White Station Middle School, TN

Meat
I love meat,
Meat is great!
It's all I eat,
Every day!

I love burgers,
I'll eat turkey,
I love steak,
Or even jerky!

Fish is good,
I like salami!
Bacon's my thing,
I need baloney!

So meat is good,
I love meat,
I eat all this,
Every week!
Camrin Richardson, Grade 6
Bernheim Middle School, KY

My Cows
Cows are very big,
And very loud,
Especially after they yell:
"Moo, Moo, Moo!" all night long!

Cows are scary to some people,
But to me, they're just big fuzz balls!
To some other people, they are ugly,
But not to me! Oh, no! They are beautiful!

Cows are very gentle,
I know from life experience,
I live on a farm,
And I've lived there *all* my life!

We have small sized to big,
The calves are the most adorable!
Especially when they're first born,
When they're learning how to stand up.
Madison Croom, Grade 6
Dyer Elementary & Jr High School, TN

A Soft Sound
A soft mixture of warmth and fear
I'm away but I'm still here

Listen close hear the wind
A soft sound coming large

There it comes the waves pushing in
Bound here to run nowhere to hide
Selinna Tran, Grade 5
Cool Spring Elementary School, NC

I Am
I am cute and fun
I wonder how I am going to be in 16 years
I hear people loving
I see people getting along
I want to become brave
I am cute and fun
I pretend I am queen
I feel powerful
I touch a tiara
I worry I am going to die
I cry when I get hurt
I am cute and fun
I understand how life goes
I say I hate JB
I dream to meet Justin Bieber
I try to become better
I hope to live long

I am cute and fun!
Trinity Wagner, Grade 4
Centennial Elementary School, TN

Winter Gloves
Why did you leave me,
Here in the snow?
Your scrawny hands will freeze,
And your fingers will too.

I'm covered with white,
Down here in the snow.
You'll come back,
And take me with you.

Your mama will send you,
For she sewed me so fine.
You never know,
Where you might find me.

So come caringly crying,
And take me home.
It's 21 degrees,
Out here in the snow.
Jessica Kreider, Grade 5
Hunter GT Magnet Elementary School, NC

Soldiers
S oldiers help us survive in life
O ffer their lives for us
L ove that soldiers give before they leave
D etermined to get home
I hope they make it home safely
E very second they fight for our freedom
R espect for the soldiers
S tand up for our country
Mika Ogborn, Grade 6
Temple Hill Elementary School, KY

Christmas

Christmas,
Jesus,
Presents.
Happy Christmas,
Fun Christmas
Loving, opening presents, Christmas.
Toys, games, cake, Christmas.

These are just a few.

Letters of Christmas,
Snowy Christmas
Joyful, family, sharing, Christmas.
Santa, sleigh, reindeer Christmas.
Excited Christmas,
Sad Christmas,
Jesus Christmas.
Don't forget trees for Christmas.

Last of all, best of all,
I like grateful Christmas.
Celina Berrios, Grade 5
Tates Creek Elementary School, KY

Black Is the Color

Black is the color
of the night
when the moon shines
the shade is bright
Black is the best
just like my choke collar
when I pull too tight
I cannot holler
I love the color black
It's devious and thrilling
I just can't get over
this cold-hearted feeling
Black is the color
I have inside
for some people
just like Mr. Hyde
black is almighty
no one can beat it
it is the ultimate
so you might as well meet it
Damien Wells, Grade 6
Bernheim Middle School, KY

Sports and School

Sports are fun to play
I could play them every day
I'd rather not go to school
It's not nearly as cool
But I guess I'll go for today.
Nicholas Peters, Grade 4
Centennial Elementary School, TN

Ice Cream Mountain

Creamy ice cream
Mountained high
Whipped cream peak
Cold as ice

Steaming chocolate fudge lava
Streaming
Down the sides
Mountain of ice cream
Mountained high

Ice cream
White as snow
Flakes of ice cream freezing cold
Maybe colder than ice

Oh no!
A spoon
A giant spoon
Sinking into the mountain
Spencer Hancock, Grade 4
Buckner Elementary School, KY

My Brother

We always stick together.
It doesn't matter wherever.
I will always love him.
It's like brother and sister in a film.

We had a great bond, I thought.
But we fight a lot.
We stand by each other.
We both love one another.

We love each other truly.
We sometimes get along smoothly.
We care for each other a bunch.
We will help each other in a crunch.

My brother can be sweet.
Hanging with him is neat.
One like him, there is no other.
Because I have the very best brother.
I love my brother!!
Kristin Rhodes, Grade 6
Bernheim Middle School, KY

Soccer

Soccer is my favorite sport.
I always feel happy and proud.
I play in hot or cold, day or night.
I love the cold fresh water that
Makes my tastes buds freeze up.
Then I am back on the fields.
Katie Fairchild, Grade 5
Longest Elementary School, KY

Homework

I don't feel like doing homework
Maybe in an hour or two
Probably not even then
Ugh, I hate having homework to do!

When my teacher assigns it
I'll almost always groan.
I get home and have to finish it
Moan, moan, moan

Eventually it'll have to be done.
I've always finished it before.
I don't like bad grades,
But doing it's a chore.

I wouldn't tell my teachers
That homework is a bore.
I'm looking forward to when school ends
So I won't have to do homework any more.
Maddy Danziger, Grade 6
White Station Middle School, TN

I Am!

I am wonderful and smart
I wonder what will become of me
I hear waves crashing upon the shore
I see green and red Christmas lights
I want hope
I am wonderful and smart
I pretend I am a princess
I feel bright
I touch my soft pillow
I worry about my father
I cry when I'm afraid
I am wonderful and smart
I understand that nobody is perfect
I say this won't last forever
I dream of becoming a teacher
I try my very best
I hope that everyone is happy

I am wonderful and smart
Audrey Lewis, Grade 4
Centennial Elementary School, TN

Ocean

Ocean, ocean, so crystal clear.
Ocean, ocean, sea shells are near.
Ocean, ocean, dolphins jumping.
Ocean, ocean, waves are bumping.
Ocean, ocean, warm and cold.
Ocean, ocean, nicknacks are sold.
Ocean, ocean, my poem is complete,
Ocean, ocean, this poem can't be beat.
Cameryn Dowdy, Grade 5
Moyock Elementary School, NC

High Merit Poems – Grades 4, 5, and 6

I Know Thanksgiving

I know Thanksgiving…

Thanksgiving is when mom starts cooking
It's when relatives start looking
It's when dad watches TV
It's when grandma kisses me.

I know Thanksgiving…

Thanksgiving is the smell of pumpkin pie
It's the noises of the baby's cry
It's the good taste of mashed potatoes
It's the phrase "Ewww tomatoes!"

I know Thanksgiving…

Thanksgiving is when relatives drive miles
It's a house full of smiles
It's the time to cook turkey
It's the noise of my stomach growling at me,

I know Thanksgiving.

Shun Dela Peña, Grade 5
Fern Creek Elementary School, KY

My Favorite Plant

I plant a seed.
It grows and grows.
It comes and it goes.
Some last 12 months and some last 6 months or so.
But my favorite one never lasts 12 months.
I don't understand
Why my favorite ones can't last 12 months.
That's the way life goes.
So I have to be happy
With the ones that last 12 months.
But when mine come around,
I am going to jump for joy.

Brianna Brooks, Grade 5
Southeast Elementary School, NC

Our Freedom

Freedom is not free,
And it will never ever be.
Soldiers stand up and fight,
And every day they give their lives.
Some people don't appreciate it,
But what would we do, if we couldn't make it.
Would you get out there and fight,
And be injured time after time?
Would you be willing to lie down and lose your life,
For people who didn't even care you died?
Please, please believe me.
Freedom is not and will never ever be free.

Toneeya Jones, Grade 6
Saint Pauls Middle School, NC

Ode to Ice Cream

Your chocolatey deliciousness fills my mouth.
You smell and feel so good.

I take a bite.
It is so cold, yet so good.

I watch them make it,
my mouth waters as I stare
at the employees and wait
for my second helping.
Tick! Tick! Tick!

It is only a minute, but it
feels like a day.

Chocolate is back in
Stock!

Devin Brader-Araje, Grade 5
Montessori Community School, NC

I Am Michael Jackson

I am Michael Jackson
I wonder what I will do with all of my money
I hear people screaming
I see guitar players
I am Michael Jackson
I pretend I am playing a guitar
I feel the guitar
I touch the pick
I worry that people will laugh
I cry because people do laugh at me
I am Michael Jackson
I understand how to make a hit record
I say I want to have fun
I dream about getting a guitar
I try to make good CDs
I hope to live forever
I am Michael Jackson

Robbie Fulmer, Grade 4
Mineral Wells Elementary School, WV

Halloween

Halloween is a time for trick-or-treating.
Kids dressing up in different costumes.
Ghost and goblins soaring around
Getting candy from house to house.
Full moon out at night
Brightens all over the streets.
Houses decorated in scary form.
Skeletons walking around.
Screams and roars from down the street.
Tonight's the night for shouts and screams
Go ahead take as much candy as you want, my pleasure.

Samantha Ellis, Grade 4
Moyock Elementary School, NC

Michelle and Brookie Bard

Michelle and Brookie Bard
They work really hard
even though they fuss and fight
they always make up every night
when she makes me mad I will tell her I am sad
when I tell her she will always say too bad
I will tell her that was mean then SLAP
Shh don't tell anyone I'm good at schemes

Brooklynn Bard, Grade 5
Longest Elementary School, KY

My Dog

I have a dog named Betsy
And she is a little chesty
She is round as a hog
And sleeps like a log
She is white with black spots
And she likes to eat a lot
She likes my mom the best
And she growls at all the rest

Chandler Caughron, Grade 5
Evangelical Christian School Ridgelake Campus, TN

Minecraft

The cows are pals
The hens love dens

Skeleton archers
Are really marchers

The mobs are fun
But they don't come in the sun

Alexander Hamilton, Grade 4
Evangelical Christian School Ridgelake Campus, TN

The Icky Sticky Snake

There once was an icky sticky snake
with a rake
he wanted to bake
but no one would touch him the icky sticky snake
went to the market to get his cake
and saw his friend Sammy the turtle
he was picking up his baking supplies
and taught the icky sticky snake to bake

Kaitlin Laymon, Grade 5
Longest Elementary School, KY

My Favorite Mom

T is for trustworthy
E is for excellent motherhood
R is for always being responsible
E is for especially being a best friend
S is for being a good sister, wife, and mom
A is for being an awesome mom!

Robyn Forde-Whitefield, Grade 4
F H Jenkins Elementary School, TN

Weekend

On the weekend I go with my friends,
Cause we never want the day to end.
On the weekend I go hiking,
Sometimes even biking.
On the weekend I go jumping into lakes,
While my mom is home baking my favorite cake.
Sometimes we even ride on a sled,
But there is nothing like getting tucked into bed!

Annalee Wilson, Grade 5
Paint Lick Elementary School, KY

Blue

Blue is the color of the sadness.
Blue is the color of a clear sky.
Blue is the color of the new Diary of a Wimpy Kid book.
Blue is the color of my sheets.
Blue is the color of moldy bread.
Blue is the color of my favorite chair.
Blue is the color of my best friend's hair.
Blue is the best.

Tayler Kee, Grade 4
F H Jenkins Elementary School, TN

Birds

Birds flying in the sky up high
You can see them in the big, blue sky
I see the nest in the tree
I wonder if they see me
Juicy worms are their favorite meal
The thought of that makes me squeal
I see their eggs oval and round
When they hatch they are no longer bound

Gray Shelton, Grade 4
Evangelical Christian School Ridgelake Campus, TN

A Mother's Love

Mommy you have shown me
many things.
You showed me how
to crawl and how to walk.
You helped me to ride my bike.
You even helped me become the little girl I am today.
But most importantly
you taught me what it means to be a daughter.

Rachel Hardee, Grade 6
Saint Pauls Middle School, NC

Winter

Winter is white
It taste like cocoa
It smells like wood in the fireplace
It looks like sledding
It sounds like kids having fun
It makes me feel chill

Will Bartel, Grade 4
Caywood Elementary School, TN

The Girl

"Ugh," she always thought "what is wrong with me?"
People teased and taunted her with lots and lots of glee.
She cut her hair, changed her clothes and watched herself daily,
Just so to others she would be satisfactory.
She was constantly hard on herself each and every day.
"You're just a girl," her friends would say "don't treat yourself this way."
"Who cares what other people say? They're living in the past."
"All that matters, is what you do to make the good times last."
The girl thought and thought about what her friends had said,
And continued to think that night as she lay in bed.
She finally fell asleep,(despite the spinning in her head),
And finally realized the next morning, what she should have said.
She told her friends she remembered a story she was told by her Great Aunt,
"When people tease and taunt you, they're usually jealous themselves,"
"So even if it's really hard to do sometimes, being teased and taunted should add to your self-worth."
The girl put a smile on her face, turned to her friends and said:
"Thanks for all you've done and everything you've said, from this day forward, I no longer hang my head!"
Now, when you read this you might ask me, "How do you know this story?"
I'd turn to you, knowing that the answer would simple be: "The reason I know this is because —"
"The Girl, was ME."

Gracelin Harvey, Grade 6
Elizabeth City Middle School, NC

I Am Inspired by Nature When…

I am inspired by nature when it is a sunny day in July, or a rainy day in April.
I am inspired by nature when flowers are blooming and butterflies are flying.
Nature always inspires me.
Nature inspires me to go outside and take a run.
I am inspired by nature when there is nothing to do inside.
Nature always inspires me.
I am inspired by nature when the wind is blowing and leaves are flying.
I am inspired by nature when birds are chirping.
I am inspired by nature when I hear the wind calling my name and can't resist going outside.
I am inspired by nature when the grass is green and the leave are too.
Nature always inspires me.
I am inspired by nature when I'm picking apples at my grandma's house.
I am inspired by nature when I go on outdoor scavenger hunts.
Nature always inspires me.
I am inspired by nature when I play basketball outside in the fall, or ride horses with my cousins.
Nature always inspires me.

Carson Greenwell, Grade 6
St Ann Interparochial School, KY

Adding a Member to Our Family

Once upon a time there were just three, it was Mom, Dad, and me.
We three — Mom, Dad, and me would go out a lot and see a movie, then go have some dinner and tea.
Then all of a sudden unexpectedly, very important news was dropped on me.
We talked about how we would no longer be just three, because we were adding on a baby to our family.
This news was a great surprise to me, but I was very happy.
For now I was very excited you see, because I would no longer be alone with just me.
No longer would we be just three, but a foursome in loving harmony.
Then discussion turned to me and how this would build more responsibility.
See, I would help in caring for my baby sister, Emily.
I admit there are times that this may overwhelm me, but the love that I see is worth it to me.

Victoria Stivers, Grade 6
Woodland Presbyterian School, TN

Legos

I like Legos because they are cool
I even like to bring them to school

I play Legos all the time
I have so many and they are all mine

I stack the Legos up really high
If they fall I give it another try

I have so many Legos I can't even count
Just by looking you can tell I have a big amount

Matthew Pennington, Grade 4
Evangelical Christian School Ridgelake Campus, TN

Fall

As the leaves change from green to gold
The weather changes too
You have to wear a coat and scarf so you don't get the flu

Roasting marshmallows over a crackling fire
Telling ghost stories with everyone
Fall is filled with so much fun
Fall is amazing
I love it the most
What's your favorite season — summer, spring, winter, fall
Whatever it is, I love them all!

Claire Waddell, Grade 5
Evangelical Christian School Ridgelake Campus, TN

Blue Time

In the evening, when I look up into the sky,
I don't see gray, nor do I see majestic orange, or royal purple.
Nor do I see light blue or flamingo pink.

I see a color more beautiful than all of those.
I see dark straight, beautiful blue,
And I call it blue time.

Blue time is like a big blue blanket,
Protecting the Earth from the massive universe.
Blue time is like a soft flower petal bringing everyone together.

Celia Adlin, Grade 4
Nature's Way Montessori School, TN

A Simple Clover

Green and small, no smell at all,
Also no sound, but the leaves are round.

With patterns circular and white,
The drops of dew on it, sparkle in the light.

Not very tall, In fact it's really pretty small
The color of it is an emerald green,
It's just a natural beauty that has to be seen.

Johanna Kastenberger, Grade 6
Baylor School, TN

Stranded

Stranded in the desert with one bottle of water
Out in the middle of the heat for one week
Communication has been cut off from everyone
Not a drop of water for five days
Getting weaker and weaker every minute
Our mouths are cracked, dry from the lack of water
Storm clouds gather overhead
Water is gold for people in the desert
Drip, drop
The rain is falling
The humidity soothes my throat
Finally, water

John Woods, Grade 6
Davidson Day School, NC

My Peaceful Bed

The neat covers on the bed,
I feel a pillow under my head.
Happy sister playing outside,
tired Mom and Dad watching TV like couch potatoes.
Sneaky sweat on my pillow.
Red blood I see from bug bites I pick,
sticky sweat on my hand.
Shining silver spit from my mouth,
I rub my soft covers to sleep,
Look at my comforter long and wide.
Feel at peace as I go to
Sleep.

Easton Crisp, Grade 6
College View Middle School, KY

Christmas

Christmas what a joy!
You might get a toy

You might even get a ball
Jesus is the best of all

Advent candles are very bright
We go to church Christmas Eve night

At Christmas time there are lots of treats
There is always something good to eat

Charlotte Godat, Grade 4
Evangelical Christian School Ridgelake Campus, TN

Winter

I know it is winter
When we have to pull out blankets and covers.
The mornings are cold waiting for the bus,
Freezing our hands and toes.
I drink hot chocolate in the cold.
Next time winter comes,
I hope it snows.

Anzaryia Cobb, Grade 4
Southeast Elementary School, NC

High Merit Poems – Grades 4, 5, and 6

Summer Time
Summer is a warm time
Blue birds are singing in their nest
The blue sky, white clouds
The warm breeze, and the cool cool creek
The noise of the waterfall
Is music in my ears
As the butterflies fly by
I thank the Lord for summer time
In Tennessee.

Mya Jones, Grade 4
Centennial Elementary School, TN

Sam and Bear
Sam and Bear were my dogs.
Sam was smart.
Bear was sweet.
Sam would be the first to eat.
Bear would open the door
Just to say I want more.
They made a mess.
They did not rest.
But they were the best.

Blake Robertson, Grade 5
Providence Academy, TN

Panama City Beach, Florida
Soft sand under my feet,
Ocean waves crash on the shore,
Lots of people splashing in the water,
The strong smell of steak from ANGIOS,
Salty water of the Atlantic Ocean,

The seashells on the seashore,
I'm happy to be on vacation,
It's like a peaceful moment.

Bess Johnson, Grade 6
College View Middle School, KY

Christmas
Christmas
Bright, sparkling
Giving, eating, playing
Remembering the price Jesus paid
Presents

Allison Breeden, Grade 4
Centennial Elementary School, TN

Man's Best Friend
Dogs are cuddly, dogs are funny.
Dogs like playing when it is sunny.
When they are done playing,
they will come in and start begging.
When they are done with their treat,
oh!! Now they will want more to eat.

Syree Johnson, Grade 4
E O Young Elementary School, NC

Silly Bears
Their slick fuzzy fur
Their blueberry eyes dart you down
The little one plays one the big one's back
They're so cute

Can't you see the glistening, snowy, fluffy fur
Showing you that they have been playing in the snow
Their little ears like notches stick out

Far ahead one of the bears see a salty snack.
They dive for it leaping
The frozen shivering cold water kicking and soaring through the ocean
They dry off and go to bed and dream their way to dreamland

Kayleigh Macumber, Grade 4
Buckner Elementary School, KY

The Beach
As I walk onto the beach I see the water, it is as blue as the sky on a sunny day.
I jump around because the sand is a hot fire beneath my feet.
The seagulls around me smell like seafood.
I jump in the water and swim.
The water burns my eyes when I open them like alcohol in an open wound.
I go fishing.
The fish are sneaky thieves who steal my bait, but can't be caught.
I leave for dinner.
The clams scream as they start getting fried and eaten.
I come back to the beach and see a lobster sunbathing lazily on a rock.
Dolphins dive deliriously down into the deeps of the sea.
I have never felt more happy and relaxed.

Kate Fullenwider, Grade 6
College View Middle School, KY

Disney
Disneyworld
You see the magnificent Cinderella Castle
The crackling explosion of Wishes
You feel the fuzzy character's hand
The roller coaster bar as you slowly creep upward
You smell fun and excitement everywhere
The wonderful smell of food when you're STARVING
You hear fading screams of Roller coaster Riders
The whining of your feet as you say 'Hurry up!'
You taste salty popcorn as the parade goes by
The cool, awesome taste of raspberry lemonade from Hollywood Studios
One man's Dream, all mankind's pleasure

Alyson Culbertson, Grade 5
Providence Academy, TN

Fudge
I walk downstairs and smell the rich dark chocolate calling my name.
It's teasing me with its richness and fame.
I take the first bite, guess what I get.
The warm dark chocolate between my lips.

Logan Watkins, Grade 5
Walton-Verona Middle School, KY

Bush Stadium
A white, bouncy baseball flying as fast as light into the outfield,
I hear the players yelling "Catch it!"
The loud crowd screaming as the white ball flies through the air,
I smell the hot dogs cooking,
I smell the tasty hamburgers cooking,
The buttery popcorn in my mouth,
The soft foam finger in my hand,
I touch the hot air as I spring out of my chair.
I feel joyful.
It's Christmas as the St. Louis Cardinals win the World Series.
Wesley Lindsey, Grade 6
College View Middle School, KY

Ode to Monkey
Monkey you are so cute
The sound you make, oh how it makes me laugh
You are so funny every move you make
You sometimes are smelly, but who cares
I love the way you eat bananas
You climb around on everything
You are my favorite animal
You are great at the monkey bars, way, way better than me
Oh how I wish that you were my best friend
Monkey please always be special to me
Addyson Messick, Grade 5
Vienna Elementary School, NC

The Pond
The orange sunset like a glowing ball of fire.
The blue water,
The martins singing.
Water splashing into the banks like hurricane winds.
Fresh-cut grass,
The fresh fall air,
The water,
The whipping water,
The rocks on my feet,
I feel totally peaceful and lonely.
Mark Myles, Grade 6
College View Middle School, KY

The Beach
There are so many things at the Florida beach like;
A couple of sails
Three or four whales
The water wears green and blue
As we say, "Woo Hoo!"
Shells jingle like bells
Sand gets on your hands
And I would say,
"Beach towels, swim suits, relaxing and all,
Oh, I wish I had it all!"
Lily Harding, Grade 4
Evangelical Christian School Ridgelake Campus, TN

The Cabin
A lake full of fresh fish as big as elephants,
My sister throwing a water balloon at me,
The laughter of my family members around the campfire,
Crickets happily singing late at night,
The clean smell of the wood from the walls,
Marshmallows roasting over the raging fire,
The rough wood of the house,
Soft, cool, ground outside is heaven on Earth,
I feel the great love of my family,
I feel the amazing competition in our water balloon fights.
Jay Carlisle, Grade 6
College View Middle School, KY

The Giant Mountain
All
mountains
are   short
and   tall,
wide   and
narrow,   just
sitting   and
doing   nothing
So very   gracefully
In the very wide and open grassy plains everywhere.
Nicholas Abbott, Grade 5
Carver Elementary School, NC

Beach Balcony
The peaceful waves crashing on the shore,
The clouds swimming across the beautiful blue sky,
Innocent children laughing as they play,
The lovely sound of waves, that are like a lullaby to me,
The fresh smell of the ocean and sand,
The wonderful smell of fresh grilled burgers,
My sweet Dr. Pepper as I sip it up,
My soft towel as I lay on a lawn chair tanning,
The soft comfort of my mother's hand,
I feel wonderfully happy and comfortable.
Maddie Wilkerson, Grade 6
College View Middle School, KY

Winter Break
It might be cold
And the snow is thick and bold.
I wonder if people sell sleds out here.
Maybe. It's cold out here.
So I will put on some nice warm jeans and put on a big coat.
Now I'm finished playing.
Now I can get some good hot chocolate with marshmallows in it.
Now I'm warm and settled.
I lay my head down on a soft pillow
And slowly dream of cute armadillos.
Jayla Brown, Grade 4
Southeast Elementary School, NC

High Merit Poems – Grades 4, 5, and 6

Christmas!!!
Christmas is my favorite time of the year.
It's time for celebration and cheer.
No children should shed a tear
The presents are here!!!
We put up our Christmas tree and put up the lights
And happily see it glow every night.
Christmas is a time for love and care
For every last one of us to share.
Kids make lists of presents they want from Santa.
If you are good he'll bring them when you're asleep.
If not, he'll give you something you don't want
A big stocking of coal for your mean, cold soul.
Rudolph's nose will glow
As Santa yells HO! HO! HO!
When you wake up on Christmas day
There will be presents under the tree!
Your mind will be full of glee!
So just remember
Be extra good in December!
Be loving, be caring
It's not about gifts it's about sharing!!

Holly Fussell, Grade 6
White Station Middle School, TN

I Am a Cat
I am a cat
I stalk my prey in the woods
As I kill the prey, I know that I am the best
Cunning, stealthy, strong, quick
I am a cat
A rabid dog finds me
When I am being chased, I trust that I am the best
Cunning, stealthy, strong, quick
I am a cat
I protect my kits from the predators
As I hear the howl of the dog, I remember that I am the best
Cunning, stealthy, strong, quick
I am a cat
All the prey has run away
As I starve in a cave, I am not sure that I am the best
Cunning, stealthy, strong, quick
I am a cat
The famine has ended, so I take a rest
When I lie in the sun, I a confident that I am the best
Cunning, stealthy, strong, quick
I am a cat

Robert Blanton, Grade 6
White Station Middle School, TN

A Zebra
There once was a zebra,
it was black and white,
it was nice but it slightly nibbled,
it had three black hooves and one odd white one.

Ashley Ford, Grade 5
Longest Elementary School, KY

Smoky Mountain Stream
A clear softly flowing stream,
Trout swimming upstream

The cold water flowing downstream,
The rustle of the leaves flowing in the wind

The fresh dew on the grass like water beads,
The clean, fresh air

The freshly grilled trout,
The clean flowing water talks to me

The smooth strong trout that I catch,
The tug on my line when a fish hits my shiny rooster tail bait

I feel at peace doing what I love,
    Just fishin'.

Nathan Hayes, Grade 6
College View Middle School, KY

Christmas Penguins
Penguins, Penguins,
Putting up trees

Puffles giving
presents to their penguin pals

Penguins, building snowmen,
Puffles and Penguins caroling

Penguins, preparing for the big day
Penguins secretly putting a candy cane under each puffle's tree

Patter, patter, the sound of
Penguins and puffles hopping to the tree

Presents everywhere
Puffles thank their owners for the big surprise.

Elijah Hughes, Grade 4
South Toe Elementary School, NC

Moms
A mom is a mom no matter where you go,
It's their forever love they must show.
Protection follows them,
Like the words to a hymn,
That has played over and over again.
Cleaning and working every day,
So we have a nice place to stay.
Making peace with everyone,
I'd give a job well done.
She has been with you through thick and thin.
She has helped you stand strong in the strongest wind.
She loves you, and you should always love her too.

Haley Wright, Grade 6
Siegel Middle School, TN

The Cost
Blood and tears,
that's the cost.
The cost of freedom.
Freedom is not,
and will never be free.
The soldiers will die.
Families will cry,
and that will always be.
Freedom is not,
and will never be free.
LouAnn Reinoehl, Grade 6
Saint Pauls Middle School, NC

Night School
What if school took place at night
And you slept during the day?
Dodge glow-ball and flashlight tag
Would be the games to play!
Classrooms lit by candle light
As you work away.
Pajamas are my uniform
With slippers that are gray!
That's how school would be…
I think I'd like it that way!
Alec Mueller, Grade 6
White Station Middle School, TN

9/11
9/11 was a very sad day
where families had very few things to say
it was hard to hear what was happening
as first plane hit
everybody thought this was a mistake
but until they saw that second plane hit
everybody burst with tears.
it's very sad to think why
everybody can't get along.
Micah Alford, Grade 5
Walton-Verona Middle School, KY

Laughter
The sound so sweet and bright,
When people feel delight,
Nothing picks you up faster,
It can only be laughter,
Nervous or cheery,
Excited or weary,
We welcome its sound,
But when it's not around,
We all feel unsound.
Keegan Vacanti, Grade 6
White Station Middle School, TN

Green
Green is the color of the coon's eyes.
When you shine the light in its face.
The green in the soldier's uniform is the camo so they can hide.
The green leaves turn into yellow when fall rolls around.
Frogs turn green in spring so they're still hidden.
Green is the color of the flower's stem when it shoots out of the ground.
Matthew Simpkins, Grade 6
Montgomery Central Middle School, TN

Summer Time!
Summer time is so divine!
I love the sun.
It's so much fun!
There's no school.
That's so cool!
The sky is so blue.
It looks brand new!
No more dew on the grass.
This is such a blast!
We party all night.
Until morning's light.
No more school food.
Which gets me in a bad mood…
It's so sunny!
The perfect time to make money!
I'll shop till I drop.
My wallet will pop!
But the end is near.
I have so much to fear!
No more playing with my friends.
I can't wait till summer comes again!
Taylor Crawford, Grade 6
White Station Middle School, TN

I Am
I am healthy and strong
I wonder why I'm the youngest
I hear dogs barking
I see puppies
I want an iPod touch
I am healthy and strong
I pretend I'm a princess
I feel sadness
I touch a rainbow
I worry about my dog
I cry when I'm scared
I am healthy and strong
I understand I get to go to college
I say "nobody is perfect."
I dream about Christopher P.
I try to be good all the time
I hope that I get my dog, Alf, back

I am healthy and strong
Casey Baxter, Grade 4
Centennial Elementary School, TN

Christmas Fun
Christmas,
Christmas,
Christmas,
Fun Christmas,
Joyful Christmas,
Nice, joyful, loving Christmas,
Playful, cold, fun Christmas.

These are just a few.

Family Christmas,
Huge Christmas,
Cool, wonderful, happy Christmas.
Joyful, giving, awesome Christmas.
Good Christmas,
Blessing Christmas,
Musical Christmas.
Don't forget snowy Christmas.

Last of all, best of all,
I like peaceful Christmas
Yoeli Wasamba, Grade 5
Tates Creek Elementary School, KY

Eleven
Eleven is my favorite number.
Why you ask?
I'll tell you now.

I am now turning 11 years old,
On the 11th day,
Of the 11th month,
In the 2011th year.
I was born 11 days early,
At 11:11 a.m.
Weighing at 11 pounds,
And 11 ounces.
I was born with 11 freckles,
And 11 strands of hair.
Now, I have hair that is 11 inches long.
I gave you 11 reasons why,
11 is my favorite number.
So tell me,
What is your favorite number?
Sarah McClellan, Grade 5
Moyock Elementary School, NC

Granny Langston, My Great Grandmother

I overheard the conversation,
It didn't make me happy,
It's never a good time,
When someone that you love is very sick,
Especially when they're 86,
And you know what's coming,
The day we went to the hospital,
And the whole family was there,
I saw her,
The preacher came,
He prayed,
A few days went by,
We kept on going to the hospital to see her,
Until the night that we got the phone call,
The last two months have been terrible,
It all started when I overheard the conversation,
Rest in peace Granny Langston.

Cassie Horner, Grade 6
Dyer Elementary & Jr High School, TN

I Am Princess Diana

I am Princess Diana. I am beautiful. I am generous.
I wonder if I will marry Prince Charles.
I hear Prince Charles coming to knock on my door.
I see his rich elegant black coat.
I am Princess Diana.
I pretend we are getting married, and there is a royal wedding.
I feel confident as I stand by his side. I will be a good princess.
I touch his soft warm hands as they touch mine.
I worry that I will not know what to say.
I cry of happiness when he asks me to marry him. "Yes, I will."
I am Princess Diana.
I understand I have just made a huge commitment.
I say "I do!" in the royal ceremony.
I dream Prince Charles and I will have children in this royal family.
I try hard to work out our many differences.
I hope that it is possible for us to have a terrific life together.
I am Princess Diana.

Trinity Phillips-Shrewsbury, Grade 4
Mineral Wells Elementary School, WV

Dogs

There are many types of dogs
Some are mixed and some are full breed
There are lazy dogs and there are active dogs
There are dogs that are cute and some aren't
They can be lovable or just very shy
There are rescue dogs and dogs for the blind
A lot of dogs can be strays but very nice
Some can be big and some can be small
Some dogs are mean, they can bite or growl
They can be skinny or they can be fat
A lot of dogs are very very soft
No matter what I love all dogs!

Savannah Hartley, Grade 5
Moyock Elementary School, NC

I Am

I am a fun and loving person.
I wonder if we are going to lose one of our planets.
I hear a person crying for help in a home.
I see a baby in the basket in the water.
I want to drive a car when I am able to drive.
I am a fun and loving person.

I pretend that I am Super Woman.
I feel leaves falling from the sky.
I touch the moon from my house.
I cry because my dad doesn't know me and I don't know him.
I am a fun and loving person.

I understand why I don't have a dad.
I say that Santa is a real person.
I dream for a pony so I can ride it.
I try to get A's on every subject in school.
I hope I don't get F's on every subject.
I am a fun and loving person.

Brittany Noland, Grade 6
Montgomery Central Middle School, TN

The Mysterious Cat

A cat once wandered near my street
He ran and leaped then landed at my feet
I picked him up and took him to my house
Where he found and caught a mouse

But the mouse escaped and ran down the road
The cat was fast, it really showed
The mouse ran by the neighbor's yard
Where their dog was standing on guard

As soon as the cat ran by
The dog started to howl and cry
As he ran after the cat too
But then I noticed the green goo

It was on my hands and the cat
So I ran home to take a bath
And once I was done I didn't go back
Looking for that silly cat

Rohini Sharma, Grade 5
Hunter GT Magnet Elementary School, NC

Life

Notice the good things in life, embrace them, enjoy them.
Don't be afraid to show your true self.
Don't pretend to be someone else.
Live your life to the fullest.
Do what you love let nothing hold you back.
Reach for the stars and grab them if you can.
Smile to the sun and live each day like your first.
And never hold back your dreams.

Isabelle Lambert, Grade 6
Sterling Montessori Academy, NC

What I Am
I am friendly and caring.
I wonder when the world will end.
I hear the laughter of my friends.
I want world peace.
I am friendly and caring.
I pretend to not care about a soul.
I feel hateful when I do.
I touch the slamming door.
I worry about the death of loved ones.
I cry when I hear about the loss of loved ones.
I am friendly and caring.
I understand we will not live forever.
I say that we will.
I dream for world peace.
I try to make people happy.
I hope that I can.
I am friendly and caring.

Ashley Weihe, Grade 6
Bernheim Middle School, KY

Wonderful Woods!!
I see huge trees like
Skyscrapers above me
I watch the creek get BIGGER
and BIGGER
As I get closer and closer
The snapping leaves and branches
As I walk among them
I listen to the beautiful birds as they sing
A grateful song
I can sniff the horrible odors
As I walk among them
The bad scent of the mold on the tree
I taste the burning leaves as we make a fire
I touch the creek as I wash the dishes
I touch the covers as I make the bed in the teepee
I feel as alive as if the world…
Was a better place

Mercedes Pierce, Grade 6
College View Middle School, KY

One Day, This World Will Turn Upside Down
One day,
this world will turn upside down.
Soon it'll make everybody so mad,
but it will make me so sad.
Soon it'll crush my heart and turn it to mush.
Then soon I'll go down into this ground.
I don't know why
that's why I'm so shy.
I just wish that I could fly.
So Jesus take me now
because now I can see,
or let me free in the open sea.

Alexander Brady, Grade 6
Saint Pauls Middle School, NC

Daytona Beach
The cold water was jumping on the shore,
sandcastles and seashells resting on the sand.

The strong waves of the water was a steady river,
kids laughing and running along the beach with joy.

The fresh ocean scent of the air is delightful,
the strong-smelling sunscreen getting sprayed around.

The ice cream as it's dripping in my mouth,
the ocean scent of dry air on my dry tongue.

The rough seashells sat still by my feet,
the warm soft sand under my feet as I walk.

The peacefulness and quietness,
soft sand under my feet and hands like a soft rug.

I absolutely love the beach!

Elyssa Lawrence, Grade 6
College View Middle School, KY

Ode to Friends
Friends; they talk your head off
But they are always there
Even if it is you they like to scare.
Having things in common is always a plus
So you can have things to discuss

They can trust you and you can trust them;
That's what makes up a true friend.
Sometimes you argue,
You may even be mean
But that does not mean you should fuss and scream

"The only way to have a friend is to be one."*
And only then will you have lots of fun.
When you're with them time flies by,
Because you know upon them you can rely.

*Quote by Ralph Waldo Emerson

Amy Stuckenborg, Grade 6
Bernheim Middle School, KY

I Love Popcorn
Ever since I was born, I've loved popcorn.
The kernels are so round, so pretty, and so gold.
I love the taste, whether it's hot or cold.
Just put it in the microwave, and get it real hot.
Watch the kernels get bigger with the sound of each pop.
Pour on some butter and a little salt, too.
Don't worry, there'll be plenty for both me and you.
Eat it at home or eat it at a movie.
Wouldn't you agree, popcorn is s-o-o-o-o-o groovy?!

Taylor Elliott, Grade 5
Briarcrest Christian School, TN

Fun at the Ice Rink
There's excitement at the ice rink,
Kids everywhere of all sorts are there.
It is also a lot of fun,
Skating, people sliding on a blanket of ice!
People having fun,
Giggling, laughing, talking, and playing.
Hot chocolate, skating, and more!
Mindy Nguyen, Grade 6
College View Middle School, KY

Band
Band
Noisy, fun
Playing, counting, watching
Flute, drums, trumpet, clarinet
Looking, sitting, listening
Loud, crazy
Orchestra
Dara Kodack, Grade 5
Hunter GT Magnet Elementary School, NC

What!
What! What is it?
Something's behind that door!
What! What is it?
I hear footsteps thumping along the floor!
What! What is it?
I'm too scared to go in!
What! Wha —
Reed Cooper, Grade 4
Nature's Way Montessori School, TN

Light versus Dark
Light is an open soul
Trying to get inside you.
Darkness will get inside you.
It will turn into rage,
sparks of anger.
Light makes you happy.
Darkness means danger!
Matilda Law, Grade 4
Nature's Way Montessori School, TN

My Best Friend
My best friend is the
peanut butter to my jelly
the reese to my cup
the straw to my berry
the pencil to my paper
but most of all you're
the best to my friend!
Riley Hayes, Grade 5
Walton-Verona Middle School, KY

Autumn
Falling colors in the breeze; red, orange, and yellow,
Softly floating from the trees; twirling like a hand waving hello.

A chilly wind bites my cheek; over the hills it shall blow,
I hear the sound of a flowing creek; winding to and fro

Chirping crickets dwell at night; they lull us all to sleep,
In the morning they take flight; and in the evening they come back to cheep.

The scent of pumpkin pie fills the air; tempting me to come,
It was almost impossible not to know it was there; I was longing for at least a crumb.

Apple cider fills my throat; as I take a drink,
the hot liquid will float; in the cup filled to the brink.

With leaves assorted like in a brochure; and frolicking, prancing deer,
I do know one thing for sure: autumn is my favorite time of year!
Alycia Love and Madeline Wujek, Grade 5
Penny Road Elementary School, NC

Meme's House
The butterflies as beautiful as fall leaves on the "butterfly" bush
I'd always catch, put in a small, glass jar and let go.

The huge picture of running horses in the carpeted basement
The loud but patient 2 yellow and white parakeets Pepaw always let out.

Pepaw coming through the door with a little surprise
Meme's beautiful flowers dancing in the wind.

Tasty breakfast on a sunny morning when I first wake up
Crispy bacon on a beautiful day
Yummy peach cobbler in the oven.

The soft feathers made of cotton on the carpet
The cold, hard basement floor on my bare feet.

I feel safe and calm at Meme's house.
Destinie Willyard, Grade 6
College View Middle School, KY

Snowy Alaska
Buildings all around me with people hustling in and out
White sparkling snow winks and waves at me as I go by
Many birds sing songs beautifully as they fly in and out of the trees
Hot dogs that are saying "EAT ME" as I pass by

Pine, oaks, leaves; it makes me feel relaxed like I was at home
Swish, as I slip across the snow covered ice
Sweet cold soda running down my ever thirsty throat
Fluffy, furry, friendly fur wraps around my unusually chilly tan fingers

I felt as small as an ant when I looked at icebergs
White freezing pieces of art all around me
Grace Thacker, Grade 6
College View Middle School, KY

Adieu, Charming Bird

Fly
Charming bird
Away you go
Waving your glorious wings
Adieu!

Brittney Kersey, Grade 5
E O Young Elementary School, NC

Blossoms Bloom

The garden in the spring, beautiful flowers,
Pink, red, and white in the warm spring air,
Plain as day, flowers in the garden,
Walking by observing a contest of colors,
Watching beautiful flowers in the spring.

Kelsey Rumage, Grade 6
College View Middle School, KY

My Tuba

My tuba is anything I want it to be
It's enormous and tough
It's made of shiny brass
It has finger holes just for me
My tuba is just the way I want it to be

Ben Charney, Grade 6
White Station Middle School, TN

Soccer

I
Love to run
Along soccer fields
In the middle of the day
Because my teammates are the best.

Rehnon Ty Larson, Grade 5
Walton-Verona Middle School, KY

Quality Convenience

On 18th and Leitchfield Road
the store,
Quality Convenience,
customers streaming in and out,
busy as a bee.

Aman Singh, Grade 6
College View Middle School, KY

Rough River Creek

Down at Rough River
A creek in the woods
Oddly shaped rocks on the ground
Like a kingdom of rocks
Water running through the rocks smoothly

Sydney Jordan, Grade 6
College View Middle School, KY

I Am

I am strong and curious
I wonder if I am special
I hear voices I don't understand
I see all the sins that have taken over the world
I want to live in a sinless world
I am strong and curious
I pretend of a very perfect world
I feel curious of why sin has come to be
I touch all the dreadful souls
I worry about how people think of me or what it is like to die
I cry about all the things people have done to me
I am strong and curious
I understand that no one is perfect
I saw that no one understands what I feel, say, or mean
I dream of why God made me this way
I try to understand but it is just too hard sometimes so I just be the best I can be
I hope for another chance
I am strong and curious

Marcus Anderson, Grade 4
Centennial Elementary School, TN

I Am Pocahontas

I am Pocahontas. I am really honest and you can trust me to keep a secret.
I wonder why there are ships and people are coming to my homeland.
I hear people saying "Hurray!" "We are free!"
I see trees, grass, and weird people in my homeland.
I am Pocahontas.
I pretend to be like the people I don't know and a supreme chief.
I feel scared if the people find me and try to kill my kind.
I grip the grass to look through and my toes touch something wet.
I worry if the people find my father and kill him with a spear.
I shout, "Father we have to leave or we'll die. Do you want that?!"
I am Pocahontas.
I understand that we aren't moving.
I say, "I believe we should get along with the other people."
I dream that the people and my kind get along.
I try to convince my father that we should go ask the people if they are hunters.
I hope that my kind and the other people live in harmony.
I am Pocahontas.

Cheonna Kerr, Grade 4
Mineral Wells Elementary School, WV

Holiday World

Roller coaster, so fast, but still possible to see.
Beware, for it is hard to stay dry on water slides because of splashing water.
Screaming here and there, too loud to cover your ears, especially when the children yell.
Water splashing from pools to playgrounds.
Fresh hot dogs refreshing the air with delightful smells.
The fresh scent of cool salt water is a breeze of thankfulness.
Dipping Dots delicious and delightful.
Funnel cakes are as warm as grandma's fresh dumplings.
Coaster carts going "screech" all day long.
Water rafts spraying people with fresh cold water.
Happy and excited.

Les Mackey, Grade 6
College View Middle School, KY

Sugar Cookies

You are oh so good
You made me eat as much as I could
Sugary and white
You bring me such delight

I mix the ingredients up
Here a pinch there a cup
Butter, eggs, salt, and flower
It was fifteen minutes but it feels like an hour

Out of the oven and oh what I've learned
To wear an oven mit so I don't get burned
I sprinkled some sugar here and there
Then I stopped to smell the wonderful air

They were tasting so good
When I turned around there my mother stood
I told her I made them myself
So she just couldn't help herself

Baylee Coots, Grade 6
Bernheim Middle School, KY

Jughead

I have a cat in my bed,
We call him by the name of Jughead.
He's gray with stripes and awful fast,
How long can his energy possibly last?

When I roll in my sleep,
He wakes me up because he attacks my feet.
He purrs and he purrs all night long.
So I have to listen to his cute little song.

By jumping off my bed, he reminds me of a Mexican jumping bean,
Amazingly he keeps himself squeaky clean.
He scratches and he paws at my dog Archie's paws,
If he was in a western movie he would be an outlaw.

But that doesn't matter anyhow,
I love him because he is the cat's meow.
Even though he's a total goofball,
He is still the best cat of them all.

Kaitlin King, Grade 6
Bernheim Middle School, KY

Puppies

Puppies are playful and happy,
Not mad but sometimes bad.
They love bones and toys,
Puppies love a lot of attention.
They love to play all day,
Until dark.
Then puppies lay in your lap as time elapses,
And morning comes and the pups come too.

Patrick Miller, Grade 5
Paint Lick Elementary School, KY

My Grandfather's Peaceful Field

Harvested crops sway in the wind
The deep, crystal, beautiful stream is the jewel in a necklace
The pretty birds sway in the wind

The fresh smell of harvested crops
The awesome smell of the fresh air
The nasty taste of burning leaves
The fresh water from the crystal stream

The rough, rocky crop left over from the harvest
The pokey roots from the trees hurt like pokey needles
I feel great and glorious with peace
I feel great with relaxation.

Lacie Mills, Grade 6
College View Middle School, KY

My Farm

Big longhorns grazing the pasture,
dogs playing in the backyard,
tractor engines roaring through the fields,
tall weeds rustling when the wind creeps through.

Fresh cut grass, floating through the air,
smoke from the bonfire as black as night,
the clean air is medicine for my lungs,
the chicken cooking on the grill,
the dirt on my go-cart tire flies away when I hit a bump.

Old wood from fallen trees, I can clear my mind
and feel free like a bird flying high in the sky.

Jacob Seidehamel, Grade 6
College View Middle School, KY

Friendship

Friendship is fun,
Friendship is nice,
Friendship is funny and an everlasting spice.

In friendship you climb trees,
You laugh and play.

Friendship is strong, like a chain, thaws like ice
Friendship brings us together in unity
That's why friendship is very nice.

Carlos Lieberman, Grade 4
Nature's Way Montessori School, TN

The Beach's Water

I see the beach's water, splashing people.
People running, playing, swimming, and laughing.
The beach's water so blue, glistening in the sun.
The tan sand miles and miles long.
Water, as blue as the clear sky.
Everyone enjoying the beach's water!

Rachel Coomes, Grade 6
College View Middle School, KY

I Am

I am pretty and a loving little sister.
I wonder if I am a good little sister.
I hear mine and my sister's laughter.
I see my sister and I arguing and fighting.
I want us to stop arguing and fighting.
I am pretty and a loving little sister.

I pretend to be the best little sister.
I feel sad when my sister and I hit each other.
I touch my sister's hand as we walk.
I worry I never get to talk to my sister.
I cry if I don't hear her voice speaking to me.
I am pretty and a loving little sister.

I understand we fight but we're sisters till the end.
I say we argue but that's what sisters do they fight.
I dream about us being in every step being their for each other.
I try not to argue but that's what sisters do.
I hope I'm the best little sister I can be.
I am pretty and a loving little sister.

Alli Verdugt, Grade 6
Bernheim Middle School, KY

Red

I smell red when I smell roses.
I can't believe how good red smells.
I can't wait till I smell red again.

I feel red when I lay against my wall.
I can feel red on some of my shirts.
I feel red when it comes out of my skin.

I see red when I walk into my room.
I see red when I look at my folder.
I see red in my mom and dad's eyes when they are mad.

Red is the color of my favorite shirt.
Red is the color of my favorite team.
Red is the color I see on someone's face when they blush.

I love red.
I love to see my face turn red when I'm mad.
I love to see people when they are mad
Because their face is so red.

Cotton Aubrey, Grade 6
Bernheim Middle School, KY

The All-Seeing Eye

I am an eyeball
My head up in the clouds
I am an oval-shaped, bloodstained
White carpet

I am immortal,
Yet my owner is vulnerable
His death renders me useless, helpless,
To the elements,
Of yonder skies.

When others poke and mock me,
I feel agony you cannot imagine.
When equals and peers poke and mock me,
I feel agony and rage beyond comprehension.

I cannot exude or express,
My feelings and sorrow,
When understanding comes to pass,
That there'll be no tomorrow.

Joshua King, Grade 5
Hunter GT Magnet Elementary School, NC

I Am

I am funny and a sports fanatic
I wonder what the future will be like
I hear the crowd cheering
I see smiling faces
I want to play basketball
I am funny and a sports fanatic

I pretend I am a pro basketball player
I feel it will take hard work
I touch a basketball
I worry about my family
I cry when I get hurt
I am funny and a sports fanatic

I understand it takes practice
I say I can do anything
I dream of playing at Madison Square Garden
I try my best
I hope to play pro
I am funny and a sports fanatic

D. J. Vittitoe, Grade 6
Bernheim Middle School, KY

Violet

I know a color a color of joy so quiet so calm can you bare any more
It's dark and beautiful like a shark.
Don't worry it's not scary
It's actually very merry.
Oh how much I hope you like it
That beautiful color violet!

McKaela Dinser, Grade 5
Walton-Verona Middle School, KY

My Sister

My sister is kind.
She can be annoying, and can be very evil!
She is very weird, but to other people she is really shy.
She tries her best at everything.
She is very energetic, and she is really, really nuts.
But I love her anyway!

Valerie Vann, Grade 5
Walton-Verona Middle School, KY

Procrastination

Procrastination is not a sensation
It is second rate to always be late
Plan your work and work your plan
Be on time whenever you can
Wake up early every day
Have a schedule and go your way
Carry a watch and check the time
Because being early is not a crime
Prioritize what matters most
Then you'll have time to coast

Andrew Cofield, Grade 5
Evangelical Christian School Ridgelake Campus, TN

Families

Families are everything.
They help you through your struggles.
They help you when you are down.
They lift you up when you have fallen.
When times are tough, they give you a helping hand.
They give you advice.
They show you kindness, hope and love.
They forgive you for anything you have done.
They listen to what you say.
Families are everything.

Austin Modlin, Grade 5
Southeast Elementary School, NC

The Tragic Event

death without a funeral
a whole cut in half to never come together again
two parts that once fit, now do not,
leaving without saying goodbye
mourning without crying
separation with no reunion
something broken that can't be fixed
a wound that can't be healed
life will never be the same

Bonnie McCary, Grade 6
Woodland Presbyterian School, TN

Glow

Glow is a bug
That lights in the night
Glow is comfort, never a fright
Glow is the campfire, warm and soft
That invites you to a comfy loft
Glow is an angel, visiting in the night
From the great star, twinkling and bright
Glow is all around you, from the ground to the sky
Glow is what keeps on shining, never going too high

Annette Stephens-Lubrani, Grade 5
Moyock Elementary School, NC

An Ode to Soccer

Oh soccer you are so much fun.
The way you make me run in the sun.
Your ball will soar just before I make a score.
Maybe it will just roll into the goal.
So therefore however hot it may be,
or how good the other team may seem
I will play soccer.
I have never thought of being a quitter
because it is the one sport I like a lot.

Michael Drury, Grade 5
West Liberty Elementary School, WV

Ode to Hunting

Hunting is something everyone should do.
Hunting is like going after a fly with a bazooka.
You have to be quiet and take your time.
Hunting is fun because if my brothers come with me
They finally shut up and toughen up.
Hunting is something.
Hunting is everything.
Hunting is fun because people don't mess with you
Because you have a gun.

Jonah Glass, Grade 6
Bernheim Middle School, KY

The Sad Moments

When the soldiers go to their jobs
Which is to fight for our country and give us freedom
They risk their lives for us and others
When they leave their families
They think they'll come back home
But sometimes they don't
When the families hear the news they just sit down and cry
When the family hears that 21 gun salute
They know that they brought another hero home.

Cassie Fields, Grade 6
Temple Hill Elementary School, KY

Wonderful Books

Books are meant to be read,
not to be colored in the color red
Oh how I stand there with a curious gaze,
as it guides me through the crazy maze.
It teaches me about amazing stuff,
I just cannot get enough.
It is time to go to bed, but
I will remember it in my head.

Ja'shaun Thompson, Grade 4
E O Young Elementary School, NC

Roses

Roses are sweet.
Roses are red they smell sweet as honey.
They are my favorite flower.

Tre Stephen, Grade 5
Mount Juliet Elementary School, TN

Christmas and Easter
Christmas
Fun, colorful
Giving, loving, unwrapping presents
Holidays, Jesus, family, gifts
Egg-hunting, egg-dying, storytelling
Eggs, pastel
Easter
Luke Brady, Grade 4
Centennial Elementary School, TN

The Old House Down Frederica Street
Down Frederica Street,
The old house stands.
Kids play everywhere.
Brown, orange, yellow, red leaves
Cover the house.
Like a warm blanket.
Alexis Wilkerson, Grade 6
College View Middle School, KY

The Wind
The wind is a deep sad moan
That shakes the trees
That knocks you over to
Get your attention
The wind is alone
Tori Wilhelm-Olsen, Grade 5
Walton-Verona Middle School, KY

Toys
Toys are like never ending things of fun.
Like the moon and stars at night,
they're a treasure chest
filled with rubies, emeralds, and sapphires,
topped with gold, pearls, and diamonds.
Bianca Jacobs, Grade 5
Walton-Verona Middle School, KY

Veterans Day
We are thankful for Veterans Day,
Because if we didn't have it,
We would have no freedom.
Veterans have saved the planet.
Thank you so much Veterans.
Madison Wood, Grade 5
Temple Hill Elementary School, KY

China
China
Fat, lazy
Sitting, sleeping, purring
In a box, on my lap
China
Michelle Bond, Grade 6
White Station Middle School, TN

Disney World
Crowds of people are swarms of bees,

Colorful teacups spinning round and round,
I think I am going to get sick!

The joyful voices of people singing in the parades,
Rapid rollercoasters screeching to a stop.
Delicious different foods from various lands in the World Showcase,
Warm nacho cheese dip dripping from my tortilla chips while I eat them.
The super sour powder candy my mother let me buy,
The smoothness of my shiny pearl just being "hatched" out of an oyster
like a butterfly from its cocoon.
My sister's sweaty hand in mine when we were standing silently in line,
I feel the awesome sensation going through the corkscrew
on the Rockin' Roller Coaster.

I feel the exciting suspense of waiting in line,
The sad bitter-sweetness of leaving the park!
Railey Abell, Grade 6
College View Middle School, KY

I Am Martin Luther King Jr.
I am Martin Luther King Jr. I want to make a difference.
I have an astonishing plan to change the United States of America.
I wonder if my plan will work?
I see lots of people mumbling. I hear them talking.
I see more and more people gathering to hear my speech.
I am Martin Luther King Jr. I will make a difference.
I pretend that I already see the world changing.
I feel extremely nervous and scared, but I believe in my "dream."
I touch the balcony and a marvelous overwhelming feeling comes upon me.
I worry. I know if given a chance my plan will work.
I shout with glory and happiness of what I see happening.
I am Martin Luther King Jr. I did make a difference.
I deeply understand that there are enough people. My plan will work.
I say that all people don't think alike, but we can get along.
I dream and see people of all races joining hands.
I try everything possible to make this dream true.
I hope that every citizen believes in themselves and my dream.
I am Martin King Jr. I made a difference.
Ronde Mullins, Grade 4
Mineral Wells Elementary School, WV

Thanksgiving
I set the table with many flavorful and delicious foods.
I like the smell of hot, roasted turkey for Thanksgiving.
I can hear all the kids arguing over who will get the turkey leg.
I reach for a soft and buttery roll to go with the juicy turkey leg.
The hot rolls make the whole house smell fresh.
I taste the sweet and spicy pumpkin pie with whipped cream for dessert.
After dinner, we all watch football on my uncle's big screen TV.
I can hear everyone cheering for their favorite team.
After a while, the feel of the soft pillow makes me sleepy.
In about an hour, I'll go back and taste more delicious food.
Andrew Huffines, Grade 5
Providence Academy, TN

The Snowflake

In my front yard
A snowflake falls,
White,
Small,
And sort of visible
Like a raindrop,
A falling snowflake

Christian Vance, Grade 6
College View Middle School, KY

Summer

Summer
Hot, thrilling
Biking, swimming, hiking
Fun in the sun, splashing in the beach
Laughing, yelling, giggling
Exciting, long
Summer

Minh Le, Grade 6
White Station Middle School, TN

The Hairy Monster

The monster I see
has humongous and hideous feet.
He smells like a pig pen,
has extremely long hair on its chin.
The sound he makes,
makes me shiver and shake.
He is the horrific hairy monster.

Brayan Aguilar, Grade 5
Carver Elementary School, NC

Sea

Day after day I see the sea,
sometimes it's calm, gentle like a baby.
Down on the bottom what I cannot see,
apparently has the most glee.
With all the fish swimming and swaying,
I hear they are laying,
…trying to get a sun tan.

Charlee Webster, Grade 5
Longest Elementary School, KY

Candy

Candy candy candy
So sweet I like candy
because I like a sweet tasting treat.

Candy candy candy
So sweet do you like candy
I do it can't be beat.

Jacob Dickinson, Grade 5
Longest Elementary School, KY

Gideon

Gideon
  adorable, young, tidy
    Sibling of
Harlan, Jasper, Eliana
    Lover of
big, long, baffling, mystery books,
long, old, funny movies, loving, friends, and family
    Who feels
happiness, when I do the right thing, joy, when someone is saved,
love, when someone does something for me,
    Who needs
help on math, because I don't have a mind for it,
friends because I would get lonely, books, because boring things befall,
    Who gives
help, to people who need it, comfort, when someone needs it,
laughter, to those who don't laugh,
    Who fears,
frightfully, fat fissures, big, fat clowns, bad economy,
    Who would like to see
more good people get saved, Christ's return, a candy factory,
Williams

Gideon Williams, Grade 5
Providence Academy, TN

My Branches Will Weep

My branches once wistful hang, like tears downward they stream,
As many horrors I've seen, my maimed leaves,
Whisper to the old man's grave.
Long ago, here on this hill, I stand, I stood,
A crown jewel in my young queenhood,
Untouched by all of nature's children
Of all perils fortunately were hidden from me,
Until I became a true weeping tree.
I've seen the bones of the wise men snap,
The blood of the women wrongly accused.
My branches weep and I want you to know,
My branches weep only for you.
And you died for those who've wasted their lives,
So I live for you, and all victims of strife,
No matter what they transform me into, my branches
Will always weep for you.
So here I tower on this hill, weeping still, weeping still,
I shall make them regret, the bloodshed, the tears wept,
Your names will ring in the air renowned.
And even my crying won't drown them out.

Cameron Voytko, Grade 5
Penny Road Elementary School, NC

The King of the Sky

The hawk soars with such grace moving at a steady pace.
His majestic wings beat high above my feet.
He dives down making a screeching sound.
His prey tries to hide, but the bird's mighty talons take him for a ride.
The hawk may have flown away, yet his elegance and grace are here to stay.

Evan Scully, Grade 5
Moyock Elementary School, NC

The Backyard Swing
I see brown robins searching for worms,
Fresh green grass swaying in the breeze,
I hear the soft squeak of the rocking swing,
Dark green frogs yelling out.

I smell freshly mowed grass,
The soft damp earth below me,
I taste the golden marigolds
traveling through the breeze,
I touch the rough and soft wood on the swing,
that is like a comfortable seat.

The changing red and yellow leaves
on the maple trees,
The swing is heaven,
I am calm, and content.

Caitlyn Williams, Grade 6
College View Middle School, KY

Mammaw's Yard
The weeping willows limbs blow
Chirping chicks so yellow with glow

The shuttling sound of happily barking dogs
The growl of the chanting bullfrogs

The crisp clean country air
The cookies I won't share

The fluffy hair of Brownie the goat
The wooden shovel while digging a moat

Always comfortable day and night
Comfortable to sleep without a fright

I love my Mammaw's yard

Drew Cockrell, Grade 6
College View Middle School, KY

Christmas Time
Christmas is coming in December
What will I get, I can't remember

A tree, a tree, as green as can be
Our tree is up, as green as I see

Ornaments up as shiny as can be
Filled with colors I love to see

Christmas is here
No one shall sneer

Everyone is here and ready
I hope we can keep things steady

Meredith Wicktom, Grade 4
Evangelical Christian School Ridgelake Campus, TN

Why the Birds Fly South
Here today, gone tomorrow
They own the sky like a pharaoh
Their wings get so dull and fragile
They can't afford to be so hollow

As they leave I sadden
For I know their return won't be sudden
Their leave is like pouring hot water on my head
Though I had a strange dream in my bed

Only if I had wings like a bird
I would be able to be free and safe
But as long as I'm doing my regular routine,
I'll always be stuck in quarantine

Now I know why they go
Well it's just how it goes it's going to snow
I can't wait for their return even though,
The cycle starts all over again, but now I know:
Why the birds fly south

Justin Martin, Grade 6
White Station Middle School, TN

Daredevil
I am a daredevil.
I wonder if I can jump 12 fire pits with a dirt bike.
I see a ramp to jump over.
I want a dirt bike with street tires.
I am a daredevil.

I pretend to let up my foot for more speed.
I feel the warm crisp air of the fire.
I touch the throttle of the bike.
I worry that I won't make it.
I cry that I might fall off the bike.
I am a daredevil.

I understand that most quit this.
I say I can do this.
I dream of flying with the birds.
I try to pump my engine.
I hope my engine does not stall.
I am a daredevil

Bryan Hicks, Grade 6
Montgomery Central Middle School, TN

Summer Vacation
At the beach with waves crashing down softly,
The soft sand squeezing my feet,
A blue, green Atlantic Ocean
White, gray sand
We saw almost 50 stingrays swimming at our feet,
That was Tampa Bay,
My favorite vacation ever.

Zachary Greer, Grade 6
College View Middle School, KY

The Talking Book

Look at me! Look at me!
Take me from the shelf

I long to reunite with those warm hands
And those sweet amber eyes

Pick me up girl
Don't hesitate
A mystery is coming your way

Pick me up
I'll take you places you never knew
You'll make the impossible, possible

Flip my pages won't you dear
A journey awaits you
With action and adventure
And a tint of humor
A picture will form in your mind

In me
You'll see the tooth fairy is true
And monkeys are really blue

With me anything is possible
'Cause I'm a book!
Ethan Bhojani, Grade 5
Hunter GT Magnet Elementary School, NC

Christmas

Christmas,
Christmas,
Christmas.
Joyful Christmas,
Happy Christmas,
Snowy, cold, lovely Christmas.
White, snowy, peaceful Christmas.

These are just a few.

Loving Christmas
Sweet Christmas,
Silly, funny, awesome Christmas.
Loving, cool, fun-filled Christmas.

Delightful Christmas,
Fantastic Christmas,
Wonderful Christmas.

Don't forget familiar Christmas.

Last of all,
Best of all
I like family Christmas.
Jaylen Richardson, Grade 5
Tates Creek Elementary School, KY

Looking Out His Window

Looking out his window,
up into the clear blue sky.
He still remembers the moment,
when he first saw her eyes.

They lit up the room
like the stars way up high.
He thought she was an angel,
and that is no lie.

The next day he called her,
he couldn't delay.
Because he was afraid
someone else would take her away.

Almost one year later,
the big question came
He asked her to marry him,
and their lives were never the same
Hannah Wilbert, Grade 6
Bernheim Middle School, KY

Uncle's House

I see dry yellow corn fields
and big oak trees
I see beautiful deer
and buzzing bees

I hear big chickens chirping
and the wind blowing hard
I hear fat toads burping
and a dog barking in the yard

I smell trails of nature trees
a dead bird on the house
the chicken feed
and the bait for the mouse

I can do all
the things I like
with people
I love
Haven Crump, Grade 6
College View Middle School, KY

Unique Art

Unique art is
Like the beautiful painting.
Bright expressive and colorful.
When working on art,
Colorful or dark,
It's the right mark.
Art is right and bright.
The charismatic art.
Naujal Wilkins, Grade 4
E O Young Elementary School, NC

Home

A house full of joy, happiness, and
liveliness
Laughter as loud as happiness
Sirens, sirens, sirens loudly down
the street
Talking through the night,
but quietly
POP! POP! POP!
Goes the popcorn quickly
and softly
Sweet, soft, warming, relaxing
smell of chocolate
Buttery sweetness of popcorn
Softness of my dog's fur
goes "Thank you"
Smoothness of the sheets like
the sandy beach
I feel happy when it's this way,
but sad when it's not
Marissa Haight, Grade 6
College View Middle School, KY

Ode to Baseball

I have a baseball in my hand
I walk down from the stand
I step on the mound
My heart starts to pound

Strike the umpire calls
2 strikes no balls
This is my time
As I hold my lucky dime

Final batter up
I'm going to get him straight up
I strike him out
He starts to pout

I'm celebrating the World Series
It's all thanks to my team
I'm so excited I'm going to explode
I hope this never ends
Tanner Johnson, Grade 6
Bernheim Middle School, KY

American

A merica
M ount Rushmore
E agle
R ed, White, and Blue
I ndependence Day
C ountry
A llegiance to One
N ation Under God
Ronnie Hill, Grade 5
Dupont Hadley Middle School, TN

Christmas

On Christmas, I see Christmas trees and snowmen.
I hear sleigh bells ringing, laughing and cheering.
I smell the winter wonderland, peppermint and gingerbread.
I love the taste of warm hot chocolate with cookies.
I feel the breezy wintry air that I love.
I see glittering lights on houses and trees.
I hear Christmas caroling and the pitter patter of the snow.
I smell Christmas cakes and warm coca.
I taste the gingerbread and nutmeg during Christmas.
Christmas is my favorite holiday.
Happy Birthday Jesus!

Hattie Bradford, Grade 5
Providence Academy, TN

Relaxation of Myrtle Beach

The warm crystal water splashing,
Dolphin fins gliding through the smooth water like a silky blanket,
The warm water dancing on the sand,
Kids screaming of joy and fun,
The saltiness of the water,
The yucky hot fish air is a rotten egg smell,
The salty nasty water,
The yucky fried fish in the pan,
The nice soft warm sand between my toes,
Soft or smooth seashells on the seashore,
I feel relaxed and calm in my peaceful place.

Hannah Straney, Grade 6
College View Middle School, KY

The Desert

The grainy hot sand of the desert floor
The hazy fumes of heat up ahead
The rattle of a rattlesnake in the sun
A wolves' choir-like howl in the moonlight
A reeking carcass left for the vultures
Smoke drifting from my fire
A medium cooked T-bone steak from my cattle
Sweet rare water tasting like chocolate
Prickly prickles from a mean old cactus
The hot deadly rays of the sun biting like sand vipers
I feel like hot grease was thrown in my face

Patrick Clapacs, Grade 6
College View Middle School, KY

Sable My Pet

My little dog is special to me because:
She loves to give kisses!
She loves to chew the stuffing out of toys!
She loves to cuddle!
She loves to sling her toys around!
She loves to go outside and wallow in the grass!
But most important, she knows when I am sad,
And comes and lays with me 'til I feel better.
That is why my dog Sable is special to me!

Jada Clayton, Grade 6
Saint Pauls Middle School, NC

Winter's Gloom and Autumn's Mist

In the winter's gloom strangely flowers bloom
Then a man and a woman come out of the blue
The woman says I love you, the man says I love you too
But we all know this isn't true
For like an iguana pretending to be the color blue
It's all make believe, like the autumn's mist is too
The autumn's mist indeed insists that the trees are a beauty
The leaves of orange, red, and yellow are divine so truly
The smell of bees making honey is a delight
The autumn insists that summer and spring are too bright
However the autumn's mist is just right

Ethan Murphy, Grade 5
Love Memorial Elementary School, NC

What Is Red

Red is warm and dark.
Red is the color of my blood when I am cut.
Rudy represents power in a war.
Scarlet is the color of the leaves in fall.
Carmine is the color of a rose in fall.
Rose is the color love at first sight.
Maroon is the color of fire when it's burning.
Vermilion is the color of a monster in a child's eyes.
Red is the color of an apple when it is ripe.
These are many things that represent
Red

Devin Christy, Grade 6
Montgomery Central Middle School, TN

My Mom

My mom is like the world to me.
She sings, laughs, and we have fun together.
If I need anything, she is there for me.
When you look in her eyes you see a glow.
I love her a little better than dad, but he don't know.
But you can't blame her,
she's so sweet and nice.
When I come home,
she has sweet homemade cookies.
Just like her.
I love my mom!

Kinsley Walker, Grade 6
Saint Pauls Middle School, NC

Skating

I like to skate fast,
I like to skate slowly.
I like to skate on blacktop,
I like to skate on snow.
I like to ramp and fly down hills,
Oh, how it hurts when I have a bad spill.
A bruise on my elbow,
A scrape on my leg.
I think I'll give skateboarding a break for today.

Cory Hamblin, Grade 5
Paint Lick Elementary School, KY

Acceptance

Acceptance.
It's shadowed by discrimination and fear.
Yet it still finds people.
Acceptance surprises us.
It makes us open and kind.
It doesn't find everyone.
Just a few lucky ones.
Acceptance does not discriminate.
We do all the discriminating.
Anyone can accept.
It's about finding the good in someone,
that might not be easy to see.
If we all tried,
we could all accept and be accepted.
Acceptance is hard.
But we all have to keep trying.
Just look past the surface.
Look inside.
Accept others and yourself.
I'm lucky.
Acceptance has found me.
Rose Dallimore, Grade 6
Baylor School, TN

Christmas

Christmas,
Christmas,
Christmas.
Good Christmas,
Joyful Christmas,
Nice, happy, enjoyed Christmas.
Blessed, delightful Christmas.

These are just a few.

Enjoyable Christmas,
Wonderful Christmas,
Fun, loving, excited Christmas.
Lovely, jolly, cold Christmas.

Comfortable Christmas,
Awesome Christmas,
Happiness at Christmas.

Last of all, best of all
I like snowy Christmas.
Naudi Mayes, Grade 5
Tates Creek Elementary School, KY

Owls

Oh how I wish I could be an owl flying
They visit my dreams why
Oh how I wish I could be an owl on high
Where I am an owl flying in the night sky
Ben Naas, Grade 5
Walton-Verona Middle School, KY

Outdoor Orchestra

The world outdoors
Performing an eternal piece
Of comfort, joy and serenity

The arioso wind
Whistling the ever-changing melody
Nature's special voice

The millions of leaves
Trembling whenever there's wind
A rustling vibrato

The spherical raindrops
Providing the steady rhythms
A wonderful percussionist

All the people indoors
Should head outside and enjoy
The outdoor orchestra's amazing music
Rachel Fan, Grade 6
White Station Middle School, TN

I Am

I am funny
I wonder if I will have a child
I hear city streets
I see people with nice houses
I want to see my dad more
I am funny
I pretend I'm slow
I feel amazing
I touch the bottom of the ocean
I worry about kids not having homes
I cried when Nana died
I am funny
I understand I have to do my homework
I say I believe what my mom says
I dream of being a football player
I try to stay on my feet
I hope to become what I want to be

I am funny
Kameron Solomon, Grade 4
Centennial Elementary School, TN

So Much Depends Upon

So much depends upon my
Good grades because if I
Have bad grades I fail school.

So much depends upon my
Personality because people
Could make fun of me or
Hurt me.
Shaun Waters, Grade 6
Bernheim Middle School, KY

The Great Fall

Looking up to the sky
Saying to myself
This is going to be fun

Walking up
Hearing the wind blow
Grabbing my sled
And whoosh!

Feeling frosty air
Coming against
My ear
My eyes are ice

Then all the air
Just flows
And everything stops

Walking up again
For the great fall
Jack Marcum, Grade 4
Buckner Elementary School, KY

An Ode to Bearry

I'd really like to share,
I know it would be fair.

I use to make dresses,
but it always made messes.

I dressed you like dog,
when we went on a jog.

When I was scared,
I knew you cared.

You were dusty teal,
but deep inside my heart you were real.

I loved you,
I hugged you.

You were kind of shy,
but you were my kind of guy.
Ally Naegele, Grade 5
West Liberty Elementary School, WV

War

On the war field
Soldiers march,
Green on black and white,
Guns shinning,
Like toy soldiers,
Guns firing.
Austin Mayfield, Grade 6
College View Middle School, KY

Dirt Bike Riding

Zoom! I zoomed so fast on my dirt bike.
I was just riding and I had two deer pop out in front of me.
I though it was so peaceful around me.

I could smell the wet dew grass.
I was just riding and I had two deer pop out in front of me.
I was like wow and had to slam on the brakes.
When I stopped I could hear my dirt bike and birds chirping.

The lighting outside was going from light to dark.
Until I saw two deer pop out in front of me.
Then everything went blank.
I was astounded by the two deer.

Thomas Embry, Grade 6
Bernheim Middle School, KY

My Old Room

Little girl toys scattered, like a tornado had just blown through,
That little blue kitchen set, so old and worn,
Daddy's soft snores, music playing softly,
Sweet, soft, quiet snores escape my puppy.

The sweet smell of pink strawberries, and green kiwis,
And silky, soft red roses,
The taste of fruit lingering in my mouth, long after eating it,
Warm chocolate, dancing across my tongue,
Cuddly, warm, soft, white puppy fur between my small, pale fingers.
My comfy quilt Grand-mommy gave me.

Feeling so safe, in the memory of my six-year-old room.

Natalie Anne Lambert, Grade 6
College View Middle School, KY

Veterans

Veterans day
is a day for our soldiers.
They fought for our country
and our state.
Iraq people wanted war against the United States.
For our richness and our freedom.
Veterans are brave and strong.
They fought for us all day long.
Veterans went to war,
and won once more.

Kennedy Flores, Grade 6
Saint Pauls Middle School, NC

Friday

F ree from school.
R eady to go!
I gnoring the teacher.
D ying to get out.
A ll day watching the clock.
Y elling in my head can't wait for school to end!

Isabella Wagner, Grade 4
Centennial Elementary School, TN

I Am

I am lovable and strong
I wonder if I will ever have a dad and mom
I hear that people are caring
I see that I was flying in an airplane
I want to be a kid
I am lovable and strong
I pretend I have a lot of money
I feel the pretty blue sky
I touch a unicorn
I worry that my Nana will die in six years
I cry when I see somebody die
I am lovable and strong
I understand that you will have to die in six years
I say people like dogs and cats
I dream to grow up and be a rock star
I try to make an effort in math and reading
I hope people will not starve to death
I am lovable and strong

Ciara Brown, Grade 4
Centennial Elementary School, TN

I Am

I am strong and smart.
I wonder what the future will be like.
I hear sleigh bells ringing.
I see Santa bringing toys.
I want an electric guitar.
I am strong and smart.
I pretend I am a rock star.
I feel a puffy cloud.
I touch the sun as it is rising.
I worry what the future will be like.
I cry when someone says Simmy.
I am strong and smart.
I understand what goes around comes around.
I say if you fail try, try again.
I dream I am a singer.
I try to succeed.
I hope I get good grades in school.
I am strong and smart.

Allie Blount, Grade 4
Centennial Elementary School, TN

I Love the Look of the Monster

The monster is the most tremendous thing you ever see.
He smells like the outdoor dumpster next door.
He has long furry hair that comes down to the top of his back.
He sounds like a roaring bear trying to break out of prison.
Oh no!!!
Here he comes
I can see him down the hallway.
He's getting closer.
Oh, never mind there is no monster
It's just my brother.

Graham Janeway, Grade 5
Providence Academy, TN

Fall
Spring,
Summer,
Winter,
Fall,
I like fall most of all,
Because of my birthday,
And the holidays.
Jessica Phillips, Grade 5
Paint Lick Elementary School, KY

Let Freedom Ring
Let freedom ring,
For Martin Luther King.
He got us freedom,
So we could live in a kingdom.
He died with a dream.
A dream that came true,
And he did it all for me and you.
Malik Atkinson, Grade 6
Saint Pauls Middle School, NC

Loved One
My mom is my loved one.
She is bright as a star in the sky.
She is as beautiful as a flower.
She can be a sour apple,
But she still cares like a mamma bear
That's why she is my
Mom!
Meagan Butler, Grade 6
Saint Pauls Middle School, NC

Leaves
Look at them all!
Some are different colors.
Some are red,
Look at the leaves.
Watch them all fall.
Some are huge,
Some are tiny.
Josh Gabbard, Grade 5
Paint Lick Elementary School, KY

New York
New York will always have a dark cloud,
Always following New Yorkers around
Because of the terrorist attack.
The Twin Towers fell.
Thousands of people died.
We will always remember
New York as a special place.
Kaitlyn Johnson, Grade 6
Saint Pauls Middle School, NC

Panama City Beach
Rushing clear waves, rides that will make you feel
Like you're dying,
It's Panama

Waves are whooshing on the sand, almost like a tiger roaring,
Kids are playing in the sand with imagination,
It's Panama

The fresh clean air of summer, there's the fear of frightened
Fish getting caught,
It's Panama

Soft sand squishing between my toes, soft, silky, smooth, slimy seaweed,
Wrapping around me as I swim in the ocean,
It's Panama

Waves dragging you under like they don't want you to leave,
It's sad to leave this long-lost beach,
It's Panama
Jessica Kirtley, Grade 6
College View Middle School, KY

I Am Martin Luther King Jr.
I am Martin Luther King Jr. I'm a preacher.
I am a member of the Civil Rights Movement.
I wonder if blacks and whites will ever be joined.
I hear the sadness of blacks being mistreated.
I see blacks being yelled at, arrested, or beaten.
I am Martin Luther King Jr. I need to do something to end this.
I pretend that I am saying a speech. People are listening and cheering.
I feel scared and nervous that my speech won't make a difference.
I have been waiting for this all my life.
I touch the microphone to say the speech.
I worry that this will not work and I will fail all of us.
I nearly cried when I thought about all I've been through all my life.
I am Martin Luther King Jr. I am going to change the world.
I understand that this will help everyone here and in the future.
I will not let everyone be treated like this for eternity.
I say the speech. I look at the giant crowd. I repeat: "I have a dream!"
I dream many nightmares of what has happened in the past. It is over now.
I try to forget about the past and hope that it will never happen again.
I am Martin Luther King Jr. I did it…I did it!
Nicholas Hayner, Grade 4
Mineral Wells Elementary School, WV

My Mom
My mom is nice, caring, smart, and mothering.
My mom is awesome and very loving.
My mom is always there for me.
My mom is so funny she makes me laugh and giggle.
She is M-I-N-E. I like to say this because she loves me each and every day.
She is sweet and generous to me and you.
Her name is Heather, that will do.
I love her and so should you!!!
Jamie Carter, Grade 6
Saint Pauls Middle School, NC

Winter

In the winter you get to have fun,
In the winter there is not a lot of sun,
In the winter you have snowball fights,
In the winter the sunlight is bright,
In the winter you get to hear the fire pop,
In the winter you drink things hot,
In the winter you get to wear gloves,
In the winter you hear turtle does,
In the winter you put up a tree,
In the winter you can go ski,
In the winter you sit by the fire,
In the winter you drink hot cider,
In the winter you see snowflakes fall,
In the winter you go to the mall,
In the winter you eat candy canes,
In the winter you play family games,
In the winter you play in the snow,
In the winter you eat cookie dough,
In the winter you have Christmas break,
In the winter you can skate on a lake,
In the winter you do a lot of things,
But the best things is waiting for spring
Lucy Rose Franklin, Grade 6
White Station Middle School, TN

Fruit

Oranges, apples, yum!
Nature gives to us some food,
Lots of sweet and sour.

Pears, limes, lemons with
Many delicious flavors.
Nature's gift to us.

Fruit, fruit, yummy fruit,
Sticky and fuzzy and hard,
I really like fruit.
Abby Priebe, Grade 5
Hunter GT Magnet Elementary School, NC

Playing Baseball

As I'm playing baseball
I hear my fans call.
"Win the game.
Tank is your name."
I pitched a strike
As fast as a quarter back says hike
I'm up to bat
wearing my hat.
I hit the ball into next fall.
I run in the dirt
as I pass by Bert.
We win the game
I'm filled with fame.
Matt Thompson, Grade 5
Longest Elementary School, KY

Happy Christmas

Christmas,
Jesus,
Presents.
Toy Christmas,
Snowy Christmas,
Cakes, pies, games for Christmas.
Presents, joy, happy Christmas.

These are just a few.

Fun Christmas,
Santa Christmas,
Sleigh, reindeer Christmas,
Excited, snowy, lovely Christmas.
Sharing Christmas,
Happy Christmas,
Excited Christmas.
Don't forget wonderful Christmas.

Last of all, best of all,
I like happy Christmas.
Linnea Burroughs, Grade 5
Tates Creek Elementary School, KY

The Pencil

I hate
Being locked away
In darkness
Waiting, wanting
To be used once more
Dreading, fearing
When my graphite stick will break
The pain is
Unbearable
Metal
Cutting into me
To find my point
Hidden inside me
Once more
Applauded
By my fellows and friends
For my new point shall
Shine beautifully
As I create
Crisp clear
Stories
Benjamin Goldman, Grade 5
Hunter GT Magnet Elementary School, NC

Grizzly Bear Snoring

I was mad as a bear
when I heard my dad snoring
I couldn't go to sleep because
of his grizzly bear snoring.
Drew Moore, Grade 5
Longest Elementary School, KY

Maybe

Maybe.
Maybe I will leap.
Maybe I will cower.
Maybe I will hit the ball.
Maybe I will strike out.
Maybe I will do well on the test.
Maybe I will miss the mark.
Maybe I will be defeated.
Maybe I will be victorious.
Maybe I will slip.
Maybe I will get back up.
Maybe I will swim.
Maybe I will cascade to the bottom.
Maybe I will score.
Maybe I will come up short.
Maybe I will be the hero.
Maybe I will let everybody down.
Maybe.
Teddy Lepcio, Grade 6
Baylor School, TN

I Am

I am polite and generous
I wonder about my life
I hear the rain falling on my roof
I see joking people
I want to know the real me
I am polite and generous
I pretend I am bigger
I feel my soft blanket
I touch my door when I open it
I worry about my grandfather
I cry about sadness
I am polite and generous
I understand life
I say I know myself
I dream about my future
I try my best in school
I hope I have a good future
I am polite and generous
Callie Anne Berry, Grade 4
Centennial Elementary School, TN

Sam Lawson

S occer player
A wesome
M anly

L ucky
A mazing
W inner
S mart
O riginal thinker
N ice
Sam Lawson, Grade 6
White Station Middle School, TN

Fall

Colorful leaves fall from the trees
Like raindrops from the sky
The colors just so glorious
Makes me want to sigh

I look around and see jack-o-lanterns
Look at me and smile
As children run around
And get candy for a while

Kaley Pearson, Grade 5
Love Memorial Elementary School, NC

The Meal

In the creek
The frog,
Green
Eyes watching
The fly,
SNAP!
As fast as lightning,
A tasty dinner

Jay Owen, Grade 6
College View Middle School, KY

The Rat and the Cat

There once was a rat,
that lived in a hat.
The bat sat on a mat,
beside a big fat cat.
The cat tried all he could,
to catch that rat,
but that rat was too fast,
and the cat was too fat.

Ramon Figueroa, Grade 6
White Station Middle School, TN

Fall Leaves

Look at the leaves,
Watch them fall,
Look at the leaves,
Look at them all.
Red, yellow, orange,
Big and small.
Red, yellow, orange,
Short and tall.

Dylan Lear, Grade 5
Paint Lick Elementary School, KY

People of the War

People of the war giving freedom,
giving lives to the USA,
we just want to say,
"We salute you today
for what you pay to the USA."

Mary Altstatt, Grade 6
Temple Hill Elementary School, KY

I Am Stephanie Meyer

I am Stephanie Meyer. I am very helpful and honest.
I hear the Breakfast Dawn Concert Series.
I see my Twilight books and movies that I have written.
I pretend that more people travel over the world to see my movies of Twilight.
I feel happy because I sold millions of Twilight books.
I touch my books and it feels like the characters are trying to get out.
I am Stephanie Meyer.

I worry about how to begin my next series.
I mumble to my husband ideas for my next series.
I understand the high anticipation for the sequel New Moon.
It was released in Sept. of 2006 and spent 25 weeks being #1.
I say I will encourage people to read more books.
I hope when I pass away people will still read my Twilight books.
I am Stephanie Meyer.

Leannda Beaver, Grade 4
Mineral Wells Elementary School, WV

I Am Davy Crockett

I am Davy Crockett. I am brave, disciplined and a goal-setter.
I wonder if Congress will take me as one of their employees?
I hear the bombs and guns. I see all the fighting of the Mexicans for Texas.
I see the Alamo catching on fire and the Mexicans cheering for glory.
I am Davy Crockett.
I will be generous and faithful.
I pretend I am not going to die.
Though I do feel scared I will die at the Alamo.
I grip the pen to sign the paper for Congress.
I understand that Texas is depending on me to make it peaceful.
I say: "I will fight for you with every breath!"
I dream that I am back home with my mother and father.
I try to really fight for my Texas.
I am going to survive and so will Texas.
I am Davy Crockett.

Kylie Campbell, Grade 4
Mineral Wells Elementary School, WV

I Learned a Lot, from a Sport

Ignoring the pain in my thighs
Sweat beads trickling down my cheeks
I really did try hard
In these last few weeks

My heart beating in my throat,
I race down the field with pride
My face smiling with excitement
I wanted to be on the field forever, not hide

Even though I get tired
I don't stop fighting for the soccer ball
This sport has taught me respect, speed, exceeding your expectations,
and that it's okay to be scared, and that's the most important of all.

Dora Wierdl, Grade 6
White Station Middle School, TN

Robot Blues
People are happy, scared and sad
Things that I know nothing about
Excited, thrilled
I just speak the same way

Loving, caring, things that I wish to do
People say that I am smart
And maybe I am, but people can do things
I cannot

I can compute numbers faster than them
But humans can walk, oh,
How I wish I could move around
Wheels get jammed, but legs cannot

Metal gets rusted, and soon useless
Humans' skin is impenetrable
And here I am, sitting here

Shielded from the terrible rain
Living forever
And watching time
Go by
Conor Mulligan, Grade 5
Hunter GT Magnet Elementary School, NC

Sisters
I was at home and
It was dark outside,
Talking to my sister.
Happy, happy, happy.

I saw tears rolling down
Her face, but I could
Tell that they were
Happy tears.
Happy, happy, happy.

We were talking about
When she was little
And when I was too.
She inspires me in
So many ways.
Happy, happy, happy.

BOOM!!! I heard the door
Open and it was
My mom,
Our moment was over
Happy, happy, happy.
Faith Smith, Grade 6
Bernheim Middle School, KY

Have Faith in Yourself
Have faith in yourself
be strong
be free
be happy
be confident
be who you want to be!

Do not give up
keep trying
keep going
keep moving
keep rejoicing
keep living your life to the fullest!

Have hope
hope…for the best of things!
Olivia Edwards, Grade 4
South Toe Elementary School, NC

Autumn
The leaves shrivel up
like grapes in the bright California sun.
Changing to the colors
of apples picked
at an orchard.
They fall gently
to the ground like
a drizzle of rain
in spring.
The air gets colder,
and puts the trees to bed.
Young children are laughing,
as they jump
into mounds of leaves.
Leaves spinning in the autumn wind,
winter is on its way.
Katie Martin, Grade 6
Woodland Presbyterian School, TN

Best Friend Advice
Don't' act like a jerk,
Don't tell me a lie,
Don't yell when you get angry,
Or you'll make me cry.

Don't' disrespect my family,
Don't make my mom stress,
Don't use all my makeup,
Or our friendship will be a mess.

Use this advice
Take care of it well,
Don't forget it,
And I hope it rings a bell.
Brooke Blair, Grade 6
White Station Middle School, TN

I Am
I am loving and caring.
I wonder who I will be when I grow up.
I hear my grandma telling me it's ok.
I see God keeping me safe.
I want peace in the world.
I am loving and caring.
I pretend to be strong when in doubt.
I feel kindness everywhere.
The touch of horses.
I worry what I can't do.
I cry when someone has past.
I am loving and caring.
I understand myself.
I say don't be a follower be a leader.
I dream to be a great person.
I try to stay weird.
I am loving and caring.
Makenna Stiggers, Grade 6
Bernheim Middle School, KY

Hawaii
People sitting on
their newly built
balconies looking
at the waves
crashing upon
the shore

I hear the seagulls
singing up in the sky
when I walk upon
the beach

The rough coconuts on
the palm tree and
when I'm there I feel
at peace when I sit
in the sand
Kelsey Trogolo, Grade 6
College View Middle School, KY

My Christmas
M erry cheery Christmas to all
Y ummy cakes and candy galore

C heer, happiness, and joy
H olly on doors,
R eindeer fly up in the sky.
I n December with its cold air,
S anta brings toys to kids everywhere.
T oys are opened on Christmas Day
M ake fruitcakes to savor always.
A ll the presents I want I get,
S tay at home and play till I can rest.
Chase Parrish, Grade 5
E O Young Elementary School, NC

Mrs. Kim
Pretty, stylish
Funny, bright, elegant
The best teacher ever
Awesomeness
Hailey Warf, Grade 4
Centennial Elementary School, TN

Christmas
Tremendous, loving
Giving, caring, sharing
The birth of Jesus
Presents
Gregory Carter, Grade 4
Centennial Elementary School, TN

Heat
H orribly uncomfortable
E xtremely bad for penguins
A gitatingly itchy
T asty when applied to marshmallows
Cole Danzer, Grade 5
Walton-Verona Middle School, KY

Mmm! Delicious Doughnuts
Soft doughnuts in my tummy.
To me they are so yummy.
Chocolatey, doughy, messy, delicious.
Make my tummy so scrumptious.
Briana Santella, Grade 5
Walton-Verona Middle School, KY

My Dog
I was all alone in the dark
Then I heard a bark
It was my dog she was in a fright
I rubbed her and she was all right
Justin Miller, Grade 5
Longest Elementary School, KY

TV
So much depends upon
That sparkling rectangular box
That provides me with
Entertainment so amazing
Jacob McKendrick, Grade 6
Bernheim Middle School, KY

The Fish
They swim in the sea as I stare at them
in the sand they watch me as I swim
in the water and play.
Natasha Laney, Grade 5
Walton-Verona Middle School, KY

It's Unfair

I am water
I sit in my bucket

warm and mucky
I was scooped from the pond
conserved and precious
scarce

I have a sister
in America
wishing to be her
No more deaths because of me

Children drink me with their hands
They savor every last drop of me

Why can't they have more of me?

It's unfair
The children in America
have so much more
Why?

I am water
I sit in my pitcher
icy and cold

I was poured from the tap
taken for granted

abundant
I have a sister
in Africa
wishing to be her
No more purifying
Aren't I clean?

Children sip me from plastic cups

They dump me in the sink
Why do they waste me?

It's unfair
The children in Africa
have so little
Why?
Kara Bringewatt and Maisie Rees, Grade 6
Davidson Day School, NC

The Ocean
The bright yellow sun shining over me.
The cool blue ocean water washing over the warm sand.

I listen to the beautiful waves rise and softly go down.
The children laughing and enjoying the wonderful scenery.

The fresh clean air surrounds me as I walk across the wet sand.
The scent of trees and wet sand lingers in the air.

Soft brown sand squishing under my feet.
The relaxing water washes over my skin while I swim slowly at peace.

I feel relaxed and peaceful.
Blanca Zendejas, Grade 6
College View Middle School, KY

Ode to Baby Girl
You tear-up and chew-up.
Oh Baby Girl, you stink like a skunk.
I hardly can breathe.
You have beautiful tan, white, and brown colors on your back.
You have hair like a hairy jungle.
Oh Baby Girl, you run like a wild hog.
You give me slobbery and wet kisses.
Oh Baby Girl, you bark, and howl like you wouldn't believe in your life.
You're a lovable dog and playful dog.
You weigh as much as a tank.
You are as old as my Grandma.
Austin Dean, Grade 5
West Liberty Elementary School, WV

I Am
I am caring
I wonder why people are abused
I hear crying
I see people are dying
I want world peace
I am caring
I pretend I am a doctor
I feel bad
I touch people that are hurt
I worry about people
I cry when people die
I am caring
I understand why people fight
I try to help people
I dream about people healing
I try to heal people
I hope for world peace
I am caring
James Coke, Grade 4
Centennial Elementary School, TN

How Great Is He
Oh my brother, how great is he?
He gets on my nerves.
He will always be some kin to me.
Such is my crazy ol' brother,
I saw him one day, just a laughing away.
How great is he,
to be at the age of sixteen.
I said how great is he.
Me and my brother we love our mother,
Oh what a loving brother.
He can be crazy,
but I will always love him.
What a silly brother
As we repeat,
"We love our mother, NO MATTER WHAT!"
We will always love her.
How great is he.
Tamia Morgan, Grade 6
Saint Pauls Middle School, NC

Snow
Snow, snow, fluffy and white.
Snow such a sight!

Snow, snow, fluffy and bright.
Snow just as light!

Snow, snow, fluffy and fun.
Snow as bright as the shining sun!

Snow, snow, fluffy for me.
Snow has fallen so I can ski!
Madison Turner, Grade 5
St Joseph Academy, NC

I Am
I am smart and funny
I wonder if something good happens
I hear the wind
I see clouds shaped in boxes
I want to fly above the clouds
I am smart and funny
I pretend I'm on the clouds
I feel the wind blowing
I touch the clouds above
I worry something bad will happen
I cry when I leave my parents
I am smart and funny
I understand the words you say
I say good luck
I dream of animals
I try my best on a test
I hope I get to see my grandparents
I am smart and funny
Chloe Lind, Grade 4
Centennial Elementary School, TN

Life
Life is short,
Life is long,
Life is fun,
Life is a pain.

Life has boys
Life has girls
Life has theaters
Life has stores
Life is hot
Life is cold
Life is new
Life is old
Life is everything people wish for
Life makes 2+2=4
Life is awesome, cool, and neat
Life isn't a fantasy
Life is real
Logan Adkins, Grade 5
Longest Elementary School, KY

My Dad
One person that dearly loves me is my dad.
Funny, kind, and caring all describe him.
I know he loves me, and I love him too.
He is one of my best friends.
He is strong to protect me,
he teaches me right from wrong.
I love his warm hugs
and his sweet smile.
If I ever lost him
I wouldn't know what I would do.
Dimitria Rozier, Grade 6
Saint Pauls Middle School, NC

S'mores
Delicious s'mores,
Being roasted,
melted chocolate
So good.

Melted marshmallows
Delicious too.

Honey covered graham crackers is next
Delicious also.

Putting them all together,
And you get a
Chocolatety,
Creamy, Crunchy,
Delicious
S'more.
Carson Strunk, Grade 4
Buckner Elementary School, KY

Cornfield
The corn,
Is as orange as the sun.
A circle as round as it can be,
Birds are chirping freely,
The corn hitting against each other,
Is what I hear.

Fresh air blows in the wind,
The fresh corn I smell.
Fresh scent of corn,
Is what I taste.
The rich soil is a soft bed.

Rough corn crops grow,
Like humans.
The smooth soil sings softly,
I'm lonely, brave, and at peace.
Kadie Boone, Grade 6
College View Middle School, KY

The Sharpening Surgery
Ouch! I broke my point!
Run me to the hospital!
My doctor is Dr. Bostitch Sharpener.
Hold me tight or I'll spin out of control.

GRIND! GRIND! Oh boy!
Ouch! I feel my point growing!
Almost done!

YES! Finally I am finished!
Pointier than ever before!
Take that you old leopard printed pencil!
Alexis Ilgandi, Grade 5
Hunter GT Magnet Elementary School, NC

High Merit Poems – Grades 4, 5, and 6

Amazing Rockets
Rockets launch in the air
to see the bright glare
from the planets and stars
can you imagine being that far?
Or could you imagine reaching Mars?
Kellen Tucker, Grade 4
E O Young Elementary School, NC

Police Officer
Police
Running, driving,
Working, talking, caring,
Safe, helpful, careful, serving,
Public servant
Xyakia Baines, Grade 5
Tates Creek Elementary School, KY

Mother
Mother
Beautiful, loving,
Smart, playful, protecting
Loves playing protecting me every day
Momma
Byron Smith, Grade 5
Tates Creek Elementary School, KY

Cars
Cars
Colorful, cool,
Driving, stopping, steering,
Loves touring across town,
Convertibles
James Broughton, Grade 5
Tates Creek Elementary School, KY

Bright Blue
Blue is the color of the clearest sky.
Blue is the color of the calmest river.
Blue is sometimes the color of my feelings.
Blue is the color of sweet fat blueberries.
Blue makes me feel happy.
Joy Osborne, Grade 4
F H Jenkins Elementary School, TN

Bright Sun
Sunlight
Our light on Earth
Our plant's great producer
It shines and heats our Earth and moon
Bright light
Robert Gregory, Grade 5
Carver Elementary School, NC

I Am Martin Luther King Jr.
I am Martin Luther King Jr. I'm helpful. I care.
I wonder why blacks and whites are so mean to each other.
I hear people clapping and cheering me on.
I see blacks and whites getting along.
I am Martin Luther King Jr. I shall make a difference.
I pretend that blacks will always be treated nicely.
I feel nervous and anxious about world peace.
I grip the church microphone. It feels cold.
I worry that my speech will not work.
I cry tears of joy when I see blacks and whites join hands.
I am Martin Luther King Jr. I am making a difference.
I understand that world peace is not going to be easy.
I proudly say my peace making speech to all the world!!!
I dream my speech will work and people all over the world will get along.
I try not to be nervous, but I am. My speech has to mean something.
I hope I make a difference not just here, but for the world.
I am Martin Luther King Jr. I have a "dream."
Dylan Sampson, Grade 4
Mineral Wells Elementary School, WV

I Am John Henry
I am John Henry. I am mighty strong and brave.
I wonder if I will beat that steam engine today.
I hear many cheering me on and some are even crying for me.
I see others hammering. Stakes are everywhere and I must drive many.
I am John Henry. I am strong and brave. I can do this!
I pretend that I win and we are finally free again.
I feel petrified!!!! I cannot let all the other workers down.
I grip the heavy hammers tightly in both hands. My heart is pounding.
I worry about what will happen if I don't beat the steam engine.
I mumble to myself, "John, it is time…"
I am John Henry strong and brave John Henry.
I understand that everyone here is depending on me to win the race.
I say in my head, "I can do this and I will!"
I dream that I beat the steam engine and it is all over.
I try harder and harder. Everyone is watching.
I hope I will survive…
I am John Henry. I am strong. I won't give up until my last breath!
Gracie Kent, Grade 4
Mineral Wells Elementary School, WV

I See My Nook
Erector set sitting cold and shiny in the corner of my room,
Books lay untouched next to my chair causing me to trip when I pass them,
Laptop is gently whirring in the background,
Radio screaming my chillin' playlist,
Metallic smelling metal tickles my nose,
Raw pinewood in the forest reminds me of my carefree days before school,
Sweet peanut butter cookies tickles my taste buds because they're so good,
Sweet Hershey chocolate that's heaven on earth,
Old homework pages that never got completed are rough and brittle,
Computer keys ready to be typed, tapped, and twisted because they laugh
at me every time I make a mistake,
Isolated and happy
Emeline Cave, Grade 6
College View Middle School, KY

I Am Helen Keller

I am Helen Keller. I am brave and generous.
I wonder why I was born so sick?
I can't hear the things that others hear.
I can't see the things that others see.
I am blind. I am Helen Keller.
I pretend that I can see and hear.
I feel terrified that I won't be able to learn.
I touch the cool water from the sink.
I worry that I won't understand my teacher.
I am excited! I can feel vibrations.
I am Helen Keller.
I understand that I need to learn.
I say my very first word.
I dream I can hear myself saying it.
I try very hard to learn everything from my teacher.
I hope someway I will be able to talk and hear.
I am Helen Keller.

Rhylea Graham, Grade 4
Mineral Wells Elementary School, WV

Colors

The sky is blue and the grass is green
Colors everywhere looking back at me

Black and yellow, yellow and black
Painting these colors on my back

Red and white and dark as night
Those are colors of my bike

Purple and pink and navy blue
I like orange and violet too

Colors, colors everywhere
I put colors in my hair

I really like colors yes I do
I really hope you like colors too

Jack Shelton, Grade 5
Evangelical Christian School Ridgelake Campus, TN

Merry Christmas

C hristmas is not all about toys
H ave you ever that about giving?
R emember when you played in the snow.
I f you are smart you won't cry.
S o if you want toys you won't pout,
T o you I am saying he's watching,
M ay I just tell you if you cry or pout,
    you won't get lots of toys or gifts.
A s St. Nicholas would say, "I have a list and I'm checking it twice,
    I'm going to find out if you have been naughty or nice."
S o if you want toys this Christmas you won't cry or pout,
    because he's watching you.

SeMarreius Keith, Grade 5
E O Young Elementary School, NC

Scouting

I love being a scout.
I get to shoot a gun.
Scouting is what I'm all about.
It's a lot of fun.

We get to build a fire.
I use a knife to whittle.
I have learned how to change a tire.
Sometimes we just piddle.

We do lots of hiking.
They have taught me how to cook.
We even go biking.
I caught a fish on a hook.

We sleep under the stars.
I work out of my book.
Working on astronomy I got to see Mars.
When I wear my uniform, you should see how I look.

Cameron Shockley, Grade 6
Bernheim Middle School, KY

My New Puppy

Floppy ears and spotted nose
That's the puppy that we chose
When she put her paws against the glass
I knew I'd found a friend at last

We bought some dog food and a toy
We found a dog bed she'd enjoy
And then when it was time to go
She stuck her head out the car window

When we got home she ran inside
All around the house she flied
She played until the sky grew dark
But when we put her in her cage she started to bark

She barked and barked the whole night long
She could be heard all the way from Hong Kong
But even though she made so much noise
We still loved her and bought her more toys

Evan McKenna, Grade 6
All Saints' Episcopal School, TN

Anger

Anger is like a raging bull,
So powerful it could break a brick wall,
It can break the best of friendships,
It's like a tornado in a trailer park,
It's like a double edged sword,
It will hurt you more than other people,
You can try to fix everything but it usually doesn't work,
Anger is a bad thing unless you can control it.

Kaleb Wilson, Grade 6
College View Middle School, KY

High Merit Poems – Grades 4, 5, and 6

A Bittersweet Holiday
Why me? I think as I sit on the table
The family watching football
Through Time Warner Cable

Why me? I think as they prepare the meal
I hate being cooked
I squirm like an eel

Why me? I think as I come out of the oven
Did they have to pick me?
There were plumper than I, more than two dozen!

Why me? I think as they fill me with stuffing
Do I have to be eaten?
I didn't do nothing!

I have a soul, I had a life,
My job, my friends, my kids and my wife

Why me, why me
Why me, oh why me?
But of course, I suppose it was destiny
Because I'm not human
I'm turkey

Ben Balint-Kurti, Grade 5
Hunter GT Magnet Elementary School, NC

Blue
Blue looks like…
A Kentucky Wildcats crowd, the ocean water,
A clear blue sky, a blueberry.

Blue sounds like…
Cheering from fans "GO BIG BLUE."
Waves crashing on the rocks "BOOM."
Wind blowing through the trees "WOOSH."
Crunching in my mouth "CRUNCH."

Blue smells like…
A sweaty gym,
Salt water and fish,
A summer day, sweetness

Blue feels like…
Throwing the ball to score,
Sand between my toes,
A soft mist from rain,
Squishy and sticky.

Blue tastes like…
Hot dogs and nachos, salt water,
Water from rain, sweet and juicy.

Zachary Johnson, Grade 6
Bernheim Middle School, KY

My Comfy, Fluffy Bed of Memories
Diving backward from my Sit n' Spin
Spreading out all my Dora toys
Reading my Rainbow Bunny book
All on my comfy, fluffy pink pillow bed

Opening presents with Auntie Jen
Playing "hide the monkeys" with my sister
Watching Star Wars movies with Papa
On my squishy, lumpy pink pillow bed

Taking naps when I was scared
Jumping with my cousins
Drying my hair with Ms. Jennifer
On my sagging, tearing pink pillow bed

Watching General Hospital with my grandmother
Painting toenails with my aunt
Scoring Red Socks games with my uncle
On my flat, ripped pink pillow bed

Filling falls out and stitches are ripped
Growing old together
Making more memories every day
My pink pillow bed of memories

Natacha White, Grade 6
Woodland Presbyterian School, TN

Green
Green,
Green is the leaves on the trees
Green is the grass on the ground
Green, green, green

Green sounds like water trickling
Green is the color of plants in the spring
Green smells like a smooth country breeze
Green, green, green

Green is a beautiful meadow
Green is a small grasshopper
Green feels like sharp needle points on the ground
Green, green, green

Green is happiness
Green is the prettiest color in the rainbow
Green is my sister's face on a roller coaster
Green, green, green

Green is my pond
Green is envy
Green is August
Green, green, green

Lexis Dunn, Grade 6
Bernheim Middle School, KY

Ode to Fishing

I love to fish; it is so very fun,
It takes the worries off your back while you are sitting in the sun.
When your bobber bounces you have a bite,
You start to jerk when it is out of sight.

At mid-afternoon you catch the big fish on a spinner,
The next day he is on your plate for dinner.
Today is a new day, we go out again,
We circle around the lake right were we began.

Oh fishing oh fishing it is so fun,
Especially when you catch the fish that weighs a ton.
Every fish is good on your plate,
Except the big ones, if you eat them you've made a mistake.

Justin Mason, Grade 6
Bernheim Middle School, KY

Colorado

Large mountains and steep hills,
houses scattered along the region.
A few cars going down the road,
birds singing far away.
The wild outdoors.
The nearby sap from the pine trees,
the wonderful smell from outside.
The grass floor.
The melting snow.
Tall tremendous trees.
This place is like paradise.
When it snows it's a gorgeous white blanket.
This place will always be a part of my heart.
I feel like this is my second home.

Ian Taylor, Grade 6
College View Middle School, KY

The Smoky Mountains

I see white clouds falling on miles and miles of green trees,
mountains, and valleys,
I hear the loud roar of the grizzly bears that is a fire truck's
siren right by you in your ear.

I smell the fresh air,
and the nature in the sky
I taste the juicy, wild berries
growing on the beautiful berry bushes.

I touch all the fresh wood
that is always growing on trees,
I'm as relaxed as a caterpillar
In its swaying cocoon

Nick Driskill, Grade 6
College View Middle School, KY

Smartphone

My pleasures are limited
So, my hand reaches into my pocket as if programmed
To the item wrapped
In a soft rubber case that
Stops the encased item from slipping.

I quickly and quietly slip it off.
Inside is a gleaming silver and black object with curved edges
I slowly push down
On the swollen button.
It is as circular and smooth as the polished aluminum on the back.

The glass display lights up
As if resurrected from the dead.
One the sheet of glass and heat sensors the time appears,
Etched into a sheet of metal dripping with water.
A sliding bar is shown below

That is patiently awaiting my eager fingertips
I slide my finger
On the smooth, plastic screen protector
Only to be flabbergasted
By the transition from reality to a completely new world, cyberspace.

Nilai Vemula, Grade 6
White Station Middle School, TN

Clown Parade

The clown parade is so much fun
We always have it under the sun

The cheerleaders cheer
You can always hear

There is music from the band
With many fans in the stand

You can play a game
You might have to aim

Kids are in the clown parade
They also serve lemonade

You play with your friends
Until the day ends

There are lots of kids, girls and boys
They always make a lot of noise

The night ends with a bang
At the football game

Gracie Plunk, Grade 4
Evangelical Christian School Ridgelake Campus, TN

What Is Green?

Green is my favorite color it is the color that I wear
It is the color of sourness, of delicious grapes.
That's what green is.

That's what green is, green is trust
The color of plants, it is vegetables.
That's what green is.

Green is the fresh cut green grass.
It is the color of so many things.
That's what green is.

Green is all sorts of food, green beans,
Also it is the color of eyes.
That's what green is.

Green is, honeysuckle vines.
The peelings of an apple.
That's what green is.

Green is snakes blending in the grass
The folder to put useful things in.
That's what green is.

Green is the sweet pears, it is nail polish. That's what green is.
Green is the color of paint, the smell of sweaty socks.
That's what green is.

Amanda Bryant, Grade 6
Bernheim Middle School, KY

Daddy

Wandering
Wondering
Blundering through
Dawdling
Questioning
Discovering new

As I walk along this well-worn road
The fields of punishment — not a pleasant abode
Little scraps of garbage flutter
Papers filled with dreams of better

Wishing
Yearning
Wanting cures
Hoping
Dying
From sneaky lures

The end has been reached,
Hospitals have been breached
Cancer isn't deadly
But I miss you, Daddy.

Theo Patt, Grade 6
White Station Middle School, TN

I Am Harriet Tubman

I am Harriet Tubman. I save people from slavery.
I hear guards yelling at me. They know my name and my purpose.
I see the slaves hurt and starving waiting in the woods for my signal.
I pretend that slavery is over and will stop.
I feel very nervous. I know that someday they will catch me.
I touch vines, trees, and I can feel them coming.
I worry that they will catch not only me but all that are with me.
I shout, "Run, run don't stop, keep on going!!!"
I understand what my people feel like.
I dream every day and night that slavery will end.
I will not give up hope!
I just get more and more to follow me to freedom.
I am Harriet Tubman.

Paige Weaver, Grade 4
Mineral Wells Elementary School, WV

Running

I love to run.
I like to run because it's a challenge.
I love the feeling of accomplishment at the end of a race.
Some people don't like running, but I love it.
I love going fast down a hill, then pushing myself up the next.
I love how when I run, I do it nonstop until the end.
As I start the race people cheer.
Sometimes it's hard, but I can't stop.
When it hurts, I just have to keep going.
As I get close to the finish I hear cheers.
It's exciting.
There is no better feeling than crossing the finish line.
Running is exciting.

Joseph Broy, Grade 6
Woodland Presbyterian School, TN

Wonderful Water Sound

My friends arguing like toddlers in a game of football
Food that is very good and yummy
A bunch of kids screaming as a big waves punches them like a bully
Waves washing in with white water
Parents tanning in Florida sun like lazy dogs
Water crashing and smashing on my body
Scents of all the saltwater when kids come in from the ocean
Very good Gatorade jumps on my taste buds
The sand massages my feet as I walk on the beach
Chomping chips after a long day at the beach

Mitchell Logan, Grade 6
College View Middle School, KY

Red Wonder

Red is the sun shining with excitement.
Red is a beautiful rose blooming in the spring
Red is a sweet bunch of tasty cherries
Red is love floating in your heart on Valentine's Day.
Red is the boiling sunset slowly going down behind the trees.
Red is the color I see in nature all around me.

Skye Chancellor, Grade 4
F H Jenkins Elementary School, TN

The Chair

Every morning I'm sat on
Is it me you don't like?
It makes me want to cry, but I don't

When you push me around I think
I have feelings you know
You treat me like dirt, but I'm just like a baby

Will you play with me Saturday?
You never do
Why bother asking, you're too busy!

We are just alike
We both have legs and feelings
What's wrong with me?

I wish you weren't always gone
From the day you bought me, I thought we were friends
I know I'm a chair, but I'm as human as you

You comfort me when you're around
Although, when you turn the lights off, I get scared
Keep them on please!

Play with me, Lillie

Ava Neijna, Grade 5
Hunter GT Magnet Elementary School, NC

Blue

Blue is the color of the sky
The color that makes you think of blueberries
You can see that people's eyes are blue
It's the color of a Bluetick Coonhound

You think of the sky when you see blue
You know it's going to be warm
I think of the clouds when I think of blue
I say blue is the brother to white

I see my Bluetick walking around
You feel her rough blue tail
She wags her blue tail
I show my blue tick in the warm sky

You and I see blueberries
You think about eating the blueberries but only to get in trouble
You touch them they are smooth
You see the color blue as you walk away

I see the blue on my paper
I can feel it smudging from the wet marker
I see the blue in his eyes
I love the color blue

Samantha Allen, Grade 6
Bernheim Middle School, KY

Nature's Reward

Maple trees blowing quietly in the wind
Large deer run swiftly across the meadow
Brown sticks snapping softly under their feet
Golden brown leaves fall like rain lightly on the ground
Shiny water is nature's dew gently quenching the thirst of life
Nature's soft air fills my mouth silently
Mother Earth creeps slowly between my slender toes
Tiny insects chirp loudly in the evening
Freshly cut grass fills the damp air
The sweet scent of nature flows lightly in the breeze
Totally calm and relaxed emotions fill my gentle soul

Brandon Pendley, Grade 6
College View Middle School, KY

Christmas

I watch the lovely snow as it falls like a balloon that has no air.
Kids are gracefully playing in the soft snow.
The icy roads are slick and wet.
I hear the soothing sound of kids laughing.
I hear the sound of snow crunching under my feet.
Children are eating smoked and roasted turkey.
They are baking sweet and sugary cookies for Santa.
They can't wait till they get to open their presents.
But the true meaning is about Jesus being born.
That's why I like Christmas.

Annika Beatty, Grade 5
Providence Academy, TN

I Love the Look of Flowers

I love the look of flowers.
They are beautiful, fancy, colorful, different.
My favorite kind is the tulip.
They come in so many colors; pink, purple, and blue.
Flowers remind me of spring and happiness.
I like them because they are living.
Bees also make sweet honey from their pollen.
Flowers have a delightful and luscious fragrance.
I love the look of one flower, a bouquet, or a field of them.
That's why I love flowers so much.

Peyton Keller, Grade 5
Providence Academy, TN

I Love the Look of Titan

I love the look of my dog.
He is so cute when he comes in with mud on his feet.
And when he sits on the furniture.
Oh how Mom gets mad.
When he looks at us with those cute little eyes.
When he gets shocked by the underground fence,
It looks so cute but yet so sad.
Oh how it makes me mad.
To him it feels so bad.
I love the look of my dog, Titan!

Courtney Riddle, Grade 5
Providence Academy, TN

High Merit Poems – Grades 4, 5, and 6

The Pizza
Pizza is my favorite meal
When we get it, my sisters squeal

I love it with pepperoni and cheese
But not red pepper, it makes me sneeze

I sometimes like it cold
But please without mold

Put hot pizza on my plate
Come over for dinner and don't be late
Christopher Cochran, Grade 4
Evangelical Christian School Ridgelake Campus, TN

Looking Out the Window on a Fall Morning
Leaves are falling,
The wind is calling,
A chill is in the air.

Will it snow?
I don't think so,
But what should I wear?

Coats and gloves,
No sun up above,
It is so hard to care.
Kayleigh Bodily, Grade 6
White Station Middle School, TN

Gulf Shores, AL
I walk to the ocean so big and blue
Palm trees as huge as the Twin Towers
The waves crashing and roaring
Seagulls cawing and looking for food
The sour smell of the salty salt water
People grilling hot dogs on the charcoal grill
Taste of BBQ hamburgers dancing around
I taste the saltiness of the fish that I'm eating
The grittiness of the sand as it glides up and down the beach
Little fish swim up and down the shallow pools
Happy and excited
Emma Fenwick, Grade 6
College View Middle School, KY

Christmas
Christmas is almost here!
It's going to be a great time of year.
Christmas is the time to worship God,
It is a time to be with family.
The reason I like Christmas is because
I like being with my family.
I like to see kids open up presents.
I like when it snows.
I like to see other kids open their presents on Christmas.
Alexis Locklear, Grade 6
Saint Pauls Middle School, NC

I Am Paul Jackson
I am Paul Jackson. I serve proudly in the USA Army.
I am on active duty. It is top secret.
I hear a helicopter, guns firing, and people screaming.
I see many hurt and wounded, some have even been killed.
I am Paul Jackson. I am here to serve my country.
I pretend that all my men made it safely to base.
I feel sad and my heart hurts inside of me.
I touch my gun beside me. It is time…I must go into action.
I worry that I may be forced to kill someone.
I cry when I see so many killed in war.
I am Paul Jackson. I am here to defend my country.
I understand that the enemies don't like us.
I say to the civilians to hide.
I dream that I am back with my unit and troops.
I try my best to make our world a safer place to live.
I am Paul Jackson. I serve you in the United States of America.
Justin Ellinger, Grade 4
Mineral Wells Elementary School, WV

Tag with Dad
Walking back to the car
For it wasn't very far
My dad tags me and says, "You're it!"
Fast. Fast. Fast.

I run up the stairs two by two
I jump for the monkey bars and missed by the inch of two
I hear a loud CRACK!
I feel a sharp pain in my left arm.
Fast. Fast. Fast.

My dad is back
He takes me back to the truck
He calls 911
The fireman were the first to come
Fast. Fast. Fast.
Shawn Conrad, Grade 6
Bernheim Middle School, KY

My Friend Noodles
Let me tell you a story.
I will start with the beginning, and finish with the end.
He is very young, blond, with brown eyes.
He likes to chase flies.
He is big, strong, and can knock you down.
He never makes my smile into a frown.
We play and run.
He always wants to have fun.
He plays with my cats, sometimes they don't care.
But other times they look at him as if they say, "Don't you dare."
Sometimes he makes my parents mad.
They look at him and say, "You're bad."
It's time to tell you who is my friend.
He is my dog Noodles, and this is the end.
Molly Castle, Grade 5
Paint Lick Elementary School, KY

Home

Giant trees waving at me,
My mom cooking,
My dad working,
Cats happily purring, right outside my door.

Radio playing softly,
Delicious, bountiful food,
On the kitchen counter,
Sweet, salty snacks,
Slipping down my throat.

Warm shower water,
Drip, drop, drip, drop,
Potatoes making my taste buds go wild,
Drinks that make me thirst no longer.
Soft comfortable blankets laid neatly upon my bed.

Smooth carpet beneath my feet,
Windows bright, like the heavens above,
Leaves flying,
Colors that are rainbows,
I feel happy and safe.

Kaylee Nacey, Grade 6
College View Middle School, KY

My Family

Ode to my family.
You are smart and funny,
You are the only one who makes me laugh when I want to cry.
You are the only one who knows how I feel inside.
I tell you all my secrets and you tell me all of yours.
We stick together through thick and thin,
We are strong, we will not bend.
We will stick together through all the lies people tell
And all the things people hide
We are strong, we will always hold on.
You are loving, caring, generous and shy, you cannot hide
We are a couple, we make two, you talk to me and I'll talk to you
We will stick together just like glue
No matter what people say.
We are durable, we will be strong.
No matter how much people try to tear us apart.
We are a family, you will always be in my heart, we are a family.
You fight for me, I'll fight for you.
We are a family, a family, a family.
Him and her, her and him.
We are a family, we will stick together until the end.

Shayla Brown, Grade 6
Saint Pauls Middle School, NC

Awesome Veterans

Thanks Veterans for fighting for our country
If you weren't fighting for us right now
we wouldn't have the freedom that we have today

Jennicka Runyon, Grade 5
Temple Hill Elementary School, KY

Peanuts

Peanuts are brown
When I put them in my mouth
I eat them like I'm going to town
I like to eat all kinds of peanuts
They are my favorite snack
I go to the store
And I buy them in a pack
The texture is so smooth
It makes me wanna groove
When I run out
I go to the store
And buy some more
They come in a lot of flavors
I only like one
The plain, salty one
You should try eating peanuts, too
They could become your favorite snack
Because I like them and you might like them too

Evan Bracy, Grade 4
Weldon Elementary School, NC

I Am

I am smart and not a quitter
I wonder what it would be like if I were the president
I hear the ocean
I see people caring
I want the world to never end
I am smart and not a quitter
I pretend I'm the king of the world
I feel great appreciation
I touch kids
I worry about people who die for our country
I am smart and not a quitter
I understand life
I say peace to the world
I dream about if I were the president
I try to get good grades
I hope I am going to marry a good woman

I am smart and not a quitter

Marco Salas, Grade 4
Centennial Elementary School, TN

An Ode to Dusty Dog

Oh Dusty dog, when I scratch you at the right spot,
your leg starts to thump.
When you see a deer pass by, that's when you start to hurry,
and that's when I start to worry.
Dad sometimes calls you a mutt,
but I just say you're a nut.
When you get really licky, it starts to get sticky,
that just means you love us.
If you get too much food,
you get in a full mood.

Emily Witt, Grade 5
West Liberty Elementary School, WV

Dogs to Humans

Talking I cannot do
But feelings I do have too
I am tired of humans treating us like babies
If you don't believe me I can show you my rabies

What is up with the two meals a day
It is hard to sit and watch you guys eating away
I would like to drink tap water too
All we want is to be treated just like you

I am sick of people dressing us like dolls
You better stop everything before revenge calls
So you better drop now
Before the human race falls

Carter Gasia, Grade 5
Hunter GT Magnet Elementary School, NC

Blue

Blue is the color of beauty!
Blue is the color of my eyes!
Blue is the color of depression!
Blue is the color of the sky!

Blue is the cool fresh air rushing past my face!
Blue is my favorite color!
Blue is the cool rain hitting the ground!
Blue is the color of a creek!

Blue is the color of the sparkly ocean!
Blue is the color of my favorite ocean!
Blue is the color of peace!
Blue is the color of the best place ever! *Kentucky!!*

Jacob Holderman, Grade 6
Bernheim Middle School, KY

God

I love God
He fills my heart with joy,
He turns night to day,
He has the whole wide world in his hands,
he gave us love.
We celebrate him on Christmas,
We worship him in church on Sunday and Wednesday,
He saved my soul from sin,
He created the world,
He has all power,
he can do all,
He is the only God, and will always be,
I take him as my only GOD.
I love God.

Preston Wilt, Grade 5
Paint Lick Elementary School, KY

The Cold Concrete Room

In the cold concrete
room, doing arts and crafts.
Bikes everywhere lined up against
the wall, a huge place full of overflowing
bins, paint, pottery, paper of all sorts. The sound
of sanding wood, then four children plunging through
the toy bins loudly. Fumes of adhesive through the day. The
toxic from the tools. I taste the memories and comfort. The
smells from the washer, the cold, chill, contagious concrete
floor on my feet. The bumpy beads are massaging
my hands. Lonely but excited and eager to
make creative loud art like a 5
year-old wanting to ride a ride
at Holiday World.

Kailey Davidson, Grade 6
College View Middle School, KY

Dolphins

My favorite animal is a dolphin
I like them because they have large tall fins

Sometimes dolphins are gray
They sometimes swim in the bay

I swam on a dolphin's fin
I had a really fun time with him

I would love to have a dolphin as a pet
The only problem is I would not have a place to keep him wet

I really like dolphins, they are blue
I really like dolphins, you should too!

Kerigan Childress, Grade 4
Evangelical Christian School Ridgelake Campus, TN

Ode to Bacon

From the beginning, I have loved bacon
When people ask for bacon, I say it's taken!
Bacon, I love your smell
Sometimes it makes me yell

Hey! Stay off my bacon!
When I say that, people become shaken
Bacon is my favorite snack
Why don't you pass me another pack

SIZZLE! CRACKLE! POP!
When it's cooking, that sound will never stop
That sound is music to my ears
It distracts me from my occasional fears

Dalton Goff, Grade 6
Bernheim Middle School, KY

My Old Home That Used to Be Mine

My parent's red brick house in front of me.
A clear reflection of me through the window like a ghost.

Silly conversations from inside the house.
Sweet laughter inside the home.

Spicy food on the grill.
Rich smoke coming out of the grill.

Sweet fresh vegetables from the garden.
Silky smooth petals on a flower like a silk scarf.

Joyful memories of all of me.

Kathleen Miller, Grade 6
College View Middle School, KY

Softball Field

Mad coaches arguing,
Young children running around,
Umpires yelling "Strike!"

Excited parents cheering,
Concession stands' tasty, tarty, treats are heaven,
The outside's fresh air.

Fresh cheesy nachos dancing in your mouth,
Soft clumpy dirt on the ground,
Sweat dripping off my face like water condensation.

I feel happy, I'm in my own world.

Mazie Coomes, Grade 6
College View Middle School, KY

The E.O.G. Test

The E.O.G. is hard you see
But if you study you will succeed
If you get As and Bs
That will make 4s and 3s
If you finish too fast,
In the teacher's eyes you finish last
Take your time, it is no race,
You get nothing if you finish in first place.
You may be nervous, you may be frightened,
But when you finish, you will be delighted.

Zachary Williamson, Grade 5
Carver Elementary School, NC

Family

F un with your cousins.
A ctivities with those who came.
Re **M** embering the good times you've had.
I nteract with your aunts and uncles.
L ove your whole family.
Y esterday will always be a memory of today.

Addison Schneider, Grade 5
Walton-Verona Middle School, KY

Nathan

Nathan, young, athletic, active
Sibling of Natania and Natadria
Lover of — Jesus Christ, who forgives my sins,
Dad and Mom, who protects me like a shepherd,
Friends, who give me company.
Who feels — happy when my friends say jokes,
Loved by my teachers,
Adored by my grandparents.
Who needs — wisdom to distinguish good from evil
Help in school to get good grades,
Patience in all things.
Who gives — kindness by sharing school supplies,
Help to Dad by weeding the garden,
Advise to my sisters when cleaning their room.
Who fears — lions that are as furry as a dog,
Bees that sting and sharks that bite.
Who would like to see — Delhi, Israel,
The Statue of Liberty.

Nathan Paul, Grade 5
Providence Academy, TN

Nature

As big as a mountain — as little as a bug
As thick as a brick — as thin as paper
As bright as the sun — as dark as night
As old as a dinosaur — as new as a baby
As tall as the sky — as short as a paper clip
As wide as the ocean — as narrow as a hallway
As hot as fire — as cold as ice
As hard as a rock — as soft as a pillow
As loud as a scream — as quiet as a mouse
As white as snow — as black as coal
As strong as an ox — as weak as a lamb
As heavy as a bear — as light as a hair
As clean as a whistle — as dirty as dirt
As fast as lightning – as slow as molasses
As hairy as an ape — as bald as an eagle
As pretty as a princess — as ugly as a toad
As nice as an angel — as mean as a witch
As wet as the rain forest — as dry as the desert

Preston Law, Grade 5
Longest Elementary School, KY

Christmas

At Christmas I can see the snow falling like a feather smiling at you
I can hear the bells ringing louder than a train whistle
I can touch the bumpy Christmas trees
I can taste the delicious ham
I can smell the fragrance of the cookies
I can see icy roads causing wrecks all over the place
I can hear people singing praises like a bird sings its love song
I can touch the beautifully wrapped presents
I can taste the tongue-blistering hot chocolate
I can smell the mouthwatering pumpkin pie

Cameron Patterson, Grade 5
Providence Academy, TN

Writing

When you write you can use your imagination.
You can write fiction or nonfiction.
Fairy tales with princesses and dragons.
Or battles with monsters vs aliens.
Writing takes you places from Planet Oogles to Unicornland.
Let writing let you dream.
Let writing survive forever!

Madison Fernandez, Grade 4
Moyock Elementary School, NC

Mario

Mario! Mario!
Help me Mario is as red as a rose
as blood
as cool water
as cool
as a dog
and as fun on a game they have in school and on TV.

Hylan Stanley, Grade 5
Longest Elementary School, KY

Veterans Day

Veterans Day is the day when we the people get together
to celebrate the ones who died for our country
to keep us safe from attack and war.

So when you hear the twenty-one gun salute
that is just a hero who passed away
by keeping our country safe.

Vicente Carrasco, Grade 5
Temple Hill Elementary School, KY

Storm

Brightness filling
Overcast stormy sky
Fascinating flashes
Overpower darkness
Booms like gunshots
Filling our ears
The earth shaking
At the war
Something
Dripping on a
Worn down tired roof
A beast covers the
Earth
His enemies
He squishes
A smacking sound
Branches hit the
Windowsills
The wind is
Howling slowly
Storms

Lauren Ashton, Grade 4
Goshen Elementary School at Hillcrest, KY

Terrible Tiger

Fierce eyes staring
Dark movements
Standing
Stripes as bold as a soldier
Stomping as loud as a stampede

Tiger
Fur as soft looking as cotton
Standing up tall

Whiskers as long as pencils
Straightened, slick
Blizzard, white, cloudy threads

Eyes meeting yours at once
Staring with darkness
Catching

One behind the other
Frightened but fierce

Colors, shady and uncomfortable
Rough and damp, dark

Feeling, going to curl you fiercely
Tangles your heart
Makes you feel, terrible

Isha Chauhan, Grade 4
Buckner Elementary School, KY

Summertime

Summertime, summertime
Fun in the sunshine
Time to cook out
But the yard needs a trim
If we get too hot
We can go for a swim

Summertime, summertime
Relax in the shade
No homework, no worries
It makes me feel like I have it made

Summertime, summertime
The grass is my rug
I rest by the trees
And watch the lightning bugs

Summertime, summertime
In the bright moonlight
I like to look at the stars
Because they are so bright

Summertime, summertime

Chloe Forbes, Grade 6
White Station Middle School, TN

I Am
I am a sister and a daughter.
I wonder when I will die.
I hear my family.
I see my sister and brother.
I am a sister and daughter.
I pretend to be mean.
I feel like my sister hates me.
I touch my tears.
I worry about my family.
I cry when I fight.
I am a sister and a daughter.
I understand why I fight.
I say I love my family.
I dream I will not fight with my sister.
I try to be a good student.
I hope to live forever.
I am a sister and a daughter.

Gretta Duckett, Grade 6
Bernheim Middle School, KY

An Ode to My Snowflake
Oh little snowflake,
you keep me gazing.

With your crystal white shapes,
they're so amazing.

Not one snowflake is the same,
but you're special to me.

Don't be ashamed,
to keep your thoughts going.

Just 1, 2, 3,
and your wish is complete.

But no matter how far you go,
be the snowflake that is special to me.

Kaylin Templeton, Grade 5
West Liberty Elementary School, WV

Sunrise
Sunrise, sunrise, sunrise
As it rises
You see all the beautiful colors
like
RED, ORANGE, and YELLOW.
The sun's so bright
And clear and near
It's so bright you can nearly
See it again
Sunrise, sunrise
I love the sunrise.
It is so bright and clear and near in sight.

Shy-Tavia McMillan, Grade 6
Saint Pauls Middle School, NC

Red
Red is the color of a cowboy's bandana.
Red is the spark of a fire cracker.
Red is the color of fire.
Red is the color that inspires you.
Red is the color of blood.

Red is the smell of an apple pie.
Red is the color of rage.
Red is the color of polka dots.
Red is the color of an explosion.
Red is the color of buffalo wings.

Red is the color of hot sauce.
Red is the color of a Corvette.
Red is the color of a fox.
Red is the color of a cardinal too.

Red is on the American flag.
Red is the color of pizza.
Red is the color of lava.
Red is the color of a shirt.

Red is the color of a rock star's hair.
Red is the color of your heart.
Red is on your face when you are mad.
Red is a sheet on a bed.

Dylan Fluhr, Grade 6
Bernheim Middle School, KY

The Night of Fright!!!
It's only
A couple more days,
Before I hit the…
Pumpkin maze!!!

It's almost here!
The night of…
CANDY!!!
The night of…
Fear!!!

I can't wait
I love it the most,
The night you can
Believe in…
Ghost!!!

It's almost time
For the night of…
Screams!!!

It's almost here
It is…
HALLOWEEN!!!

Wilson Tinnell, Grade 4
Buckner Elementary School, KY

The Best Mom I've Ever Had
Mommy, oh mommy
You care such a lot
You always have told me
We are like two peas in a pot
You clothe me
You bathe me
You always put me first
You always let me tell my problems
Even if they're the worst
We were all made
But you were a piece of art
In which God would never let us fall apart
And since God's made us one
I'm so very glad
And now I know you're the best mom
I've ever had

Erica McKenzie, Grade 6
Saint Pauls Middle School, NC

Winter
The leaves are falling to the ground
Different colors, red and brown
It's getting colder every day
The grass is starting to look like hay
The birds are flying towards the south
That's what winter is all about
Staying warm is hard to do
The cold wind blowing all around you
The animals are nestled in their bed
Hibernating as if they were dead
The pretty white snow falls to the ground
Kids will go outside and run around
Laughing, playing, and snowballs flying
So much fun, no one is sighing
People usually don't get out
That's what winter is all about

Cody Reagan, Grade 4
Centennial Elementary School, TN

The Wonderful Creation
The wonderful creation of our
world living beneath our feet
our freedom lives upon our
sides waiting for us to take in
the freedom beside us.

The wonderful creation living
beneath our feet the Lord our
Savior the man we thank every day
for the first person we
as people have seen.
He's the man who created us all
of our Holy Father living above us
listening to our prayers.

Abigail Hudgins, Grade 4
South Toe Elementary School, NC

I Am

I am an angel to my mom and dad.
I wonder about a lot of things.
I hear the sound of an ocean current.
I see the population growing every day.
I want to have a wonderful history.
I am an angel to my mom and dad.

I pretend to fly in fluffy marshmallows.
I feel the crisp breeze blowing on my body.
I touch the clouds in the blue sky.
I worry about my family.
I cry if something bad happens to anyone in my family.
I am an angel to my mom and dad.

I understand what people can go through in life.
I say I believe in God.
I dream for a better life.
I try to get good grades in school.
I hope I decide to have a good education.
I am an angel to my mom and dad.

Cheyanne Hobbs, Grade 6
Montgomery Central Middle School, TN

Freedom

I am the boy who loves his country.
I wonder what the world will be like in the future.
I hear the cannon on the Fourth of July.
I see heroes who fight for our freedom.
I want my country to be free forever.
I am the boy who loves his country.

I pretend to fight for my country.
I feel freedom when I see the flag.
I touch happy feelings to see free people.
I worry if my country will lose its freedom.
I cry when soldiers die.
I am the boy who loves his country.

I understand we fight hard for freedom.
I say we will win the war.
I dream to stay free.
I try to fight.
I hope we will win.
I am the boy who loves his country.

Dustin Trotter, Grade 6
Montgomery Central Middle School, TN

My Garden

If I had a garden, I'd grow everything I like to eat.
Some things would be tart; some things would be sweet.
Tangerines are tart, and strawberries are sweet.
Those are just two fruits I like to eat.
Tomatoes and potatoes are two things I like to eat too.
Gardening is my favorite thing to do.

Jazir Mickins, Grade 5
Southeast Elementary School, NC

My Ode to Jesus

Jesus is my very best friend.
He is always by my side and will never give up on me.
It if weren't for Jesus I don't know what I would do.
When I feel upset and lonely I think of Jesus.

He took the nails for me and you;
He died on the cross and took our sins
As far as the east is from the west.
Then three days later after Jesus died on the cross
He rose from the grave normal, perfect, and healthy.

Jesus heals the sick.
Let's the blind see.
He will bless us as long as we do right.
If he didn't give up on me he won't give up on you.

Payton Stice, Grade 6
Bernheim Middle School, KY

I Love the Look of San Francisco

I like the look of San Francisco, CA
I see the boats going in
And out
From the ocean, to the ocean
I see the Golden Gate Bridge
It is red and big
I also see tall buildings and people
Walking on the streets
I hear airplanes going in and out of
The airport
I see people on the streets with a shopping carts,
They are homeless
I feel very sorry for them
Only God has a good plan
For them

Stephanie Bailey, Grade 5
Providence Academy, TN

The Surprise

Woke up one bright morning
from a really fun sleep over

Walked sleepily downstairs
Friends eating warm sweet pancakes
"yum" I said as I stuffed them in my mouth

After a breakfast fit for a *queen* my family arrived
A smirk on my brothers face
He dragged me to the back trunk

And then I saw it a big BLACK...
Dog kennel
We were finally getting a dog
What a surprise.

Kaylee Hardin, Grade 4
Buckner Elementary School, KY

Amazing Apple Tree
Apple tree blossoms
Gracefully sways with the wind
Amazing beauty
Robert Susewell, Grade 5
E O Young Elementary School, NC

Nature
Nature is so fun!
To play in leaves and flowers.
Have fun in nature!
Taylor Vineyard, Grade 4
Centennial Elementary School, TN

Trees
Trees move side to side
Their leaves are so beautiful
Oh, how I love trees
Celie Evans, Grade 5
Walton-Verona Middle School, KY

Grass
Nice swishy feeling
It feels coolish on my feet
Can you guess? It's grass
Chapin Johnson, Grade 5
Walton-Verona Middle School, KY

Weeping Willow
Tall with long straight leaves
They blow like waves in the sea
This is where I'll be
Megan Wells, Grade 5
Walton-Verona Middle School, KY

Index

Aaron, Taylor ... 211
Abbott, Nicholas ... 222
Abdurahman, Adil ... 174
Abell, Railey ... 232
Abeln, Kate ... 168
Aboulmouna, Lorina ... 80
Adkins, Logan ... 244
Adkins, Mandie ... 67
Adkins, Natalie ... 105
Adlich, Madison ... 98
Adlin, Celia ... 220
Aguilar, Brayan ... 233
Ahlers, Matthew ... 20
Alam, Naima ... 114
Alexander, Melissa ... 99
Alford, Micah ... 224
Algee, Brandi ... 65
Alghali, Amina ... 66
Allen, Angel ... 83
Allen, Aquella ... 157
Allen, Peyton ... 97
Allen, Samantha ... 250
Allen, Shaye ... 131
Alsip, Brienna ... 203
Altstatt, Mary ... 241
Alvey, Rebekah ... 123
Amagliani, Laymon ... 212
Anderson, Alisa ... 23
Anderson, Christina ... 138
Anderson, Derek ... 13
Anderson, Marcus ... 228
Anderson, Sarah ... 18
Andrews, Kolotita ... 91
Angle, Emily ... 106
Archer, Corey ... 109
Argo, Will ... 167
Armes, Kelsey ... 50
Armstead, Katie ... 37
Armstrong, Jennifer ... 78
Arndt, Michaela ... 185
Arnold, Cameo ... 21
Arnold, Katie ... 92
Arnwine, Logan ... 194
Arora, Srishti ... 133
Arrington, Micah ... 145
Ashton, Lauren ... 255
Assadnia, Sophie ... 182
Atkinson, Malik ... 239
Attkisson, Jesse ... 17
Au, Ruby ... 37
Aubrey, Cotton ... 230
Aubrey, Skylar ... 134

Ayres, Coire ... 145
B., Monquall ... 61
Bagley, MoKyus ... 168
Bailey, Chelsea ... 210
Bailey, Dylan ... 169
Bailey, Hannah ... 120
Bailey, LeeAnn ... 46
Bailey, Stephanie ... 257
Baines, Xyakia ... 245
Baker, Dereka ... 149
Baker, Jessica ... 66
Baker, Megan ... 209
Baker, Sarah ... 128
Baldwin, Laura ... 42
Balint-Kurti, Ben ... 247
Balke, Laura ... 49
Ball, Kathrine ... 41
Ball, Martha ... 95
Ballard, Kiana ... 24
Bandel, Sarah ... 25
Banh, Tollina ... 181
Banister, Williesha ... 126
Banner, James ... 86
Bannister, Kalissa ... 182
Bansal, Sarthak ... 161
Barbour, Josh ... 122
Barbrey, Taylor ... 121
Bard, Brooklynn ... 218
Barkley, Grant ... 171
Barlow, Benjamin ... 81
Barnett, Olivia ... 128
Barrach, Emily ... 211
Bartel, Will ... 218
Bartkowiak, Natalia ... 171
Bartley, Courtney ... 68
Bartram, Allison ... 19
Bauer, Abby ... 105
Baughan, Katherine ... 101
Bauman, Alicia ... 185
Baxter, Casey ... 224
Bayless, Cheyanna ... 182
Baylor, Sarai ... 165
Beamer, Kelsey ... 30
Beason, Shelby ... 79
Beatty, Annika ... 250
Beauchamp, Kayla ... 108
Beaver, Leannda ... 241
Beavers, Terrence ... 210
Beckham, Kayla ... 131
Beckman, Alex ... 75
Beebe, Tyler ... 119
Beeler, Leslie ... 28

Belanger, Noah ... 56
Belcher, Brooke ... 31
Belk, Montgomery ... 175
Bell, Caitlin ... 165
Bell, Emma ... 107
Bell, Micayla ... 199
Bellefant, Shaniya ... 138
Bennett, Racquel ... 156
Benson, Diamond ... 119
Benson, Hannah ... 198
Berrios, Celina ... 216
Berry, Callie Anne ... 240
Berry, Dylan ... 28
Bess, Shelby ... 100
Bhojani, Ethan ... 235
Billings, Andrew ... 165
Billips, Eugene ... 63
Bird, Ashby ... 16
Bisset, Jada ... 91
Blackburn, Brooklyn ... 129
Blair, Brooke ... 242
Blaisdell, Victoria ... 51
Blakeney, Nate Mo. ... 120
Blanton, Robert ... 223
Blevins, Madelyn ... 185
Blevins, Renée ... 44
Blount, Allie ... 238
Bodily, Kayleigh ... 251
Bogdal, Sarah ... 38
Boggis, Tommy ... 127
Bolen, Karlee ... 180
Boles, Daniel ... 39
Boling, Sara ... 42
Bolton, Ja'Rae ... 8
Bolyard, Joanna ... 53
Bond, Katelyn ... 133
Bond, Michelle ... 232
Bonner, Allexa ... 79
Bonner, Caitlin ... 32
Boone, Kadie ... 244
Boos, Allyson ... 92
Booth, Courtney ... 69
Bosak, Emily ... 48
Bosley, Amy ... 169
Boultinghouse, Will ... 200
Bowman, Brittany ... 200
Boyd, Makayla ... 149
Boyles, Andrew ... 153
Bozeman, Tyler ... 16
Bracy, Evan ... 252
Brader-Araje, Devin ... 217
Bradford, Hattie ... 236

Bradley, Phillip 33	Calef, Ezra 119	Coble, Sloane 125
Brady, Alexander 226	Cambron, Connor 130	Cochran, Christopher 251
Brady, Luke 232	Campbell, Kylie 241	Cockrell, Drew 234
Bragg, Matthew 126	Campbell, Madissen 184	Cofield, Andrew 231
Branch, Janey 105	Canal, Joey 212	Coke, James 244
Brasel, Tori 175	Canary, Savana 201	Cole, Deandre 111
Braxton, Claire 28	Cardenas, Jenifer 44	Cole, Taylor 54
Bray, Dillon 72	Cardinal, Jeanne 69	Coleman, Alexandra 52
Breeden, Allison 221	Cargile, Jeffrey 125	Coles, Georgia 164
Brenin, JT 99	Carlisle, Jay 222	Coley, Nora 183
Brennan, Conor 130	Carman, Addi 213	Colley, Madison 199
Brennan, Jessica 91	Carrasco, Vicente 255	Collier, Rebecca 12
Brewer, Daniel 84	Carroll, Kaylyn 155	Collins, Carenna 162
Brewer, Elizabeth 203	Carroll, Veronica 164	Collins, Joshua 136
Bright, Evan 195	Carter, Aryelle 196	Comella, Alec 164
Bringewatt, Kara 243	Carter, Brianna 13	Connell, Blake 95
Brink, Maria 9	Carter, Gregory 243	Conrad, Shawn 251
Brooks, Brianna 217	Carter, Jamie 239	Coomes, Mazie 254
Brooks, Chloe 207	Carter, Mae 51	Coomes, Rachel 229
Broome, Drew 200	Carvelli, Corey 178	Cooper, Eli 198
Broughton, James 245	Carver, Cory 140	Cooper, Emily 201
Brown, Ciara 238	Castevens, Kayla 85	Cooper, Reed 227
Brown, Gabrielle 14	Castle, Molly 251	Coots, Baylee 229
Brown, Ivory 32	Catlett, Brent 206	Corbin, Hunter 117
Brown, Jason 181	Caughron, Chandler 218	Corcoran, Alexandra 93
Brown, Jayla 222	Cave, Emeline 245	Cordova, Mariano 203
Brown, Kennedy 107	Challa, Anup 148	Corey, Cameron 158
Brown, Mikayla 143	Chance, Cole 170	Correa, Maria 91
Brown, Shayla 252	Chancellor, Skye 249	Costain, Chase 112
Brown, Sierra 22	Chandler, Jared 27	Cotter, Destiny 97
Brown, Tamika 191	Chandler, Jeffrey 25	Couch, Samantha 28
Broy, Joseph 249	Chandler, Rebecca 134	Cowan, Robby 67
Bruner, Jade 8	Chapman, Keenan 177	Cowart, Jason 191
Brunner, Nicole 16	Chappell, John 185	Cozart, Hannah 77
Bryant, Amanda 249	Charm, Lois 57	Craig, Chandler 167
Bryant, Andrew 50	Charney, Ben 228	Crain, Destiny 33
Bryant, Sarah 118	Chauhan, Isha 255	Cravens, Autumn 154
Bryant, Sarah 130	Cheek, Daniel 169	Crawford, Gardazly 117
Buchko, Megan 158	Chen, Amy 133	Crawford, Taylor 224
Buck, Ivy 107	Cheramie, Hannah 156	Craycroft, Michaela 150
Buck, Sarah 69	Cheshire, Tiffany 11	Crenshaw, LaRae 129
Buck, Taylor 165	Childress, Kerigan 253	Crisp, Easton 220
Buday, Cali 209	Chiozza, John 204	Crisp, Samantha 174
Bullock, Zachary 123	Christensen, Lily 192	Criswell, Siara 184
Burage, Kayla 164	Christy, Devin 236	Croom, Aubrie 201
Burford, Austin 127	Chunn, Zoe 111	Croom, Madison 215
Burgess, Hunter 184	Cischke, Adam 175	Crowe, Austin 209
Burns, Haley 104	Clapacs, Patrick 236	Crowell, Emma 90
Burns, Mariana 42	Clapper, Avery 194	Crumley, Spencer 58
Burris, Amber 21	Clark, Amy Nicole 207	Crump, Haven 235
Burroughs, Linnea 240	Clark, Mackenzie 120	Culbertson, Alyson 221
Busby, James 154	Clarke, Alina 18	Cunningham, Savanna 115
Butler, Meagan 239	Clay, Nicole 115	Curry, Anna 136
Butts, Destiny 140	Clayton, Jada 236	Curry, Corey 107
Butts, Lydia 83	Cline, Molly 193	D., Alec 9
Cabell, Ryan 96	Clinton, Jerriney 69	Daley, Wayne 214
Calcote, Cade 100	Clinton, Noah 139	Dallimore, Rose 237
Caldwell, Kat 116	Cobb, Anzaryia 220	Dancy, Iman 195

Daniel, Derek 91	Douglass, Dominique 75	Fields, Dillon 47
Daniel, Zachary 121	Dowden, Meredith 13	Fields, Holly 168
Dann, Mary Alice 80	Dowdy, Cameryn 216	Figueroa, Ramon 241
Danzer, Cole 243	Downey, Timmy 174	Figures, Angelica 36
Danziger, Caroline 156	Downs, Hannah 125	Flay, Buddy 8
Danziger, Maddy 216	Driskell, Mackenzie 161	Flood, Andy 171
Darpel, Samantha 173	Driskill, Nick 248	Flores, Kennedy 238
Darwesh, Bako 130	Drury, Michael 231	Floyd, Kelsie 169
Dash, Anisha 184	Du, Robin 92	Fluhr, Dylan 256
Daugherty, Sarah 159	Dubites, Diana 183	Flynn, Adam 124
Davidson, Kailey 253	Duckett, Gretta 256	Flynn, Austin 124
Davis, Abigail 25	Dudley, Bryan 123	Flynn, Gabrielle 109
Davis, Leah 106	Dufour, Rachel 56	Flynn, Isabella 98
Davis, Madison 93	Duke, Haley 45	Flynn, Seth 155
Davis, Marissa 14	Dunn, Lexis 247	Forbes, Chloe 255
Davis, Sydney 27	Dupeire, Teagan 132	Ford, Ashley 223
Davis, Tare 180	Durden, Cody 201	Ford, Maggie 136
Davis, Tronjay 80	Dyke, Kaitlyn 85	Forde-Whitefield, Robyn 218
Dawson, Nataly 94	Eakin, Carter 33	Fortune, Parris 165
de Figueiredo, Madeline 154	Eban, Elizabeth 136	Foster, Jevonta 20
De Lilly, Aaron 37	Edmonds, Kiera 177	Foster, Kaleigh 208
Dean, Austin 243	Edwards, Olivia 242	Fountain, Zachary 172
Deardorff, Dana 148	Edwards, Taylor 182	Fowler, Brooke 65
Deaton, Lindsey 95	Edwards, Unique 193	Fox, Mollie Grace 197
Dees, Maris 206	Edwardson, Emma 98	Foye, Nathaniel 147
Deese, Santana 95	Edwardson, Grace 101	Fracchia, Anna 212
Deglow, Paige 167	Ehlman, Catherine 147	France, Will 191
Dela Peña, Sharmaine 120	Eichenberger, Sarah 128	Frank, Kyra 92
Dela Peña, Shun 217	Ellinger, Justin 251	Franklin, Alex 14
Deng, Wing 184	Elliott, Brooklyn 97	Franklin, Lucy Rose 240
Denny, Haylee 196	Elliott, Kat 46	Franzen, Rob 52
Denton, Carrie 155	Elliott, Taylor 226	Freeman, Rachel 52
Denu, Liberty 145	Ellis, Samantha 217	Fullenwider, Kate 221
Derenoncourt, Jasmine-Rose 107	Ellis-Gainous, Katlyn 124	Fuller, Madison 214
Derezinski-Choo, Natasha 106	Embrey, Benjamin 117	Fulmer, Robbie 217
Desai, Amishi 81	Embry, Thomas 238	Fulton, Kelcee 64
Dew, Laura 54	Ensor, Shelby 212	Fussell, Holly 223
Dharsandia, Jay 113	Escobar, Angelica 172	Gabbard, Josh 239
Diallo, Mariam 70	Evans, Celie 258	Gabbard, Tori 30
Dickerson, Tiara 76	Everett, Steven P. 26	Gaertner, Tejes 192
Dickinson, Jacob 233	Exley, Alexandria 68	Galindo, Sean 137
Dickinson, Louie 190	Ezekiel, Makenna 141	Gallop, George 208
Diggs, Hilda 45	Fahr, Lama 145	Galvan, Alvaro 53
Dill, Julianna 192	Fair, Harold 158	Gardner, Kinsey 58
Dinser, McKaela 230	Fairchild, Katie 216	Garland, Britney 96
Dischell, Caroline 37	Faith, Kristen 83	Garland, Luciey 139
Dixon, Kathryn 28	Faiz, Fatima Ezzahra 170	Garner, Haley 152
Dombrowski, Allison 117	Fan, Rachel 237	Gasia, Carter 253
Donlon, Erin 116	Farmer, Amber 25	Gast, Audrey 193
Donlon, James 197	Farmer, Simon 139	Gaudette, Briley 144
Donnell, Cassie 93	Fedders, Caroline 114	Gauze, Daisha 44
Dorsey, Craig 119	Fedoronko, Faith 148	Geiger, Courtney 41
Doss, Garrett 190	Felton, Jonathon 205	Genovese, Hope 110
Dotson, Brooklyn 62	Fenwick, Emma 251	Gerdes, Carley 98
Dotson, Margie 175	Fenwick, Seth 211	Gerling, Claire 122
Doubrley, Zoe 199	Fernandez, Madison 255	Ghodsi, Saaman 151
Dougherty, Zachary 41	Ferraro, James 67	Gilliam, Saige 48
Douglas, Tori 208	Fields, Cassie 231	Gilliland, Emily 145

Gilmore, Kasey ... 40	Hamblin, Cory ... 236	Henson, Jennifer ... 132
Givens, Nadia ... 59	Hameed, Shilan ... 86	Hernandez, Gabriel ... 146
Glass, BrinLee ... 36	Hamer, Margaret ... 169	Herrera, Paola ... 13
Glass, Jonah ... 231	Hamilton, Abigail ... 109	Hester, Dylan ... 201
Glick, Sarah ... 12	Hamilton, Alexander ... 218	Hickman, Hannah ... 96
Godat, Charlotte ... 220	Hamilton, Dylan ... 207	Hickman, Sierra ... 178
Goff, Dalton ... 253	Hammond, Olivia ... 141	Hicks, Bryan ... 234
Goldey, Casey ... 131	Hancock, Spencer ... 216	Hicks, Kaitlynn ... 157
Goldman, Benjamin ... 240	Haney, Brandon ... 207	Higazy, Linda ... 13
Good, Chastity ... 51	Hannah, Rosa ... 131	Higazy, Magi ... 19
Goodall, James ... 22	Hans, Amanda ... 119	Higginbotham, Ethan ... 106
Gooding, Darin ... 149	Hanson-Colvin, Madeleine ... 55	Hill, Abigail ... 125
Goodwille-Contreras, Jasmine ... 38	Hardee, Rachel ... 218	Hill, Jenna Grace ... 22
Goodwin, Alexander ... 195	Hardin, Kaylee ... 257	Hill, Ronnie ... 235
Goodwin, Courtney ... 37	Harding, Lily ... 222	Hillyer, Mikhaila ... 110
Gordon, Esther ... 155	Harney, Destini ... 117	Hilton, America ... 114
Gorman, Haley ... 166	Harper, Melissa ... 122	Hincks, Frannie ... 210
Gorrell, Lane ... 129	Harper, Michael ... 108	Hinds, Arniecia ... 41
Gould, Jordan ... 116	Harris, Amber ... 86	Hixson, Abigail ... 101
Gowan, Asha ... 21	Harris, Blair ... 178	Hoagland, Brielle ... 160
Graham, Jessica ... 50	Harris, Gizelle ... 29	Hobbs, Cheyanne ... 257
Graham, Rhylea ... 246	Harris, Jessica ... 211	Hobbs, Tiara ... 61
Gramling, Amelia ... 24	Harris, Kerri ... 109	Hodgens, Kurtis ... 109
Grant, Jamonte ... 100	Harris, Kiara ... 108	Hodges, Adam ... 182
Graves, Mackenzie ... 20	Harris, Kyriunna ... 67	Hodges, Olivia ... 129
Gray, Mary Catherine ... 177	Hart, Lee ... 39	Hoffman, Alyssa ... 58
Gray, Victoria ... 23	Hartin, Lana ... 48	Hogan, Terrence ... 68
Green, Detravia ... 71	Hartley, Savannah ... 225	Hogewood, Hannah ... 31
Green, Jonathan ... 163	Harvey, Gracelin ... 219	Hoke, Kynadee ... 119
Green, Sierra ... 92	Hatcher, Jaleen ... 71	Holbrook, Nathan ... 26
Greene, Isaiah ... 154	Hatcher, Richard ... 96	Holderman, Jacob ... 253
Greenwell, Carson ... 219	Hatten, Vertina ... 92	Holland, Abigail ... 113
Greer, Zachary ... 234	Hatter, Kate ... 103	Holland, Andrea ... 101
Greever, Hanna ... 206	Hawkins, Ashley ... 58	Holland, Jeanette ... 165
Gregory, Robert ... 245	Hayden, Rionne ... 170	Holland, Leslie ... 35
Gresham, Zoe ... 110	Hayes, Brianna ... 167	Holland, Rebekah ... 102
Griggs, Kelsey ... 61	Hayes, James ... 124	Hollingsworth, Hannah ... 198
Grimes, Andrew ... 80	Hayes, Logan ... 205	Holloway, Cortni ... 11
Groff, Megan ... 52	Hayes, Nathan ... 223	Holstine, Brooke ... 184
Gross, Jacob ... 180	Hayes, Riley ... 227	Hong, Xena ... 36
Gross, Kirby ... 11	Hayner, Nicholas ... 239	Hooks, Henry ... 190
Gruber, Sara ... 197	Hazlett, Tristan ... 99	Hopkins, Michael ... 10
Gruner, Abby ... 147	Hearn, Davis ... 153	Horne, Alesha ... 203
Gudiseva, Sairam ... 148	Hearn, Kiana ... 157	Horner, Cassie ... 225
Guevara, Crystal ... 127	Hearn, Zoe ... 191	Horney, Caroline ... 148
Gullett, Hunter ... 169	Heath, Julia ... 110	Horton, Kamron ... 105
Gwyn, Megan ... 183	Heavrin, Katie ... 181	Horton, Lauren ... 26
H., Devan ... 70	Heck, Cody ... 149	Housley, Raven ... 30
H., Keantay ... 85	Hedrick, Madison ... 214	Howell, Brooklyn ... 182
Hacker, Alex ... 185	Hefler, Chris ... 130	Hudgins, Abigail ... 256
Hacker, Sam ... 180	Hefley, Hanna ... 70	Hudnall, Kristen ... 110
Hadaway, Tyler ... 215	Heilig, Jeremy ... 179	Hudnall, Victoria ... 131
Hager, Brooke ... 38	Hemming, Hannah ... 126	Huffines, Andrew ... 232
Haight, Marissa ... 235	Hendricks, Asia ... 32	Huffman, Holly ... 198
Hall, Alex ... 198	Hendricks, Keely ... 163	Hughes, Alex ... 15
Hall, Brooke ... 66	Hennies, Ethan ... 117	Hughes, Caroline ... 76
Hall, Kylie ... 117	Henry, Sion ... 94	Hughes, Diana ... 174
Hall, Makenna ... 146	Hensley, Lashonda ... 201	Hughes, Elijah ... 223

Index

Humphrey, Gatlin 207
Hunt, April 57
Hunter-Fleming, Kashanus 150
Hupp, Katherine 9
Hupp, Lauren 30
Hurst, Katlyn 160
Hutcheson, Annastasia 207
Hutchinson, Kyra 30
Hutton, Jessica 131
Huxley, Corryne 74
Hvasta, Braden 210
Hyde, Christina 123
Hyre, Dallas 157
Ihler, Zach 160
Ilgandi, Alexis 244
Ingram, Allison 193
Irvin, Meg 16
Irvine, Jacob 42
Irwin, Corey 35
Jackson, Alex 123
Jackson, Heather 84
Jackson, Nazire 196
Jacobs, Bianca 232
Janeway, Graham 238
Janssen, Scott 193
Jeffries, McKinlee 197
Jenkins, Jawon 57
Jenkins, Jedidiah 154
Jennings, Abbie 108
Jennings, Anna 115
Jennings, Kathryn 149
Jenrette, Donte 59
Johns, Ashley 40
Johnson, Bess 221
Johnson, Chapin 258
Johnson, Jordan 90
Johnson, Justin 65
Johnson, Kaitlyn 239
Johnson, Kimberly 47
Johnson, Myranda-Lynn 10
Johnson, Savana 196
Johnson, Syree 221
Johnson, Tanner 235
Johnson, Tierra 164
Johnson, Trikeria 43
Johnson, Zachary 247
Jolly, Malea 157
Jones, Amber 151
Jones, Ashley 211
Jones, Brianna 63
Jones, Caroline 135
Jones, Dalton 104
Jones, Daniel 143
Jones, Hayley 213
Jones, Mya 221
Jones, Spencer 29
Jones, Sydney 125
Jones, Toneeya 217
Jones, Trevor 143
Jordan, Sydney 228
Joshi, Arati 99
Joy, Levi 199
Julian, Lacey Dylan 72
Justice, Jake 205
Justice, Shane 69
Kamau, Hekima 194
Karaouch, Saad 103
Karimpour, Kamellia 195
Kastenberger, Johanna 220
Kaul, Smiti 137
Kee, Tayler 218
Keelin, Kylie 137
Keen, Mary 18
Keith, SeMarreius 246
Keller, Elena 118
Keller, Peyton 250
Kelley, Connor 191
Kelly, Chris 135
Kelly, Grace 103
Kennedy, Antonious 78
Kent, Gracie 245
Kerr, Cheonna 228
Kersey, Brittney 228
Key, Emily 27
Kidd, Chantel 213
Kidwell, Lindsey 62
Kidwell, Lindsey 62
King, Caitlin 204
King, Joshua 230
King, Kaitlin 229
Kinney, Reese 100
Kinniburgh, Rose 118
Kirby, Tanner 161
Kirk, Zach 111
Kirkland, Nicholas 20
Kirtley, Jessica 239
Klausing, Caroline 40
Klopfenstein, Abigail 150
Knack, Benjamin 23
Knotts, Bryton 44
Kodack, Dara 227
Koella, Grace 110
Kolb, John 152
Korgar, Ashleyh 82
Kouser, Hamza 124
Kramer, Julianne 74
Kreider, Jessica 215
Kriss, Jordan 212
Krohn, Christopher 208
Krupia, Brandon 39
Kummerle, Laura 83
Kunkel, Maddy 124
Lackey, Savannah 181
Lacroix, Taylor 174
Lafon, Tori 152
LaGarce, Destiny 65
Lambert, Adrienne 202
Lambert, Caitlin 138
Lambert, Isabelle 225
Lambert, Natalie Anne 238
Lane, Rebecca 43
Laney, Natasha 243
Lanier, Ma'Lesha 112
Lanning, Justine 104
Larson, Rehnon Ty 228
Latham, Elijah 206
Lavender, Jacob 121
Law, Matilda 227
Law, Preston 254
Lawrence, Elyssa 226
Lawrence, Justice 132
Lawson, Brian 144
Lawson, Sam 240
Lawyer, Natalie 74
Lay, Jacob 84
Lay, Nichole 27
Laymon, Kaitlin 218
Le, Minh 233
Leak-Kent, Hannah 166
Lear, Dylan 241
LeBaron, Victoria 97
Lee, Davies 183
Lee, Elizabeth 47
Lee, Yon-Soo 26
Legg, Kasidi 153
Lehman, Josie 202
Lemmons, Hayley 83
Lemon, William 196
Lepcio, Teddy 240
Lewis, Audrey 216
Lewis, Carrington 166
Lewis, Jacob 130
Lewis, Jordan 31
Lewis, Karia 213
Liberto, Jason 121
Lichtefeld, Hannah 102
Lieberman, Carlos 229
Likens, Mason 209
Liles, Allison 138
Lill, Arielle 191
Lillie, Sara 146
Lim, Adrienne 53
Lind, Chloe 244
Lindon, Briana 207
Lindsey, Wesley 222
Little, Kasiya 200
Littlepage, Keeley 193
Lobach, Anna Laura 115
Lockhart, Jessica 33
Locklear, Alexis 251
Locklear, Kaitlyn 197
Lofgren, Tommy 53
Logan, Daylan 202
Logan, Mitchell 249

Lollis, W'Raven 102
Long, Alyssa 173
Long, Ryan 170
Long, Sean 34
Loomis, Tiffany 176
Lopez, Graciela Stephany Arreola 162
Louden, Stanford 132
Love, Alycia 227
Loveless, Corbin 81
Lovett, Renn 67
Lovin, Briauna 135
Loyd, Michael 29
Ludovicy, Lee 180
Luna, Carlos 190
Lundy, Annah 205
Lyons, Mason 45
Lythgow, Trevor 59
Mackey, Les 228
Mackin, Travis 94
Macumber, Kayleigh 221
Maddox, Logan 214
Majmudar, Parth 62
Maliwat, Noel 113
Malla, Janak 77
Mandrekas, Brianna 178
Mankins, William 26
Mann, Britton 149
Mann, Morgan 150
Mapp, Mickie 59
Maras, Jayme 202
Marble, Latonya 34
Marcum, Jack 237
Markovich, Keith 111
Marksberry, Evan 208
Martin, Justin 234
Martin, Katie 242
Martin, Kirstin 120
Martin, Mary 44
Martin, Serenity 17
Martz, Rebecca 49
Mason, Justin 248
Massenburg, Jordan 132
Massey, Kimberly 98
Mathis, Lillie 213
Matthews, Tyler 86
Mattison, Taelor 198
Mauk-Olson, Camille 174
Mavilla, Vaishnavi 192
Mayberry, Caitlyn 210
Mayes, Naudi 237
Mayfield, Austin 237
Mayo, Alexandra 39
McAdams, Colton 210
McBroom, Cole 27
McCarson, Lucas 204
McCarty, Kaleigh 148
McCary, Bonnie 231
McCauley, Sara 170
McClellan, Hannah 115
McClellan, Sarah 224
McConnell, Briana 152
McCourt, Katherine 10
McCoy, Brandon 127
McCoy, Katie 56
McCurry, Pauline 134
McGarry, John 162
McGhee, Darian 124
McGill, Shelby 100
McIlvaine, Naomi 72
McKendrick, Jacob 243
McKenna, Evan 246
McKenzie, Erica 256
McKenzie, Paige 209
McLellan, Austin 202
McLeod, Alexis 98
McLeod, Shannon 109
McMillan, Shy-Tavia 256
McNelly, Breana 64
Medani, Doha 24
Medlin, Gabriel 122
Megeed, Hedaya 20
Melton, Hannah 76
Mendelson, Maxwell 192
Mendenhall, Allen 69
Menzies, Peter 12
Merriman, Savanna 176
Messick, Addyson 222
Metcalf, Hannah 185
Methvin, Sarah 52
Meyer, Katie 169
Meyerhoffer, Alissa 202
Michaud, Amy 141
Mickins, Jazir 257
Mikels, Alisha 97
Mileski, Julia 126
Miller, Jacob 183
Miller, Justin 243
Miller, Kathleen 254
Miller, Lily 204
Miller, Micah 81
Miller, Patrick 229
Miller, Tori 113
Mills, Lacie 229
Mills, Selby 70
Milner, Gabrielle 184
Mitchell, LaAndrea 64
Mitchell, Michaela 124
Mitchell, Norah 173
Modlin, Austin 231
Mohn, Aly 111
Molina, Crystal 118
Molinet, Elizabeth 59
Mona, Ramsey 127
Moncrief, Hannah 151
Moore, Cameron 128
Moore, Drew 240
Moore, Jake 181
Moore, Joel 54
Morehead, Andy 214
Morgan, Brandon 74
Morgan, Hailey 51
Morgan, Justin 48
Morgan, Tamia 244
Morrell, Aaron 33
Morris, Cheyenne 103
Morris, Joshua 62
Morris, Zoey 153
Morrow-Elder, Hunter 54
Morton, Rodney 81
Mosier, Kynzee 192
Mosteller, Danielle 60
Mountz, Becca 168
Mourneau, Lindsey 146
Mueller, Alec 224
Mulligan, Conor 242
Mullins, Ronde 232
Murch, Cody 103
Murley, Drew 40
Murphy, Ben 78
Murphy, Clara 86
Murphy, Ethan 236
Murray, Kaitlin 52
Mustard, Bailie 114
Muyengwa, Dzidzai 37
Myers, Evan 205
Myles, Mark 222
Naas, Ben 237
Nacey, Kaylee 252
Naegele, Ally 237
Nasritdinova, Umida 152
Neblett, Katlynn 150
Neijna, Ava 250
Nelms, Tanner 53
Nelson, Ashley 59
Nelson, Emilee 196
Nesmith, JaQuan 168
Nethery, Hunter 105
Newberg, Caroline 118
Newborn, Blair 57
Newcomb, Shaina 113
Newkirk, Zan 49
Newton, Keenan 112
Nguyen, Mindy 227
Nguyen, Nicholas 105
Ni, Helen 84
Niattianandam, Arvind 215
Nicely, Dallas 214
Nicely, Dalton 207
Nicely, Natalie 203
Nichols, Cheyenne 106
Nieto, Madeleine 119
Niner, Kyle 144
Nixon, Charlotte 151
Njie, Mirian 148

Index

Noble, Kayla 128
Noe, Katie 194
Noland, Brittany 225
Norman, Brent 152
Northern, Brad 23
Norton, Colbie 110
Norton, Sean 72
O'Brien, Cameron 204
O'Leary, Kathryn 158
Ogborn, Mika 215
Oglesby, Trace 126
Ohlwein, Matthew 78
Oliver, Kyle 155
Oppong, Akua 90
Orgel, Hannah 121
Orosz, Lindsay 102
Osborne, Joy 245
Osuala, Cheyenne 160
Owen, Jay 241
Owens, Tyler 147
P., Shaun 139
Padgett, Alea 200
Padinha, Marisa 80
Page, Kevin 172
Palmer, Samantha 161
Pardue, Andrew 9
Parish, Sidney 96
Park, Kennedy 199
Parker, Katelyn 118
Parkerson, Rhiannon 161
Parks, Caylan 45
Parrill, Isaac 83
Parrish, Chase 242
Patel, Amit 166
Patel, Radha 9
Patt, Theo 249
Patterson, Ahdonnica 55
Patterson, Cameron 254
Paugh, Kaitlyn 156
Paul, Nathan 254
Pauley, Kayla 96
Payne, Morgan 34
Pearson, Kaley 241
Pendley, Brandon 250
Penn, Jaelynn 159
Pennington, Matthew 220
Pentony, Madison 179
Peragine, Sarah 35
Peralta, Michael 51
Perkins, Alyvia 55
Perkins, Tori 193
Peters, Nicholas 216
Petty, Christian 193
Pfeifer, Emily 64
Phillips, Catherine 190
Phillips, Gabriela 36
Phillips, Jessica 239
Phillips, Robin 108

Phillips-Shrewsbury, Trinity 225
Phongsa, Ling-ling 50
Pierce, McClain 176
Pierce, Mercedes 226
Pierson, Alyx 123
Pittman, Kezionne 167
Piwonka, William 82
Pleasant, Michelle 12
Plowman, Rebekah 12
Plunk, Gracie 248
Poff, Madison 180
Pollard, Jack 194
Poole, Jacob 198
Pope, Phoenix 64
Porras, Nick 136
Porter, Elizabeth 16
Portilla, Claire 109
Poteet-Berndt, Caroline 117
Powers, William 185
Prabhu, Sanjana 83
Prasad, Divya 126
Prater, Christian 107
Price, Justin 74
Price, Kassidy 53
Priebe, Abby 240
Prier, Davion 114
Pritchard, Madison 179
Pullum, Deea 61
Quinones, Nicole 63
Qureshi, Arhum 194
Rader, Shelby 196
Rahman, Meead 171
Rains, Timothy 160
Rakers, Tyler 212
Ramasubramanian, Karthik 39
Ramser, Emily 31
Ramsey, Cameron 171
Raper, Sydney 200
Rashad, Maya 172
Ratcliffe, Makayla 112
Ratliff, Kayla 176
Ratzman, Athena 122
Rawl, Davida 144
Ray, Alia 151
Raynes, JannaBeth 140
Reagan, Cody 256
Redmon, J'Shaun 212
Rees, Maisie 243
Regan, Lexus 122
Reinoehl, LouAnn 224
Reitz, Madison 184
Renn, Marlee 131
Rhea, Joshua Cole 197
Rhodes, Kristin 216
Rials, Rachel 39
Richardson, Amanda 36
Richardson, Camrin 215
Richardson, Jaylen 235

Rico, Ana 22
Riddle, Courtney 250
Riggleman, Melissa 45
Riley, Taylor 49
Ripley, Brittany 130
Ripple, Meghan 9
Risinger, Taylor 60
Ritchie, Kelsey 177
Roark, Kaycee 54
Robertson, Blake 221
Robertson, Christopher 196
Robinson, Natwiya 204
Robinson, Victoria 105
Robling, Bailey 109
Rodriguez, Leodan 103
Roedel, Payton 71
Rogers, Jack 164
Rogers, Kailee 105
Rogers, Madeline 137
Rogers, Molly 155
Rohmann, Breanna 178
Rokvic, Giannina 56
Romes, Sam 179
Rooney, Raquel 116
Root, Morgan 128
Rorie, Alyssa 209
Rose, Kaitlyn 212
Ross, Erica 73
Ross, Kimberly 104
Rowley, Jacqueline 185
Rowlinson, Olivia 159
Roy, Emily 129
Royal, Alda 25
Rozier, Dimitria 244
Rumage, Kelsey 228
Rumbaugh, Brooke 156
Runyon, Jennicka 252
Russell, Grayson 176
Russell, Marisa 139
Russell, Savannah 94
Russo, Jordan 42
Sabra, Yusef 175
Safford, Vendela 131
Sagerdahl, Will 150
Salas, Marco 252
Salcevski, Adelina 55
Salomon, Aaron 158
Sampson, Dylan 245
Sanchez, Brenda 61
Sands, Regan 95
Sanford, Lindsey 104
Sansone, Taylor 94
Santella, Briana 243
Saucier, Mycalyn 40
Saunders, Elesia 15
Savage, Cody 85
Sawh, Michael 154
Sawyers, Kristen 81

Sayani, Aasim	16	
Scavo, Marisa	57	
Schaffstein, Johnny	151	
Schickling, Susan	118	
Schlader, Jillian	47	
Schneider, Addison	254	
Schranze, Ian	15	
Scott, Emma	82	
Scott, Eric	42	
Scott, Tierra	113	
Scully, Evan	233	
Seagroves, Christiny	140	
Segposyan, Katherine	186	
Seidehamel, Jacob	229	
Selby, Hank	162	
Sellers, Dylan	181	
Sellers, Whitney	22	
Selukar, Subodh	49	
Sermersheim, Lucy	176	
Sewell, Kendall	205	
Shahan, Ilea	167	
Shannon, Hannah	178	
Sharma, Rohini	225	
Sharp, Laura	12	
Sheaffer, Samantha	146	
Shean, Eden	202	
Sheffield, Damaris	199	
Shelton, Gray	218	
Shelton, Jack	246	
Shelton, Jared	190	
Shelton, Natalie	15	
Shelton, Thomas	138	
Shepherd, Erica	60	
Sheppard, Evan	215	
Sherlock, Gage	121	
Shockley, Cameron	246	
Shoffner, Alison	79	
Shostak, Mariya	31	
Shwer, Hayley	149	
Sichel, Ethan	204	
Sidhu, Tarana	158	
Siler, Hope	32	
Silva, Noah	104	
Silvels, Sherrese	147	
Simmons, Blessen	211	
Simmons, Keagan	203	
Simmons, Nakei'Briana	203	
Simpkins, Matthew	224	
Simpson, Ariel	93	
Simpson, Danny	142	
Simpson, Layne	200	
Sims, Kaleb	205	
Sims, Tanishia	63	
Singh, Aman	228	
Singh, Bhavna	71	
Singleton, Kaitlyn	75	
Siskind, Eden	35	
Siva, Nanda	66	

Skeens, Shawna	185	
Smith, Austin	132	
Smith, Bristol	113	
Smith, Byron	245	
Smith, Drake	206	
Smith, Faith	105	
Smith, Faith	242	
Smith, Julian	48	
Smith, Katelin	85	
Smith, Leigha	181	
Smith, Savannah	50	
Smith, Val	201	
Smithers, Cassidy	140	
Smoak, Rachel	15	
Snyder, Steven	211	
Socarras, Jose	143	
Solomon, Kameron	237	
Song, Christina	111	
Souza, Jesse	58	
Spahr, Destiny	147	
Spangler, Jordan	129	
Spears, Everett	48	
Spillman, Samantha	71	
Sprigg, Becca	22	
Sriraman, Swamynathan	29	
Stafford, Dakota	60	
Stanhope, Staci	185	
Stanley, Dalton	200	
Stanley, Hylan	255	
Stanley, Samantha	173	
Stazzone, Scott	161	
Steele, Zachary	32	
Steinauer, Elizabeth	17	
Stephen, Tre	231	
Stephens-Lubrani, Annette	231	
Stevens, Mackenzie	182	
Stevens, Taylor	15	
Stice, Payton	257	
Stiggers, Makenna	242	
Stillwell, Elizabeth	68	
Stivenson, Faith	79	
Stivers, Victoria	219	
Stobaugh, Reed	193	
Stokes, Savannah	153	
Stone, Bethany	212	
Stone, Jayde M.	174	
Story, Skye	208	
Stotts, Aurora	63	
Stover, Christian	205	
Straney, Hannah	236	
Stratman, Katie	112	
Strawn, Rachel	197	
Street, Kassidy	209	
Strickland, Cody	130	
Strunk, Carson	244	
Stuckenborg, Amy	226	
Sucher, Kelsey	100	
Sucher, Nathan	112	

Summers, Ashly	41	
Summers, Jalen	180	
Sumpter, Robert	31	
Sumser, Austin	118	
Suresh, Pavithra	43	
Susewell, Robert	258	
Sutton, Amanda	24	
Sutton, Mallory	101	
Sweeney, Erin	184	
Sweet, Kayla	65	
Sweitzer, Madison	145	
T., Marcus	85	
Tabeling, Kirk	173	
Tabor, Brittany	33	
Taghavi, Omid	73	
Tannenbaum, Maxx	91	
Tanner, Robbie	195	
Tant, Heather	169	
Tassos, Jennifer	136	
Tate, Asha	66	
Tate, Natasha	97	
Taylor, Alexis	10	
Taylor, Ian	248	
Taylor, Nya	65	
Telkamp, Dylan	162	
Templeton, Kaylin	256	
Terrell, Bradly	180	
Testerman, Mayson	104	
Thacker, Grace	227	
Thaman, Lily	134	
Thayer, Brittney	83	
Thetford, Libby	214	
Thomas, Abby	8	
Thomas, BreAnna	10	
Thomas, MaryKate	55	
Thomas, Sharon	132	
Thomas, Tori	93	
Thompson, Evan	142	
Thompson, Ja'shaun	231	
Thompson, Matt	240	
Thurman, Luke	204	
Tidwell, Mallory	104	
Tinnell, Wilson	256	
Torres, Soett	171	
Towell, Mallory	19	
Townsend, Kristen	77	
Tran, Angela	161	
Tran, Selinna	215	
Tritt, Arden	19	
Trogolo, Kelsey	242	
Troiano, Angelica	157	
Trotter, Dustin	257	
Tucker, Darius	150	
Tucker, Jessica	18	
Tucker, Kellen	245	
Tucker, Tiphanie	8	
Tunstull, De'Quan	144	
Turner, Hallie	193	

Index

Turner, Jeremiah 45
Turner, Madison 244
Tyler, Jerry 211
Tyree, Blake 30
Tyrone, Brittany 43
Tyser, Lauren 27
Utley, Michael 176
Vacanti, Keegan 224
Vaillancourt, Monique 124
Van, Danyka 194
Van Dyne, Mitchell 168
Vance, Christian 233
Vance, Jacob 134
Vang, Ashley 135
Vann, Valerie 230
Varner, Shelby 139
Vaughn, Jessica 40
Vemula, Nilai 248
Verdugt, Alli 230
Versteeg, Genevieve 63
Villers, Christian 166
Vineyard, Taylor 258
Vinson, Kianna 50
Vittitoe, D. J. 230
Voehringer, Ryan 207
Volyanyuk, Bohdan 62
Voyles, Hannah 17
Voytko, Cameron 233
Waddell, Claire 220
Wagner, Isabella 238
Wagner, Nathan 140
Wagner, Trinity 215
Wagoner, Kara 28
Walker, Dustyn 175
Walker, Kinsley 236
Wallace, Samantha 47
Walls, Parker 109
Waltenburg, Brendan 198
Ward, Daniel 197
Ward, Linda (Lynn) 122
Warf, Hailey 243
Warman, Abagail 200
Warner, Casey 179
Warnock, Taylor 183
Wasamba, Yoeli 224
Washington, Tiana 134
Waters, Shaun 237
Watkins, Logan 221
Watts, Antonia 60
Weathers, Lachelle 145
Weaver, Paige 249
Webb, Hannah 41
Webb, Richard 18
Webster, Charlee 233
Weeks, Esme 204
Weihe, Ashley 226
Weinhold, Michael 67
Wellington, Wyatt 99
Wells, Damien 216
Wells, Emileigh 166
Wells, Megan 258
West, Leah A. 19
Westcott, Amber 200
Whelan, Elizabeth 209
Whitaker, Miya 162
White, Bless 113
White, Brooke 130
White, Emily 138
White, Michelle 8
White, Natacha 247
Wicktom, Meredith 234
Wierdl, Dora 241
Wilbert, Hannah 235
Wilbur, Brianna 60
Wilder, Dylan 138
Wiles, Bethany 76
Wiley, Savannah 115
Wilhelm-Olsen, Tori 232
Wilkerson, Alexis 232
Wilkerson, Maddie 222
Wilkins, Naujal 235
Wilkinson, Jared 127
Willett, Amber 125
Williams, Caitlyn 234
Williams, Chase 24
Williams, Donavon 106
Williams, Ethan 185
Williams, Gideon 233
Williams, Grace 195
Williams, LaDestinee 72
Williamson, Riley 135
Williamson, Ryan 90
Williamson, Zachary 254
Williford, Justin 138
Williford, Kaitlin 142
Willis, Harold 201
Willoughby, Jeremy 14
Willyard, Destinie 227
Wilson, Annalee 218
Wilson, Catena 90
Wilson, Danielle 101
Wilson, Gage 202
Wilson, Hannah 43
Wilson, James 142
Wilson, Kaleb 246
Wilson, Lane 191
Wilson, Nikkita 76
Wilson, Thomas 78
Wilt, Preston 253
Wimberly, Jacklyn 191
Winebarger, Brianna 86
Wines, Cole 149
Winfree, Kelsey 156
Wisswell, Savanah 202
Witt, Emily 252
Witt, Robert 100
Wix, Elizabeth 202
Woggon, Erin 119
Wolsey, Kaitlynn 62
Wong, Jacquelyn 94
Wood, Brittany 161
Wood, Casey 213
Wood, Dawson 205
Wood, Liberty 108
Wood, Madison 232
Woods, Aaron 17
Woods, John 220
Woods, Madison 149
Wooldridge, Edward 23
Woosley, Christopher 204
Wooten, Rya 80
Wordsworth, Aleah 175
Worley, Nadine 29
Worthy, Ellen 119
Wright, Coral 96
Wright, Elijah 35
Wright, Haley 223
Wright, Marcus 90
Wu, Xiya 135
Wujek, Madeline 227
Yarborough, Bryton 201
Yeo, Nathan 102
Yeomans, Heather 32
Young, Christopher 21
Young, Lloyd 172
Young, Natalie 206
Young, Spencer 36
Young, Taylor 68
Yu, Bryant 73
Zakharenko, Savely 18
Zamudio, Samantha 104
Zendejas, Blanca 243
Zhang, Helen 11
Zhao, Bob 97
Zhu, Xuyi 74
Zidaroff, Zach 144
Ziemer, Alex 159

Author Autograph Page

Author Autograph Page

Author Autograph Page

Author Autograph Page

Author Autograph Page

Author Autograph Page

Author Autograph Page

Author Autograph Page

Author Autograph Page

Author Autograph Page

Author Autograph Page

Author Autograph Page